Avibhāga–Bhedābheda

Avibhāga–Bhedābheda

(Indivisible Difference and non-Difference)

In the Vijñānāmṛtabhāṣyam of Vijñānabhikṣu: A Thread that Unites Divergent Aspects of Reality

RAJU FELIX CRASTA

MLBD ®
PUBLICATIONS

Motilal Banarsidass Publications

MOTILAL BANARSIDASS
PUBLICATIONS
4741/23, Ansari Road, Daryaganj, New Delhi - 110002 (India)
Email: mlbd@mlbd.com | sales@mlbd.com
exports@mlbd.com | publications@mlbd.com
Website: www.mlbd.com

Avibhāga–Bhedābheda
by
Raju Felix Crasta

First Edition Published in 2022

Published in India by Motilal Banarsidass Publications

ISBN : 978-93-91759-04-9 (HB)

Printed and bound in India

TABLE OF CONTENTS

CHAPTER FOUR

CHAPTER FIVE

FOREWORD

Right from the Master's Programme in Philosophy till his doctoral milestone, Raju Felix Crasta has undertaken an arduous and fascinating Indological journey. He has shown tremendous and admirable amount of required patience, passion and perseverance. Indeed, Crasta has extracted nectar, having churned the difficult and complex field of Indology in general and *Avibhāga-Bhedābheda* of Vijñānabhikṣu in particular. In spite of experiencing scarcity of resources like the translations and critical studies, Crasta has come oust with a critical, creative and relevant doctoral thesis. Now that the fruit of his research is seeing the light of the day in the form of publication, I feel immensely joyful as a guide of the thesis. I heartily congratulate the author and wish him all the best for the future intellectual ventures.

The thesis titled "*Avibhāga-Bhedābheda* (Indivisible Difference and Non-Difference) in the Vijñānāmṛtabhāṣyam Of Vijñānabhikṣu: A Thread that Unites Divergent Aspects of Reality," is a timely and significant contribution to the world beset with conflicts due to lack of integration between difference and non-difference. Raju's thesis proposes creative ways of harmonizing these two extremes harmoniously without compromising the importance of both the aspects of reality.

I see a bright and promising future for Raju Felix Crasta. Since there is no translation of the text, I hope he would undertake it with the critical edition of the text. I wish the author all the best for the important task of Indological publications. May he become an instrument of creating unity amidst diversity.

SHUBHAMASTU

Dr Henry D'Almeida, SJ

Preface

The *Vedānta* is the end of the Vedas. It can be understood in three levels: the *Advaita*, the *Dvaita* and the *Dvaitādvaita*, in other words *Abheda, Bheda* and *Bhedābheda* respectively. Though traces of these three categories are foreshadowed in the Vedic literature, they are developed into a full-streamed philosophy later during the years each with distinct scholars and later by their followers. The first two philosophical positions are much known by people than the third category. Each category has its own philosophical positions and at times differences within its followers.

The category under study in this book is the third Vedāntic position, the Bhedābheda. Within this School of thought, there are several thinkers with distinct philosophies of converging and diverging opinions. The position under study here is the lesser-known philosophy, the Avibhāga Bhedābheda proposed by Vijñānabhikṣu, a 16th Century thinker. This is a unique and novel concept under the Bhedābheda tradition with a wide range of applications.

This work is an updated version of my doctoral dissertation submitted to the faculty of Philosophy, Jnana-Deepa (Pontifical Institute of Philosophy and Religion, Pune), defended on January 22, 2019, for the Degree of Doctor in Philosophy (Ph.D).

A Sanskrit verse states, *"na hīkṣulehanenaiva jñātā ikṣuraso bhavet na cekṣudaṇḍaṁ niṣpiḍya labdho nekṣurasobhavet,"* "By merely licking the outer surface of sugarcane, one cannot taste and enjoy its sweetness; without squeezing it, one cannot savour the sugarcane" (Vyāsatīrtha's *Ślokatātparyacandrikā*, 29). The journey so far has not been less than a *sāgaramanthana*, 'churning of the ocean' of Indian scriptures, with several ups and downs, squeezing and wheezing at times to get a drop of delicious nectar. It was not possible to attain this just admiring from outside. As I bring down the curtain to this work, I stand indebted to all those who stood beside me in my journey.

I thank the Almighty God for the showers of blessings and grace. It was He who instilled in me the courage to stand alone, dig deeper, see the unseen, and discover the hidden wisdom. I prostrate unto His feet and offer this work in gratefulness and love.

Guru stands next to God. It is he who shows the path. My guru, Dr Henry D'Almeida, SJ, a moving encyclopaedia of Indian Philosophy inspired me to dive into this ocean knowing my strength and weakness. He encouraged me and gave me every possible help. His erudite and meticulous corrections, critical acumen, inspiring insights, valuable suggestions, discussions, and importantly his journey along my side made the most satisfying thing in my life. My heartfelt gratitude goes to him.

I am thankful to Jnana-Deepa (JD) for whetting my philosophical thirst, right from the beginning of my philosophical journey and quenching it. I thank the President Dr Selvarathinam, SJ, the Dean of the faculty of Philosophy Dr Kuruvilla Pandikattu, SJ, the Chairman of the Doctoral Committee Dr S. Francis and other members of the committee, the Registrar Dr Jose Thayil, SJ, the Librarian Fr. Biju Vadakkumchery, SJ and his collaborators, the Treasurer of the institution, the Post-graduate Block Moderator, and all the officials and staff of JD for their unflinching support.

I extend my sincere thanks to the Most Rev. Felix Toppo, SJ, the former Bishop of Jamshedpur and the present Archbishop of Ranchi, and the Chancellor of St. Albert's College for placing his trust and sending me for higher studies. I am grateful to the erstwhile and present Apostolic Administrators of Jamshedpur Diocese: Rev. Fr. Augustin Topno and Rev. Bishop Theodore Bilung SVD respectively, and their collaborators for the encouragement. I thank the Rector, Staff, and colleagues of St. Albert's college Ranchi for their encouragement and support.

I am deeply indebted to the help given by Dr Antony Samy for his painstaking and careful reading of the drafts of my thesis to embellish the language. I place on record my earnest thanks to Dr Ivan D'Souza for his technical assistance and also to Fr. Joby T. OP, Fr. Varan V., Fr. Ivan M. MST, and Fr. Franclin SVD for suggestions and assistance.

I record my genuine gratefulness to the Church-in-Need for the generous and timely financial aid needed for my studies. Their big-hearted help facilitated the smooth completion of my studies for which I ever remain thankful. I also remember with fondness and gratitude the members of my family, friends, colleagues, students, and others. My heart wells up with joyful thanks to one and all. May God be praised unceasingly!

Raju Felix Crasta

Bishop's House, Golmuri, Jamshedpur

KEY TO TRANSLITERATION AND PRONOUNCIATION

अ	a	o as in son
आ	ā	a as in palm
इ	i	i as in ink
ई	ī	ee as in feel
उ	u	u as in pull
ऊ	ū	oo as in shoot
ऋ	ṛ	r as in bright
ॠ	ṝ	prolongation of r as in bright (rarely used)
लृ	lṛ	combination of l and r (rarely used)
ए	e	ay as in May
ऐ	ai	ai as in aisle
ओ	o	o as in over
औ	au	ow as in how
•	ṁ (*anusvāra*)	m as in hum
:	ḥ (*visarga*)	h a as oh!
क	ka	c as in cut
ख	kha	kh as in inkhorn
ग	ga	gu as in gum
घ	gha	gh as in loghut

ङ	ṅa	ng as in cling
च	ca	ch as in check
छ	cha	tch as in match
ज	ja	ju as in jump
झ	jha	dge as in hedge
ञ	ña	ng as in singe
ट	ṭa	t as in Tata
ठ	ṭha	t as in bitter (hard accent)
ड	ḍa	d as in darling
ढ	ḍha	dd as in headder
ण	ṇa	n as in under
त	ta	t as in French t
थ	tha	thu as in thumb (hard accent)
द	da	thu as in thus
ध	dha	the as in breathe
न	na	na as in nasty
प	pa	pa as in papa
फ	pha	pha as in loop-hole
ब	ba	bu as in but
भ	bha	bh as in abhor
म	ma	mu as in munch

य	ya	ya as in Yama
र	ra	ra as in Ratan
ल	la	la as in Lalit
व	va	va as in vast
श	śa	sh as in Prashant
ष	ṣa	sho as in show
स	sa	sa as in Salomi
ह	ha	hu as in humming
ळ	ḷa	la as in Kerala (But with Malayalam accent)
क्ष	kṣa	ksha as in riksha
ज्ञ	jña	jña as in jñānadeepa

ABBREVIATIONS

AU	Aitareya Upaniṣad
AbU	Amṛtabindu Upaniṣad
AV	Atharvaveda
BCE	Before Common Era
BG	Bhagavadgītā, Bhagavad Gītā
BP	Bhāgavata Purāṇa
BS	Brahmasūtra of Bādarāyaṇa
BSB	Brahmasūtrabhāṣya of Madhva
BSBBh	Brahmasūtrabhāṣya of Bhāskara
BSSBh	Brahmasūtrabhāṣya of Śaṅkara
BU	Bṛhadāraṇyaka Upaniṣad
BUBh	Bṛhadāraṇyaka Upaniṣad Bhāṣya of śaṅkara
CE	Common Era
CU	Chāndogya Upaniṣad
Ed.	Editor, Edited by, Edition
GP	Garuḍa Purāṇa
IU	Īśavāsya Upaniṣad
KaU	Kaṭha Upaniṣad
KauU	Kauśītaki Upaniṣad
KeU	Kena Upaniṣad

KP	Kūrma Purāṇa
KU	Kaivalya Upaniṣad
MaiU	Maitrī Upaniṣasd
MaU	Māṇḍukya Upaniṣad
MB	Mahābhārata
MnU	Mahā Nārāyaṇa Upaniṣad
MS	Mīmāṁsā Sūtra
MuU	Muṇḍaka Upaniṣad
P	Page(s)
PU	Praśṇa Upaniṣad
RV	Ṛgveda
SPB	Sāṅkhyapravacanabhāṣya of Vijñānabhikṣu
SU	śvetāśvatara Upaniṣad
SuU	śuka Upaniṣad
Trans.	Translator, Translated by
TU	Taittirīya Upaniṣad
VAB	Vijñānāmṛtabhāṣyam
VP	Viṣṇu Purāṇa
YV	Yajurveda
YVV	Yogavārttika of Vijñānabhikṣu

GENERAL INTRODUCTION

What a chimera is a reality in which humans interact! Reason, experience and the mystery abound it. It leads to wonder and appreciate the all-inclusive Absolute. Conversely, it compels one to accept the fact of its plurality of existence. There is fundamentally an inherent unity and at the same time discernible plurality. How do we comprehend this enigmatic *status quo*? In what relation unity and plurality can co-exist, and what is their interrelation? Is unity real and diversity an illusion? Empirically, what is the status of, and the relationship between the sentient and insentient world with it? Is the philosophical Absolute Reality the same as the Absolute of religion which endorses it, or are they different? If it is the same, can one tradition accommodate the other within its fold with all its diversities and uniqueness? Questions multiply when I delve into the heart of the ontology of Vedāntic philosophy, especially the philosophy of Vijñānabhikṣu.

The Context

I grew up in a multi-religious neighbourhood. As I became an adult, the fascination and taste for religious harmony and interconnectivity became the dynamic force of my philosophy. However, the present socio-religious scenario of the country has disturbed the cordial fabric of society, orienting it stealthily into intolerance. The liberating perspective of religions and their universalistic scriptural outlook is regarded in suspicion both by the insiders as well as by the outsiders. The majoritarian religion of the country, Hinduism, known for 'accommodation and hospitality'[1] over the centuries is now repressing its intent and fervour. Further, its plethora of beliefs and forms encompass a tremendous diversity of India since centuries as known by the term '*sanātana dharma*,'[2] eternal faith that espouses the concept of all-embracing and all-inclusive feeling. However, the present 'one-religion, one-culture, and one-nation' meme pose a great threat to this universalism. This threat is triggered not only by the 'religion nation' point of view but also provoked by the philosophical and intellectual tenets. The medieval religious and intellectual culture are founded on accommodative principles could be a saving figure here.

At the same time, material culture is unseating the transcendence. Religion and its practices are getting commercialized rather than catering to the spirituality of people. The modern technocratic innovations, artificial intelligence, genetic culture and globalization turn all the social communion and interactions topsy-turvy. More people are becoming agnostics, atheists and non-religious.[3] At this juncture a question emerges, 'can the scripture give us an alternative where the divine is recognized at the same time culture, pluralism and accommodation, no matter which religion one endorses, is respected?' This implies that there has been a deviation in every religion from adopting an integral approach. Scriptures and their messages have been the inspiring forces of unity and mutual understanding in every culture.

Upholding and re-appropriating their central message is the need of the hour. Therefore, the question posed in this dissertation is, "*What is the inseparable thread that unites the divergent aspect of reality?*" A non-differentiating relationship that exists in the form of the divine essence is the uniting feature of every uniqueness and difference. This is a remarkable emancipatory aspect found in the scripture, tradition or any religion that can be the healing remedy for various divisions in society. *Avibhāga Bhedābheda* concept of Vijñānabhikṣu can harmoniously accommodate different traditions, cultures, ideologies, differences without compromising one's uniqueness. This foundation is established in his commentary on the *Brahmasūtras* of Bādarāyaṇa called the *Vijñānāmṛtabhāṣyam*.

The Research Question and Hypothesis

Scripture is not the monopoly of a particular religion. By its very nature, the truth contents of it are universal. Vijñānabhikṣu taking this insight, comments on the *Brahmasūtras* of Bādarāyaṇa to show that the Hindu scriptures are proposing a pluralistic *weltanschauung* (world-view). His commentary on the *Brahmasūtras* known as *Vijñānāmṛtabhāṣyam* proposes an inseparable union (*avibhāga*) of the self and the world with the Absolute exhibiting an integral vision of the reality. A closer textual analysis illustrates a theistic integral non-dualism and a purposeful divine intervention brought in by Vijñānabhikṣu in this seminal work at a time when Hinduism was in danger of its existence and had the challenge of unifying diverse creeds. Integral theism can be a healing remedy to bring about a harmonious difference in the present world.

Rooted in one's tradition, without disregarding other creeds, and refuting materialistic and agnostic trends of the time, Vijñānabhikṣu embarked on a commentary of the *Brahmasūtras* from the *Sāṅkhya* perspective to uphold the *integral theism as an inseparable thread to unite divergent aspects of reality, and simultaneously maintaining the differences*. What binds therefore religions, traditions and culture is the penetrating divinity. This work in North India came at a time when the Moghul dynasty was at its zenith; the religious renaissance in the form of Bhakti traditions was widespread; Buddhism and Jainism had remarkable influence in society; Islam and Christianity were making their presence felt, and agnostic and atheistic trends were challenging the existing ritualism and clericalism of the majority religion.

Presently, we recognize discordant notes among the people in the name of gods, divisions within and without in the religions, idolatrous practices, the deification of animals, pseudo reasonings, growing intolerance and the material tendencies of religious practices. The majority religion needs a reformation as any religion requires. This reformation has to come from within. The scriptures compel to be re-read and interpreted keeping the present time in mind. The integral theism of Vijñānabhikṣu has the vista of making people realize the sacredness of relationships to live a harmonious life with all the uniqueness and differences.

Therefore, we presuppose that *a non-differentiating relationship in the form of divine essence existing at the core of the being threads the divergent views and unique features in a community creating an integral vision*, like an umbrella that shelters different people under its hood.

The Objective

One neither needs to abandon one's tradition and creed nor needs to embrace the other in order to dialogue and have a harmonious life. 'Mono-culture and mono-religion' archetype is against the very nature of any religious belief. The seeds of truth are present everywhere. Every scripture upholds in its deepest core an integral and accommodative *weltanschauung*. Therefore, hatred, ill-feeling, and queasiness towards other cultures and traditions within and without religion are not divine sanctions. Being rooted in one's own culture with a firm belief in one's creed can have a fruitful relationship with the other. Mutual accommodation and respect are the keys for a healthy society. Therefore, the objective of this research is to establish a foundation for an integral vision to understand the point of arrival and departure without infuriating anyone and to have a divine *darśana* in everything.

The Methodology

The methodology used here is exegetical and analytical. By *exegetical,* we mean that the issue is viewed from the hermeneutical perspective both in its primary and derivative meanings. Further, it is examined from the viewpoints of the author and others to have a wider perspective. By *analytical*, we imply that the issue is presented systematically as it is, critically investigated, setting aside any biases and preconceived assumptions. Therefore, it is a direct investigation and descriptive in form.

Here, we directly harp on the primary resources. Nuances from the original texts are absorbed and critiqued using several secondary sources such as books, articles, electronic materials, and discussions with scholars of different grades. At times, the descriptive and reflective trajectory could not be avoided rather than being evaluative to make the work lucid and palatable.

A detailed bibliography at the end, a glossary of frequently used words, and standard transliteration aimed at the reader to have better exposure to the related textual studies. All the non-English words are transcribed with diacritics and italics except for persons, places, and terms frequently used in the English language.

The Review of Literature

So far nothing substantial has been done in this field. There is no complete translation of *Vijānāmṛtabhāṣyam*, the book under our scrutiny in any languages of the world. What is accessible so far is only a part of the translation in English by John Borelli known as, "*The Theology of Vijñānabhikṣu: A Translation of His Commentary on Brahma Sūtras 1.1.2 and an Exposition of His Difference-in-Identity Theology.*"[4] Being theological in its nature, the dissertation of Borelli aims to proffer a foundation for the "tripartite division"[5] of theological writings of both the East and the West. By tripartite division, he meant to divide the thought patterns of both the East and the West with *bheda*, *abheda* and *bhedābheda* or identity, difference and difference-in-identity respectively. However, this is a handy secondary source for any researcher, to begin with.

Two more works in line with Borelli are Kanshi Ram's *Integral Non-Dualism*[6] and Andrew J. Nicholson's *Unifying Hinduism.*[7] The former is a critical exposition of Vijñānabhikṣu's system of philosophy without any practical significance. And the latter is a survey of the *Vedāntic* philosophy in which Vijñānabhikṣu's *Avibhāga-Bhedābheda* is a part, showing how they all can be encapsulated in a single system of belief known as 'Hinduism.' Further, Nicholson shows how Vijñānabhikṣu's philosophy is an attempt to unify the entire Hinduism. Both these works base themselves on the *Vijñānāmṛtabhāṣyam* to enumerate the philosophy of Vijñānabhikṣu.

However, the first scholarly work on Vijñānabhikṣu is done by Sureścandra Śrīvāstava under the title, "*Ācārya Vijñānabhikṣu Aur Bhāratīya Darśan Me Unkā Sthān* [*A Study of Vijñānabhikṣu and His Place in Indian Philosophy*]."[8] There are three important things Śrīvāstava places before us through this work: the biographical details of Vijñānabhikṣu, the basic contents of his teachings available so far, and a vague place of Vijñānabhikṣu in Hindu thought pattern. But this is only the first major introduction to the thinker in modern time with a special focus on the date of composition and the basic idea. Secondly, the work being a dissertation submitted to Allahabad University is unavailable to the common readers since it is not placed in the public domain. This is written in the Hindi language, and therefore it is as if extant to the readers.

Among the other thinkers and writers, Surendranath Dasgupta is worth mentioning. He has dedicated a major section in the third volume of his five volumes in *A History of Indian Philosophy*[9] to Vijñānabhikṣu and his philosophy. He has contributed to the general idea of Vijñānabhikṣu, Brahman and world, individual self, nature of experience, the relationship between *Sāṅkhya* and Vedānta, criticism of *Sāṅkhya* and *Yoga* and finally the basic tenets of *Īśvara Gītā* (the second part of the *Kūrma Purāṇa*).

Another interesting work worth referring to here is done by Hayavadana Rao. He has summarized Vijñānabhikṣu's philosophy in 28 pages, more prominently the first *sūtra* in his 888 pages long introduction to the *śrīkarabhāṣya*.[10] In his work, Rao has placed Vijñānabhikṣu around in the middle of the 17th century, without any substantial pieces of evidences. Sarvepalli Radhakrishnan has a short introduction to Vijñānabhikṣu in his *The Brahma Sūtra: The Philosophy of Spiritual Life*.[11] However, he has depended largely on Hayavadana Rao.

Among the other works of the thinker, only *Sāṅkhya* and *Yoga* are translated and commented upon especially by Ramshankar Bhattacharya and Goswami Prahallada Giri, F.E. Hall, Richard Garb, T.S. Rukmani, Anima Sen-Gupta, Jadunath Sinha and Shiv Kumar.

Apart from these, Mircea Eliade in his book *Yoga: Immortality and Freedom*[12] has references in several places to the works of Vijñānabhikṣu, especially to the works on *Yoga* and *Sāṅkhya*. A detailed bibliography on the available primary and secondary sources of Vijñānabhikṣu is furnished at the end.

The present work is a philosophical one. Apart from affirming the unificatory dimension of Hinduism, the book aims at critically exposing the practical application of Vijñānabhikṣu's key concept, the *Avibhāga-Bhedābheda*. Without limiting the *Vedāntic* text itself to Hinduism, the care is taken to interpret the idea with a panoramic perspective. This approach can be a tool to re-read any scripture from an integral approach, i.e., scriptures can be read as accommodating diverse cultures and traditions without any prejudices. In a deeper sense, religion should be an inclusive enterprise, promoting religious and social harmony, ushering in an all-encompassing liberation.

Limitations

I have foreseen and underwent many difficulties and limitations during my research. They are:

1. Lack of deep knowledge on the Sanskrit language is a handicap in my research. Though the language employed by Vijñānabhikṣu is classical Sanskrit, he has utilized the Sanskrit language of the time in many places. It enjoins a real in-depth knowledge of both classical and modern Sanskrit to get to the original nuances that Vijñānabhikṣu intends. The reading becomes all the more tedious due to the unavailability of any prevalent translations of the time. However, a determined effort is made to read the original writings with the help of limited knowledge of Sanskrit and secondary resources.

2. Indian philosophy is rich and complex with diverse canons both in terms of *śruti* and *smṛti*. To know is to invest thevwhole of one's life, yet insufficient. The use of diverse

canons by Vijñānabhikṣu especially from the lesser known *smṛti* complicates the research into indigestible lumps.

3. One requires to be an insider to give a balanced interpretation and critique, or else the interpretation will be mired in a bloghole. Being an outsider, at times my convictions and upbringing has consciously or unconsciously imbued the hermeneutical circle of the text. Though I have tried to be neutral, yet in many places, it has become unavoidable and palpable.

4. The very nature of Indian philosophy is a *jugalbandi* (entwined twins) of philosophy and theology or reason and faith. When reason fails to answer a query faith resolves in, and when faith fumbles to satisfy reason rescues it and vice-versa. Getting acquainted with this realm and attempting a satisfying explanation at times is a herculean task.

The Structure of the Book

The present book is divided into five chapters. The first two chapters deal with the historical overview of *Bhedābheda Vedānta* in line with *Advaita* (*abheda*) and *Dvaita* (*bheda*). *Bhedābheda*, in a primitive theistic sense, was already present in *Vedic* literature. This monotheistic undercurrent was further appropriated by the *Upaniṣads* and the later writings in Hinduism. As the thought pattern becomes more complicated later during the *Vedāntic* period a better clarification was sought. *Bhedābheda* doctrine is the result of such prolonged investigation. As a result, a separate class of *Vedānta* evolved over the centuries. Thus, this chapter gives a historical background for *Avibhāga-Bhedābheda*.

The third chapter gives an immediate background to the philosophy of Vijñānabhikṣu. The Socio-cultural, historico-philosophical and religious situation of the time is probed before giving a detailed biography and works of the author.

The fourth chapter examines the *Avibhāga-Bhedābheda* of Vijñānabhikṣu as propounded in his commentary on the *Brahmasūtras*. Without limiting to one particular *sūtra* as Borelli did, this chapter will cull out the concept used by the thinker throughout the book. As the chapter advances the non-distinguishing relationship, the crux of unifying aspect of differences and uniqueness are scrutinized using *tattvamasi* concept and various other relationships.

The integral theism or the *Avibhāga-Bhedābheda* as envisaged in the previous chapter was the need of the hour in the 16th century. Vijñānabhikṣu in his erudite style formulates it through his commentary on the *Brahmasūtras*. The fifth chapter critiques and appropriates this concept. During the operation, care is taken to place Vijñānabhikṣu in the context in order to make him meaningful to the present ambiance.

The general conclusion sums up the findings of the thesis with an orientation to further opening or scope for the future research. The present work delineates a further scholarship on the unexplored areas of Vijñānabhikṣu. Thus, the entire research is like burrowing a hole in the sand—the deeper one digs the center, the wider the periphery it creates.

---

[1] The issue, 'the Vedic culture being accommodative' is very much debatable. Though the Vedic dictum "*ekaṁ sat viprā bahudhā vadanti*" endorses accommodation, yet the Aryan culture to which Vedas are the custodians, has swallowed up indigenous socio-religious culture. Looking at the Aryan invasion theories, the absorption of local deities and cultures endorsed in the *smṛti* literature and even with the language patterns one can easily state that it is not an accommodative religion. The understanding of '*sanātana dharma*' as understood today, has come much later. In this book, I have presupposed that the Vedic religion is accommodative. The etymological meaning of the word 'Hindu' has a broad vision. "*hīnaṁ dūṣayati*" means, the one who condemns immoral standards or "*hīnaṁ dūrayati iti hindu*" one who keeps away vices is a Hindu. Bhīmācārya Jhalakīkar, *Nyāyakoṣaḥ or Dictionary of Technical Terms of Indian Philosophy*, 2015 ed. s.v. "hinduḥ."

[2] *dhṛīyate loko'nena,* that which holds many worlds; *dhārati lokam,* holds the world; or *dhṛ+man*, beholding the other. Vaman Shivram Apte, *The Student's Sanskrit-English Dictionary*, 1991 ed.; Vaman Shivram Apte, *A Sanskrit English Dictionary*, 2015 ed. See under the word, "dharma," "dhṛ" and "man."

[3] According to the latest *Global Index of Religiosity and Atheism*, there is a rise in number of non-religious in India. As against 87% saying they were religious in the same survey in 2005, the percentage has fallen to 81% in 2015, a drop in 6% in seven years. Kounteya Sinha, "More Indians have stopped believing in God: Survey," in *Times of India*, e-Paper 27 May 2013. Available on https://timesofindia.indiatimes.com/world/uk/More-Indians-have-stopped-believing-in-God-Survey/ articleshow/20284261.cms, accessed on 26 December 2018. The census of India also proves this fact. The number of 'no religion' over the years has doubled from 0.43% in 1951 to 0.72% in 2001 to 0.9% in 2011. C. Chandramouli, "Census of India 2011–A Story of Innovations," Press Information Bureau, Government of India, 23 August 2011.

[4] John W. Borelli, "The Theology of Vijñānabhikṣu: A Translation of His Commentary on Brahma Sūtras 1.1.2 and an Exposition of His Difference-in-Identity Theology" (PhD Dissertation, Fordham University, 1976).

[5] Borelli, "The Theology of Vijñānabhikṣu," viii, 13.

[6] Kanshi Ram, *Integral Non-Dualism: A Critical Exposition of Vijñānabhikṣu's System of Philosophy* (New Delhi: Motilal Banarsidass Publications, 1995).

[7] A.J. Nicholson, *Unifying Hinduism: Philosophy and Identity in Indian Intellectual History* (Columbia University Press, 2010).

[8] Sureścandra Śrīvāstava, *Ācārya Vijñānabhikṣu Aur Bhāratīya Darśan Me Unkā Sthān* [*A Study of Vijñānabhikṣu and His Place in Indian Philosophy*] (Allahabad: Lokabharati Prakashan, 1969).

[9] Surendranath Dasgupta, *A History of Indian Philosophy*, vol. 3 (London: Cambridge University Press, 1940), 445-95. Also see, Surendranath Dasgupta, "Vijñānabhikṣu," in *Encyclopedia of Indian Philosophies, vol 15: Bhedābheda and Dvaitādvaita Systems,* 417-460. Edited by M. M. Agrawal, Karl H. Potter (Delhi: Motilal Banarsidass Publishers, 2013).

[10] C. Hayavadana Rao, ed., *The Śrīkara Bhāṣya: Being the Vīraśaiva Commentary on the Vedānta Sūtras by Śrīpati*, 2003 ed., 2

vols., vol. 1 (New Delhi: Akshaya Prakashan, 1936), 153-180. This *bhāṣya* is a *Śaiva* text.

[11] Sarvepalli Radhakrishnan, *The Brahma Sūtra: The Philosophy of Spiritual Life* (London: George Allen and Unwin, 1960), 94-95.

[12] Mircea Eliade, *Yoga: Immortality and Freedom*, translated by Willard R. Trask (London: Routledge and Kegan Paul, 1958). This book is originally published in 1954 in French language with the title, *Le Yoga: Immortalite et Liberte*.

Chapter One
AN OVERVIEW OF THE *BHEDĀBHEDA-VEDĀNTA*

Darśana is the foundation of the mystical life. India has been the country where *darśana* and *dharma* co-existed since time immemorial. The enigma of *satya* and *mithya* of the physical existence, and the understanding of *saguṇa* and *nirguṇa* of the Absolute with its revealing and concealing aspects are the bones of contention in all the philosophical discourses. Added to this is their inter-intra relationship. This relationship is not a new insight for the ancient seers. However, it has become the central theme in the later *Mīmāṁsā* tradition, known as the *Vedānta*.

The word '*vedānta*' literally means 'the end of the *Veda*.' Understood from a broader sense, it refers to the later part of *Mīmāṁsā*, one of the six Orthodox Schools (*āstika darśana*) of the Indian Philosophy. The former part of *Mīmāṁsā*, known as the *Pūrva Mīmāṁsā* proposes tools for the "rational inquiry"[1] of the *Vedas* (and the scriptures in general). The necessity for rational inquiry is due to the unintelligible, incongruous, self-contradictory and apparently meaningless sentences[2] along with straightforward and lucid texts of the scriptures. This is also proof for the *Bhedābheda* outlook in the scripture. Therefore, Jaimini composed the aphorisms known as the *Mīmāṁsā Sūtras* and maintained the interpretative tools to explain the *karmakāṇḍa* (*Saṁhitā* and

Brāhmaṇā) part of the *Vedas*. In contrast, Bādarāyaṇa in the similar fashion codified the *jñānakāṇḍa* part of the *Vedas* (*Upaniṣad* and *Āraṇyakā*), naming them the *Brahmasūtras*, the aphorisms describing the nature of Brahman, *jīva*, and *jagat*, and together with their relationship. This came to be known as the *Vedānta Darśana* or the *Uttara Mīmāṁsā*. Therefore, the *Vedānta* is nothing but the philosophical speculations of the *Vedic* literature.

Based on the acceptance of the reality, the *Vedānta* can be classified into three prominent traditions: *Advaita*, *Dvaita* and *Dvaitādvaita*,[3] i.e., the School considers reality as one (*eka* or *advitīya* or *abheda*), dual (*dvitīya* or *bheda*), and both different and non-different (*Bhedābheda* or *Dvaitādvaita*), respectively. The chief proponent of the monistic interpretation is Śaṅkarācārya. The dualistic interpretation is championed by Madhvācārya. However, there is no one chief proponent to be singled out as *the first and the key proponent* of the *Bhedābheda*.

The inability to single out the exclusive proponent is due to the nature of Reality and the scriptural foundation itself. This is its strength and not its weakness. Therefore, one can find very much the *Bhedābheda* tradition both in *śruti* and *smṛti*, and in Reality.

This chapter provides a historical overview of the *Bhedābheda* tradition beginning from the *Vedas*, the *Upaniṣads* and the *Vedāntic* traditions in two chapters. The first chapter demonstrates a divine inseparable thread running in every aspect of reality to make it one whole despite certain unique features as found in the *Vedas*, the *Upaniṣads* and the *Bhagavad Gītā*. This will also imply the inseparable relationship inherent in it. The second chapter, continuing from the first sifts the same relationship from various *Bhedābheda* traditions over the centuries.

1.1 *Bhedābheda* in the *Vedic* Literature

At the outset, the *Vedic* religion is said to be polytheistic due to a vast number of deities, to which the hymns are addressed and attributed to. However, it is not the right thing to categorically affirm it so. There is a basic monotheistic flow in Vedic literature. Max Müller thinks that the right thing to address the *Vedic* religion is '*kathenotheism*,' "the consciousness that all the deities are but different names of the same godhead breaks forth indeed here and there in the Vedas."[4] The *Ṛgveda* affirms it, "They call him Indra, Mitra, Varuṇa, Agni; then he is the beautiful-winged heavenly Gurutman: that which *is One the wise call it in diverse manners*: They call it Agni, Yama, Mātariśvān... Wise poets make the beautiful-winged, *though he is One, manifold by words*" (RV 10.114-15, 121).[5] This 'One' effects everything. The *Nāsadīyasūkta* explicates, "That one breathed, windless, by its impulse. Other than that there was nothing beyond" (RV 10.129.2).[6] The reality of the Supreme Being is depicted to be one with the world yet otherwise. As a result of this inseparable oneness, Dasgupta moots the origin of the theory of *Bhedābheda*, tracing it to *Puruṣasūkta* of the *Ṛgveda*. Brahman is not only identical with the creation but also greater and distinct from this.[7]

Brahman as neuter gender, in the sense of creative power or the principal cause of all things, does not occur in the *Ṛgveda.* But it is found in *Atharvaveda* and several *Brāhmaṇas.* The *Atharvaveda* declares, "The oldest or greatest Brahman which rules everything that has been or will be... Heaven is said to belong to Brahman alone" (AV 10.8.1). The *Śatapatha Brāhmaṇa* discloses, "Brahman is called the firstborn, the self-existing, the best of the gods, and heaven and earth are identified with it" (*Śatapatha Brāhmaṇa* 8.4.9.3).[8]

Yāska in his *Nirukta* postulates that "There is One Supreme Being and all other *Devatās* are His limbs only" (*Nirukta* 7.4).[9] But this one Supreme Soul is variously praised, on account of His omnipotence. Other *devatās* are but *pratyāṅgas* (various manifestations) of this one Supreme Soul.[10] Dayānanda Saraswati understands the word '*devatā*' in the Vedas to refer to 'One Supreme Lord.' The deities mentioned are merely different names, indicating the most important attributes of the Supreme.[11] He supposes, "Agni, Varuṇa, Āditya, Mātariśvā and Indra may mean anything in different contexts but they also mean Supreme Being (Brahma) [sic], described under different names. They are different names of one Lord."[12] Besides he reiterates, "The Vedic Hymns are chanted *to One Deity under many names,* names which are used, and even designed, to express His qualities and powers."[13] RV 10.164.10 poses a specific question, "*kasmai devāya*?" (Who is that God?), and answers it as "*prajāpatiḥ*" (He is the *prajāpati,* the Lord of the people). Further, it clarifies that He (*prajāpati*) is none but "the only

Lord of creation, the only king, who fixed heaven and earth." A similar rendering can also be noted in the *Atharvaveda*, "He, who is soul-giving, strength-giving, of whom all, of whom even the gods, wait upon instructions; who is the Lord of these bipeds, who of quadrupeds—to what god may we pay worship with oblation."[14] Several other statements prove that there is only one Supreme Reality and all other deities are either part of it or names of its attributes. In fact, Dayānanda Saraswati in his *Ṛgvedādi-Bhāṣya-Bhūmikā* determines all the deities mentioned in these verses as qualities of Brahman. Therefore, the Vedic religion advocating plurality as understood by several European scholars is flawed. It is the only emanation of the One and only One God. All plurality is only imaginary (an idea), which is already expressed clearly and distinctly in RV 1.164.46 "*ekaṁ sadviprā bahudhā vadanti*."[15]

The following are the few references from the Vedas to ascertain this fact.[16]

- "Many are Thy names O Agni, Immortal, God, Divine, Jātavedas."[17]
- "Indra moves multiform, in His wonderful creation."[18]
- "Even He is Agni, He is Āditya, He is Vāyu, He is Candrama; He is Śukra, He is Brahma, He is Āpa, He is Prajāpati."[19]
- "He is Āryamā, He is Varuṇa, He is Rudra, He is Mahādeva; He is Agni, He is Sūrya, He is verily Mahā Yama."[20]
- "Neither second, nor third, nor yet fourth, is He called. He is called neither fifth, nor sixth, nor yet seventh. He

is called neither eighth, nor ninth, nor yet tenth. He is the Sole, the Absolute One, the One alone. In Him, all gods become simple and One."[21]

This characterizes the Vedic praxis as monotheistic. This Absolute One is concretely portrayed multifariously. The *Taittirīya Upaniṣad* expresses it, "*bahusyām prajāyeyeti*," "let me be many" (TU 2.6). The 'Absolute One' is referred to as '*puruṣaḥ*' in the Vedas. In fact, this Sanskrit word denotes humans as a class of beings now.[22] Etymologically, it connotes a deeper reality. *Nyāyakoṣa, the Dictionary of Technical Terms of Indian Philosophy* defines *puruṣa* in terms of *Sāṅkhya* as, "*anubhayātmakaḥ puruṣaḥ*,"[23] the one who has neither *prakṛti* nor *vikṛti*. That is, *puruṣa* is neither the cause nor the effect or neither evolving nor evolute.[24] This implies that it lacks action (*niṣkriyatva*) and possesses eternity (*anāditva*). Thus, *puruṣa* is a transcendental agent which either directly or indirectly involved in the creation of objects in the world.

Both Apte and Suryakanta track down the word to the root *pra/pṛ/pṛī*.[25] All these three roots mean 'pervasion' or 'filling.' This suggests *pṛ*, referring to that which "pervades the body or the world" or "all-pervasive," to be precise *nitya, vyāpaka*, and *apariṇāmī*.[26] 'That which pervades everything' cannot be a limited being like a human being, but the Unlimited or the One Supreme existence, in short, the Soul.[27] Rightly so, Vijñānabhikṣu understands and identifies *puruṣa* to represent the Supreme existence while referring to the highest self of the Reality, i.e., the Brahman. Therefore, *puruṣa* means the Supreme Being, the Creator in the primary sense. While elucidating the significance of the *Puruṣasūkta*, the Vedic hymn, Subhash Anand underpins this aspect as follows:

> He [*Puruṣa*] pervades all and is beyond the boundaries of time. Thus the *Puruṣa* is none other than the Supreme Being, seen in the hymn as self-sacrificing. Thus the *Puruṣa-sūkta* is a myth, a story of primal realities and foundational events. It is trying to tell us something very real about ourselves: our existence is rooted in a mystery, in *Puruṣa* and to the extent we understand this mystery and embody it in our life, our life will be worthwhile.[28]

Therefore, the *Puruṣa* is the Supreme Soul, the cause for *all—surāsura* (divine and non-divine), *naranāri* (men and women), *jīvajantu* (human and non-human), and *jīvājīva* (living and non-living). Furthermore, it is the foundation (*adhiṣṭhāna*) of all that exists.

'That which pervades' needs a locus to pervade. The *Bṛhadāraṇyaka Upaniṣad*, the part of the *Yajurveda* in its second chapter considers the pervading space (*ākāṣa*) as Brahman. It is in this space everything moves and exists like the spider emanating its web from its body and moving in its web, or the sparks come out from the fire,[29] or as the light enlightens the world or as the light that shines within the human being.[30] From this discriminating mark (*liṅga*), Brahman is shown to be *ākāśa* as the *Brahmasūtras* confirm it, "*ākāśastalliṅgāt*" (From His discriminatory mark of *ākāśa*,

BS 1.1.22). Vijñānabhikṣu also supports this, "space as its mark, is the Supreme Brahman,"[31] so too is *prāṇa* in the body.[32] Therefore, both material and transcendental forms are the *locus operandi* of Brahman.

The object of pervasion is *prakṛti*. The root word of *prakṛti* can again be traced back to *pra/pṛ/pṝ* as in the case of *puruṣa* along with *kṛ*. Āpte defines *prakṛti* as "*prakaroti iti prakṛtiḥ*."[33] *Prakṛti* is 'that which induces to do something' (derived from the root word *kṛ*). Further, Monier-Williams explains the use of the root *pra* along with a locative word to mean 'to cause to work, engage upon, entrust with, appoint to.' *Pra,* as an indeclinable participle, has the meaning of 'before, forward, in front and forth' in connection with an active verb, a verb denoting motion or action. Thus, from the combination of the roots *pra/pṛ/pṝ + kṛ/kri + ti,* we get the word *prakṛti* which could mean the substratum in/on which the Supreme Soul pervades or fills in both immanently and transcendentally. In the words of Monier-Williams, "*prakṛti* is the personification of the will of the Supreme Being (Soul) in the creation."[34] The *Sāṅkhya darśana* distinguishes *puruṣa* and *prakṛti* as two primordial eternal elements (*padārtha*) from which everything came into being. Here, *prakṛti* is viewed *jaḍa* as an active principle and the material cause of everything. 'That which is filled' or 'pervaded' cannot be in the vacuum but a substratum. When the substratum is filled with 'that which is pervaded' then it gains momentum. The substratum here is active and feminine (therefore, *prakṛti* is a feminine gender) through which the creation flows forth. The creation is nothing but the divine pervasion in the matter.

From the above explanation, we infer that the Vedic notion of the 'One Supreme Soul' pervades the whole of creation. In other words, Brahman is manifested as the space and the *prakṛti* as the substratum, the locus.

This directs us to the *Sāṅkhya* doctrine of *satkāryavāda*, where Brahman is at once *nimitta kāraṇa* (efficient cause) and *upādāna kāraṇa* (material supportive cause). In other words, there is a non-difference between material cause and its effect. The effect pre-exists in the material cause subtly, as the curd existed in the milk or the pot in the clay. It is the *nimitta kāraṇa* that brings out this effect like the potter brings out the pot from the clay. The material supportive cause is necessary for the continued existence and activity. The dependence of the effect on the efficient cause ends the moment the effect is fashioned. The pot will remain ever even if the potter dies. This leads us to the immanence, the organic unity, and the continued existence of the material cause. Thus, *satkāryavāda* is the basis for *Bhedābheda* philosophy.[35]

The pervasion of the Supreme Soul can neither be separated from that which it is pervaded, nor the pervaded and the pervading are identical. The Vedic seers designate the 'pervaded' as the '*hiraṇyagarbha,*' 'the golden embryo' (RV 10.121). *Hiraṇya* means gold, and *garbha* means womb, therefore, *hiraṇyagarbha* is the 'golden womb.' The womb is the place where creation takes place and is sustained. Similarly, God is the place where creation takes place and is sustained. Brahmā and Viṣṇu are also called *hiraṇyagarbha* as one creates and the other sustains it. *Hiraṇya* can also mean knowledge. Knowledge precedes any creation. Therefore, God is the womb of all knowledge. Therefore, a complicated entwined meaning of *Bhedābheda* is noticed here. The words of Sāyaṇa are very relevant here to epitomize the layers of meaning deposited in the composite word.

> '[H]e is in whose belly the golden seeds or egg exists like an embryo.' This seed of fire is placed in the waters of the womb; it is also the embryo with which the waters become pregnant (v.7). So, too, Agni is the child of the waters but also the god who spills his seed in the waters. These are interlocking rather than contradictory concepts; in the late Vedas, the father is specifically identified with the son. Furthermore, the egg is both a female image (that which is fertilized by seed and which contains the embryo that is like the yolk) and a male image (the testicles containing seed). Thus the range of meaning may be seen as a continuum of androgynous birth image: seed (male egg), womb (female egg), embryo [and] child.[36]

Vijñānabhikṣu has recognized this relationship clearly and therefore enunciates this in terms of the father-son relationship in his commentary (VAB 1.1.2, p.27). Creation and creator are not two different aspects. The son is the continuation of the father and the father is the originator of the son. But, both are not the same physically as individuals.

However, the son surely has some fatherness in him. Modern scientific technology informs us that genes inherited by the son are the combination of the genes of father and mother. That is why a human being will always deliver a human child and an animal will bear its kind.

Another important and "the latest hymns of the *Ṛgveda*,"[37] the *Puruṣasūkta* while illustrating the creation relates to us the primordial sacrifice of *puruṣa* as the cause of the whole of creation—human beings, plants and animals, earth, gods, air, fire, rituals and sacrifices—coming into existence (RV 10.90). The verse 5 is significant here, "From him *Virāj* was born and from *Virāj* came the Man. When he was born, he ranged beyond the earth behind and before."[38] *Virāj* is the female active creative principle. It is later replaced by *prakṛti* or *pradhāna*, or material nature, the matter of *puruṣa* in *Sāṅkhya* philosophy.[39]

Puruṣa can be understood as a 'person.' Person is the one who is endowed with freedom and will. In other words, a person is a being with certain capacities or attributes such as reason, morality, consciousness or self-consciousness, and also a part of a culturally established structure of social relations such as kinship, ownership of property, or legal responsibility. The very concept of *puruṣa* as a person excludes "isolation, alienation, and solipsistic solitariness and expresses inter-connection and unity,"[40] asserts Raimundo Panikkar. Further, he presents, "*Puruṣa* is not only the cosmic Man; it is also the personal aspect of the whole reality."[41] Śaṅkara's definition of *puruṣa* is worth noting here, "*pūrvamauṣadi iti puruṣaḥ*"[42] that is, "one who has burnt or combusted previously." One becomes the *prajāpati* by totally burning one's sins and thus becomes a *puruṣa*.[43] According to *Advaita*, one becomes Brahman by totally removing ignorance, by following the path of knowledge. In the opinion of Vijñānabhikṣu becoming Brahman in the visible world is to become *brahmacāri*. In the *Yogasārasaṅgraha* quoting *Aśvamedhaparva* he spells out, "One who has passed over all disciplinary action and has his basis on *Brahma* alone, he moves about in the world as a *Brahma* himself, is called a *brahmacāri*. *Brahma* is his fuel, *Brahma* is his fire, and his seat also the *Brahma*, *Brahma* his water and his preceptor *Brahma* and he is himself fixed on *Brahma*."[44] This points out that every self-realized conscious being is a visible embodiment of the divine whom the scriptures call *yogarūḍha, sthitaprajña, paramahaṁsa, arhant, buddha, sant,* and so on.

The above description underscores two aspects of *puruṣa*: i. the immanence and transcendence, *ii.* the phenomenal world with all in it as its embodiment. Subhash Anand has a better insight here. According to him, the concept of *sahodara-sahodarī, bandhutva, materia* (matter)/*mātrā* and *mater*/*mātṛ* could be seen as *Bhedābheda* relation in nature. [45] Therefore, *puruṣa* and *prakṛti* are not only two polarities of reality but also inter-depending aspects. Later, the *Upaniṣads* infer and develop this idea of *puruṣa* as Brahman. Thus, Brahman has two-fold existences: *ātman* and *brahman*, that is, immanent and transcendent natures respectively. For Vijñānabhikṣu, *ātman* is like the son of the father, in the sense of part and whole.[46] Here, one does not discover a single well-articulated system of thought rather identifies strands interwoven into a single whole. However, the relationship between *ātman*, *Brahman* and *jagat* which is expressed feebly in the *Vedas* is investigated as an important element in all the *Upaniṣads*. The *Vedānta* further surveys it as the key issue. Therefore, immanence and transcendence are not something beyond one's imagination, but a concrete reality expressed in every sentient and non-sentient being.

This transports us altogether to another realm, that every being is endowed with transcendence and will, basically share something common. They are the divine inheritance, common substratum, and locus. Therefore, they are one family yet individuals have different roles to play to conserve the organic unity of the whole.

1.2 *Bhedābheda* in the *Upaniṣadic* Literature

The opening verse of the *Īśa Upaniṣad* declares, "All things whatsoever move in this universe and the universe itself; is pervaded or clothed by the Lord. Thou should enjoy by abandonment, covet not anybody's wealth."[47] The Lord is both a substantial and efficient cause of the *lokāloka*. It is in and through Him we live, move and have our being. The existence of any being is clothed in the Lord which supports the understanding of *adhiṣṭhāna* in *Vedāntic* literature.

Every being is a manifestation of the divine and is at its core divine, for it has been created not only by the Supreme but also out of the Supreme like a 'spider weaves its web.'[48] The prospect and potentiality of discovering the divine lie in every sentient being. That's why it is prompted, *ātmā vā are dṛṣṭavyaḥ, śrotavyaḥ mantavyaḥ ca*—self alone is to be seen, heard and meditated. Thus, there is a basic *abheda* in the reality, which is difficult to break apart (*avicchedaḥ*) from it. Therefore, the reality basically is *avibhāgādvaita* which is the basic teaching of the *Upaniṣads*. However, this teaching can be verified on two levels: *bheda* and *abheda*.

1.2.1 *Bhedatva* in the *Upaniṣads*

There are several verses and occurrences in the *Upaniṣads* incorporating duality and plurality. One of the famous verses, appearing in three principal *Upaniṣads*, is "*dvā suparṇā sayujā sakhāyā samānaṁ vṛkṣam pariṣasvajāte tayor anyaḥ pippalaṁ svādvatti anaśnannanyo abhicākaśīti.*" It means, "Two birds, companions (who are) always united, cling to the self-same tree. Of these two, the one eats the sweet fruit and the other looks on without eating" (MuU 3.1.3).[49] The same aphorism is found also in the *Śvetāśvatara Upaniṣad* 4.6-7. The alike with a slight modification also occur in *Kaṭhā Upaniṣad*, "There are two selves that drink the fruit of the *Karma* in the world of good deeds. Both are lodged in the secret place (of the heart), the chief seat of the Supreme. The knowers of Brahman speak of them as shade and light as also (the householders) who maintain the five sacrificial fires and those too who perform the triple Nāciketa fire"[50] (KaU 1.3.1). The *Ṛgveda* also mentions a similar aphorism in 1.164.20.[51] According to Ranade, the bird which relishes the fruit is the individual soul and that which looks on is the Universal Soul.[52] In any case, they represent two distinct beings.

Further, we can also distinguish between the Supreme Being, and the individual being and matter, "There are two unborn ones, the knowing and the unknowing, the one all-powerful, the other powerless"[53] (SU 1.9). Though they are two distinct individuals, they are one aspect of the Supreme Being. That's why Dr. Radhakrishnan insists, *jīveśvara-prakṛti-rūpa-trayaṁ brahmam*—the individual souls, the personal god and *prakṛti* or nature are all contained in Brahman.[54]

Individual beings possess certain qualities, functions, etc. Whatever is perceived by the senses is possible to indicate to others. This insinuates that there must be a being or a thread devoid of all these characteristics, like *jāti-guṇa-kriyā-viśeṣaṇaiḥ* (genus, quality, function or relationship). The *Kena Upaniṣad* expounds, "There the eye goes not, speech goes not, nor the mind; we know not, we understand not how one can teach this."[55] Similar references can be seen in KaU 6.12, MU 3.1.8, and TU 2.4. The Supreme Being is not dependent on mind, life and senses, for, its being. He is an independent reality and the individual souls are dependent on Him.[56] Clearly, a dualistic understanding is seen in the *Upaniṣads*. In the *Śvetaśvatara Upaniṣad* it is more towards *ātman* and *prakṛti*, while in other *Upaniṣads,* it is between human being and divine[57] (*apara* and *para*). Thus, the *Upaniṣads* speak about a *svatantra* reality and a *paratantra* reality. This does not negate the unitary aspect of both as in the case of *tat* and *tvam* of *tattvamasi* in the *Chāndogya Upaniṣad* (CU 6.8.7).

1.2.2 *Abhedatva* in the *Upaniṣads*

In the beginning, Brahman was alone without a second existing. He desired to be many, and thus creation came into being[58] (CU 6.2.1,3). The Being, that existed prior to its manifestation (*idam*), was without any limitations (*upādhis*). There was no second being. This is also disseminated in the *Taittirīya Upaniṣad*, "non-existent, verily, was this (world) in the beginning. Therefore, verily, was existence produced. That made itself a soul."[59] A similar statement also can be noted in CU 3.19.1, "That the Sun is Brahman is a prevailing teaching. This world, in the beginning, was non-existent. *Sat* termed as *tat* (that), alone existed. It subjected itself to becoming."[60] The 'non-existent' here signals the world before it comes into being. The manifested condition of the world is called *sat*. *Sat* is that which exists, and that which exists is *Being*. This *Being* reveals (be-ing) or manifests itself (*svataḥ pramāṇyam*). The revelatory function of existence is shown in its verbal form in the Western Philosophical thought, that is, Be-ing. This is not a new aspect of Indology. The equivalent form of Be-ing is Brahman.

Brahman should be known from its etymological sense. The word *brahman* comes from the root *bṛh*, or *vṛh*, meaning 'to break forth, to grow, to increase, to expand, to swell,' etc.[61] The Truth/*Sat* is continuously manifesting in its both existent and non-existent form. Truth is manifested more as one goes deeper, namely, its revelation expands (the verbal form). The more we endeavour to know, the more we know that how less we know. Thus, there is a non-difference between what is expressed as existence and unexpressed as non-existence. The *Ṛgveda* states that in the beginning there was neither being nor non-being.[62] Whatever is created by this Being is part and parcel of it, and therefore, there is a total *abheda* between the created and creator.

In the beginning, this world was Brahman and then everything came into being.[63] This being desired to be many, and thus, the creation came to be and therefore, whatever in the creation is its embodiment. Hence, the *Taittirīya Upaniṣad* enunciates:

> He (the supreme soul) desired. Let me become many, let me be born. He performed austerity. Having performed austerity He created all this, whatever is here. Having created it, into it, indeed, He entered. Having entered it, He became both the actual and the beyond, the defined and the undefined, both the founded and the non-founded, the intelligent and the non-intelligent, the true and the untrue. As the real, He became whatever there is here. This is what they call the real.[64]

Appropriately, we see two clear aspects of Brahman: transcendental and immanent, actual and beyond or *sat* and *tyāt*. The transcendental Brahman willed, thought and created. The incomprehensible divine becomes a concrete reality, revealing itself into many-ness in the phenomenal world.

The *Bṛhadāraṇyaka Upaniṣad* beautifully propounds the phenomenon of One becoming Many yet remaining one integral whole. In the beginning, this world was *puruṣa*, and this *puruṣa* alone existed. Then, He wished to be many to have delight. Therefore, He embraced as if the couple would do and caused Himself to fall (*patati*). With the fall, He became two equal parts whom He called *pati* (husband) and *patni* (wife) like the two halves of a split pea. *Pati* embraced *patni* and became united with her, and thus human beings were produced. Later, from this primordial couple every other being—cow, bull, mare, stallion, she-ass, he-ass, hoofed animals, goats, ewe, rams—whatever exists in pairs, down to the ants came into existence.[65] This indicates to us that every human being in its essence is the embodiment of the divine, but not a complete one. The completion transpires when the husband and wife (male and female) begin to procreate (come together). Both the *pati* and *patni* are equal parts of the divine, and the two are "not separate and the theory is not one of the final dualism,"[66] but one integral reality. What proceeds from this is the new creation which is the continuation of the parent body and simultaneously there is discontinuity. This integral unity is asserted in the *Bṛhadāraṇyaka Upaniṣad* as, "This self was verily Brahman at first. It knew only itself as 'I am Brahman.' Because of that, it became all."[67] Though Śaṅkara advocates here *abheda*, he does not negate the close affinity between creation and creator, "Because, I myself have created this whole world and therefore it is not different from me."[68]

The manifold beings are only scintillations from Brahman. All that exists now are coming from this Brahman. The *Muṇḍaka Upaniṣad* corroborates, "many kinds of beings issue forth from the immutable and they return thither too"[69] like "a spider moves along the thread, as small sparks come forth from the fire, even so from this Self come forth all breaths, all worlds, all divinities, all beings."[70] A similar rendering is also perceived in the *Maitrī Upaniṣad*, "from him, indeed, who is in the self come forth all living creatures, all worlds, all the [V]edas, all the gods and all beings."[71]

Vijñānabhikṣu endorses this view. According to him, there are multiple *puruṣas* in the world, but they are all related in a relationship of father-son or as part and whole relation (*aṁśa-aṁśībhāva*[72]). Put succinctly, there is only One *Puruṣa* as identified in a gift of unbounded energy. All the other revealed *puruṣas* have their origin in this One, and the hidden one is pervading in all.[73] The *Praśna Upaniṣad* compares this great *Puruṣa* to the central hub of the chariot's wheel and its spokes as other *puruṣas*.[74] The same thing is attested by the *Bṛhadāraṇyaka Upaniṣad*, "Just as the spokes of a wheel are held together in the naval of the wheel, similarly in the Supreme Soul are centered all these beings, all gods, all worlds and all individual souls. The Supreme Soul is the king of all" (BU 3.5.15). The *Gītā* too validates this view, "Nothing higher than me exists, O Arjuna. On me all this universe is strung like pearls on a thread" (BG 7.7).

The *Muṇḍaka Upaniṣad* identifies the Self with the Supreme Person and the universe. There is no distinction between Brahman and this universe. Explicitly, this universe has no separate existence apart from the *Puruṣa*.[75]

In the *Śvetaśvatara Upaniṣad*, Brahman (*eko devaḥ*) is

equated with Rudra who is assigned with the three-fold duties: creation, protection and maintenance. The *Upaniṣad* declares, "Truly Rudra is one, there is no place for a second, who rules all these worlds with this ruling powers... that one God, who has an eye on every side, a face on every side, an arm on every side, a foot on every side, creating heaven and earth forges together by his arms and his wings" (SU 3.1-2).[76]

The *Kauśītaki Upaniṣad* enlists with a couple of imageries to authenticate the *ātman* and Brahman as closely knit entities. It remarks, "Just as a razor is laid in a razor-case or a bird is pent up in its nest, even so, is this Conscious Being placed in the body up to the very nails, up to the very hair of the body" (KauU 4.20). Further, the *Śvetāśvatara Upaniṣad* holds that just as oil is hidden in sesame seeds or ghee in curds, just as water is hidden in springs, or fire in the churning sticks, even so, is the *ātman* immanent in the body. The *ātman* is reckoned to be all-pervasive like butter in milk, rooted in self-knowledge and penance (SU 1.15-16).[77] The inter-penetration of *jagat* and Brahman is portrayed in the *Muṇḍaka Upaniṣad* as, "From Him, all the seas and the mountains, from him flow rivers of every kind; from him are all herbs and their juice too; by which, together with the elements, the inner souls are upheld" (MuU 2.2.9). The knower penetrates the whole world and becomes the All.

Hence, the divine immanence and transcendence revealed in the Vedas continue to become vivid in all the *Upaniṣads*. Though the revelation seems to be primeval, it is perennial and yet looks afresh like the days and nights.[78] The *Upaniṣads* equip us to integrate the past-present-future in one continuum, and to live in time as well as in eternity. The *Upaniṣads* is nothing but the continuation of the Vedic revelation. For example, the *Bṛhadāraṇyaka Upaniṣad* is the fourteenth section of the *Śatapatha Brāhmaṇa*. Scholars have classified the *Upaniṣads* as either part or continuation of the Vedas.[79] However, scholars like Radhakrishnan deem some of them as "The Principal Upaniṣads"[80] as their authority stems from their antiquity and non-sectarian nature unlike many of the minor *Upaniṣads*.[81]

The *Upaniṣadic* revelation of *Bhedābheda* is further elucidated by the *Vedāntic* thinkers. Now we briefly explore how this revelation is articulated by various schools of *Vedānta* with special reference to the *mahāvākya tattvamasi* beginning from the *Bhagavad Gītā*.

1.3 *Bhedābheda* in the *Bhagavad Gītā*

The *Bhagavad Gītā*, one of the *prasthānatrayī*[82] of the *Vedānta* philosophy with 700 *ślokas* in 18 chapters is regarded either as *śruti* or *smṛti*[83] or both. It is known also as, 'the Sacred Song,' 'the Divine Song,' or 'the Song of the Lord'[84] for two reasons: the song sung by the Lord Kṛṣṇa Himself and its evocation of the sacredness or divine truth. It is also called the *Upaniṣad* (*Gītopaniṣad*) for two reasons: from the etymological sense (*upa+ni+ṣad* = near+down+sit), sitting near the teacher to listen to his teaching. Arjuna sits near Kṛṣṇa and listens to his exhortation. From the fact of its contents, the BG illustrates the relation between the Absolute Being and *jīva-jagat*. As far as the contents of the *Gītā* are concerned, Chandra Kumar Jhā views the purpose of the book as to educate Arjuna regarding a few issues he is facing.[85] The despondency (*viṣāda*) of human beings is represented by Arjuna with the inability to have a discriminatory knowledge between *nitya* and *anitya* (*nityānityavastuvivekajñāna*), i.e., the inability to distinguish the relationship between *jīva, jagat* and *paramātman*, inability to know the difference between *pṛthak śarīra* and *apṛthak ātman*, nature and effect of *triguṇātmic prakṛti*, the relationship between *jñāna* and *karma*, etc.[86] This implies that the basic content of the *Gītā* is the mutual relationship between *jīva, jagat* and *Brahman*.

The *Bhagavad Gītā* is influenced greatly by the *Vedas* and *Upaniṣads*. The concept of "*ekaṁ sat viprā bahudhā vadanti*"[87] of the *Ṛgveda*, the *Vedic* and *Upaniṣadic* ideals of harmony (*ṛta*), tolerance, spiritual unity, etc. can very well be deciphered here. The doctrines of *Sāṅkhya* philosophy, the *Vedic* nature of the tree of knowledge in the form of *Vaṭavṛkṣa* (banyan tree), nature of *Brahman—saguṇa* and *nirguṇa—varṇadharma*, etc. concepts in the *Gītā* are very much *Vedic* and *Upaniṣadic*. S. Prabhavananda writes that the *Gītā* is, "[the] ideal of harmony and universality to its logical conclusion in the process of blending, synthesizing, and harmonizing conflicting metaphysical ideals and conceptions of spiritual disciplines."[88] So the relationship cited above can be distinguished in different ways.

The rich cultural, religious and social content is in itself a legacy. However, as scripture, containing conflicting texts has steered the eminent scholars of both the East and the West over the centuries, to comment and re-comment on different points of view, and initiating a philosophical debate as well. It is Śaṅkarācārya for the first time perused the *Gītā* from *abheda* tradition and wrote an extensive commentary. Later, Madhvācārya approached it with *bheda* interpretation. Meanwhile, the scholars like Rāmānuja, Nimbārka, Caitanya and others explicated it from both *bheda* and *abheda* forms.[89] Surendranath Dasgupta advocates the *Bhagavadgītā* as well as the *Purāṇas* and *Pañcarātras,*[90] in essence, to be in the *Bhedābheda* tradition. In his words, "The *Bhagavadgītā*, which is regarded as the essence of the *Upaniṣads*, the older *Purāṇas* and *Pañcarātras*... are more or less on the lines of *Bhedābheda*."[91]

In the *Bhagavad Gītā*, there are many citations where Lord Kṛṣṇa declares 'I am the Supreme Lord, I am everything, everything emanates from me and I am distinct from everything. I am omniscient and you are not. I should be worshipped by falling at my feet and you should surrender to me for which I will reward you with *mokṣa*.' There are also many references where Arjuna glorifies Lord Kṛṣṇa as the Supreme Lord with his transcendental form. Sanjaya also extols Kṛṣṇa's form. Further, there are also statements testifying that *ātman* is eternal, everything is *ātman*. On the contrary, Arjuna doesn't understand his *nirguṇa* aspect but worships his transcendental form in the disposition of an insignificant *bhakta*. There are direct pronouncements to substantiate the *jīvātman* as the energy of the *paramātman*, whereas the *paramātman* is distinct from *jīvātman* and material energy (*bhumir apo*). There are clear assertions to authenticate the *jīvātman* as an *aṁśa* of the *paramātma* (*mamaivaṁśo*). There are both mutable and immutable things in reality.[92]

Commenting on the *Advaitic* tradition, Pathikonda Viswambara Nath proposes that the eighteen chapters of the *Bhagavad Gītā* establish the unity between *tvam* (human being) and *tat* (*Paramātman*) through *asi* (*jñāna*). He moots, "The essence of *Bhagavadgītā* is to make one realize *tat tvam asi* aspect of Him.... (1) The first six chapters deal with '*tvam*,' (2) The second six chapters deal with '*tat*' and (3) the last six chapters deal with '*asi*'."[93] Counter to this, Madhvācārya differentiates between *Paramātman* and *ātman*. In his commentary on the BG, known as *Gītātātparyanirṇaya,* interprets that by no means there can be unity (*aikya*) between Brahman and *ātman*. The words like *aham, brahma, asmi, tat, tvam, asi* in *ahaṁ brahmāsmi, tattvamasi* sentences speak only *bheda*. Hari is *aheya* (one who is ever-present), and therefore, he is '*aham*; he is boundless, slayer of evil, and possessor of knowledge and therefore he is *asmi*; he is *guṇaparipūrṇa* (completion of *guṇa*), and therefore, he is *brahma*, and he is *tejasvī* and therefore *tvam*. All the *kriyāvācya, dravyavācya* and *guṇavācya* words determine Hari as the *paramamukhyavṛtti* (super primary). Therefore, they endorse *bheda* and not *abheda*.[94]

1.4 *Bhedābheda* in the *Vedāntic* Literature

Advaita, aviccheda, avibhāga and *anyonyābhāva* in the *Upaniṣads* can be summarized in the forms of four well-accepted great sentences, called the *mahāvākyas.*[95] The *mahāvākya* is linked with the essence of the individual Self and the Supreme Being. Various commentators have tried to answer it from their perspective. This hermeneutical exercise to solve the textual puzzle is not a mere commentatorial ingenuity and resource, but also a philosophical enterprise. This is explicit and definite in the philosophical stand taken by different *ācāryas*. This is the strength of the Indian Philosophical culture. The criterion, however, in the *Vedāntic* tradition[96] is, the message they contain, the *akhāṇḍārtha.*[97] The exploration on the *mahāvākya* by the *Vedāntic* teachers is based on this inclusive understanding of these Great Sentences of the *śruti* texts.

1.4.1 The Four *Mahāvākyas*

There are four sentences—though isolated from within the sentences—accepted as the *mahāvākyas* by most of the *Vedāntic* thinkers.[98] They are the following:

i. *Prajñānaṁ Brahma* (Consciousness is Brahman). It is segregated from the *Aitareya Upaniṣad* of the *Ṛgveda* 3.1.3.

ii. *Ahaṁ Brahmāsmi* (I am Brahman). It is detached from the *Bṛhadāraṇyaka Upaniṣad* of the *Śukla Yajurveda* 1.4.10.

iii. *Tattvamasi* (That Thou Art). It is disjoined from the *Chāndogya Upaniṣad* of the *Sāmaveda* 6.8.7.

iv. *Ayamātmā Brahma* (This *Ātman* is Brahman). It is taken from *Māṇḍūkya Upaniṣad* of the *Atharvaveda,* 2nd *mantra*.

The aforementioned four aphorisms represent four different Vedas and are "the quintessence of *Upaniṣadic* wisdom."[99] The first aphorism declares the nature of the finite and the infinite self, while the remaining three relate essential identities between them. By getting rid of adventitious adjuncts from the finite self, one can reach the state of *ekamevādvitīyam* (CU 6.2.1) or *ekarasa*. The sixth chapter of the *Chāndogya Upaniṣad* is about the oneness of the *ātman* with the Brahman. This becoming One is termed as '*ekarasa*' by the *Advaitavādins*.[100] What prevent one to reach this state are the impurities accumulated in terms of *ariṣaḍvarga* (six-fold enemies such as *kāma* (lust), *krodha* (anger), *lobha* (greed), *moha* (attachment), *mada* (pride), and *matsara* (jealousy)), *mamakāra* (mine-ness) and *ahaṅkāra* (ego) from the past and the present existence of the self. Venkatarama Iyer expresses this well, "a mind which is pre-occupied, which is therefore not free to receive new ideas or a mind which is not sufficiently alert, will fail to grasp the truth of even the objects that are external to it and which are consequently open to observation and experiment."[101]

1.4.1.1 *Prajñānaṁ Brahma* (Consciousness is Brahman)

This aphorism is taken from the *Aitareya Upaniṣad,* a part of the *Aitareya Āraṇyaka* and belongs to the *Ṛgveda* 3.1.3. This *Upaniṣad* has three chapters, dealing with the creation of the primordial self. The finite self, created from the infinite, entails the assistance of a teacher to reach back to its origin. The knowledge which reaches one back to its origin is *brahmajñānam* or the *prajñānam.*

The *Upaniṣad* attempts to answer a question posed at the beginning, "Who is *ātman*?" As an answer, it enumerates from different physical, psychical and mental functions, and considers all these as names of consciousness. Next, it examines from all the metaphysical aspects like gods, primal elements and concludes consciousness (*prajñānam*) as the substratum of Brahman. *Prajñāna* also connotes *wisdom, knowledge* or *understanding.*[102] And fittingly, Brahman is defined as wisdom.

This *mahāvākya* is also called the *lakṣaṇā-vākya. Lakṣaṇā* refers to "a quality or a distinguishing characteristic."[103] The grammarian, Bhartṛhari uses the word *lakṣaṇā* as "indicated meaning" and Śabara defines it as, "means by which something is perceived."[104] This implies that *prajñāna* is a distinguishing attribute of the Supreme Reality by which it has to be identified.

Knowledge or wisdom is one of the distinct characteristics of any scripture, besides its identity with the divine. Knowledge leads one from untruth to truth, from darkness to light, from death to life as the *Upaniṣadic* seer chants, "*asatomā sadgamaya, tamasomā jyotirgamaya, mṛtyormā amṛtamgamaya*" (BU 1.3.28). When the contents of the scriptures become a lived experience, true liberation takes place; if not, one remains in darkness or bondage. Vijñānabhikṣu asseverates, "Only through experience one passes out from the fear of the worldliness."[105] This lived experience is the joy in essence. The joy is obtained when one contemplates on the indwelling spirit (*antaryāmī*), the

Brahman who is in the innermost cave of the being, as the *Chāndogya Upaniṣad* relates, "This *Ātman* dwells in the depth of my heart. It is Brahman."[106] The contemplation involves the meticulous performance of rituals with the merits achieved through them, owing to all the existence to the highest Existent with spontaneous self-expression which is necessarily a good act. The spontaneous ejaculation or the enfoldment of the creative urge is an act of re-creation.

1.4.1.2 *Ayamātmā Brahma* (This *Ātman* is Brahman)

The aphorism, *Ayamātmā Brahma* is taken from the *Māṇḍūkya Upaniṣad,* part of the *Atharvaveda* with 12 passages. It especially deals with the *AUM mantra,*[107] consciousness and four states of awareness—waking state, dream state, sleep state and conscious state. Further, it asserts unequivocally the absolute *One Reality* and its *attributelessness* (*nirguṇatva*).[108]

The original statement goes like this, "*sarvaṁ hyetad brahma, ayamātmā brahma, so'yamātmā catuṣpāt,*" viz., "Everything verily is Brahman, this self is Brahman, that this self has four feet" (MāU 1.2). *Sarvaṁ hi* refers to animate and inanimate, visible and invisible, objective and subjective, and moving and unmoving world. This aphorism parallels the previous aphorism of the *Māṇḍūkya Upaniṣad,* "This everything is *AUM* letter."[109] In AUM, there is the inseparability of *śabda* and *artha* (word and its meaning), and further, it implies the Supreme Reality in its inseparable *nirguṇa-saguṇa* form. The individual self is related to it. We can very well infer a *non-dualistic dualism* here. Therefore, *sarvaṁ hi* alludes to an intrinsic relationship within the duality expressed above.

In this sense, *AUM* could be a *mahāvākya*, denoting the totality of the Reality. *AUM* is the sound of the infinite, the essence of all the *mantras*, the *śabdabrahman*, the ultimate reality and the essence of the Vedas. According to Sadānanda, a *mahāvākya* is "a proposition conveying identity by virtue of the three relations of its terms,"[110] that is, *the declaration of the identity of the individual Self with the Supreme Self* is the criterion. In this sense, *AUM* cannot be called the *mahāvākya*, but it can refer to its culmination.

AUM stands for creation, preservation and dissolution.[111] The *Chāndogya Upaniṣad* uses a similar word, *tajjalān,*[112] a composite of four words: *tat+ja+la+an* indicating the Supreme Being. *Tat* means *that; ja* indicates *janma* (birth); *la* signifies *laya* (dissolution or absorption), and *an* suggests *moving* or *breathing.*[113] In other words, AUM is that which or from which all is born, all is absorbed and from which all breathe or live closely. Consequently, *tajjalān* specifies *Brahman.* Brahman is that One who causes to exist, preserves and dissolves the existence, i.e., everything origins and ends in Him alone.[114]

This aphorism is the *abhyāsa vākya,* "the statement of practice."[115] Apte defines *abhyāsa* as, "repetition in general, repeated exercise or practice, habit, custom and proximity,"[116] namely one has to constantly keep in mind throughout one's existence on earth that the *ātman,* a person possesses, is nothing but the spark of the fire, or the part of the whole.

1.4.1.3 *Ahaṁ Brahmāsmi* (I am Brahman)

The aphorism, *Ahaṁ Brahmāsmi* is taken from the *Bṛhadāraṇyaka Upaniṣad* of the *Śukla Yajurveda* 1.6.10. This *Upaniṣad* has six chapters and describes the *prāṇa* as the creator; dialogues of Gārgī, Ajātaśatru, Yājñavalkya, Maitreyi and Janaka; morality, creation, eternity and many other philosophical issues. The *ātman* is delineated as not different from Brahman. Brahman is presented as the beginning and becoming of all.

"Brahman, indeed, was this in the beginning, it knew itself only as '*I am Brahman*.' Everything else was later."[117] In this aphorism, '*aham*' (I) and '*asmi*' (am) indicate a conclusive pronouncement of a person's self-realization. The self-realized person declares the union of *ātman* with Brahman keeping subjective-objective duality simultaneously abolishing the duality and maintaining an *avibhāgādvaitic* unity. Whoever knows 'I am Brahman' becomes Brahman, the Ultimate Reality. This union and identification is a deep mystical or intuitive experience of the aspirant (*anu-bhava*, after the world). Since this statement is the ultimate declaration of identity of the aspirant who has experienced and realized the oneness with the Supreme Being, it is called "the statement of experience," the *anubhava-mahāvākya*.[118]

1.4.1.4 *Tattvamasi* (That Thou Art)

The aphorism, *Tattvamasi* is taken from the *Chāndogya Upaniṣad* of the *Sāmaveda*. It deals with the identity of *Brahman* with the sentient being. The son, Śvetaketu is taught about this relationship by the sage and father Uddalaka in the words, "*sa ātmātattvamasi.*"

The *Chāndogya Upaniṣad* begins directing the priests to perform their sacred duties and to discern the hidden wisdom signifying their performance and recital as a brute ritual. This sublimation of ritualism gradually leads to perceive the entire life system as a *yajña*. This is to comprehend the reality as divine (*sarvamkhalvidaṁ brahma,* CU 3.14.1). It is followed by the inquiry into what Brahman or the reality is, and the answer arrived at is *tattvamasi*. Once this is realized in oneself, the person reaches the state of *idaṁ sarvam,* one's divine self (CU 3.12.1), a leap takes place from the self-identity to everything which eventually leads to the world of *becoming* (Brahman).

Before we enter into the details of different Vedantic thinkers on this aphorism, let's look into its background.

1.4.2 The *Upaniṣadic* Background to *Tattvamasi*

Śvetaketu upon his father's insistence goes to a *gurukula* and studies for twelve long years and returns at the age of twenty-four as a proud and arrogant student.[119] His father notices it. Three words are used here to describe the condition of Śvetaketu, *mahāmanāḥ* (one feels greater than the other, which leads one to arrogance), *anūcānamānī* (one who thinks of oneself as a great orator) and *stabdhaḥ* (stubborn, feeling of superiority in the presence of others). Often, when one begins to learn becomes unhappy whether one can cope with the unseen forces, surroundings, mind, etc. After the education, the polarity changes, the person acquires the behaviour of '*I am better than the other,*' '*I have studied,*' '*I know it all.*' This is a kind of pride Śvetaketu is crammed with. Learning gives humility and humility gives knowledge.[120] The humbling experience of the *upaniṣad,*[121] expected of him, has not yet been achieved.

To remove his pride and arrogance, and to test his knowledge, his father puts across a philosophical question. "Did you ask for that teaching, through which what is unheard becomes heard, what is unthought of becomes thought of and what is unknown becomes known?"[122] The son gets a first tremor here. He feels his education is not yet complete and therefore, mellows down and pleads for the answer, "of what nature reverend teacher is that teaching?"[123] Father replies with three metaphors, 'with a single clod of clay all that is made of clay is known, through a single ingot of gold all that is made of gold is known, through a single nail clipper all that is made of iron is known, all that perceived is but mere a name.' Śvetaketu replies, 'that thing the teachers did not know. Had they known it, why they did not tell me?'

A proud person never acknowledges one's weakness, and always will blame others. A good teacher always knows how much to give, whom to give, what to give, when to give and how to give. Gradually, Śvetaketu realizes it and begs his father to teach. Father becomes the teacher and teaches the son employing nine analogies. Each analogy ends with the phrase, "*sa ya eṣo'ṇimaitadātmyamidaṁ sarvam tatsatyaṁ sa ātmā* ***tattvamasi*** *śvetaketo iti bhūya eva mā* *bhagavānvijñāpayatviti tathā somyeti hovāca.*" This key sentence can be called 'identifying sentence,' which appears, therefore, nine times through nine analogies in the same chapter, i.e., 8.7, 9.4, 10.3, 11.3, 12.3, 13.3, 14.3, 15.3, and 16.3. The nine analogies[124] are a bird tied with a string, the juice of various flowers and honey, rivers emptying themselves into the sea, the tree is cut, the breaking of *nyagrodha* fruit, salt dissolved in water, the blindfolded and waylaid traveller, the sick man at the death bed, and a man accused of theft and subjected to the trial by the fire ordeal.

1.4.3 *Avibhāga-Bhedābheda* in *Tat-Tvam-Asi*

Divine is inter-penetrating in the reality and therefore everything appears divine. The understanding of the interpenetration of the divine by the people from different traditions demarks the interpretation of *tattvamasi.* The Supreme Reality appears divine everywhere or appears different from the appearing objects. This can be verified in the following way.

1.4.3.1 *Kevalādvaita Vedānta*

Brahman is truth (*satya*)*, the world is an illusion* (*māyā*) *and jīva and Brahman are none but the same*[125] sums up the *Kevala Advaita* of Śaṅkara. This doctrine reveals that the true Reality is One, i.e., the individual Self and Brahman are one. This is the core teaching of all the *Upaniṣads. Satyam*[126] means that which exists all the time without undergoing any change and exists in all the three states of consciousness (waking state, dream state and deep-sleep state). Therefore, the Absolute Reality is birthless, deathless and changeless which is referred to as '*Brahman.*' Thus, Śaṅkara is the advocate of *abheda-vāda.*

Śaṅkara explores *tattvamasi* chiefly in three places, viz., the *Chāndogyopaniṣadbhāṣya, Vākyavṛtti*[127] and the *Upadeśasāhasrī.*[128] In all these three works, there are three main strategies worked upon. They are *neti-neti mārga* (method of negation), *śāstra mārga* (method of the scriptural assertion) and *bhāgatyāgalakṣaṇā mārga* (or *jahadajahallakṣaṇā mārga,* the *reject-accept method*). In his *Vākyavṛtti*, Śaṅkara states,

> Having thus ascertained the meaning of the term 'thou' one should reflect upon what is meant by the word 'that'—employing both *the method of negation and also the direct method of scriptural assertion* [No. 28]. In the statements like 'that thou art' etc., the *reject-accept method is to be employed* as in the sentence 'He is this man.' No other method can be applied [No. 48].[129]

Though Śaṅkara asserts that "no other method can be applied," he has used other methods also like, *sādhanatraya: śravaṇa, manana* and *nidhidhyāsana; adhikaraṇa, māyā-avidyā,* etc.

Neti-neti (*na-iti, na-iti* – not-so, not-so) is a *Vedic* analytic method of negation to affirm Brahman.[130] In this method, the seeker negates one's identification of self with all the worldly things. Through a gradual process, the seeker negates the mind and transcends all the worldly experiences till nothing remains but the Self.[131] The concept is to express, something "inexpressible"[132] when no other definition applies to it. This is denying the body, name, form, intellect, senses and all the limiting adjuncts (superimposed), discovering what remains, the true "I," like peeling off the sheaths of onion, that is, one de-sheaths the layers of *pañcakośas*[133] to reach the ultimate pure essence. The *Avadhūta Gīta* confirms this: "By such sentences as 'That thou art,' our Self is affirmed. Of that which is untrue and composed of the five elements—the *śruti* (scripture) says, 'Not this, not this.'"[134] Thus, one dis-identifies the self and achieves the union with the Absolute. Another way of expressing *neti-neti* is to address the non-attributiveness of the Supreme Reality. "In the Beginning, this was being alone, one only, without a second" (CU 6.2.2). One cannot encapsulate Brahman with adjectives, for it is *nirguṇa*. Therefore, the *Upaniṣad* expresses it as, '*not thus, not thus* or *not this, not this*.'

The real import of the meaning of *tattvamasi* can be enclosed by adopting *bhāgatyāgalakṣaṇā* or it can be also called *jahadajahallakṣaṇā*. Two words in the sentence refer to the same and at the same time negate certain aspects. The *Vākyavṛtti* illustrates it in the following way:

> The direct meaning of the term *tvam* is pure consciousness with the internal organ and the reflection of consciousness in it. Likewise, the direct meaning of the term *tat* is Pure Consciousness with *māyā* and the reflection of consciousness in it. On account of the incongruity involved in one part of their import, the idea of identity of consciousness cannot be established. Therefore, by abandoning that

incongruent portion which has relation to invisibility and visibility, etc., there remains only Absolute Pure consciousness which is common to both *tat* and *tvam*. This speaks of the identity of *jīva* and *Īśvara,* the real purport of the *Upaniṣadic* text: *Tattvamasi*.[135]

If the direct word meaning throws up inconsistency with what is pointed out by other proofs and shreds of evidences, the sense consistent with its word meaning that is intelligently suggested by the term, is to be accepted—and this is its suggestive meaning, the *lakṣaṇā*. Thus, a reject-accept method is to be employed as in the sentence, 'he is this man.'[136] In the example, both 'he' and 'this' refer to the same man. So also, in the example, 'the village is burnt,' the village has not burnt whole but refers to the 'part of the village' as burnt.

The statement has to be, therefore, understood in its totality, *akhaṇḍārtha*,[137] as a *partless single essence*. According to *Vedāntasāra* of Sadānanda,[138] *akhaṇḍārtha* is established by delimiting the adjuncts (*upādhi*) as in the case of *so'yam devadattaḥ*. What is delimited is the contrary meaning, arising from *tat* and *tvam* from *vācyārtha*. At the end of the process of delimitation *akhaṇḍa caitanya* is achieved, that is *abheda* between *tat* and *tvam*.[139] This is the *lakṣaṇārtha*.

The word '*tvam'* is to be taken not as the physical body, but as the witness-self (*sākṣin*) of the nature of reality, consciousness and bliss. The connective verb employed here is '*asi'* which is in the indicative mood. In that sense, the utterance in an indicative sentence is opposed to relational or in the meaning of qualification.

Consequently, according to Śaṅkara, *tattvamasi* is to be interpreted from *jahadajahallakṣaṇā* method, where the primary meaning of the words are partly suppressed and partly retained. The *'tvam'* signifies the individual self, conditioned by the present 'now' and present 'here'; and the word *'tat'* denotes the unconditioned and unrelated self. The differences between the two words, *'tat'* and *'tvam'* are said to be sublated to reach pure identity.

Śaṅkara does not reject the primary meaning (*vācyārtha*). The *vācyārtha* gives us *bheda*. But the reality is not *bheda*, it is *abheda*. When *mukhyārtha* cannot be established in the words, having *samāna adhikaraṇa* (like *tattvamasi, so'aham*), then *lakṣyārtha* is taken up. This is because at the *vyāvahārika* level the reality is *mithyā*. In the *vācyarūpa, jīva* is limited and Brahman is unlimited and there cannot be *abheda*.[140] Therefore, to achieve *abheda, lakṣaṇārtha* has to be accepted. In the same way, in *tattvamasi*, though there is *bhedā* between *tat* and *tvam, abheda* has to be accepted for the sake of confirmation of *ātmattva* in Brahman.

The primacy of the secondary meaning in contrast to the primary meaning in the words conveying contradictory meaning in a word gets rooted in the *Viśiṣṭādvaita* where both primary and secondary meanings are established without having any contradiction. It is discussed below.

1.4.3.2 *Viśiṣṭādvaita Vedānta*

Rāmānuja (1017-1137 CE), the proponent of the

Viśiṣṭādvaita tradition holds that the reality is qualified non-dual, characterized by attributes. Brahman is the Supreme Reality. *Jīva* and the world are real and inseparably associated (*apṛthaksiddha*) with Brahman. God exists and all else is a manifestation or attribute of God. In other words, the *Viśiṣṭādvaita* inculcates the *advaita* or oneness of God, with *viśeṣa* or attributes.

The hermeneutical strategy of Rāmānuja can be best understood from the phrases, *samānādhikaraṇyam* and *śarīra-śarīrī sambandha*. *Samānādhikaraṇyam*, translated as 'apposition' keeps the things juxtaposed, in short, having the same referent. The attribution of the 'blue-ness' and the 'lotus-ness' in the 'blue-lotus' (*nīlakamala*) is applied to one and the same substance. According to Rāmānuja, *samānādhikaraṇyam* is defined as, "The application of two terms to connote one meaning under the aspects of two modifications."[141] Anima Sen Gupta verbalizes that, "According to the rules of grammar, when attributive words formed by *prakṛti, pratyaya,* etc., and having different senses, are predicated of one and the same substances, which is their common substratum, it is known as apposition (*samānādhikaraṇyam*)."[142] In this way, as in the 'blue-lotus,' the relation existing between both the things is the 'relation of inseparability' which leads to the state of oneness, *ekībhāva*. This methodology can be further existentially explained as *śarīra-śarīrī sambandha* or *ātma-śarīra-bhāva,*[143] an organic unity of body-soul relation. "The soul as the body of Brahman remains inseparably related to it and every moment of the soul is directed by God to fulfillment of the divine purpose."[144] Rāmānuja spells out the relationship between soul and body as "the relationship between substratum and dependent entity incapable of functioning separately," "the relationship between transcendent controller and controlled," "the relationship between principal and accessory," and "soul and body."[145]

According to Rāmānuja, the individual soul as a category is inferior to *nirguṇa Brahman* and can never be absolutely identical with the latter. There is a natural and essential difference between the *nirguṇa Brahman* and individual soul since the soul is *śarīra* of the *śarīrin* or the *āṁśa* of the *āṁśin*. Therefore, when one refers to the body, in fact, the person names the soul and when mentioning the soul, to the Supreme Soul as well. This can be represented as follows:

tat = *nirguṇa brahman, saguṇa barahman*

tvam = soul, body, sentient and insentient being

asi = the relation (*samānādhikaraṇyam*)

Here, the question emerges, if both (*tat* and *tvam*) share the same referent, then how is it that they are not totally identical? For which it is answered, "*The identity is only from practical point of view*. Ontologically speaking, God and individual soul are different, although they always stand in a relation of the inseparable union."[146] This again alerts us that there is 'something' that connects the metaphysical to the empirical.

Tat and *tvam* refer to *Brahman* under two different aspects. The *tat* aspect is *nirguṇa omniscient Brahman* who is omniscient. *Tat* also includes the personal *Brahman* who is *saguṇa*. *Saguṇa* is the indwelling soul in the body. In this respect, *tvam* is equated with *tat*. This indicates, that "Brahman whose body is individual soul connected with the non-intelligent matter"[147] is *tvam* who is addressed as Śvetaketu. Grammatically, the statement *tattvamasi* denotes the single reality existing in two modes, as the *samānādhikaraṇya* definition goes.

The *practical identity purpose* of the *Viśiṣṭādvaita* referred above retains the individuality of *tat* and *tvam* unto liberation. (Śaṅkara differs here, who views, with the liberation the soul is merged into Brahman like water merges in the sea and become one). This understanding surfaces only from the implied sense, *lakṣyārtha*. Put another way, the word *tat* stands for Brahman who resides in Śvetaketu in the form of *ātman*. According to *Viśiṣṭādvaita,* word alludes to God as a *viśeṣaṇa* (adjective). Therefore, it is not a necessity one takes it from an implied sense. As the adjectives necessarily refer to the noun, so too the beings in the world inseparably related to the *Brahman,* the substratum. Therefore, they are treated as one.

Śruti goes very well along with this. But, if *śruti* were wrong, it would contradict the *Upaniṣadic* statement, "May I become many." This is precisely the reason why there is a *bheda* at the core. Secondly, in "*aitadātmyamidaṁ sarvam,*" "*sarvam*" is to be understood as, "the world, including the intelligent souls" (*cetana-miśraṁ prapañcam*) and "*idam*" is to be grasped as, "*Brahman, the ātman of the world.*"

This gives way for the reconciliation of *bheda* and *abheda* and is very well supported by *śarīra-śarīri-bhāva* as a combination of transcendence and immanence. Therefore, *Viśiṣṭādvaita*'s body-soul relationship applies at the level of both macrocosm and microcosm, and unites them together as a cosmic whole.

Vallabha's *Śuddhādvaitic* interpretation of *tattvamasi* comes closer to Rāmānuja. If Rāmānuja interprets it as 'You are His part' or 'You are God's part,' Vallabha explicates it as 'you are in essence God' or 'Soul is an essence of Brahman.' This is because Vallabha splits *tattvamasi* into two parts: *tattvam* and *asi*, where *tattva* refers to the essence or state of *tat* (Brahmanhood). *Tvam* in *tattvamasi* does not allude to the second person singular form but a termination conveying the sense of state, added to *tat*. The meaning, therefore, is that the soul is an essence of Brahman as its part or *aṁśa*.[148]

Rāmānuja simultaneously attempts to demonstrate the *abheda* of Brahman (Brahman modified by all, because all constitute his body, abides in variety), and *bheda* from the world (because Lord, *Jīva* and world is categorically different in form and nature). There are *Upaniṣads* revealing difference as well as non-difference as characteristics of Brahman. The *Śvetāśvatara Upaniṣad* speaks of the individual self as different from that which actuates it to act. In another context, the same *Upaniṣad* asserts Brahman as the *kāraṇa* and as the Lord of that which rules the senses, and the one who rules and the ruler of the senses must be quite different from another. There are also *vākyas* like *tattvamasi* of the *Chāndogya* that emphasizes non-difference like *ayamātma brahma* of the *Bṛhadāraṇyaka Upaniṣad.*[149] Further, the relationship of *bheda* and *abheda* is supported by various relationships: *śarīra-śarīrī sambandha, amśa-amśī sambandha, rakṣya-rakṣyaka sambandha, seśa-śeśī sambandha, prakāra-prakārī sambandha*—the relationship between substratum and dependent entity incapable of functioning separately, the relationship between transcendence controller and the thing controlled, the relationship between the principal and the accessory.

While Śaṅkara's elucidation is more appealing to intellect, Rāmānuja's explanation attracts more the heart. Certain questions may pop up here: how can God remain the same while parts are subjected to change as they are related to God as parts and whole? Does God subject to misery and evil in the world from which the souls suffer? If so, he is not God at all. Often equating Brahman with *cit* and *acit*, Rāmānuja has really reduced Brahman to finite self, and transcendence of God seems to be sacrificed.

1.4.3.3 *Dvaita Vedānta*

Madhvācārya (1238-1317 CE), the proponent of *Dvaita* Vedānta holds that Brahman, the Supreme Being is the only *svatantra* (independent) reality. *Jīva* and the *jagat* are eternally separate and real. They always depend on Brahman. The relationship between Brahman and *jīva* is that of *bimba-pratibimba-bhāva* (mirror-image-relation). Therefore, Madhva's entire thesis is *the majesty of Brahman as the highest purport.*[150] His highest purport and is *Viṣṇusarvottamatva* or the absolute sovereignty of Viṣṇu, which can be termed as, *Viṣṇusarvottama Madhvaḥ*, in line with Rāmānuja's understanding.

Madhva formulates his strategy on certain presuppositions. Some of them are, i. Hari is Supreme (*Hariḥ paratarah*), Lord Viṣṇu (Hari) is *sarvottama* and *parabrahman* can be known only through scriptures who is different and distinct from both sentient and non-sentient beings. ii. All souls depend on Him (*jīvagaṇāḥ harer anucarāḥ*). iii. World is real (*satyam jagat*). iv. Difference (*bheda*) is fundamental (*tattvatobhedaḥ*), the very nature of the entity. There are five-fold *bhedas*: *Brahman-ātman, Brahman-jagat, ātman-ātman, ātman-jagat* and *jagat-jagat*.

Through *tattvamasi* concept, Madhva elucidates his philosophical stand mainly employing two techniques: *padaccheda* technique (a division of words according to grammatical rule) and *prakaraṇa saṅgati* (contextual relevance). Madhva scrutinizes the keywords of the text from morphological and semantic angles to get to the original meaning. This becomes evident when one compares the *bhāṣyas* of the *Brahmasūtra* written by Śaṅkara and Madhva.[151] For example, Śaṅkara understands the *samanvaya* in *Samanvayādhikaraṇa*, the opening *adhyāya* of the *Brahmasūtra* from 'the secondary power of words' or *lakṣaṇā*, whereas Madhva considers it as an exegetical method (*tātparyaliṅga*). The idea of Madhva is to seek maximum affiliation of scripture in the most primary, intimate and plenary sense in a text. For Śaṅkara, it is the conventional understanding (*rūḍhi*) that matters.[152]

Madhva splits the conjoined sentences as *atat-tvam-asi* (not that-thou-art) based on *savarṇadīrgha sandhi* between the final long vowel in the preceding word *ātmā* followed by the initial short vowel of the following word *atat*. According to the compound, if there is an '*a*' *kāra* (sound) in the last syllable of the first word and *'ā' kāra* (long sound) in the beginning of the next word or vice-versa, then the resulting combination '*a*' *kāra* is omitted. Hence, grammatically the formulation is read as "*ātmā-atat-tvam-asi*" (*ātmātattvamasi*). This reading is favourable since it does not necessitate the dependence on the *lakṣaṇā* (secondary meaning) for either *tat* or *tvam*. For Dvaita, *lakṣana* is optional. The secondary meaning of *tat* brings about the association, relation, being a source of another, dependence, resemblance between Brahman and *jīva*, etc.[153] Here, the dependency of the *svatantra tattvas* is vital to understand the whole reality.

According to the *Dvaitavāda*, the *Advaitic* reading is insufficient and is not according to the *śāstras*. This brings us to the *prakraṇa saṅgati*, the context. The contextual discourse itself offers a *bheda* between *tat* and *tvam*. It can be found in Śvetaketu's ego. He did not know that he was under the control of the Supreme God. If one were to tell him that 'you are Brahman,' it would heighten his pride and ego. Therefore, the father's declaration has to be understood as 'you are not that' or 'you are totally under His control.' In a broader understanding, it can be inferred that Śvetaketu represents every human being who considers themselves 'supreme.' As a consequence, the scripture aims at the learned people to convey a philosophical message to humbly surrender to the *Sat* or *Tat* to whom all else is subject (*aitadātmyamidaṁ sarvam*). The grammatical explanation 'not that' (*atat*) doesn't go against Pāṇini's grammatical rule. Secondly, Śaṅkara does not explain how the world is unreal, or that Śvetaketu is identical with *Sat*. Even the *Bhagavadgītā* in chapter 15, Kṛṣṇa states that *Paramātman* is higher and different from the *kṣara* and *akṣara*. The world is real and the difference is real.[154]

One has to see the text as a whole (*akhaṇḍārtha*) from *adhikaraṇa* point of view.[155] The whole teaching expresses the dependence of *jīva* and *jagat* on the Brahman. Nowhere has it showed the identity. B.N.K. Sharma articulates this in the following way:

> The whole cosmos, of which we as individual souls form part, is metaphysically dependent, as reality, on One Supreme Power which sustains everything in the cosmos including the souls; that the cosmos lives, moves because of that Being and derives all its powers and potencies from that great Source, and therefore the philosophical message of the text *Tat tvam asi* is the dependence of the cosmos on Brahman as a reality and not its identity with Brahman.[156]

Nine illustrations justify his reading. Besides, the reading, '*atat-tvam-asi*' directly and categorically conveys the truths of '*jīveśvara-bheda.*'

The illustration of 'the bird's coming back to rest' signifies that though the bird is in rest with the lord, it is utterly helpless without the protective benevolence of the Supreme. The analogy of 'the honey collected' exemplifies that the living beings, though existing in the *Sat* is in an inseparable relation, fail to realize and know not that they are all existing in the Supreme Being. The insentient beings may flop to recognize the dependency, but not the sentient human beings. The example 'the sap oozing from the cut tree' exhibits that bereft of the immanence of the supreme power within, the *jīvātman* (*tvam*) would be a non-living being (*jīva*). It is the Brahman who gives life to the *jīva* and makes what it is, a living being (*jīvayati iti jīvaḥ*). The presence of the Supreme has to be grasped in one's life- experiences just as the presence of salt is inferred from the taste. The case of the man in the sickbed reveals his experience of utter helplessness and so his total relyiance on the unseen power of God. A traveller waylaid and blindfolded manifests that rebirth causes one to be in ignorance. The grace of God, instruction of a teacher and *sādhanas* liberate the person. The analogies of robbery, theft and ordeal caution Śvetaketu and all the human beings appropriately at the end of instruction, against any entitlement to any identity of essence or status with the Supreme Being. Therefore, *Dvaita Vedānta* discloses deep-rooted theism in Reality and a foundational relation with different aspects of it.

1.4.3.4 *Svābhāvika-Bhedābheda Vedānta*

The philosophy of Nimbārkācārya is known as *Svābhāvika-Bhedābhedavāda*, the theory of *natural difference and non-difference*. This School accepts three principles:

paramātman or *puruṣottama*, the *jīva* and the *jagat*. Scriptures speak about the natural differences and non-differences of *jīva, jagat* and Brahman. *Bhagavān* Vāsudeva or Brahman (or Kṛṣṇa) is different and non-different from all, the world and individual selves. He is the object of desire or consideration. There is also a *Svābhāvika-Bhedābheda* between a worshipper and Brahman as part (*aṁśa*) and whole; and between the material world and Brahman as material cause and instrumental cause. In the ordinary understanding, there is a natural relationship between a devotee and God.

The world is a modification or *pariṇāma* of Brahman. Souls and the world are dependent on Brahman. The nature of *jīva* is consciousness. *Jīva* is of the nature of light, as Brahman itself is of the nature of light.

Brahman is the cause and the soul, the effect. There is a difference between the cause and its effects just like the sea and its waves and sun and its rays, yet they have something common between them. Brahman is the whole and soul is the part. Part and whole cannot be identical. Brahman is the object to be worshipped, to be known, to be attained; the soul is the knower, worshipper and attainer. There is always a difference between them. Brahman is the inner controller, dwells within and the controller.[157]

This is proved by the fact that the effect is completely dependent on the cause for its very being and existence, that the effect can exist solely when the cause itself exists and never otherwise. The effect which belongs to a posterior time is present in the cause. The fact is that the effect and the cause, the part and whole are neither absolutely distinct nor non-distinct, but the relation between them is a relation of both difference and non-difference.[158] This difference and non-difference is natural like a snake and its coil.

The strategy used by this school to explain *tattvamasi* is *jahadajahallakṣaṇā*[159] and *padacchedavṛtti*. According to Nimbārka, in *tattvamasi* the peculiar attributes of the soul and Brahman are overlooked, while both are regarded in their common features alone.

However, *cit* and *acit* are non-different from Brahman. The *cit* and *acit* co-eternal realities have Brahman as the essence like a golden earring made from gold. They have their existence and activity under the control of Brahman. Moreover, whatever is under the control of something else for its existence and activity is non-different from it like sense-organs are non-different from the *prāṇa*. They are pervaded by Brahman and whatever is pervaded by something else is non-different from it. Nonetheless, *cit* and *acit* are different from Brahman, for there is an essential difference between the nature of these and Brahman. Brahman is the controller, and *cit* and *acit* are the enjoyer and the enjoyed respectively.

Abheda is established by using the technique of *jahadajahallakṣaṇā* and *upakrama-upasamhāra aikya* technique. The former is used as usual by other *Advaitins*. The latter is explained by considering the whole of the verse, "*etadātmyamidaṁ sarvaṁ tat satyaṁ sa ātmā* ***tat tvamasi*** *śvetaketo.*" Here, the word *tat* is a masculine referring to *etad* of *etad-ātmyaṁ* to denote the *ātman* as part of the *paramātman* and so there is *tādātmya* between them. This *tādātmya* is *sambandharūpaka aikya* (relational unity). The whole of creation is *etadātmyaṁ,* His Soul (the Soul of *Hari*).[160]

Bheda is established by using *padacchedavṛtti.*[161] *Tattvamasi vākya* has to be understood by dividing the words as '*sa ātmātat tvamasi*' as *jīvā* is different from Brahman. However, there is both *bheda* and *abheda* within *atat* like the word '*abrāhmaṇa*' means other than *brāhmaṇa* (*brāhmaṇa bhinna*) and *brāhmaṇa* like (*brāhmaṇa sadṛśa*).

Brahman is always a liberated soul. It is *tat.* The liberated soul is *brahmasvarūpa;* therefore it is different (*bhinna*), but in the liberation it is identical (*abhinna*). This is the nature (*svabhāva*) of reality. Hence, the theistic relation within and without of the creation is natural.

1.4.3.5 *Acintya-Bhedābheda Vedānta*

Śri Caitanya's *Vaiṣṇava Vedāntic* tradition contemplates the reality to be *Acintya-Bhedābheda,* incomprehensible difference and non-difference. It is hard to determine the meaning of *śruti* based on reasoning. The power of Brahman is beyond the scope of reasoning. The non-considerable one is the Lord *Puruṣottama* beyond *prakṛti.* He possesses unlimited powers. *Jīva* and *jagat* are his powers which are non-different and different from the Lord. The *bheda* and *abheda* are beyond consideration. For the Caitanya School, devotion to Brahman surpasses everything.

The Caitanya system does not esteem *tattvamasi* to be the *mahāvākya* as Śaṅkara would like to see. For them, *tattvamasi* depicts partial utterances found in the Vedas as it does not follow the *lakṣaṇā vṛtti*.[162] Those sentences are called *Mahāvākyas* which depict the eternal word or *Śabdabrahman* like *Oṁkāra*. The *Oṁkāra* is the supreme word, the reservoir of all the energies of the Supreme Lord. *Tattvamasi* is the only secondary word. Consequently, *tattvamasi* represents only a partial representation of the divine. Then, the text has to be read from the beginning of the section.

In the *tattvamasi* text, the meaning of the indivisible essence is implicated by abandonment of the contradictory portions, that is, finite cognition and infinite cognition. Finite cognition belongs to *tvam* (individual soul) and infinite cognition belongs to *tat* (Brahman). Explicitly, *tat* is Brahman and *tvam* is *jīva*. Even so, *asi* does not imply identity but copulative and indicates the body of love between Brahman and *jīva*.[163] As a corollary,

i. there is absolute oneness between *tat* and *tvam* understood by using the form of predication or co-ordination;

ii. the meaning of absolute oneness comes in by way of sublation of the opposite portions of their meaning;

iii. the sublation of the opposite portions of the meaning is brought to light utilizing the process called *lakṣaṇā vṛtti*[164] or the implication attached to the two words as in the case of 'this is that *Devadatta*.'

This implies that Brahman exists in two different modes or aspects of the same thing. Otherwise, the entire principle of coordination would be given up. The word *tvam* in the text which stands in coordination to *tat* must be understood in the sense of the same omniscient Brahman in so far as having its part or body in individual souls linked with the unintelligent matter. If we assign the natural meaning to *tat* and *tvam*, it would not hamper any meaning in arriving at a relation between Brahman and *jīva*.

Therefore, *tattvamasi* means,

> There is sameness between the two self in so far as both are knowledge and bliss and both are eternal. There is difference at the same time for while one is infinite, the other is finite, the one is regulator and the other is a thing regulated, the one is pervasive, the other is pervaded, the existence of one is absolutely real that of the other is relative.[165]

This interpretation is accepted to avoid all conflicts with other *śruti* texts. Bhaktivedānta Prabhupāda reckons, "The words of *tattvamasi* also found in the Vedic hymns... *tattvamasi* means that the living entity is a spiritual particle of the Supreme Spirit, but it is not the chief motif of the *Vedānta* or *Vedic* literatures."[166] Therefore, *identity is expressed, but the identity has to be understood not in the sense of absolute oneness, but in the sense of identity amidst diversity*. This endorses, there is some difference between the absolute and the individual soul, besides sameness in some aspects. At the same time, they are relational.

Summary

The one complex reality is observed by scriptures as many. The divine is seen as an inseparable thread that unites and relates with these diverse aspects. Though this thread is not amenable to ordinary senses, it can be made meaningful in the existential dealing with various spheres of it. The *Bhedābheda Vedānta* makes it clear.

---

[1] Swami Vikrant, *Classical Indian Philosophy* (Bangalore: Kristu Jyoti Publications, 2007), 44.

[2] N.V. Thadani, *Mīmāṁsā Sūtra of Jaimini: Text with Translation in English and Notes* (Delhi: Bharatiya Kala Prakashan, 2007), vi.

[3] *Nyāyakoṣa* lists *Viśiṣṭādvaita* as the third school, while I refer to *Dvaitādvaita* in its place so as to include different schools within this tradition. "*uttaramīmāṁsā ca vedāntadarśanam it ucyate. tatrāpi mukyatvena trīṇi darśanāni dvaita advaita viśiṣṭādvaita pratipādakāni.*" Jhalakīkar, *Nyāyakoṣaḥ,* s.v. "darśanam."

[4] Fredrich Max Müller, *The Vedas* (Calcutta: Susil Gupta Limited, 1956), 27. *Kathenotheism* is "a form of polytheism characteristic of the Vedic religion, in which one god at a time is considered supreme." The word is coined in German by Max Müller in 1865 from Greek *kath hena* 'one by one' (*kata* means 'according to' and *en* refers to 'one'), and theism refers to god. Müller also coined the nearly synonymous henotheism (1860, from Greek *henos* 'one') for 'faith in a single god' as distinguished from exclusive belief in only one god, in writings on early Hebrew religion. He has also formed a word *adevism* (from Sanskrit *deva* 'god') for 'disbelief in the old gods and legends.' *Online Etymology Dictionary,* s.v. "Kathenotheism." Available on https://www.etymonline.com/, accessed on 25 August 2016.

[5] Müller, *The Vedas*, 28. The stress is added. *indraṁ mitraṁ varuṇamagnimāhuratho divyaḥ sa suparṇo garutmān. ekaṁ sadviprā bahudhā vadantyagnina yamaṁ mātarariśvānamāhuḥ.* RV 1.164.46.

[6] Wendy Doniger O'Flaherty, trans., *The Rig Veda: An Anthology: One Hundred and Eight Hymns, Selected, Translated and Annotated,* 2000 ed. (New York: Penguin Books, 1983), 25.

---

[7] *"sa bhūmiṁ viśvato vṛttvā atyatiṣṭhadhṛśāṅgulam... etāvānasya mahimā ato jyāyāṁśca puruṣaḥ... pādo'sya viśvā bhūtāni tripādasyāmṛtaṁ divi...."* "He is spread all over the universe, and is beyond the count with ten fingers... This *puruṣa* is much greater than all his greatness in what all we see." *Puruṣasūkta* 1 and 3. Also see, Surendranath Dasgupta, *A History of Indian Philosophy*, vol. 2 (Delhi: Motilal Banarsidass, 1973), 105.

[8] Müller, *The Vedas*, 6.

[9] *"ekasyātmano anye devāḥ atyaṅgāni bhavanti."* *Nirukta* 8.4. As translated by, Svāmī Dayānanda Saraswatī, *Ṛgvedādi-Bhāṣya-Bhūmikā: Being an Introduction to the Commentary on the Four Vedas*, translated by Parmanand (New Delhi: Meharchand Lachhmandas, 1981), lii.

[10] *mahābhāgyaddevatāyā eka eva ātmā bahudha stūyate. ekasyātmano'nye devāḥ pratyaṅgāni bhavanti. Nirukta* 7.4. Saraswatī, *Ṛgvedādi-Bhāṣya-Bhūmikā*, lxxxvi.

[11] Saraswatī, *Ṛgvedādi-Bhāṣya-Bhūmikā*, lxxviii.

[12] Saraswatī, *Ṛgvedādi-Bhāṣya-Bhūmikā*, lxxxvi.

[13] Saraswatī, *Ṛgvedādi-Bhāṣya-Bhūmikā*, lxxxviii. Original stress.

[14] *"ya ātmadā baladā yasya viśva upāsate praśiṣaṁ yasya devāḥ yo'syeśe dvipado yaś catuṣpadaḥ kasmai devāya haviṣā vidhema."* AV 6.2.1. As translated by C.W.J. Van Der Linden, *The Concept of Deva: In the Vedic Age of the Indian Literature* (Utrecht: Drukkerij Vesta, 1954), 118.

[15] Saraswatī, *Ṛgvedādi-Bhāṣya-Bhūmikā*, 84.

[16] The translation of these Vedic verses are taken from, Saraswatī, *Ṛgvedādi-Bhāṣya-Bhūmikā*, lxxxvii.

[17] *"agne bhūrīṇi tava jātavedo deva svadhāvo'mṛtasya nāmā."* RV 3.20.3.

[18] *"indro māyābhiḥ puruṣa īyate."* RV 6.47.18.

[19] *"tadevāgnistadādityastad vāyustadu candramāḥ, tadeva śukraṁ tad brahma tā āpaḥ sa prajāpatiḥ."* YV 32.1.

[20] *"so'ryamā sa varuṇaḥ sa rudraḥ sa mahādeva: so'gniḥ sa u sūryaḥ sa u eva mahāmayaḥ."* AV 13.4.4.

[21] *"na dvitīyo na tṛtīyaścaturtho nāpyucyate; na pañcamo na ṣaṣṭhaḥ saptamo napyucyate; nāṣṭamo na navamo daṣamo*

---

nāpyucyate... sa eṣa eka ekvṛd eka eva; sarve asmin devo ekavṛto bhavanti." AV 13.4.14-21.

[22] In fact, in the *ṚGVEDA* and later *Atharvaveda* and *Taittirīya Saṁhitā* do use the words '*puruṣa'* and *pūruṣa'* to refer humans as a class of beings (*jātivācaka śabda*). In *Atharvaveda,* the humans are made up of five parts, in *Aitareya Brāhmaṇa* it is six to twenty five mythical parts. See, RV 7.104.25; 97.4.5,6; 165.3; AV 3.21.1; 21.5; 8.2.25, etc. Arthur Anthony Macdonell and Arthur Berriedale Keith, *Vedic Index of Names and Subjects* (Varanasi: The Chowkhamba Vidyabhawan, 1912), s.v. "puruṣa."

[23] *"anubhayātmakaḥ puruṣaḥ." "Puruṣa* is of neither kind." Jhalakīkar, *Nyāyakoṣaḥ,* s.v. "puruṣa." Also, Shashiprabha Kumar, Santhosh Kumar Shukla and Ram Nath Jha, eds., *Dārśanik Sampradāy-Koś: Dictionary of Concepts in Indian Philosophy* (New Delhi: D.K. Printworld and Jawaharlal Nehru University, 2014), s.v. "na prakṛti na vikṛti."

[24] Mādhavācārya, *Sarvadarśanasaṅgraha,* Translated by E.B. Cowel and A.E. Gough (London: Trubner and Company, 1882), 223. Metaphysically speaking the Sāṅkhya School accepts only two categories: *puruṣa* and *prakṛti.*

[25] Apte, *The Student's Sanskrit-English Dictionary,* s.v. "pra/pṛ/pṛī." Apte, *A Sanskrit English Dictionary,* s.v. "pra/pṛ/pṛī." The meanings of these root words are explained later in this section.

[26] Apte, *The Student's Sanskrit-English Dictionary,* s.v. "*pṛ*." *Sanskrit-Hindi-English Dictionary*, 2002 ed., s.v. "pṛ." William Dwight Whitney, *The Roots, Verb-Forms and Primary Derivatives of the Sanskrit Language* (New Delhi: Motilal Banarsidass Publishers, 2006), s.v. "pṛ."

[27] *Śiśupālavadha* and *Raghuvaṁśa* confirm this in 1.33 and 13.6.8 respectively.

[28] Subhash Anand, *Hindu Inspriation for Christian Reflection: Towards a Hindu-Christian Theology* (Anand: Gujarat Sahitya Prakash, 2004), 3.

[29] *"yatraiṣa etat supto'bhūd ya eṣa vijñānamayaḥ, vijñānamayaḥ puruṣaḥ, tad eṣām prāṇānām vijñānena vijñānam ādāya ya eso'ntar-hṛdaya ākāṣaḥ tasmiñcete, tāni yadā gṛhṇāti atha haitat puruṣaḥ svapiti nāma. tad gṛhīta eva prāṇo bhavati, gṛhītā vāk, gṛhītaṁ cakṣuḥ, gṛhītaṁ śrotraṁ, gṛhītaṁ manaḥ."* BU 2.1.17. "When this

being fell asleep thus, then the person who consists of intelligence, having by his intelligence taken to himself the intelligence of these breaths (sense organs) rests in the space within the heart. When the person takes (senses), he is said to be asleep. When the breath is retrained, speech is restrained, the eye is restrained, the ear is restrained, the mind is restrained." Radhakrishnan, *The Principle Upaniṣads*, 189.

[30] *"atha yad ataḥ paro divojyotirdīpyate viśvataḥ pṛṣṭeṣu sarvataḥ pṛṣṭeṣva anuttameṣūttameṣu lokeṣvidaṁ vāva tad idam asminnantaḥ puruṣe jyotiḥ."* CU 3.13.7. "Now the light which shines above this heaven, above all, above everything, in the highest worlds beyond which there are no higher, verily, that is the same as this light which is here within the person." Radhakrishnan, *The Principle Upaniṣads*, 390.

[31] *"tatra ayaṁ nirṇayaḥ: ākāśaḥ prakṛteḥ (te) paraṁ brahma, kutaḥ? talliṅgāt."* VAB 1.1.23, p.87.

[32] *ata eva prāṇaḥ*. VAB 1.1.23, p.89.

[33] Apte, *The Student's Sanskrit-English Dictionary*, s.v. "prakṛti."

[34] Apte, *A Sanskrit English Dictionary*, s.v. "prakṛti." Similarly, *Śakti* or personified energy of wife of a deity is represented as Lakṣmī or Durgā.

[35] For more details see, Joseph Satyanand, *Nimbārka: A Pre-Śaṅkara Vedāntin and His Philosophy* (New Delhi: Munshiram Manoharlal Publishers, 1997), 291-92.

[36] O'Flaherty, *The Rig Veda*, 27.

[37] Arthur A. Macdonnell, *A Vedic Reader for Students*, 1976 ed. (Madras: Oxford University Press, 1917), 195. For details on interpolation of *Puruṣasūkta* see, Victor Borde, *Puruṣasūkta: An An A-Religious Inquiry into a Sacred Text* (Indiana: LifeRich Publishing, 2021).

[38] O'Flaherty, *The Rig Veda*, 30.

[39] The same hymn has two references for *Virāj*. RV 10.90.5; 10.130.5. "From him *Virāj* was born, and from *Virāj* came the man." "The *Virāj* metre was the privilege of *Mitra* and *Varuṇa*; the *Triśṭubh* metre was part of the day of Indra." O'Flaherty, *The Rig Veda*, 30, 33.

[40] Raimundo Panikkar, *The Vedic Experience–Mantramañjarī: An Anthology of the Vedas for the Modern Man and Contemporary Celebration* (London: Darton, Longman and Todd, 1977), 73.

[41] Panikkar, *The Vedic Experience–Mantramañjarī*, 73.

[42] Śankarācārya, *Bṛhadāraṇyakopaniṣad: Sānuvāda Śāṅkarabhāṣyasahita*, translated by Shattkarbashaya (Gorakhpur: Gita Press, 1950), 167. Shattkarbashaya translates this in Hindi as, "*pūrv me oṣaṇ kiyā isiliye 'puruṣ' kahlāyā*."

[43] Śankarācārya, *Bṛhadāraṇyakopaniṣad*, 167.

[44] "*apetavratakarmā tu kevalaṁ brahmaṇi sthitaḥ, brahmabhūtaścaraṅlloke brahmacārīti kathyate. brahmaiva samidhastasya brahmāgnibrahma viṣṭraḥ, āpo brahma gururbrahma sa brahmaṇi samāhitaḥ.*" *Aśvamedhaparva* 26.16.17. Vijñānabhikṣu, *Yogasārasaṅgraha of Vijñānabhikṣu: Sanskrit Text with Hindi and English Translation*, translated by Ram Shankar Bhattacharya and Goswami Prahlad Giri (Varanasi: Bharatiya Vidya Prakashan, 1989), 52,54,56. Here the word '*brahma*' refers to *Brahman*.

[45] Anand, *Hindu Inspriation for Christian Reflection*, 3-6.

[46] *ato jīvā brahmāṁśā bhavanti. "ātmā vai jāyate putraḥ" iti śrutyā putre pituravibhāgalakṣaṇā-bhedavajjīve'pi brahmaṇo'vibhāga lakṣaṇābhedasya 'bahusyāṁ prajāyaye' ityadi śrutyāsiddher iti.* VAB 1.1.2, p.27. "Souls are parts of Brahman. By scriptural texts like "the self is indeed born like a son" (KauU 2.11) and like "let me be many, let me produce" (CU 6.2.3) the non-difference of Brahman and the soul, defined as non-separation, is established to be like the non-difference between a father and a son, which is defined as nonseparation." For translation, see, Borelli, "The Philosophy of Vijñānabhikṣu," 55. This echoes *Kauśītaki Upaniṣad* 2.11 where it says, "You are born from every limb of mine, you are born from the heart, *you, my son, are my self indeed*, may you live hundred autumns." Radhakrishnan, *Principal Upaniṣads*, 768. Also see, *Śatapatha Brāhmaṇa*, 14.9.8.4. Thus, the glory of latter is also the glory of former (BU 6.4.8), "With power and glory, I give you glory. Thus two become glorious." Radhakrishnan, *Principal Upaniṣads*, 323.

[47] "*Īśavāsyamidaṁ sarvaṁ yatkiñca jagatāyaṁ jagat; tena tyaktena bhuñjithā mā gṛdhaḥ kasyasviddhanam.*" IU 1. Pathikonda Viswambara Nath, *Tat Tvam Asi: The Universal Message in the Bhagavadgītā*, 2 vols., vol. 1 (Delhi: Motilal Banarsidass Publishers, 1998; reprint, 2002), xxiv-xxvi.

[48] Madhu Khanna, ed. *Thirty Minor Upaniṣads*, 2011 ed. (New Delhi: Tantra Foundation, 1914), 100-104. Also see, "*yathorṇa-nābhiḥ*

sṛjate gṛhṇate" "as a spider sends forth and draws in its thread." MuU 1.1.7.

[49] Sarvepalli Radhakrishnan, *The Principal Upaniṣads* (London: George Allen and Unwin Ltd., 1953), 622, 686, 733.

[50] *"ṛtam pibantau sukṛtasya loke guhāṁ praviṣṭau parame parārdhe, chāyā-tapau brahma-vido vadanti, pañcāgnayo ye ca tri-ṇāciketāḥ."* KaU 1.3.1. Radhakrishnan, *The Principal Upaniṣads*, 621.

[51] "Two birds, joined together, clutch the same tree. One of them eats the sweet fruit; the other looks on without eating." RV 1.164.20. O'Flaherty, *The Rig Veda*, 78.

[52] R.D. Ranade, *A Constructive Survey of Upanishadic Philosophy: Being an Introduction to the Thought of the Upanishads*, 1968 ed. (Bombay: Bharatiya Vidya Bhavan, 1926), 151. For Madhvācārya, the *dvaita* proponent, this is an important text to show *bheda* between Brahman and *ātman*.

[53] *"jñājñau dvāv ajāv īśanīśāv ajā hy ekā bhoktṛ-bhogyārtha-yuktā anantaś cātmā viśva-rūpo hy akartā trayaṁ yadā vidnate brahmam etat."* SU 1.9.

[54] Radhakrishnan, *The Principal Upaniṣads*, 714.

[55] *"na tatra cakṣur gachati na vāg gacchati no manaḥ, na vidmo na vijānīmo yathaitad anuśiṣyāte."* KeU I.3. Radhakrishnan, *The Principal Upaniṣads*, 582.

[56] This is the basic understanding of *Dvaitavedānta*.

[57] Warren Matthews, *World Religions*, 2010 ed. (Belmont: Wadsworth, 2007), 73.

[58] *"sad eva, somya, idam agra āsīd ekamevādvitīyam... tadaikśata, bahusyām prajāyeyeti, tat tejo'sṛjata."* CU 6.2.1 and 3. "In the beginning, my dear, all this was Existence, the one only without second.... It is completed: May I be born as many. It thus brought forth fire from Itself." Swami Muni Narayana Prasad, trans., *Chāndogya Upaniṣad: With the Original Text in Sanskrit and Roman Translation, Translation with an Extensive Commentary*, Rediscovering Indian Literary Classics, No. 15 (New Delhi: D. K. Printworld (P) Ltd., 2006), 404, 409. Also see, Radhakrishnan, *The Principal Upaniṣads*, 447-449.

[59] *"asad vā idam agra āsīt, tato vai sad ajāyata, tad ātmānaṁ svayam akuruta."* TU 2.7. Radhakrishnan, *The Principal Upaniṣads*, 548-549.

[60] Prasad, *Chāndogya Upaniṣad*, 261.

[61] Apte, *A Sanskrit English Dictionary*, s.v. "brahman." Whitney, *The Roots, Verb-Forms and Primary Derivatives*, s.v. "bṛh."

[62] See, *Nāsadīya Sūkta* of RV 10.129; *Śatapatha Brāhmaṇa* 2.1.17.

[63] *"brahma vā idam agra āsīt, tat ātmānam evāvet ahaṁ brahmāsmīti tasmāt tat sarvam abhavāt."* BU 1.4.10. "Brahman, indeed was this in the beginning. It knew itself only as 'I am Brahman.' Therefore, it became all." Radhakrishnan, *The Principal Upaniṣads*, 168. *"brahma ha vā idam agra āsīt, eko'nantaḥ."* MaiU 6.17. "Brahman, indeed was this in the beginning, one and eternal." *"asad vā idam agra āsīt. tato vai sadjāyata."* TU 2.7. "Verily was non-existent, this world in the beginning. Therefrom, was the existent born." Prasad, *Taittirīya Upaniṣad*, 142.

[64] TU 2.6. See, Radhakrishnan, *The Principal Upaniṣads*, 548. Original parenthesis.

[65] *"ātmaivedam agra āsīt puruṣavidhaḥ... sa vai naiva reme; tasmād ekākī na ramate; sa dvitīyam aicchat; sa haitāvān āsa yathā strīpumāṁsau sampariṣvāktau; sa imam evātmānaṁ dvedhāpātayat, tataḥ patiś ca patnī cābhavātām... tato manuṣyam ajāyanta... sā gaur abhavat, ṛṣabha itaras tāṁ sam evābhavat...."* BU 1.4.1-4. A parallel account of this story is already present in the *ṚGVEDA* in its *Puruṣasūkta*.

[66] Radhakrishnan, *The Principal Upaniṣads*, 164.

[67] *"brahma vā idamagra āsīt, tadātmānamevāvet. ahaṁ brahmāsmī'ti. tasmāt sarvam abhavat."* BU I.4.10. Anonymous, *The Bṛhadāraṇyaka Upaniṣad: Containing the Original Text with Word-by Word Meanings, Running Translations, Notes and Introduction* (Madras: Sri Ramakrishna Math, 1968), 61-62.

[68] *"ahaṁ hi yasmādidaṁ sarvaṁ jagadsṛṣṭi sṛṣṭavān asmi tasmād iti arthaḥ."* Śankarācārya, *Bṛhadāraṇyakopaniṣad*, 181.

[69] *"akṣarād vividhāḥ bhāvāḥ prajāyante tatra caivāpi yanti."* MuU 2.2.1.

[70] *"sa yathorṇanābhiś tatntunoccaret, yathāgneḥ kṣudrā vispuliṅgā vyuccaranti, evam evāsmad ātmanaḥ sarve prāṇaḥ, sarve lokāḥ, sarve devāḥ. Sarvāni bhūtāni vyuccaranti."* BU 2.1.20. Radhakrishnan, *The Principal Upaniṣads*, 190.

[71] *"tasmād vā etasmād ātmani sarve prāṇāḥ, sarve lokāḥ, sarve*

vedāḥ, sarve devāḥ, sarvāni ca bhūtāny uccaranti." MaiU 6.32. Radhakrishnan, *The Principal Upaniṣads*, 842.

[72] In fact, the *aṁśa-aṁśī sambandha* is the crux of Vijñānabhikṣu's *vedāntic* flow.

[73] *"bahavaḥ puruṣā brahmantutāho eka eva tu" iti praśne – bahavaḥ pururṣā rājan sāṅkhyayoga vicāriṇām...iti anena puruṣa nānātvam eva vicārato vyavasthāpya vyāsoktaṁ puruṣa aikyaṁ pitāputravad avibhāgena upapāditam."* VAB 1.1.2, p.27. "There are many spirits for *Sāṅkhya* and *Yoga* investigators... since it has been determined that the manifoldness of Spirit is logically tenable, the oneness of Spirit is taught by Vyāsa to be possible through nonseparation like with father and son." As translated by Borelli, "*The Philosophy of Vijñānabhikṣu*," 56.

[74] *arā iva rathanābhau kalā yasminpratiṣṭitāḥ. taṁ vedhyaṁ puruṣaṁ veda mā vo mṛtyuḥ parivyathā iti*. PU 6.6. Know that *puruṣa* who ought to be known, in whom the *kalās* are centered like the spokes in the nave of a wheel... in order that death may not harm you. As translated by Chinmayananda, *Prasnopanisad*, 188.

[75] *"puruṣa evedaṁ viśvaṁ karma tapo brahma parāmṛtam." "na viśvaṁ nāma puruṣād anad kiñcid asit."* MuU 2.1.10. "The person himself is all this. Work, austerity and Brahmā beyond death." "The universe has no separate existence apart from the person." Radhakrishnan, *The Principal Upaniṣads*, 682.

[76] *"eko hi rudro na dvitīyāya tasthuḥ ya imāṁllokānīśata īśanībhiḥ, pratyaṅjanān tiśṭhati sañcuko ca anatakāle saṁsṛjya viśva bhuvanāni gopāḥ. viśvataścakṣuruta viśvatomukho viśvatobāhuruta viśvātaspāt, saṁ bāhubhyām dhamati sampatatrair-dhyāvābhūmī janayandeva ekaḥ."* SU 3.1-2.

[77] *"tileṣu tailaṁ dadhanīva sarpir-āpaḥ srotaḥsvaraṇīśu ca agniḥ, evam ātmātmāni gṛhyate'sau satyenainaṁ tapasā yo'nupaśati. sarvavyāpinam ātmānam kṣīre sarpirivārpitam, ātmavidyātapomūlaṁ tadbrahmopaniṣat param."* SU 1.15-16.

[78] *"sanātanam enam āhur utadya syāt punar navaḥ aho rātre prajāyete anyo anyasya rūpayoḥ."* AV 10.8.23.

[79] *Aitereya, Kauṣītaki, Ātmabodha, Nādabindu, Nirvāṇa, Mudgala, Akṣamālikā, Tripurā, Saubhāgya and Bahvṛca Upaniṣads* are part of the *ṚGVEDA; Īśa, Bṛhadāraṇyaka, Jābala, Hamsa, Muktika, Sarvasāra, Nirālamba, Kaivalya, Amṛtabindu, Skanda, Paiṅgala, Adhyātma,*

Subāla, Tejobindu, Brahma, Śārīraka, Garbha, Nārāyaṇa, Kalisantāraṇa, Bhikṣuka are part of the *Yajurveda; Kena, Chāndogya, Vajrasūci, Dhyānabindu, Maitrī Upaniṣads* are part of the *Sāmaveda; Praśna, Muṇḍaka, Māṇḍūkya, Sītā, Sūrya, Gaṇapati, Nāradaparivrājaka, Śāṇḍilya Upaniṣads* are part of the *Atharvaṇa Veda*. Madhu Khanna has classified 108 *Upaniṣads* under four Vedas. For more details see, Khanna, *Thirty Minor Upaniṣads*, 4-5.

[80] The number varies from ten, eleven, thirteen or eighteen depending on the authors. Śaṅkara comments about ten and calls them *Mukhya Upaniṣads*. Robert Ernest Hume speaks of thirteen. The traditional eleven are: *"īśā-kena-kaṭha-praṣna-muṇḍaka-māṇḍūkya-taittirī-aitareyaṁ ca chāndogyaṁ bṛhadāraṇyakaṁ tathā."* Srisa Chandra Vasu, *A Catechism of Hindu Dharma* (Allahabad: Sudhindra Natha Vasu, 1919), 4. Radhakrishnan considers eleven and to which he adds two*: Śvetaśvatara, Kauśṭika and Maitrī. Fourteenth to eighteen are Subāla, Jābāla, Paiṅgala, Kaivalya* and *Vajrasūcikā*. See, Robert Ernest Hume, *The Thirteen Principal Upanishads* (New York: Oxford University Press, 1921); Radhakrishnan, *The Principal Upaniṣads*.

[81] Radhakrishnan, *The Principal Upaniṣads*, 6.

[82] The *Brahmasūtras*, the *Upaniṣaads* and the *Bhagavad Gītā* together constitute the *prasthānatrayī*, the three-fold authoritative foundation of the *Vedānta*. The *Brahmasūtras* are the *nyāyaprasthāna*, the *Upaniṣads* are the *śrutiprasthāna* and the *Gītā* is the *smṛtiprasthāna*.

[83] *Smṛti*, literally "that which is remembered," refers to a specific body of Hindu religious scripture, and a codified component of Hindu customary law. The literature which comprises the *smṛti* was composed after the *Vedas* around 500 BCE. *Smṛti* is the second source of authority for *dharma*. The first source of *dharma* is *śruti*: the *Vedas* or Revelation. Scholars have commonly translated *smṛti* as "tradition." Although *smṛti* is also considered a written source; it differs from *śruti* in that *smṛti* does not have divine origins. The *smṛti* texts have become a binding element of "sacred literature" which includes the six *Vedāṅgas, the Itihāsas: the Mahābhārata* and the *Rāmāyaṇa*, as well as, the *Purāṇas*. Robert Lingat, *The Classical Law of India*, translated by J. Duncan M. Derrett (Berkeley: University of California Press, 1973), ix.

R.N. Minor thinks that even though the *Gītā* was never considered a part of *śruti*, it was regarded by the *Vedāntins* as one of the three great texts which deserved and required commentary along with the *Upaniṣads* and the *Vedānta Sūtras*. Robert N. Minor, *Bhagavad-Gītā: An Exegetical Commentary* (Columbia: South Asian Books, 1982), xv-xvi.

All the schools of Indian philosophy do not consider the Gītā in the same manner. For example, Nyāya School regards it as *śruti*, whereas the *Mīmāṁsā* school as *smṛti*. It is *smṛti* because of its setting in the *Mahābhārata*. It is *śruti* mainly because of its *Upanisadic* content, as the *Gītopaniṣad*. In any case, labelling the *Gītā* as *śruti* is more appropriate because of its contents and *Upaniṣadic* nature which were widely known at the time of its composition. If such were not the case, then the author of the *Gītā* (whosoever may be) would not be able to use the *Upaniṣadic* contents in its setting. This indicates that the *Gītā*, especially the knowledge in it, is quite ancient. Incidentally, Chapter IV of the *Gītā* indicates in the beginning that the knowledge in the *Gītā* is very ancient and used to be transmitted through oral tradition, implying that the *Gītā* is truly an *Upaniṣad* and therefore a *śruti*.

[84] R.C. Zaehner, *The Bhagavad-Gīta: With a Commentary Based on the Original Sources* (Oxford: Oxford Univesity Press, 1969), 6.

[85] Chandra Kumar Jha, *Śrīmadbhagavadgītā: Ek Trik-Śāstrīya Pariśīlan* (Kurukshetra: Nirmal Book Agency, 2014), 62.

[86] Jha, *Śrīmadbhagavadgītā*, 62.

[87] "Truth is one, wise call it by many names." RV 1.164.46.

[88] S. Prabhavananda, *Vedic Religion and Philosophy* (Madrass: Sri Ramakrishna Math, 1983), 107.

[89] For the chronological and tradition-wise list of various commentaries on the BG see, Jha, *Śrīmadbhagavadgītā*, 16-21. Here he enlists the extant commentary of Vijñānabhikṣu mentioned in the *Sarvadarśanasaṅgraha* of Mādhavācārya.

[90] *Pañcarātra* School is also known as *Bhāgavata* or *Sāttvata* or *Ekāntika* School in *Vaiśṇava* tradition. Probably, it has a non-Vedic origin along the Vedic times. The prominent issues here are: i. *Jñāna*: knowledge regarding God, soul, creation, liberation and prominently on occultism containing knowledge of secret powers of letters, syllables formulas and figures, ii. *Yoga*: meditation to acquire secret knowledge, iii. *Kriyā*: rules to be followed in the making of idols,

temples, etc. iv. *Caryā*: rules regarding worship, rituals, duties and festivals. See, S.R. Bhatt, *The Philosophy of the Pancharatra: Advaitic Approach* (Madras: Ganesh and Company, 1968), 7.

It is possible that *Bhedābheda* tradition has taken inspiration from this Philosophical School. Vijñānabhikṣu has used the name *Pañcarātra* quite often in his work.

[91] Dasgupta, *A History of Indian Philosophy*, 105.

[92] See, BG 5.29; 7.7; 7.10; 7.19; 9.17; 10.8; 10.20; 10.23;15.15; 15.18; 7.4; 15.7; 2.19; 2.20; 15.6.

[93] Nath, *Tat Tvam Asi*, xxxiv.

[94] K.T. Pandurangi and Krishnacharya Upadhyaya, ed., *Gītātātparyanirṇayaḥ*, vol. 1 (Bangalore: Dvaita Vedanta Studies and Research Foundation, 2007), 122-23, 53.

[95] Some *Advaitins* enumerate six such sentences – *ahaṁ brahmāsmi, ayamātmā brahma, tattvamasi, prajñānaṁ brahma, sarvaṁ khalvidaṁ brahma* and *so'ham*. Anonymous, "Six Mahāvākyas," The Hindu Universe. Available on http://hindunet.org/scriptures/mahavakyas/index.htm, accessed 30 November 2016. I have used *Mahāvākya* as singular and *Mahāvākyas* as plural, though the plural is *mahāvākyāni*.

[96] *Bhedābheda* in the *Upaniṣadic* Philosophy cannot be explained without having recourse to the four *mahāvākyas*. Explaining the *mahāvākyas* is incomplete without having explained *tattvamasi* in detail according to different *vedāntic* proponents. This will suffice to explain the *Bhedābheda* in the *Upaniṣads*. Therefore, I have explained only *tattvamasi* in detail before giving the gist of other three *mahāvākyas*. This will also initiate us to familiarize with the kinds of philosophy different *vedāntic* teachers expound.

[97] Swami Nikhilananda, *Vedāntasāra of Sadānanda with Introduction, Text, English Translation and Comments* (Almora: Advaita Ashrama, 1931), 97.

[98] Though well accepted ones are only four, there are several such aphorisms. Some of them are, *sarvaṁ khalvidaṁ brahma* (CU 3.14.1, All of this is Brahman), *so'ham* (IU 16, He I am), *brahma satyaṁ jagat mithyam* (Brahman is truth and the world is unreal), *ekameva advitīyaṁ brahma* (Brahman is indeed one). CU 6.2.1-2. *satyaṁ jñānaṁ anantaṁ brahma* (Brahman is real, knowledge and infinite).

TU 2.1.1. See, Samaya Sri Vidyatantra, "Mahavakyas: The Great Contemplations." Available on http://www.swamij.com/mahavakyas.htm, accessed on 7 December 2016. Karl Potter's work, *Mahāvākyavivaraṇa* recognizes 12 *Mahāvākyas*. See, Karl Potter, *Encyclopedia of Indian Philosophies* (Dehli: Motilal Banarsidass Publishers, 1981), s.v. "Advaita Vedānta up to Śaṁkara and His Pupils."

[99] M.K. Venkatarama Iyer, "The Methodology of the Upaniṣads," in *Studies in Vedānta Philosophy*, edited by R.K. Panda (Delhi: Bharatiya Kala Prạkashan, 2002), 69.

[100] Shyama Kumar Chattopadhyaya, *The Philosophy of Sankar's Advaita Vedanta* (New Delhi: Sarup and Sons, 2000), 320.

[101] Iyer, "The Methodology of the Upaniṣads," 71.

[102] Apte, *The Student's Sanskrit-English Dictionary*, 1991 ed. s.v. "Prajñāna."

[103] *Dictionary of Spiritual Terms*, s.v. "Lakṣaṇā."

[104] *"lakṣyate yena tallakṣaṇaṁ, dhūmo lakṣaṇamagneriti vadati."* As quoted by K.D. Tripathi, "Lakṣaṇā," in *Kalātattvakośa: A Lexicon of Fundamental Concepts of the Indian Arts*, edited by Kapila Vatsyayan (Delhi: Motilal Banarsidass Publishers, 1988), 137.

[105] *"anubhava anantaram eva sa vidvān saṁsāra bhayād uttīrṇo bhavati."* VAB 1.1.19, p.84.

[106] *eṣa ma ātman antḥhṛdaya etad brahma*. CU 3.14.4. Also the *Bhagavad Gītā* states, "The Lord resides in the heart of all individual beings and turns them round and round on the wheel of his *Māyā*." BG 18.61.

[107] AUM, also written as AUṁ, Oṃ, OM and ॐ is understood to be the primordial sound. It also refers to the Supreme Spirit.

[108] Swami Sharvananda, *Māṇḍūkyopaniṣad: Including Original Verses, Constructed Text (Anvaya) with a Literal Word by Word Translation, English Rendering of Each Stanza, Copious Notes, Introduction and a Summary of Gauḍapāda's Kārikā*, Upaniṣad Series (Madras: Sri Ramakrishan Math, 1943), 3-4.

[109] *"aumityetadakṣaramidaṁsarvaṁ."* MāU 1.

[110] *"atha mahāvākyo varṇyate. idaṁ tattvamasivākyaṁ sambandhatrayeṇākhanḍārthabodhakaṁ bhavati."* Nikhilananda,

Vedāntasāra of Sadānanda, 97.

[111] Anonymous, "Aum or Om," *The Hindu Universe.* Web online, available on http://www.hindunet. org/aum/, accessed on 7 December 2016.

[112] *sarvaṁ khalvidaṁ brahma tajjalani iti śānta upāsīta.* CU 3.14.1. Swami Muni Narayana Prasad translates this as, "Everything here verily is Brahman. From It everything is born, into It everything dissolves; in It everything lives moving about." Prasad, *Chāndogya Upaniṣad*, 223.

[113] Sveta Uppal, *Vedapārijāta* (New Delhi: NCERTC, 2014), 92. Also see, *Prasad, Chāndogya Upaniṣad*, 223.

[114] The work of a disciple and a teacher ends in the investigation of the *Mahāvākya*, as it is the culmination of "*the sanctification of the mind*," says P.D. Mehta. See, P.D. Mehta, *The Heart of Religion*, 1987 ed. (London: Element Books Limited, 1976), 44. Italics mine.

[115] Vensus A. George, ed., *Self-Realization (Brahmānubhava): The Advaitic Perspective of Shankara*, edited by George F. Mclean, Indian Philosophical Studies (Washington: The Council for Research in Values and Philosophy, 2001), 51. The original spelling is retained.

[116] Apte, *The Student's Sanskrit-English Dictionary*, s.v "abhyāsa."

[117] *brahma va idam agra āsīt, tadātmānam evavet, ahaṁ brahāsmīti, tasmāt tatsarvam abhavāt.* BU 1.4.10. "Brahman, indeed was this in the beginning. It knew itself only as 'I am Brahman.' Therefore, it became all." Radhakrishnan, *The Principal Upaniṣads*, 168.

[118] George, *Self-Realization* (*Brahmānubhava*), 51.

[119] *sa ha dvādaśavarṣa utpetya caturviṁśativarṣaḥ sarvānvedāndhītya mahāmanā anūcānamānī stabdha eyāya taṁ ha pitovāca śvetaketo yannu somyedaṁ mahāmanā anūcānamānī stabdho'syuta tamādeśamaprākṣyaḥ.* CU 6.1.2. He, having studied twelve long years, retuned at the age of twentyfour conceited, proud and and arrogant. His father told him, "O Śvetaketu, my dear, I find you conceited, proud of having become learned man and arrogant."

[120] "*vidyā dadāti vinayaṁ vinayād yāti pātratāṁ, pātratvāddhanamāpnoti dhanāddharmaṁ tataḥ sukham.*" Knowledge gives humility, from humility one attains character; from character one acquires wealth; from wealth good deeds (righteousness) follow and

then happiness. "*tatra avidyā-dhvaṁsataḥ—avidyā-dhvaṁsato bodho vidyodaya-puraḥsaraḥ, aśeṣa-kleśa-viśrānti-svarūpāvagamādi-kṛt.*" Śrīla Rūpa Gosvāmī, *Śrī Bhakti Rasāmṛtabindu,* 2.4.180. *Bodha* arising from destruction of ignorance: "Enlightenment occurs after the appearance of knowledge, which occurs after the removal of ignorance. This enlightenment consists of realizing one's identity with *brahman*, which destroys unlimited suffering." Śrīla Rūpa Gosvāmī, *Śrī Bhakti-Rasāmṛta-Sindhu: The Eternal Ocean of Nectar of Devotion*, vol. 1., translated by Gaurahari Dāsānudās Bābājī (http://esotericteaching.org), 302. Available on https://archive.org/details/SriBhakti-rasamrta-sindhu/, accessed on 24 September 2018.

[121] The meaning of the word *upaniṣad* is *upa+ni+ṣad* = near+down+sit, that is, sitting at the feet of the *guru* and learning. In fact the humbling experience is very much lacking in the contemporary Indian Spiritualdom. Most of the spiritual leaders or *gurus* think that they are the sole custodians of truth and only they are the authority on the scriptures and religion. What they preach is the orthodoxy.

[122] *uta tamādeśamaprakśāmyaḥ, yenāṣrutaṁ śṛtutaṁ bhavatyamataṁ matavijñātaṁ vijñātam?* CU 2.1.2-3.

[123] *iti kathaṁ nu bhagavḥ sa ādeśo bhavatīti.* CU 6.1.3.

[124] For the detailed study see, Swami Vimalananda, *Tat Tvam Asi: Notes on Chāndogya Upaniṣad, Chapter Six* (Mumbai: Central Chinmaya Mission Trust, 2000; reprint, 2013).

[125] *brahma satya jaganmityā jīvo brahmaiva nāparaḥ*. This is commonly known *Advaitin* dictum and found in a text ascribed to Śaṅkara called, *Brahmajñānavalīmālā*. Śaṅkara, *Brahmajñānavalīmālā,* 20. Available on https://sanskritdocuments.org/doc_z_misc_shankara/brahmajna.pdf, accessed on 15 August 2019.

[126] *Advaita* has a beautiful way of explaining '*satyam.*' *Satyam* consists of three syllables: *sa, ti* and *yam*. The first and the last means real and the second is unreal. The unreality is enclosed on both the sides by reality: the present moment is evanescent, enclosed on both the sides by an eternity which is real: we move from eternity to eternity, halting for a short while in the caravansary of the present and it is wonderful to notice that the whole of the "*satyam*" has been

supposed to have come out of the primeval waters. See, Ranade, *A Constructive Survey of Upanishadic Philosophy*, 55-56.

[127] Śaṅkarācārya, *Ādi Śaṅkarācārya's Vākya Vṛtti* (Mumbai: Chinmaya Mission, 2010). Available on http://www.astrojyoti.com/vakyavritti.htm. Part of this book is also translated by Satya Sarada Kandula and is available in his blog. See, Satya Sarada Kandula, "Tat Tvam Asi: Vakya Vritti of Sri Adi Sankaracharya," in *Old Thoughts* (2010). Available on https://oldthoughts.wordpress.com/ philosophy/tat-tvam-asi-vakyavritti-of-sri-adi-sankaracharya/, accessed on 12 December 2016. In fact, there is a doubt regarding the authenticity of the authorship. Mostly, it is ascribed to Śaṅkara. It mainly explains purport of the *Mahāvākya Ahaṁ Brahmāsmi* and *Tattvamasi*.

[128] Śaṅkarācārya, *A Thousand Teachings, the Upadeśasāharsī of Śaṅkara: Translation with Introduction and Notes*, trans., Sengaku Mayeda (Tokyo: University of Tokyo Press, 1979).

[129] See, Śaṅkarācārya, "Ādi Śaṅkarācārya's Vākya Vṛtti," no. 28,48. Italics mine.

[130] This is similar to the Western concept, '*via-negativa*' used in Apophatic theology. An equivalent recent terminology could be 'bracketing' or phenomenological reduction.

[131] Swami Vishnu Devananda, *Meditations and Mantras*, 2003 ed. (Delhi: Motilal Banarsidass Publishers, 1978), 119.

[132] Pavel G. Somov, *The Lotus Effect: Shedding Suffering and Rediscovering Your Essential Self* (Oakland: New Harbinger Publications, 2010), 34.

[133] It is called the *pañcakośa prakriyā*. The concept of *pañcakośa* (the theory of five sheaths of the self) can be found in the *Taittirīya Upaniṣad* (TU 2.1-9). It shows how *Upaniṣads* have spiritualized human personality in its very nature, forming the core of very existence of every living being and pursuing the path of Spirituality in every manifestation. *Pañcakośa* explains human personality in five layers: the bodily self or the *annamayakośa*, the biological self or *prāṇamayakośa*, the psychological or *manomayakośa*, the intellectual self or *vijñānamayakośa* and the spiritual self or *ānandamayakośa*. The *ānandamayakośa*, the highest stage of individual self, consists of bliss and within all the other sheaths. The realization of *ānandamayakośa* leads to God-realization or *brahmānubhava*. So the

spirituality which forms the core of the cosmic world, exists within every human being and thereby an individual need to unite himself with God to make room for spirituality but to realize one's own real nature which we often forget due to ignorance.

[134] *"tattvamasyādivākyena svātmā hi pratipāditaḥ, neti neti śrutirbrūyād anṛtaṁ pāñcabhautikam."* *Avadhūta Gītā* 1.25. Rishi Dattatreya, *Dattatreya, Song of the Avadhut: An English Translation of the Avadhut Gita with Sanskrit Transliteration*, translated by Swami Abhayananda (abhayananda@bellsouth.net, 2009), 30. The saying, "That thou art," affirms the reality of your own true Self. The saying, "Not this, not this," denies the reality of the five composite elements.

[135] Śaṅkarācārya, "Ādi Śaṅkarācārya's Vākya Vṛtti," no. 44-46.

[136] Śaṅkarācārya, "Ādi Śaṅkarācārya's Vākya Vṛtti," no. 47-48.

[137] *Akhaṇḍārthavākya* is a proposition that employs demonstrative and has an indivisible meaning. Such sentences are self-complete. On the contrary, *saṁsargāvagāhivākyas* are the one's which employ descriptive, classificatory and relational expressions. They are incomplete as they do not satisfy the conditions of *ākāṅkṣā*.

[138] *Vedāntasāra*, 'the Essence of Veda,' is a 15th century *Advaita* text written by Sadānanda Yogendra Saraswati. It contains six chapters in which fourth chapter deals with the de-superimposition of *tattvamasi*. For translation and text, see, Nikhilananda, *Vedāntasāra of Sadānanda*, 168.

[139] *"tasmād yathā 'so'yaṁ devadattaḥ' iti vakyaṁ tadartho vā tatkālaitatkālaviśiṣṭa devadatta lakṣaṇasya vākyārthasyāṁśe virodhāt viruddha-tatkālaitatkāla viśiṣṭatvāṁśaṁ parityajyāviruddhaṁ devadattāṁśamātraṁ lakṣyati tathā 'tattvamasi' iti vākyaṁ tadarthāvā parokṣatvāparokṣatvādiviśiṣṭa caitanyaikatvalakṣaṇasya vākyārthasyāṁśo virodhād viruddha-parokṣatvāparokṣatvādi viśiṣṭatva aṁśaṁ parityajyā viruddham akhaṇḍa caitanyamātra lakṣayati."* *Vedāntasāra* 4.169.1-2. See, Nikhilananda, *Vedāntasāra of Sadānanda*, 169. In conclusion, the meaning of the sentence, "This is that Devadatta," is that present and past qualify the same person, Devadatta. Due to the contradiction in the literal meaning, present and past, the qualified portion may be abandoned and the non-conflicting portion regarding Devadatta is retained. To apply this, consider "Thou art That." The import is that remoteness and closeness, etc. qualify the same consciousness. Due to the

contradiction in the conflicting portion, of the literal meanings, remoteness and closeness, this qualified portion may be abandoned. The non-conflicting portion regarding the pure eternal Consciousness alone stays as the implied meaning.

[140] *Vivekacūḍāmaṇī*, no. 243-246. Śaṅkarācārya, *Vivekacūḍāmaṇī* (Tamil Nadu: Tiruchengode Chinmaya Mission, no date). Available on http://www.advaitin.net/PranipataChaitanya/Viveka chudamani%20eBook%20FinalFinal1.pdf, accessed on 10 January, 2017.

[141] *"dvahoḥ padayoḥ prakāradvayamukhenaikārthaniṣṭhatvam."* Johannes Adrianus Bernardus Van Buitenen, *Rāmānuja's Vedārthasaṁgraha* (Michigan: Deccan College Postgraduate and Research Institute, 1956), 109.

[142] Anima Sen Gupta, "Ramanuja on 'Tat Tvam Asi'," *Philosophy East & West* 12, no. 2 (1962): 129. For Śaṅkara, *samānādhikaraṇyam* would be bare unity established by abandonment of attributes, between Brahman and *ātman*.

[143] Yoshitsugu Sawai, "Rāmānuja's Hermeneutics of the Upaniṣads in Comparison with Śaṅkara's Interpretation," *Journal of Indian Philosophy* 19, (1991): 91.

[144] Gupta, "Ramanuja on 'Tat Tvam Asi'," 129.

[145] *"pṛthak-siddhy-anarhādhārādheya bhāva," "niyantṛ-niyāma-bhāva," "śeṣa-śeṣī-bhāva," "śarīra-śarīrī-bhāva."* Van Buitenen, *Rāmānuja's Vedārthasaṁgraha*, 85. Also see, P.N. Srinivasachari, *The Philosophy of Viśiṣṭādvaita* (Madras: The Adyar Library and Research Centre, 1970), 93-97, 123-126.

[146] Gupta, "Ramanuja on 'Tat Tvam Asi'," 30. Italics mine.

[147] *acid-viśiṣṭa-jīva-śarīrakaṁ brahma*. Van Buitenen, *Rāmānuja's Vedārthasaṁgraha*, 109. Also see, Sawai, "Rāmānuja's Hermeneutics of the Upaniṣads," 94.

[148] Jethala G. Shah, *Shri Vallabhacharya: His Philosophy and Religion* (Anand: The Pushtimargiya Pustakalaya, 1969), 133-135.

[149] V. Varadachari, *Antiquity of the Term Viśiṣṭādvaita* (Madras: Ramanuja Research Centre, 1974), 57-58.

[150] B.N.K. Sharma, *Brahamasūtras and Their Principal Commentaries: Critical Exposition*, vol. 1 (Delhi: Munshiram Manoharlal Publishers, 1974), 22. *"ataḥ sarvapramāṇaviruddhatvāt na*

abhede tātparyaṁ vākyasya kintu viṣṇoḥ sarvottamatva eva mahātātparyaṁ sarvāgamānām." Śrī Ānandatīrtha, *Viṣṇutattvavinirṇaya of Śrī Ānandatīrtha*, translated by K.T. Pandurangi (Bangalore: Dvaita Vedanta Studies and Research Foundation, 2011), 26.

[151] Sharma, *Brahamasūtras and Their Principal Commentaries*, 11.

[152] C.R. Krishna Rao, "The Supreme Text: Tattvamasi - That Thou Art," *Dharmaprakash Journal* 11, no. 9-10 (1982): 28. B.N.K. Sharma, "Tat Tvam Asi," *Dharmaprakash Journal* 11, no. 11 (1982). Sharma, *Brahamasūtras and Their Principal Commentaries*, 10.

[153] B.N.K. Sharma, *Mahātātparya of Mahāvākyas and Other Advaita Śrutis* (Bangalore: Anandatirtha Pratisthana of Akhila Bharata Madhva Mahamandal, 1999), 177-78.

[154] *"viśvaṁ satyaṁ, satyaṁ bheda."*

[155] Vijñānabhikṣu also endorses this view.

[156] Sharma, "Tat Tvam Asi," 18.

[157] Umesh Mishra, *Nimbārka School of Vedānta* (Allahabad: Tirabhukti Publications, 1966), 20-29.

[158] Jadunath Sinha, *The Philosophy of Nimbarka* (Calcutta: Sinha Publishing House, 1973), 148-149.

[159] Nimbārka & Śrīnivāsa, *Vedānta-Pārijāta-Saurabha of Nimbārka and Vedānta-Kaustubha of Srinivāsa: Commentaries on the Brahmasūtras*, translated by Roma Bose, 1943 ed. (Calcutta: Royal Asiatic Scoeity), 100.

[160] *Bhāratīya-Darśan-Bṛhatkośa* (Delhi: Sharada Publishing House, 2012), s.v. "Tat Tvamasi."

[161] *sa ātmātat tvamamityatrātatvaṁ chedhyaṁ padaṁ buddaiḥ, sādṛśyādi nana bodhyaṁ nirmuktatvādinā hareḥ*. See, 'Jñāna,' *Bhāratīya-Darśan-Bṛhatkośa*, s.v. "Tat Tvamasi." This does not mean that the process is like Madhva, rather it is the division of words according to grammar.

[162] *Lakṣaṇā-vṛtti* is the potency of words whereby they on the sublation of the literal or natural import signify something connected with the natural meaning and this potency is different from the natural potency of words.

[163] A.K. Majumdar, *Caitanya: His Life and Doctrine* (Bombay:

Bharatiya Vidya Bhavan, 1969), 270. Also see, Girindra Narayan Mallik, *The Philosophy of Vaisnava Religion*, vol. I (Lahore: Motilal Banarsidass Publishers, 1927), 202.

[164] Bhaktivedānta Swami Prabhupāda, *Teachings of Lord Caitanya* (Bombay: Bhaktivedānta Book Trust, 1974), 224.

[165] Mallik, *The Philosophy of Vaisnava Religion*, 204.

[166] Prabhupāda, *Teachings of Lord Caitanya*, 227.

Chapter Two

BHEDĀBHEDA IN THE *BHEDĀBHEDA-VEDĀNTA* TRADITIONS

The *Bhedābheda* is a tradition or a family of philosophies in the *Vedānta* without having a single founder, unlike *Advaita* or *Dvaita*.[1] In general, it has some commonalities like "the relation between individual self (*jīvātman*) and Brahman as one of part and whole; the doctrine that the phenomenal world is a real transformation of Brahman (*pariṇāmavāda*); and the doctrine that liberation can only be attained through a combination of knowledge and ritual action (*jñānakarmasamuccayavāda*), not by knowledge alone"[2] which make this tradition rich, says Nicholson. Vijñānabhikṣu emulates the *Bhedābheda* tradition, but with a modification. He repudiates the direct transformation of Brahman (*sākṣātpariṇāmavāda*) and illusory appearance (*vivartavāda*), "I am going to refute the direct transformation and the illusory appearance of Brahman."[3] At the same time, each thinker within this tradition has significant philosophical disagreements regarding the precise meanings of the philosophical terms, *bheda* and *abheda*.[4] Here, we survey briefly the proponents of this philosophy to enter the world of Vijñānabhikṣu. This also would clarify the relational aspect within the reality, their uniqueness and divergences.

2.1 Scholars Before Bādarāyaṇa

Some scholars have regarded the *Brahmasūtras* of

Bādarāyaṇa's (4 CE) as one of the foundational texts common to all the *Vedānta* schools, written from a *Bhedābheda* point of view. This claim is debated by many, especially by the *Advaita* School proponents.[5] Bādarāyaṇa himself mentions three *Bhedābheda* proponents in three different *sūtras* in the *Brahmasūtras*, *"pratijñāsiddherliṅgaṁ* ***āśmarathyaḥ****, utkramiṣyata evambhāvādityo* ***auḍulomiḥ****, avasthiteriti* ***kāśakṛtsnaḥ****"* (BS I.4.19-22). Besides these three people, there were also people like Kaśyapa, Asita, Devala, Garga, Jaigīṣavya, Parāśara, and Bṛugu who could be *Bhedābheda* proponents.[6]

It is possible to perceive Bādarāyaṇa himself as a *Bhedābhedavādin*. Citing a few aphorisms as examples from the *Brahmasūtras* suffices to prove this fact. For example, the following aphorisms illustrate *bheda*, "On account of difference" (VAB 1.1.17), "It is a part because of the declaration of difference" (VAB 2.3.43), "But Brahman is something else on account of description of differences" (VAB 2.1.22).[7] Some aphorisms advocate identity as well as difference. "Everything originates from the self" or it can be understood as, "everything is identical with the self" (VAB 4.1.3), "from the virtue of brightness that depends on the light" (VAB 3.2.28), "non-difference from the declaration of *śrutis"* (VAB 4.2.15) and "from the fact of inseparability seen (in the scriptures)" (VAB 4.4.4).[8] These are only a few, there are many more such examples to endorse Bādarāyaṇa as a *Bhedābhedavādin*.

The available textual excerpts from the commentaries

relate Āśmarathya, Auḍulomi and Kāśakṛtsna were, in fact, *Bhedābhedavādins,* whom Bādarāyaṇa too ascribes. Vācaspati Miśra in his *Bhāmati ṭīkā* approves this fact in the following manner, "Just as spark is neither very much different from the fire nor non-different from it, so too *jīvātman* is neither different nor non-different from *paramātman.*"[9] Further, he notifies, "Prior to *mukti* there is *bheda* between *jīvātman* and *paramātman,* and after the *mukti* as *abheda* as there is lack of cause for it."[10] "Just as there is neither difference nor non-difference in the meaning of *ākāśa* as *aṁśa,* so too between *jīvātman* and *paramātman.*"[11]

This signals that *Bhedābheda* thought existed before Bādarāyaṇa. Śaṅkara claims that Kāśakṛtsna as the propounder of monism.[12] Nonetheless, irrefutably this philosophy, as one of the foundational claims of *Vedānta* philosophy and as 'the philosophy' of the *Upaniṣads,* existed at the time of Bādarāyaṇa. Srinivasachari recognizes Bhāskara in this aspect, "*Bhedābheda* is the central truth of *Vedānta.*"[13] The central claim of this philosophy is the inquiry into the nature of the ultimate reality and its relationship with sentient and non-sentient beings. Here, we investigate various *bhedābhedavādins.*

2.1.1 Āśmarathya

We have the proof about Āśmarathya in the *Brahmasūtras, abhivyakterityāśmarathyaḥ* (BS 1.2.29), *pratijñāsiddherliṅgamāśmarathyaḥ* (BS 1.4.20). *Abhivyakti* means manifestation. The divine manifests Himself. His revelation is spatially limited.[14] By saying *'abhivyakta,'* Āśmarathya conveys that the Lord has to be seen manifesting in the creation like a mark (*liṅga*), just as the effect is to be seen in the cause.[15] This thought is akin to the *Chāndogya Upaniṣad* where it is assumed that the infinite Supreme Self exhibits itself (*abhivyakti*) as the size of a thumb and index finger to the worshipper (CU 5.18.1). The *Bṛhadāraṇyaka Upaniṣad* declares, "When *ātman* has been known, this all is known" (BU 2. 4-5). The sage Āśmarathya emphasizes the Universal Soul manifesting itself in the individual beings present in the limited spaces like the human heart for the sake of finite beings. Verse 29 has the reference to 25 (*vaiśvānaraḥ sādhāraṇa śabdaviśeṣāt,* BS 1.2.25), where *vaiśvānara* is understood to be Brahman and commonly as the Self.

In BS 1.4.20, Āśmarathya articulates the non-difference between the individual and supreme self to be a sign indicative of the fulfillment of the declaration. *Jīva* and Brahman are correlated as effect and cause respectively. They are different yet non-different from each other. Had the individual soul quite different from Brahman, then by the knowledge of the Brahman everything else would've been known.

Therefore, there is an assertion of *Bhedābheda*, that *ātman* is somehow similar and non-similar with 'all this known.' That's why, Āśmarathya elucidates the *Bhedābheda* relation between *vijñānātma* and *paramātma*, knower and known. The Jaimini's *Mīmāṁsa Sūtra* 6.5.16 too acknowledges him, "*anirupte'bhyudite prākṛtībhyo nirvapediti Āśmarathyaḥ taṇḍula bhūteṣvapanayāt*".[16] Śrīnivāsa in the *Vedānta Kaustubha* points Āśmarathya's opinion of *bheda* and *abheda* between *ātman* and *paramātman* as between cause and effect. "Since the effect is non-different from the cause, being born from it and so on, non-difference between the two, too, is equally a fact.... The individual souls being non-different from the Supreme Soul as His effect, by the word "individual soul" the Supreme Soul is designated"[17] (BS 1.4.20).

2.1.2 Auḍulomi

Three references relate to Auḍulomi in the *Brahmasūtras*: "*utakramiṣyata evaṁ bhāvādityauḍulomiḥ*" (BS 1.4.21), "*ārtijyatmiyauḍulomistasmai hi parikrīyate*" (BS 3.4.45), and "*citi tanmātreṇa tadātmakatvādityauḍulomiḥ*" (BS 4.4.6). When the *ātman* departs from the body, upon death, it attains the status of Brahman (BS 1.4.21). It is the duty of the *ṛtvik* (priest) as he is paid for it. This stipulates the labour of the priest to be purchased by the sacrifice so that the fruit of the whole performance is attained by the sacrifice (BS 3.4.45). The liberated *ātman* communicates itself solely as pure consciousness. That is its pure nature (BS 4.4.6).[18]

According to Auḍulomi, the individual self has the nature of pure consciousness (*cit* or *caitanya*), and upon liberation, it gets united with Brahman as it is made of pure consciousness. In the bondage as in *saṁsāra,* it remains distinct and non-different, like 'the rivers giving up their name and their form, flow out and disappear into the ocean and become one' (MuU 3.2.8). He speaks about the cause of *Bhedābheda* as the difference in the material reality.

Auḍulomi speaks of a relation of *bheda* and *abheda* existing between *jīva* and Brahman, *bheda* is in the state of *saṁsāra* and *abheda* in the state of *mukti*. *Jīvātman* is the pure form of consciousness.[19] "On account of its attaining the state of Brahman, the Supreme Soul is denoted by a term denoting the individual soul.... On this view, there is a difference between the individual soul and Brahman during the soul's state of bondage and non-difference during its state of release."[20] This view is also buttressed by Vijñānabhikṣu in his *Vijñāmṛtabhāṣyam*. He enlightens, that at the time of departure from the *paramātman*, the *jīvātman* is like *prāṇā* as *paramātman*; at the time of production they are one like husband and wife in procreation, and at the time of destruction or death they separate from each other and exhibit *abheda* relationship as they exhibited in the world and in dealings (VAB 1.4.21).[21] In this way, Vijñānabhikṣu favours the *Bhedābheda* of Auḍulomi through his *Avibhāga-Bhedābeda*. Quite the reverse, according to Vācaspati Miśra, Bādarāyaṇa has integrated Auḍulomi to rebut the teachings of Atreya of *Mīmāṁsā* School.

2.1.3 Kāśakṛtsna

Among various *Vedāntic* scholars, there is a contretemps whether Kāśakṛtsna is an *Advaita* or a *Bhedābheda* proponent. If Śaṅkara considers him as an *Advaitin*, Bhāskara Bhaṭṭa reckons him as *Bhedābhedavādin*. Despite that in reality, when compared the *bhāṣyas* of Bhāskara, Madhva,

Śrīkāṇṭa, Rāmānuja, Nimbārka and Caitanya he is understood more of a *Bhedābheāvādin* than an *Advaitavādin.*[22] There is an illustration about him in the *Brahmasūtras* 1.4.22, "*avasthiteriti kāśakṛtsnaḥ.*" Kāśakṛtsna regards that because of the universal self abiding in everything,[23] *ātman* is considered to be Brahman.

Kāśakṛtsna is referred to and quoted in other places also. Śaṅkara identifies him '*śrutyanusāri*' or '*tattvavetta ācārya,*' Pātañjali recognizes him in his *Mahābhāśya* 4.1.14, 4.1.93 and 4.3.15.[24] Sadāśivendra Saraswati, an Advaitic proponent, estimates, "Kāśakṛtsna thinks [the statement about the identity at the beginning of the text is in order] because of the existence of the supreme Self as [an] individual soul."[25] At this instant, Brahman Himself appears like the individual Self with a limiting adjunct. *Paramātman* controls the *jīvātman* through his abiding presence in the latter's *antaḥkaraṇa.*[26] Subsequently, Kāśakṛtsna proposes a relation of the controller and the controlled (*niyamya-niyanta sambandha*). ""On account of abiding" of the Supreme Soul in the individual soul, an object to be controlled by Him, as its soul... by a term denoting the individual soul, the Supreme Soul is denoted, so thinks the teacher Kāśakṛtsna, a knower of the object controlled, as well as of the controller."[27] The *Bṛhadāraṇyaka Upaniṣad* correlates that any being is not for the sake of the being, but for the sake of the Self. It is like, the husband is dear not for the sake of husband but for the sake of the Self, so too the wife, children, or any other work (BU 2.4.5, 4.5.6). Likewise, the individual self is not for the sake of individual existence, but for the sake of the Universal Self.

The word, '*avasthiter*' would epitomize the existence of *jīva* and *jagat* as "conditioned temporally and spatially" by the existence of the cause of it, the Brahman. As a consequence, the individual self is either a part of the supreme self or is a constitutive element or *aṁśa* of it as stated in BS 2.3.43, "*aṁśo nānāvyapadeśāt.*"

There are two more individuals—Bādari and Kārṣṇājini—besides the above three names discussed in the *Brahmasūtras* could be entitled *Bhedābhedavādins*. We describe below briefly them.

2.1.4 Bādari

Ācārya Bādari lived in the same place where Bādarāyaṇa lived, in Badravana. Bādari is referred to in the *Brahmasūtras* in four places 1.2.30, 3.1.11, 4.3.7 and 4.4.10.[28] Bādarāyaṇa speaks about the relationship between *Ātman* and *Brahman* in the *vaiśvānarādhikaraṇa* (BS 1.2.24-32). While explaining this relationship, he equates *vaiṣvānara* to be Brahman[29] exhibiting as *ātman* for the sake of worship. This is because the *sthūla śarīra* of Brahman is unable to contain within the worship. Therefore, Brahman has to be taken in terms of *ātman* as *sūkṣma śarīra*, thinks Bādari (BS 1.2.30, *anusmṛter bādariḥ*). Again in *kṛtatyādhikaraṇa* (BS 3.1.7-11), Bādari is brought in by Bādarāyaṇa to relate the meaning of *caraṇa* (feet) with *pāpa-puṇya* (good and bad deeds, VAB 3.1.11, p.229), specifically, good behaviour or act (*sukṛta*) of people as people of good feet. People of good feet are those born with good deeds as a result of *puṇya* and people of bad feet are those who are born of bad behaviour (*duṣkṛta*).

As follows, Bādari describes *Bhedābheda* relationship as *upāsya-upāsaka sambandhabhāva* (worshipped and worshipper relation) between *jīva* and Brahman. Distinctively, there is a close affinity between one's life here in the world with its past and present as well as the good and bad deeds of the past. In view of that, there is no discrimination between a person born of higher class or lower class. He believed in equal rights amongst all the classes of the society regarding divine worship, including *śūdras*. It is at this point Jaimini condemns him. Fortunately or unfortunately, we have insufficient facts to corroborate this view.

2.1.5 Kārṣṇājini

There is a reference to *ācārya* Kārṣṇājini in BS 3.1.9, "*caraṇāditi cennopalakṣaṇārtheti kārṣṇājiniḥ.*" It discloses, "If it were asserted that on account of conduct (the assumption of residual *karma* is not necessary for a rebirth) (we say) not so, (for, the word 'conduct' is used) to denote indirectly (the remaining *karma*). So thinks Kārṣṇājini."[30] Kārṣṇājini has been also referred to in Jaimini's *Mīmāmsā Sūtra* 4.3.17 and 6.7.35 since he was a scholar of *Karma Mīmāṁsā*. The *Mīmāṁsā Sūtra* 4.3.17 states, "Purpose, action, and results are all connected like the limbs of the body, so says Kārṣṇājini."[31] Again in 6.7.35, he articulates, "When we speak of the law of man, we speak of the law of the human race, because it would be improper to speak of it as such if it referred only to an individual."[32]

In the *Brahmasūtras,* he is referred to the ritual aspect. He aims to say that mere rituals will not cancel out one's collected *karmas* or the remaining *karmas* (*sañcita* and *prārabdha*), but one's good conduct (*śīla*) will. This is in line with Vedas, "The Vedas do not purify the man who is devoid of good conduct."[33] Secondly, there is a close bond between human-made law and law imprinted in the very life of human. Thirdly, there is a connection between the rituals and actions performed with their impending fruits. That's why, in a way, he advocates a kind of '*jñānakarmasamuccayavāda*,' where both action and conduct are essential for the salvation, which is *Bhedābheda* way of explaining the ultimate aim. Thus, there is a necessary unseen interconnection between the rituals and conduct of the present with the future.

2.2 Bhartṛprapañca's *Bhedābheda*

Practically, nothing is known about Bhartṛprapañca due to the unavailability of his writings except through the refutation of Śaṅkara in his commentaries on the *Bṛhadāraṇyaka Upaniṣad* and the *Brahmasūtras*. However, he must have been one of the important proponents of the *Vedānta* philosophy and the commentator of the *Upaniṣads*. Despite the non-availability of his works, some fragmentary records have been extracted from the commentaries of Śaṅkara, Sureśvara, Madhusūdana and Ānandagiri. He is also the commentator of the *Brahmasūtras*, the *Kaṭhopaniṣad*, and the *Bṛhadāraṇyaka Upaniṣad*.[34] Professor Hiriyanna has collected his available excerpts and presented them in the *Proceedings of the All-India Oriental Conference*.[35] Hajime

Nakamura, the Japanese indologist and historian dates him around 550 CE.[36] Basing on these details, we can infer the possible date of Bhartṛprapañca as before Śaṅkara.[37]

From the available secondary resources, we can infer Bhartṛprapañca to be one of the original proponents of *Bhedābhedavāda Vedānta*. This doctrine is a kind of dualistic monism in which both *bheda* (dualism) or difference and *abheda* (monism) or non-difference is accepted between Brahman and the *jīvas* in the world. The *jīvas* or the individual souls with their world, evolving out of Brahman, are both *different and non-different* from it. The reality is both unity and multiplicity: in Brahman it displays as One, and in the world, it displays as Many. There is the multiplicity of lives, but there is only one Supreme Being. These multiplicities of lives exist in Brahman and therefore, it is understood to be many, but in one form. It is like the waves and the foam or the bubbles surfacing in the ocean are all identical as water, but different as waves or bubbles. In its divine form, it is *abheda, advaita* and *eka*; and in its multiplicity of the existence in *jīva*, there is *bheda, dvaita* and *aneka* in form. Therefore, this system is called *Bhedābheda, Dvaitādvaita* and even *Anekāntavāda*.[38]

In agreement with Bhartṛprapañca, *advaita* is the ultimate teaching of the *Upaniṣads*. Brahman has two aspects: *para* or the higher Brahman and *apara* or the lower Brahman. Though distinct and real like *'ghaṭa'* and *'paṭa,'* they are at the same time equal as opposed to the *vivarta* nature of the reality of *Kevala Advaita*. In the words of Hiriyanna, "the two things related being equally real, the relation also is real."[39] Given that, both relation and related are real as in the case of the *mahāvākya tattvamasi.*

Śaṅkara differentiates common knowledge or the empirical knowledge from metaphysical knowledge and considers the latter to be superior to the former, whereas, for Bhartṛprapañca, both the empirical and the revealed knowledge are equally valid and similar. As a result, he acknowledges three *pramāṇas*: *pratyakṣa* or direct perception, *anumāna* or inference and *śabda* or the verbal testimony. He recognizes the reality of the world experienced through the sense organs, and hence there is a need for *karma* or actions including rituals. Further, he admits a combination of knowledge and action (*jñānakarmasamuccaya*) as a means to *mokṣa* or liberation. *Karma* or desire-less action leads to *apavarga* or freedom from *saṁsāra. Jñāna* initiates in the destruction of *avidyā* or ignorance, culminating in identity with Brahman, the ultimate Truth. This is attested in the Scriptural revelation of creation, *truth as diversity*. Brahman should exhibit both *dvaita* and *advaita, unity-in-diversity*. The *Upaniṣads* persevere with '*ekam*' through knowledge and action. Both *jñāna* and *karma* are fundamental for the attainment of *mokṣa* and therefore, neither of them is superior nor inferior.[40] This is a path-breaking facet in the *vedāntadarśana* in view of the welfare of the world (*jagatkalyāṇa*).

One of the noteworthy aspects is the resemblance between an evolutionary theory of Bhartṛprapañca and the

Sāṅkhya. In the process of evolution, the Brahman, differentiates into manifold things of experience which are both *identical with and different from* it. Subsequently, it is the Brahman who is the ultimate cause of evolution. Brahman expands into *Īśvara*, *jīva* and *jagat* and at the same time remains one whole. *Īśvara* is the inner ruler, but lower to Brahman. Later Brahman exhibits as *jīvas* and *sākṣins*. From here, everything diversifies. This view is known today as *Brahma-pariṇāmavāda*.[41]

As indicated by Bhartṛprapañca, there are eight states of Brahman as critiqued by Śaṅkara[42] in his *Bṛhadāraṇyaka Upaniṣad Bhāṣya* (BU Bh 3.8.12). The unity and plurality of *Ātman* (*ekāneka*) is to be comprehended as the relationship between 'cow' and 'cowness'—the substance and universality. The cause is intrinsic in the effect, like a snake and its coil or sun and its rays. The whole pervades the parts and the universal is realized in and through particulars. The quiet ocean shows itself as an ocean filled with waves and ripples maintaining its self-identity.[43] In the same way, Brahman unfolds himself as *para* and *apara* states in the world gradually. In His evolution, Brahman asserts himself as *Īśvara*, *jīva* and *jagat*: the inner ruler of all and phenomenal realities.

In his *Bṛhadāraṇyaka Upaniṣad Bhāṣya* Śaṅkara confirms:

> Therein some declare – *Inner ruler* (*antaryāmin*) is [a] slightly agitated state (of the imperishable Brahman) of an immovable nature corresponding to the great ocean. Excessively agitate state of the perishable

> Brahman is a *Knower of the field* (*kṣetrajña*) who does not know the Inner ruler; in such a way manner [sic] they postulate another *five states – thus there are eight states of Brahman*, they say.[44]

Further, he sustains, "In this manner, distinguished by limiting adjunct of the body and organs of *hiraṇyagarbha, avyākṛta, devatā, jāti, piṇḍa*, men, animals, spirits, etc., one becomes of such a name and of such a form."[45] Along these lines, Brahman is manifested in eight states: *piṇḍa* (individual), *jāti* (class), *virāj* (a wide-ruling one or a wide-shining one), *sūtra* (string), *daiva* (divine or divinity), *avyākṛta* (unevolved or unexpounded), *sākṣin* (witness) and *kṣetrajña* (knower of the field). Instead of *kṣetrajña, hiraṇyagarbhha* or *parabrahman* or *akṣara;* and instead of *sākṣin, antaryāmin* is also used by these commentators.[46] The highest state is, beyond these eight states, *parabrahman* who manifests himself in the world in these *apara* states. In the opinion of Śaṅkara, to reach the ultimate state one has to diversify oneself from all the limiting adjuncts – emancipating from all stains, ego, distinctions, actions, etc. through the *neti-neti mārga*. But, Bhartṛprapañca's evolutionary process appears to be from epistemology to metaphysics and leading to cosmological level, that is, from cognition (*sākṣin*) to *antaryāmin* to *jāti, piṇḍa, sūtra, virāj* and *daiva* respectively. All these eight states of Brahman are modes and not illusory aspects.[47]

From the above investigation, we can infer that the *Vedāntist* underscores the unity of Being using the substance and universal relation, though at times considers Brahman as distinct from *jīva* or *jagat*. Brahman is present in everything and rules everything from within and everything is His manifestation. Bhartṛprapañca elevates healthy co-ordination between knowledge and action (*jñānakarmasamuccayavāda*) leading to salvation.

2.3 Lakulīśa's *Bhedābheda*

Kanti Chandra Pandey familiarizes another *Bhedābhedavādin* from the Pāśupata tradition of Śaivism,[48] known as Lakulīśa or Nakulīśa. His *Bhedābheda* tradition is known as *Lakulīśa Pāsupata darśana* or *Nakulīśa Pāsupata darśana*. Lakulīśa must have lived in the first half of the second century Common Era. Later, his religion and philosophy thrived in the present states of Gujarat, Rajasthan, Uttarakhand, Uttar Pradesh and Orissa.[49] *Pāśupata* tradition spots him to be the 28th incarnation of the Lord Śiva. There are a few temples dedicated to his name in these places, where his naked statue is found in *padmāsana* position with an erect phallus and a mace (*lakula*) in hand.

There is a close semblance of this philosophy with *Taittirīya Āraṇyaka*. The *Pāśupata* doctrine of Lakulīśa is divided into five parts: *kāraṇa* (cause, also called *pati*), *kārya* (effect, also called *paśu*), *vidhi*, *yoga*, and *duḥkhānta*. *Kāraṇa*, *pati* and Brahman are synonymous in meaning in this tradition. Like a seed is the cause of a tree, so too, Brahman is the cause of everything, its beginning, preservation and dissolution.[50] He has the power of knowledge and action. *Kārya* or *paśu* is eternal and is controlled by *kāraṇa*. It is of three types: *cit, acit* and *cetana*. In other systems, *kārya* or effect is altogether a new beginning, but here it is eternal. *Vidhi* leads to the presence of God from where there is no return, whereas other systems understand it to be a method or Vedic prescription of going to heaven.[51]

There is a profound relationship between *kāraṇa* and *kārya* (*pati* and *paśu*). *Kāraṇa* is *sat* or real. Their relation is that of difference and non-difference (*bheda* and *abheda*). There are pluralities of beings like stars in the sky. Their existence is not separate, but closely knit like the holes in a honeycomb. *Kārya* is the manifestation of *kārana*. Thus, the causality of Lakulīśa *Pāsupata* is based on *satkāryavāda*. He holds that "all effect exists as identical with the Lord's power (*śakti*) from which he manifests them at will."[52] *Pati* freely creates everything. It is only through Him creation becomes active.

Liberation concurs not only the cessation of miseries like *Nyāya-Vaiśeṣika*, but also in the attainment of the powers of knowledge and action (*jñānakarmasamuccaya*). God, being the efficient cause is independent. Through rituals and devotions, one draws closer or gains nearness (*sāmīpya*) to God. As a result, this system though understood to be *Bhedābheda*, seems to be proximate to *Advaita*. Śaṅkara is more sympathetic towards it, unlike any other system. The reason could be both Lakulīśa and Śaṅkara hail from Śaiva tradition.

2.4 Bhāskara's Aupādhika-Bhedābheda

The exact date of Bhāskara is inaccessible. Mr. Dvivedin

gathers together as many as twenty Bhāskaras in the preface to the book on *Bhāskara Bhāṣya.*[53] Śaṅkara does not speak about Bhāskara but Vācaspati Miśra does. However, Bhāskara has criticized *Advaitic māyāvāda* and the unrealistic nature of the empirical reality along with Buddhist's views. In his *Bhāṣya*, Bhāskara counters the people who follow Buddhism, *māyāvāda* and other such commentators.[54] In another instance, Śaṅkara is indirectly accused of using Buddhist doctrine.[55] This entails that Bhāskara whom we intend to investigate must have lived after Śaṅkara (or maybe the contemporaries), and most probably a contemporary to Miśra.[56] Nonetheless, Rāmānuja has criticized Bhāskara in his work. This insinuates Bhāskara must have lived and composed his works sometime between 9-11th centuries CE, preferably in the 9th century. His commentary on the *Brahmasūtras is* called the *Brahmasūtrabhāṣyam* or the *Śārīramīmāmsaka-bhāṣyam.*[57] There is another book attributed to him, the *Siddhāntaśiromaṇiḥ.*[58] Both these books are available only in Sanskrit.

The reality, according to this scholar, is both *One and Many—abhinna* and *bhinna*. The *One* is the unconditioned absolute and uncaused cause. But what is manifested as the manifold is the absolute, conditioned by the *upādhis*[59] or the delimiting adjuncts. That's why this system is called *Aupādhika Bhedābheda.* The absolute becomes the relative and is immanent in it. The finite self is the Brahman but limited by the metaphysical and moral imperfections of *avidyā, kāma* and *karma*. *Mukti* consists in removing the barriers, transcending the boundaries of *saṁsāramaṇḍala* and embodying the absolute or attaining *ekībhava*.[60]

The self when purified and perfected can know the unknown. Brahman is unknowable to the discursive reason, but the beatified soul becomes Brahman, dissolving its separate consciousness. There is no contradiction or boundary line between the finite and the infinite. Like the sun and its rays, the soul is one with the self. The higher includes the lower and explains it.[61]

Reflecting along with Bhāskara, Srinivasachari discloses, "Reality or Brahman is an identity that is immanent in difference and constitutes them."[62] Brahman is immanent in the *prapañca*. Brahman is also the *kāraṇa* of the *prapañca*. It is also the ground of all relations and presuppositions. The *prapañca* is sustained by Brahman and not vice-versa. However, the finiteness of the *prapañca* as the predicate tempers the conditions of Brahman.

Brahman is real. Whatever that exists are the effects (*kārya*) of Brahman who is the cause (*kāraṇa*) of it, like clay is the cause of all the objects made of clay. For the *Advaitavādins*, both effect and cause are identical, because the effects, in reality, are only the expression of the real, they do not exist at all or are mere *vikalpa*.[63] Bhāskara counters it with a question, 'how can cause and effect be identical?' The words indeed expressed denote the practicality of the objects. But the effects, in reality, are the stages of manifestation, modification and existence of the cause itself. Effects are transient, come and go, but the cause remains permanent as the ground of real manifestation. That's why it is said clay alone is true. The effect is only a state of cause, and therefore both identical and different from it. This is even proved by the *śrutis* as in the case of *tattvamasi* statement or one cannot negate fire-ness from fire.[64]

The *bheda* has a identity within *abheda* like the sea and its waves or the identical fire which can either illuminate or burn or be both. Similarly, the effect is the real manifestation of the power of the cause. Thus, all that is one is also many, and the one is neither absolute identity nor absolute difference.[65] To explain this indisputable relationship between the finite self and the infinite, Bhāskara employed several examples from the *Vedas* and *Upaniṣads*. It is Bhāskara, who for the first time epitomized, that *Brahman is identical and immanent in differences and constitutes them* and that *Bhedābheda principle is the semantic axis of the Vedānta and Upaniṣads*. This becomes clear when we scrutinize the examples in his work.

The following statements expound on the relationship between Brahman, world and soul in a better way.[66] Bhāskara proves the non-difference or *abheda* in terms of the following śruti texts: "Thou art That" (CU 6.8-6, BSBBh 2.1.14); "There is no other seer but he, there is no other hearer but he, there is no other perceiver but he, there is no other knower but he. This is thy Self, the ruler within, the immortal" (BU 3.7.23); "This self is Brahman" (BU 2.5.19); "The fishermen are Brahman, the slaves are Brahman. Brahman are these gamblers; men and women are Brahman" (*Brahma Sūkta Saṁhitā Upaniṣad*); "Thou art the old moving with stick" (SU 4.3), etc. texts. Difference or *bheda* is illustrated from the following *śrutis*, "There are two unborn one knowing, the other not knowing, one strong the other weak" (SU 1.9); "The Lord of Nature and the souls, the ruler of the qualities, the cause of bondage, of existence and the release from *saṁsāra"* (SU 6.16); "He is the cause, the Lord of the Lords of the organs" (SU 6.9); "One of the two eats the sweet fruit, without eating, the other looks on" (SU 4.6; MuU 3.1.1); "Having known Him only, one passes beyond death" (SU 3.8); "He who dwells within the self" (BU 3.7.22); "He should be sought, He should be meditated upon" (CU 8.7.1); "He whom one eternal intelligent fulfills the desires of many eternal intelligent beings" (KaU 2.5.13), "Embraced by the all intelligent self, he knows nothing that is without, and nothing that is within" (BU 4.3.21). The *Bhedābheda* is characterized in the following texts, "He who knows Brahman becomes Brahman" (MuU 3.2.9); "But when the self has become all for him, where could he see another" (BU 4.5.15); *"Sadvidyā"* (the knowledge of existent, CU 6). In *Sadvidyā,*[67] he asserts the principle of identity-in-difference in the relation between Brahman and the world of *cetana* and *acetana.*

From the above statements, first and foremost, ensue that the reality is *One* and it cannot be divided into two separate categories.[68] Though *bheda* and *abheda* are seen as two different portions like space inside the pot and space outside, they are only imaginary, *kalpanāmātram.*[69] Similarly, they may seem to be two contradictory aspects like heat and cold, but there is no contradiction here.[70] There permeates a unity or *abheda* in the differences. For example, in the relation between *cause and effect* or *clay and pot* or *this pot is made of clay,* the effect is surely enclosed in the cause and continues to be so. Secondly, the *Bhedābheda* is built on the integrity of normal experience, satisfies the tests of reasoning and *śruti,* executing full justice to the philosophical demands of monism and pluralism without in any degree sharing their defects. The absolute manifests itself in the finite and gives meaning to it. In the above example, clay cannot be negated in the pot and similarly, a potential pot cannot be negated in the clay. The universality of the effect is concealed in the cause itself. The phenomenal reality complements both universality and individuality. It is only in the abnormal state such as psychic and physical disorders one perceives two things concurrently like the illusion of two moons (*dvicandrabhrama*). One must reallocate from the symbols to the symbolism that they point to. Then only the reality will become meaningful.

However, Bhāskara's system of *Aupādhika-Bhedābheda* is not much viable in spite of his refutation of *avidyā* and *jagannmithyatva* of Śaṅkara as he recoils with the latter. Bhāskara's *Bhedābheda* relation is effective only in the *baddha sthiti* (bound state) and not in the *mutka sthiti* (released state). In his *bhāṣya,* he maintains that *jīva* is united with Brahman in the released state (*avasthiteriti kāśakṛtsnaḥ* BSB Bh 1.4.21), which is nothing but *Kevala Advaita* view.[71] There is another person who can go along with Bhāskara. He is Yādavapraśa flourished in the 11th century CE. Through his concept of *Brahmapariṇāmavāda,* he has tried to overcome the discrepancy of dualism created by the concept of upādhis as real by Bhāskara. He feels that the upādhi is inherent in Brahman. He equally emphasizes *bhedā* and *abhedatva* than Bhāskara. In his system, there is no difference between *cit* and *acit*, and everything is sentient.

Later, *upādhi* reckons the reason for the individual soul's being different from Brahman (BSBBh 2.3.18-23)—which is nothing but *māya* of Śaṅkara—and upon removing it effects in *ekībhava*, the total unity as the *ghaṭākāśa* and *maṭhākāśa* amalgamate upon breaking the pot (*upādhi*). Similarly, the atomic size of the individual self is regarded as '*aupādhika*,' and '*vibhutva*' is regarded as its real nature. Whatever be the critique, one cannot deny the fact of something permanent in the reality which proffers continuity to the transient effect.

2.5 Nimbārka's *Svābhāvika-Bhedābheda*

Nimbārka, the Telugu *Vaiṣṇava Brāhmin* was born in Nimbpur, a small village in Bellary District and later known to have settled at the Bank of Godāvari River in Andhra Pradesh. The exact date of his birth is disputable. However, most probably, he lived after Śaṅkara either before or during Rāmānuja. This indicates a date somewhere between the 12th and the 14th centuries CE.[72]

The Absolute or Brahman for Nimbārka is Kṛṣṇa,[73] who is omniscient, omnipotent, the ultimate cause and all-pervading Being. All that is articulated about Brahman in the *śāstras* is about Śrīkṛṣṇa and is to be understood as Śrīkṛṣṇa alone.[74] Quoting the *Bhagavadgīta*, he spells out in his commentary on the *Brahmasūtras*, "The Lord [Kṛṣṇa] is in the heart of every being" (BG 18.61). Hence, there is a difference between *jīva* and *paramātman*, the individual soul and Supreme Soul.[75]

Nimbārka's *'Kṛṣṇaism'* or "Brahman in *śāstras* is about Śrīkṛṣṇa and is to be understood as Śrīkṛṣṇa alone" can lead to two kinds of understandings: orthodox teaching and divine permeation. The former is monopolizing the scripture to suit one's ideology. This is detrimental in a country that promotes diverse views, varied and accommodative cultures. All the same, every tradition advances one's views and adheres to them. Though this orthodox view may not be an intended meaning by Nimbārka, the second understanding augments the theology. It reinforces that divine is present everywhere and in everything, "the heart of every being."

This Absolute Brahman transforms itself into the world in various forms of *jaḍa* and *jīva* (*acit* and *cit*), the matter and spirit.[76] It is like the *prāṇa* or the life-force remaining itself independently, divulges into various conative and cognitive functions of the body. For example, it is like a spider weaving its web out of its own body without getting transformed or like the hair on the head and hair on the body of a person,[77] so too Brahman, without changing, transforms itself into the world of matter and spirits. Brahman is the material and determining cause of all other beings. Nimbārka proclaims, "Brahman alone is the material cause of the world, as well as its efficient cause"[78] (BS 1.4.23, *prakṛtiśca pratijñādṛṣṭānta anuparodhāt*, Brahman is the material cause and the efficient cause on account of the absence of conflict concerning the initial proposition and the illustration). The very existence and movement of all the beings depend on Brahman. Thus, Brahman is both *saguṇa* and *nirguṇa*, and immanent and transcendent. He is transcendent because He is beyond and more than the mere aggregate of *cit* and *acit* being; and immanent because He resides in the heart of *cidācit* beings, and being inner controller (*sarvaniyantā*).[79]

The nature of Brahman both within and outside the *prapañca* is *Bhedābheda*. It is the nature of Kṛṣṇa, that whatever exists is different and non-different from Him.[80] He is Supreme Being, the locale of all auspicious qualities, possesses unthinkable attributes, the greatest among the greatest, omnipresent, omniscient, omnipotent, superior, cause of everything, the unequaled, all-pervasive, sum of all knowledge, great, etc. Therefore, he is believed to be *binna* and *abhinna*.[81] *Śruti* enlightens the *bheda* and *abheda* relationship of Brahman with the world and the individual selves. Vāsudeva or Kṛṣṇa is different and non-different from all.[82]

According to Nimbārka, only *Bhedābheda* nature of Brahman can resolve and expound the non-dualistic and dualistic *śrutivākyas*. Brahman has a peculiar nature. It is 'natural,' *svābhāvika* to Brahman. It is not by imposition or supposition that it can at once be *One and Many*. The nature of Brahman is such that it is at once *One with and Different from* the world of matter and spirits.[83] Therefore, Nimbārka's system is called *Svābhāvika Bhedābhedavāda*.

Considering Brahman from only the *Dvaita* or *Advaita* standpoint is untenable as the former will end up determining Brahman as the only determining cause or the latter only as *nirguṇa* which is not acquiescent to the ordinary perception. The absolute *nirguṇa* reality cannot be the locus of any illusion and at the same time, any means of devotion will be contradicting the reality. To an ordinary human being, *nirguṇa* does not make any sense, but *saguṇa* does. Therefore, by its very *svabhāva*, Brahman is both *dvaita* and *Advaita*, *nirguṇa* and *saguṇa*.[84]

Answering *Advaita* critique who holds *the Nimbārkite's bheda has no locus*,[85] Mādhava Mukunda articulates, '*bheda is not in a relationship but in the adhikaraṇa itself* or *it is the locus itself*.'[86] Therefore, the *bheda* is the mode of the object[87] or the relation itself. The apprehension of the mode of the object connotes the comprehension of all differences existing in it. Knowing Brahman indicates, knowing both its *saguṇa* and *nirguṇa* aspects and yet the reality will not be completely known. For example, a piece of wood can be known in a particular manner, say a plank. But it can remain unknown in its different aspects. One can utilize it as a stand, a chair, an instrument and as a weapon. The pure Brahman is self-luminous in itself yet its attribute of unity or difference remains fully unknown to the knower. Correspondingly, Being is one (*Avibhāga*) expressed in many like *fire and spark* or *water and its ripples*.[88]

Rebutting the *tādātmya* of *Jīva* and Brahman of the *Kevala Advaita*, Nimbārka states that the existence of one cannot direct and verify the existence of the other. Even though two identical sons (twins) look similar, they are two separate individualities. But at the same time, can we nullify certain harmony between them? We cannot. *Jīva* and Brahman are two orders of being—*para* and *apara*. Despite that affirming the identity would mean affirming the duality. Duality and difference hinge on the comprehension of their differences. This difference impedes establishing the identity.

Brahman is the "sum total of all auspicious qualities," "*samastakalyāṇaguṇaika rāśitvam*." This settles to a certain extent the existence of evil in the world. It is true that there is a contradiction here. How can an auspicious Being contain inauspiciousness? In other words, can a good being contain evil? The Lord is not devoid of negative qualities but only auspicious qualities. The evil and vices that exist are only for the sentient beings. This paves the way for the dependency of sentient beings on the Lord who is both sentient and insentient.

The *Advaitic* notion of reality gives us the reason why there is *manyness* in reality. The Bhāskara's system of *upādhis* spells out the external distinctions of reality. But, the Nimbārka's system relates with the way for the *integral wholeness*. In the words of Srinivasachari, "the philosophy of Nimbārka is a kind of monism and pluralism and preserves the integral experience of *Bhedābheda*. The universal or the whole is immanent in the particular and yet remains beyond, without losing its wholeness."[89] This deliberation prompts one to affirm the mysterious nature of reality. Vijñānabhikṣu develops a similar concept in his system and names it *avibhāgādvaita* which will be dealt with in the coming chapters.

One cannot gloss over Rāmānuja's *Viśiṣṭādvaita* while dealing with Nimbārka. There are a lot of similarities between them: *cit* and *acit* aspects, the concept of *śakti* and *śaktimān* (power and powerful), *śarīraśarīrī bhāvasambandha* and *śaktimadbhāvasambandha*, elements of *bhakti*, preference for *prapatti* or self-surrender, *vyūha* and *avatāra*, etc. While Rāmānuja considers *cit* and *acit* as the body of Brahman, Nimbārka envisages them as powers of Brahman. It seems to be an abridged version of the former.

2.6 Caitanya's *Acintya-Bhedābheda*

Caitanya Mahāprabhu (1486–1534), well-known as the incarnation of Viṣṇu among his followers, born in West Bengal is the founder of *Gauḍīya Vaiṣṇavism.*[90] He did not compose any philosophical or theological treatise, unlike other *ācāryas*. The legacy of this school is being continued by ISKON movement. Caitanya Mahāprabhu refuted Śaṅkara's unrealistic view of *jagat* and opted for Madhva's *dvaita* aspect of reality. But, soon departed from the latter and proposed the reality as *Acintya-Bhedābheda*. *Acintya* means inconceivable. He proposes a reality that contains inconceivable difference and non-difference. His teachings are encapsulated as ten maxims called *daśamūla*.

The relationship between the creator and the created or the Brahman and the *Jīva* is beyond the comprehension of human beings (*acintya*). Brahman is simultaneously *one with and different* from His creation like a molecular particle of sunshine or fire. According to Bhaktivedānta Swami

Prabhupāda, "One who knows God, knows that the impersonal conception and personal conception are simultaneously present in everything and that there is no contradiction. Therefore, Lord Caitanya established His sublime doctrine: *acintya bheda-and-abheda-tattva*—simultaneous oneness and difference."[91] The analogy used for the elucidation is *sun and the sunshine where both are parts of the same reality*, but there is a great difference between having a beam of sunshine in one's room and being close to the sun itself. Qualitatively the sun and the sunshine are not different, but as quantities, they are very different.

This analogy is applied to the living beings and God: the *Jīva* being a similar quality to the Supreme Being, but not sharing the qualities to an infinite extent, as would the Personality of Godhead himself. Hence, there is a difference between the souls and the Supreme Lord. This indicates that the reality is *panentheistic.*[92]

Vijñānabhikṣu concurs with Caitanya. While explaining the *avibhāga* relationship, Vijñānabhikṣu explains the infinite dwelling of the divine in the world, through the meaning of the *ekavākya "etadātmyamidaṁsarvam"* with *ardhajaratīyanyāya.*[93] From the external look at one part of a woman may look like an old lady, but looking at the black hair of the same lady may appear young. Similarly, looking at certain aspects of *jīva* or *ātman*, they may appear or give the impression of Brahman. Both of them point out the same reality, the perceived depicting the unperceived. Further, exemplifying *puruṣa* and *prakṛti*, one conscious and the other unconscious form speaks of their similar relation with Brahman. All in the highest states are in Brahman. After the creation, *purūṣa* and *prakṛti* are in a lower state, as both *vyakta* and *avyakta* form in time. This denotes that everything is not God, but God is in everything.

Summary

Śaṅkara's strong metaphysical appeal, rigid application of logical norms and social stratification monopolized medieval *Vedāntic* thinking and still continues. However, this restricted *abheda* approach to reality also incited strong rejoinders from different parts of the country: reaction not only to the one-sided metaphysical approach but also to the issue of liberation. Śaṅkara, as a devout believer belonging to the higher rung of the caste hierarchy never desired the salvation to be open to all. It may be due to the social requirement or his prejudiced time frame of mind. For instance, the intend of his *śūdra* exclusion from salvation mentioned in the *Apaśūdrādhikaraṇa* of his *Brahmasūtrabhāṣya* itself is self-explanatory.[94] Ditto can be noticed with *Dvaita* proponent, Madhvācārya regarding this issue. Scriptures cannot be the monopoly of one kind of interpretation. And to claim that 'this is the only way' to comprehend is against the very nature of the revelation of any scripture. By its very nature, scriptures are revelatory and emancipatory. And they cannot be the sole property of one of a kind of people. Any unnatural treatment to any system is bound to bring a reaction.

The first one to counter to the unreality of *bheda* of

Śaṅkara is Rāmānujācārya. Rāmānuja retorts the reality is not an abstract concept in which the non-difference completely loses its identity, but a synthetic unity of both substance and attribute by the relation, *apṛthaksiddhi*. The attribute is different from the substance in the sense that it inheres in it though the latter cannot be equated with any particular attribute as a mere assemblage of them all, but is something over and above. This necessitates that substance and attribute, the unity and plurality are real and form an organic whole. The relation between them is non-difference (*abheda*) and not total identity (*tādātmya* as claimed by Śaṅkara). Conforming to the *Viśiṣṭādvaita* tradition, Śrīkaṇṭha (the *Śaiva* proponent) also endorses similar view.[95] Bhāskara sets off with the very intent of the text and then contemplates the whole reality as difference and non-difference, unity and plurality. For him, at the causal state of Brahman, specifically during salvation and dissolution, there is a complete identity between *Jīva* and Brahman. But during *saṁsāra,* there is a difference.

It is at this point, the latter *Bhedābhedavādins* reclaim scriptural integrity. They have succeeded moderately though they might have failed to some extent. Caitanya's *Acintya Bhedābheda* has brought social revolution reasonably in bringing equality among the people, but the over-enthusiasm of traditionalism has prevailed over the renewed vigour of the modern times, repositioning back to the hierarchical structure.

Both *śruti* and *smṛti* literature behold theism as a

foundational thread binding both transcendent and immanent. The Absolute Reality is concealed to the ordinary senses, yet manifestations of it can be discerned and experienced in every aspect. *Bhedābheda Vedānta*, without a single proponent to explain this truth, clarifies it clearly as the philosophy grew over the years. Kāśakṛtsna and Āśmarathya spoke of this divine manifestation in terms of soul abiding in everything in the creation. Due to their similar class (*sajātīyatvata*), *ātman* and Brahman are understood to be the same. Though they are identical, they are not the same. The former (*ātman*) is controlled and the latter (*Brahman*) controller (or worshipper and worshipped) due to its dependency on the latter. In their *sāṁsāric* existence, they are different; and in their *mukta* state, they are non-different. To get away from *saṁsāra,* rituals and good conduct are necessary. In so far as the object of the reality is real, its relationship is also real.

What makes them relational is their ontological status, namely, they are related as substance and universal relationship, just as there is cowness in cow or stoneness in stone, so too, the universal principle of Brahman (Brahmanness) is existing in *Ātman* due to its *sajātiyatvata*. Therefore, one can convey Brahmanness in every *Ātman*.

Another important component is that every effect has a deeper relationship with the cause. Theistically speaking, the effect is identical with the power of the Lord, by which He manifests Himself in the creation. But due to the limiting factors, the Absolute manifested is not grasped in the multiplicity of reality. The limiting adjuncts block the Real. Vijñānabhikṣu reinvents this truth in a capsule form known as *Avibhāga-Bhedābheda* in his commentary on the *Brahmasūtras.*

---

[1] *Internet Encyclopedia of Philosophy*, s.v. "Bhedābheda Vedānta." Available on http://www. iep.utm.edu/bhed-ved/#SH2b, accessed on 15 September 2016.

[2] *Internet Encyclopedia of Philosophy,* s.v. "Bhedābheda Vedānta."

[3] *brahmaṇaḥ sākṣāt pariṇāmavādaṁ vivartavādaṁ ca tatraiva nirākariṣyāmaḥ*. VAB 1.1.2, p.18.

[4] *New World Encyclopedia*, s.v. "Bhedabheda." Available on http://www.newworldencyclopedia. org/entry/Bhedabheda#cite_ref-2, accessed on 15 January 2018.

[5] Surendranath Dasgupta, *History of Indian Philosophy*, vol. 2, 1992 ed. (Cambridge: Cambridge University Press, 1923), 42; Hajime Nakamura, *A History of Early Vedānta Philosophy,* vol. 1, translated by Sengakul Mayeda Trevor Leggett, Taitez Unno and others (Delhi: Motilal Banarsidass, 1989), 500.

[6] Lalit Krishna Goswami, *Śrī Nimbārka Vedānta* (Prayāga: Nimbārka Peeṭha, 1965), 55.

[7] "*bhedavyapadeśācca*." VAB 1.1.17, p.72. "*aṁśo nānāvyapadeśānyathā cāpi daśākitavāditva-madhīyata eke*." VAB 2.3.43, p.195. *"adhikaṁ tu bhedanirdeśanāt*." VAB 2.1.22, p.156.

[8] "*ātmeti tūpagacchanti grāhayanti ca.*" VAB 4.1.3, p.305. *"prakāśāśrayavadvā tejasvāt.*" VAB 3.2.28, p.249. "*avibhāgo vacanāt*." VAB 4.2.16, p.320. "*avibhāgena dṛṣṭatvāt*." VAB 4.4.4, p.332.

[9] As quoted by, Goswami, *Śrī Nimbārka Vedānta*, 50.

[10] As quoted by, Goswami, *Śrī Nimbārka Vedānta*, 51. "*āmukterbheda evasyājjīvasya ca parasya ca. muktestu na bhedo'sti bhedahetorbhāvataḥ*."

[11] Goswami, *Śrī Nimbārka Vedānta*, 51.

[12] Tripta Gupta, *Vedānta Kaustubha: A Study* (Delhi: Sanjay Prakashan, 2000), 16.

[13] P.N. Srinivasachari, *The Philosophy of Bhedābheda*, Revised and Enlarged, 1950 ed. (Madras: Adyar Library, 1934), 12.

[14] Sadāśivendra Saraswati (Avadhūta), *A Commentary on Bādarāyaṇą Brahmasūtra Named Brahmatat'tvaprakāśikā*, translated by S. Kothandaraman, vol. 1 (New Delhi: B.R. Publishing House, 2009), 76,148. Also see, Shridhar Majumdar, *The Vedanta Philosophy*, 2000 ed., Chowkamba Sanskrit Studies, 108 (Varanasi: Chowkhamba Sanskrit Series Office, 1926), 80, 169.

[15] *kāryaurḥ kāraṇamabhivyajyate liṅgarūpeṇa* (BS 1.2.29). Vijñānabhikṣu, *Brahmasūtra Vijñānāmṛtabhāṣyam*, edited by Kedāranātha Tripāṭhī, Prācyavidya Series (Varanasi: Banaras Hindu University, 1979), 108.

[16] Certain words have to be treated as exceptions, such as *taṇḍula* (rice), says Āśmarathya. *Mīmāṁsā Sūtra* 6.5.16. The context is, when the common meaning of a word is not satisfactory, and a different interpretation is required, then a special case is applied. Here '*taṇḍula*' is best form a grain and therefore, refers to *prakṛti* or the nature. Thadani, *Mīmāṁsā Sūtra of Jaimini*, 169, 196.

[17] Śrīnivāsa, *Vedānta-Pārijāta-Saurabha*, 253.

[18] (Avadhūta), *A Commentary on Bādarāyaṇa Brahmasūtra* vol.2, p.507, 587. Also see, Majumdar, *The Vedanta Philosophy*, 170, 637, 749.

[19] *"brahmaṇi cidrūpe upāsannaḥ pratyagātmā cinmātreṇa rūpeṇāvirbhavati."* Goswami, *Śrī Nimbārka Vedānta*, 208.

[20] Śrīnivāsa, *Vedānta-Pārijāta-Saurabha*, 253-54. BS 1.4.21.

[21] *auḍulomistvācāryo manyate paramātmanyapi jīvaprāṇayorliṅgamupapadhyate utkramaṇa ārambhakāle jīvaprāṇayorevambhāvāt paramātmabhāvāt, yathā maithunakāle strīpuṁsayorekībhāva iti arthaḥ. tathā ca maraṇakāle paramātmāvibhāgādanyadāpi tadbheda vyavahāreṇa jīvaprāṇadharmau brahmaṇyucyete, loke tathā vyavahārād iti bhāvaḥ.* VAB 1.4.21, p.138.

[22] Bijendra Kumar, *Bhedābheda Darśana* (Delhi: Bijendra Kumar, 2013), xii.

[23] Majumdar, *The Vedanta Philosophy*, 171. Also see, (Avadhūta), *A Commentary on Bādarāyaṇa Brahmasūtra*, 149.

[24] Goswami, *Śrī Nimbārka Vedānta*, 55.

[25] (Avadhūta), *A Commentary on Bādarāyaṇa Brahmasūtra*, 149.

[26] *"jīvātmani svaniyamye "antaḥ praviṣṭaḥ śāstājanānām" ityādau prasiddhasya paramātmano niyantṛtvena avasthiter hetorniyamyapadenopakramādau niyantuparigraha iti kāśakṛtsno manyatesma."* BS 1.4.22. Goswami, *Śrī Nimbārka Vedānta,* 51. According to the scritpural sources like 'having entered,' *Jīvātma* that is under its control, due to the fact of having control, from that which controled need to be understood as controlling, thinks Kāśakṛtsna.

[27] Śrīnivāsa, *Vedānta-Pārijāta-Saurabha*, 256.

[28] *"anusmṛter **bādariḥ**."* BS 1.2.30, p.108. "For the sake of meditation, says Bādari." *"sukṛtaduṣkṛte eveti tu bādariḥ."* VAB 3.1.11, p.229. "However, good and evil works are nothing but this, says Bādari." Vijñānabhikṣu comments here, "***bādaristvācāryo** aśuddhi kṣayadvārā yāgāṅgatvavad dṛṣṭadvārādi (pi) śubhāśubhayoni hetutvaṁ caraṇasyecchan sukṛtaduṣkṛte eva caraṇasyārthaḥ prayojanaṁ iti manyate."* VAB 3.1.11, p.229. *kāryaṁ bādarijasya gatyupapatteḥ.* VAB 4.3.7, p.327. "It is not absolute Brahman but relative Brahman, to whom soul is conducted by his escorts, opines Bādari." *abhāvam bādarirāha hyevam.* VAB 4.4.10, p.334. "Released soul neither possesses a body nor senses and bases the opinion on scriptures, thinks Bādari." Stress is mine.

[29] *vaiśvānare parameśvarasya anucintanīyatvena vaiśvānaradharmāḥ parameśvarasya upalakṣakā ityato na virodha iti bādarirācāryro manyata iti arthaḥ*. VAB 1.2.30, p.108.

[30] (Avadhūta), *A Commentary on Bādarāyaṇa Brahmasūtra*, 314. Also see, Hajime Nakamura, *A History of Early Vedānta Philosophy*, vol.1, 369-70.

[31] *"kratau phalārthavādamaṅgavatkārṣṇājiniḥ."* *Mīmāṁsā Sūtra* 4.3.17. Thadani, *Mīmāṁsā Sūtra of Jaimini*, 100.

[32] *"sa kulyaḥ syāditi kārṣṇājinir ekasminn sambhavāt."* *Mīmāṁsā Sūtra* 4.3.17. Thadani, *Mīmāṁsā Sūtra of Jaimini*, 182-83.

[33] *Vasiṣṭasmṛti* , 6.7.35. As quoted by, Nakamura, *A History of Early Vedānta Philosophy*, vol.1, 371.

[34] Ramamurti Sharma, *Bhāratīya Darśan Kī Cintandhārā*, Chowkambha Prācyavidhyā Granthamālā (Delhi: Chowkambha Orientalia, 1999), 320.

[35] M. Hiriyanna, "Fragments of Bhartrprapanca," in *Proceedings of the All-India Oriental Conference 3* (1924). Reprinted in M. Hiriyanna,

Indian Philosophical Studies, vol. I (Mysore: Kavyalaya Publishers, 1957), 6-16. Also see, M. Hiriyanna, "Bhartrprapañca: An Odd Vedāntin," in *Indian Antiquary* (Mysore: Kavyalaya Publishers, 1924), 77-86. M. Hiriyanna, *Indian Philosophical Studies*, vol. 2 (Mysore: Kavyalaya Publishers, 1972), 79-94. Ivan Andrijanić, "Quotations and (Lost) Commentaries in Advaita Vedānta: Some Philological Notes on Bhartṛprapañca's 'Fragments'," *Journal of Indian Philosophy* 43, no. 2 (2015). Available on http://link.springer.com/journal/volumesAndIssues/10781, accessed on 25 January 2017.

[36] Hajime Nakamura, *A History of Early Vedānta Philosophy*, vol. 2, 131.

[37] Hiriyanna, *Indian Philosophical Studies*, vol.2, 61.

[38] Sharma, *Bhāratīya Darśan Kī Cintandhārā*, 320-21. Here, *anekāntavāda* should not be misunderstood with the Jain metaphysics. Here it simply means 'manyness' in the reality itself.

[39] Hiriyanna, *Indian Philosophical Studies,* vol.1, 81.

[40] Sharma, *Bhāratīya Darśan Kī Cintandhārā*, 321. Also see, *Brahmasūtra Śānkarabhāṣya* 2.1.14.

[41] Hiriyanna, *Indian Philosophical Studies,* vol.1, 87-92. Also see, Hiriyanna, *Indian Philosophical Studies,* vol.2, 6-7.

[42] Though Śaṅkara did not specify whose views he is critiquing, there is strong evidence that it is about Bhartṛprapañca. Sureśvara (*Bṛhadāraṇyako'paniṣad Vārttikā* 1.4.487) and Ānandagiri (*Bṛhadāraṇyako'paniṣad ṭīkā* 3.8.12) who have critiqued Bhartṛprapañca very much also mention these eight states. Ānandagiri's commentary on Śureśvara's *Bṛhadāraṇyako'paniṣad Vārttikā* called *Śāstraprakāśikākhya ṭīkā* (1.4.1043) eight states of Brahman are attributed to Bhartṛprapañca. For the detailed discussion see, Ivan Andrijanic, "Bhartṛprapañca and the Eight States of Brahman," *Revista Científica Guillermo de Ockham* 14, no. 1 (2016): 57-67.

[43] Srinivasachari, *The Philosophy of Bhedābheda*, 179-180.

[44] *"tatra kecid ācakṣate. parasya mahāsamudrasthānīyasya brahmaṇo akṣarasya apracalitatva rūpasyeṣat pracalitāvasthāntarayāmī atyantapracalitāvasthā kṣetrajño yastaṁ na vedāntaryāmiṇāṁ tathānyāḥ pañcāvasthāḥ parikalpayanti tathāṣṭāvasthā brahmaṇo bhavantīti vadanti."* BUBh 3.8.12. As quoted

by Andrijanic, "Bhartṛprapañca and the Eight States of Brahman," 59. The emphasis is given.

[45] *"tathā hirṇayagarbhāvyāṛktadevatājātipiṇḍamanṣyatiryakpretādikārya-kāraṇopādhibhir viṣśiṭas tadākhyas tadrūpo bhavati."* BUBh 3.8.12. As quoted by Andrijanic, "Bhartṛprapañca and the Eight States of Brahman," 60.

[46] Andrijanic, "Bhartṛprapañca and the Eight States of Brahman," 59-61.

[47] Srinivasachari, *The Philosophy of Bhedābheda*, 181.

[48] For detailed philosophical position of *Lakulīśa Pāśupata*, refer to, Tribuvan Prasad Upadhyaya, ed., *Bhāskarī: An English Translation of the Īśvara Pratybhijñā Vimarśinī with an Outline of History of Śaiva Philosophy*, vol. 3 (Lucknow: Superintendent, Printing and Stationery, 1954), xxvii-xxix, cxii-cxlvii. This book gives also certain details of philosophy closer to *Bhedābheda* philosophy within *Śaiva* and *Vaiśṇava* traditions like Śrīpati, Śrīkaṇṭha, Bhāskara, Rāmānuja, and so on. Also see, Madan Mohan Agrawal, *The Philosophy of Nimbārka* (Varanasi: Chowkhambha Surabharati Publication, 1982), 57-61. Kumar, *Bhedābheda Darśana*, xiii-xvi.

[49] For more details see, Maheshwar P. Joshi, "Śaṅkarācārya, Lakulīśa-Pāśupatas and Uttarākhaṇḍa," *Annals of the Bhandarkar Oriental Research Institute,* vol. 70, no. 1/4 (1989). B.P. Majumdar, "Lakuliśa-Pāśupatas and Their Activities in Medieval India," *Proceedings of the Indian History Congress* 13, (1950). R. Ananthakrishna Sastri, ed. *Pasupata Sutras with Pancarthabhashya of Kaundinya* (Trivandrum: The Oriental Manuscripts Library of the University of Travancore, 1940). Mādhavācārya, *Sarva-Darana-Saṁgraha*, Parimal Sanskrit Series. Edited by K.L. Joshi (Delhi: Parimal Publications, 1997), 142-153. Mādhavācārya, "Nakulīśa Pāśupata System" in *Sarvadarśanasaṅgraha*, Translated by E.B. Cowel and A.E. Gough (London: Trubner and Company, 1882): 103-111.

[50] Sastri, *Pasupata Sutras*, 8.

[51] Minoru Hara, "Nakulīśa-Pāśupata-Darśanam," *Indo-Iranian Journal* 2, no. 1 (1958): 30.

[52] Upadhyaya, *Bhāskarī*, cxii.

---

[53] Bhāskarācārya, *Brahmasūtrabhāṣyam*, edited by Vindhyesvari Prasada Dvivedin, 1915 ed., Chowkamba Sanskrit Series nos. 70, 185 & 209 (Banaras: Chowkambha Sanskrit Book Depot.), 3, 8. Srinivasachari, *The Philosophy of Bhedābheda*, 3-7.

[54] *ye tu bauddha matāvalambino māyā vādinas te'pi anena nyāyena sūtrakāreṇaiva nirastā veditavyāḥ* (BSBBh 2.2.29). Bhāskarācārya, *Brahmasūtrabhāṣyam*, 124.

[55] *tathā ca vākyakāravṛttikārabhyāṁ syād dadhyādivat iti vigītaṁ vicchinnamūlaṁ māhāyānika bauddha gāthitaṁ māyāvādaṁ vyāvarṇayanto lokān vyāmohayanti.* BSBBh 1.4.25. Bhāskarācārya, *Brahmasūtrabhāṣyam*, 85. Also see the way Bhāskara refutes *māyāvāda* and affirms the *Bhedābheda* in BSBBh 2.1.14-27 is a proof for his rebut against Śaṅkara. Bhāskarācārya, *Brahmasūtrabhāṣyam*, 92-105.

[56] Hajime Nakamura gives a chronology of the *vedāntic* thinkers after an elaborate discussion as follows: Bhartṛhari (450-500), Maṇḍanamiśra (670-720), Śaṅkara (700-750), Sureśvara (720-770), Padmapāda (720-770), Bhāskara (750-800), Sarvajñātman (750-800), Vācaspatimiśra (-841-). See, Nakamura, *A History of Early Vedānta Philosophy*, vol.1, 88.

[57] At the end of every chapter he signs off as, "*iti bhāskarīya brahmasūtrabhāṣye,*" "Thus is Bhāskara's commentary on Brahmasūtras." At the conclusion of the complete commentary he signs off as, "*iti śrībhagavadbhāskarācāryapraṇīte śārīrakamīmāṁsābhāṣye caturtha adhyāyasya caturthaḥ pādo'dhyāyaśca samāptaḥ.*" "Thus is the end of fourth chapter of fourth section of Bhāskara's commenatary of *śārīraka mīmāṁsā* (*Brahmasūtra*)." Bhāskarācārya, *Brahmasūtrabhāṣyam*, 249.

[58] See, Bhāskarācārya, *Brahmasūtrabhāṣyam*. Bhāskarācārya, *Siddhāntaśiromaṇiḥ*, edited by Muralidhar Thakur, 1950 ed., Kāshī Sanskrit Series 149 (Banaras: Jaya Krishna Das Haridas Gupta).

[59] For Śaṅkara, *upādhi* is *apāramārthika* or *mithyā*. It makes an apparent distinction between things which are really identical and real; and so is not itself ultimately real. The *ākāśa* inside the pot (*ghaṭākāśa*) appears to be different from the ether outside of the field (*maṭhākāśa*). When one removes this *upādhi* by breaking the pot, *ākāśa* will become absolutely identical with the *ākāśa* outside. Before the creation the *jīva-jagat* is absolutely merged in Brahman without

any distinction. During creation, *jīva-jagat* becomes different from Brahman. Thus *binnābhinna* is in time. At the time of *pralaya*, again, they become identical with Brahman. The original state of the reality is *abheda* and it is *svābhāvika*, because Brahman is cause, *jīva-jagat* is its effect. But *bheda* is not original or eternal, but real. Only during the *kāryāvastha*, the time of *saṁsāra*, they remain different, otherwise they remain identical.

[60] Srinivasachari, *The Philosophy of Bhedābheda*, 5-6.

[61] Srinivasachari, *The Philosophy of Bhedābheda*, 11.

[62] Srinivasachari, *The Philosophy of Bhedābheda*, 12.

[63] *vācā kevalaṁ ārabhyate vikārā-jātaṁna tu tattvato'sti yato nāmadheya mātram etat... śabda-jñāna'nupāti vastu-śūnyo vikalpa it, tathā ca'vastutayā anṛtaṁ vikāra jātam* (BSBBh 2.1.14). Bhāskarācārya, *Brahmasūtrabhāṣyam*, 93.

[64] *yathā somyaikena mṛtpiṇḍena sarvaṁ mṛṇmayaṁ vijñātaṁ syād vācārambhaṇaṁ vikāro nāmadheyaṁ mṛttiketyeva satyamiti vātho vāg indriyasya ubhayam ārambhaṇaṁ vikāro nāmadheyaṁ ca vikārobhidheya upapattistadabhidheyaṁ nāmadheyaṁ ubhayamālabhyaṁ vāgvyavaharaḥ pravartate ghaṭena udakam āhare'it mṛṇmayamity asya idaṁ vyākyānam... kāraṇam eva kāryātmanā ghaṭavad avatiśṭhate... kāraṇasyā avastha mātraṁ kāryaṁ vyatirikta avyatririktaṁ śukti rajatavad āgamāpāyadharmitvāc ca anṛtam anityam iti ca vyapadiśyate... nyāyasūtraṁ laukika parīkṣakāṇāṁ yatra buddhisāmyaṁ sa dṛṣṭānta iti api yāgād anger agnitvam iti...aitadātmyam idam sarvaṁ tat satyaṁ sa ātmā tattvamasi... atha nāmadhyeaṁ satyasya satyamiti....* BSBBh 2.1.14. Bhāskarācārya, *Brahmasūtrabhāṣyam*, 93.

[65] *abhedadharmaśca bhedo yathā mahodadher abhedaḥ sa eva taraṅgādy ātmanā vartamāno bheda iti ucyate na hi taraṅgādayaḥ pāṣāṇādiṣu dṛśyante yasyaiva tāḥ śaktayaḥ śakti śaktimatośca ananyatvaṁ anyatvaṁ copalakṣyate yathā'gner dahan prakāśanādi śaktayo bhedāḥ yatha ca vāyoḥ prāṇādivṛttibhedena bhedaḥ. tasmāt sarvam eka anekātmakaṁ na atyantam abhinnaṁ bhinnaṁ vā.* BSBBh 2.1.14. Bhāskarācārya, *Brahmasūtrabhāṣyam*, 101.

[66] Srinivasachari picks up several statements from the commentary of *Bhāskara Bhāṣya* to prove this point. See, Srinivasachari, *The Philosophy of Bhedābheda*, 13-15.

---

[67] The *sadvidyā* – defines Brahman as *sat* without a second externalizing itself as the manifold of material things and thinking things. Brahman is the unconditioned, beyond the categories of time, space, and causality; but, by its infinite *śakti*, it finitises itself into thinkers and things. Brahman thus exists in three forms known as *kāraṇa, kārya* and *jīva*.

[68] Vijñānabhikṣu differs here: *puruṣa* and *prakṛti* are two modes of the Supreme Being.

[69] *yathā ghaṭākāśaḥ paṭākāśa iti ākāśasya bhedavyapadeśaḥ kalpanāmātreṇa iti.* BSBBh 1.1.17. Bhāskarācārya, *Brahmasūtrabhāṣyam*, 26.

[70] *śītoṣṇayor yathā parasparaṁ virodhastathā bhedābhedayoḥ kimidamucyate nāsti virodha.* BSBBh 1.1.4. Bhāskarācārya, *Brahmasūtrabhāṣyam*, 17.

[71] Gupta, *Vedānta Kaustubha*, 20-21.

[72] Nimbārkācārya, *Brahmasūtra Nimbārkabhāṣyam: Vedāntakaustubha Vedāntakaustubhaprabhā Bhāvaadīpikā Vyākhyātrayopetam*, edited and translated by Madan Mohan Agrawal, 2000 ed., Vrajajīvana Prācyabhāratī Granthamāla, vol. 1 (Delhi: Chaukambha Sanskrit Pratishthan), vii. According to *Nimbārka sampradāya*, Nimbārka lived in the year 3096 BCE at the time when the grandson of Arjuna was on the throne. However, the date is mythical. Madan Mohan Agrawal in his introduction to *Nimbārkabhāṣya* places Nimbārka before Śaṅkara, that is, 750 CE. Bhandarkar proposed him as a philosopher after Rāmānuja and maintained the date of his demise as 1162 CE. Some dated around the 13th Century. However, S.N. Dasgupta regarded Nimbārka's era around the middle of the 14th Century. Alternatively, S.A.A. Rizvi assigns the date between 1130 to 1200 CE, whille Jadunath Sinha counts him as a 13th century philosopher, and Tarachand presumes him to be a younger contemporary of Rāmānuja. The most generally accepted date is given by Dasgupta. See, R.G. Bhandarkar, *Vaisnavism, Saivaism and Minor Religious System* (Varanasi: Indological Book House, 1913), 62-63. Dasgupta, *A History of Indian Philosophy*, 399-400. Jadunath Sinha, *The Philosophy of Nimbarka*, 2. Srinivasachari, *The Philosophy of Bhedābheda*, 183. Gupta, *Vedānta Kaustubha: A Study*, 7-8.

[73] *śrīkṛṣṇaṁ vanda iti anvayaḥ.... svarūpeṇa guṇaśaktyādibhiśca bṛhattamaḥ sarveśvaraḥ śrīkṛṣṇa eva brahmapadārthaḥ sa ca śrīkṛṣṇa*

śabdena atra abhihitaḥ. Nimbārka Bhāṣya 1.1.1. Nimbārkācārya, *Brahmasūtra Nimbārkabhāṣyam*, 2. 'It refers to praising Śrīkṛṣṇa... in the form He is quality and power, greater, and is Lord of all, He is the Brahman and is to be declared by the word Śrīkṛṣṇa.'

[74] *'yato vā imāni bhūtāni jāyate* (TU 3.1.1), *etasmājjāyate prāṇo manaḥ sarvendriyāṇi ca* (MU 1.3; KU 15), *sadeva somyedamagra āsīt, ekam evam advitīyaṁ brahma* (CU 6.2.1), *tadaikṣata bahu syā prajāyeya* (CU 6.2.3) *ityādi vacanānāṁ sākṣāt eva śrīkṛṣṇo'nvayaḥ. Nimbārka Bhāṣya* 1.1.1. see, Nimbārkācārya, *Brahmasūtra Nimbārkabhāṣyam*, 2. 'That from which beings are born,' 'from the Supreme Brahman are born life, mind and all organs of perception and action,' 'in the beginning, my dear, all this was Existence, the one only without a second,' 'He contemplated, may I be many,' etc. statements verily refer to Śrīkṛṣṇa alone.

[75] *"īśvaraḥ sarvabhūtānāṁ hṛddeśe'rjuna! tiṣṭatī iti smṛteśca jīvaparamātmanobhedo'sti"* BSVPS 1.2.6. Nimbārkācārya, *Śrībrahmasūtra Śrīnimbārkabhāṣyam: Vedānta Pārijātasaurabh of Nimbārkācārya and Vedāntakaustubha of Śrīnivāsācārya*, edited by Duṇḍirāja Śāstri, 1989 ed., Kashi Sanskrit Series (Banaras: Chowkamba Sanskrit Series Office), 51.

[76] *tattvaṁ tāvantrividhaṁ-cidacidbrahmabhedāt*. Nimbārkācārya, *Śrībrahmasūtra Śrīnimbārka-bhāṣyam*, 7. Reality is three types – conscious, unconscious and divine.

[77] Śrīnivāsa, *Vedānta-Pārijāta-Saurabha*, 259. Also see, RV 1.105.9; 2.11.8; 3.23.4; MuU 1.1.7.

[78] *"prakṛtir upādānakaraṇaṁ cakārānanimitakāraṇaṁ ca paramātmaiva, "uta tamādeśam-aprākṣya yenāśrutaṁ śrutaṁ bhavatyamataṁ matavijñātaṁ vijñātaṁ bhavati" iti pratijñāyā, yathā somya ekena mṛtpiṇḍena sarvaṁ mṛnmayaṁ vijñātaṁ syāt" iti dṛṣṭāntasya ca sāmañjasyāt." Vedānta Pārijāta Saurabha*, 1.4.23. Roma Bose, *Vedāntapārijātasaurabha of Nimbārka*, 255. 'The material cause,' as well as 'the efficient cause,' indicated by the particle "and" (in the sutra), is none but the Supreme Soul, because then alone the initial proposition: "Did you ask for that instruction whereby the unheard becomes heard, the unthought becomes thought, the unknown becomes known?" (CU 6.1.3), as well as the illustration: "Just as, my dear, through a lump of clay, all objects made of clay may be known" (CU 6.1.4) are explicable.

[79] Nimbārkācārya, *Śrībrahmasūtra Śrīnimbārkabhāṣyam*, 144.

[80] *sarva bhinna abhinno bhagavān vāsudevo viśvātmaivajijñāsā viṣayaḥ*. Nimbārkācārya, *Brahmasūtra Nimbārkabhāṣyam, 70.*

[81] *brahma ca acintya ananta niratiśaya svābhāvika bṛhattamsvarūpaguṇādi āśrayabhūtaḥ sarvajñaḥ sarvaśaktiḥ sarveśvaraḥ sarvakāraṇarūpaḥ samānātiśayaśūnaḥ sarvavyāpakaḥ sarva-vedaikavedhyaḥ śrīkṛṣṇaḥ eva "bṛhati bṛṁhayati tasmāducyate paraṁ brahma."* Nimbārkācārya, *Śrībrahmasūtra Śrīnimbārkabhāṣyam*, 5.

[82] Shailaja Bapat, *A Study of the Vedānta in the Light of Brahmasūtras* (Delhi: New Bharatiya Book Corporation, 2004), 119.

[83] Dasgupta, *A History of Indian Philosophy*, vol.1, 406.

[84] This is the reason why people venerate several deities in the Hindu tradition. Every family will have a house deity, called *kuladevata*, which is unique to every family. These deities give meaning to their spiritual life.

[85] *bhedasya na adhikaraṇa svarūpam*. Srinivasachari, *The Philosophy of Bhedābheda*, 185. Also see, Dasgupta, *A History of Indian Philosophy*, vol.1, 417.

It is noteworthy that Nimbārka does not refute any *vedāntins*, be it *Dvaita*, *Advaita* or other *Bhedābhedavādins* in his *bhāṣya, Nimbārka Pārijāta Saurabha*. His commentary is terse and short requiing other sub-commentaries to find his refutations.

[86] Dasgupta, *A History of Indian Philosophy*, vol.1, 417.

[87] *brahma abhinno'pi kṣetrajñaḥ svasvarūpato bhinna eva.* BS 2.1.22. As quoted by Srinivasachari, *The Philosophy of Bhedābheda*, 184.

[88] *avibhāge'pi samudra-taraṅgayoriva sūrya-tatprabhāyoriva tayor vibhāgas syāt.* BS 2.1.13. Srinivasachari, *The Philosophy of Bhedābheda*, 185. *Avibhāga* is like the wave in the sea, and sun and its sparks both are non-different.

[89] Srinivasachari, *The Philosophy of Bhedābheda*, 185.

[90] *Gauḍīya* refers to the Gauḍa region, the present day Bengal-Bangladesh. *Vaiṣṇavism* refers to the worship of Viṣṇu or Kṛṣṇa as the Supreme Being. This sect gives more prominence to *Bhakti* or devotional worship and incarnations of Viṣṇu. The famous '*Hare Rama Hare Kṛṣṇa*' movement belongs to this group.

---

[91] A.C. Bhaktivedanta Swami Prabhupada, *Bhagavadgītā As It Is* (California: Bhaktivedanta Book Trust, 1972), 7.

[92] *Panentheism* is the belief that the divine interpenetrates every part of the universe and extends timelessly beyond it. In contrast, pantheism holds that the divine and the universe are identical. Panentheism differentiates between the divine and non-divine with their significances. The universe and the divine are not ontologically equivalent. God is viewed as the soul of the universe, the universal spirit present everywhere, in everything and everyone, at all times.

[93] *'sarvagatvādanantasya sa evāyamahaṁ sthitaḥ.' iti viṣṇupurāṇādāvapi* (VP 1.19.15). *ato avagamyate–śrutayo api abhedaṁ vibhāga lakṣaṇameva bodhayanti, ekavākyatvāt 'etadātmyam idaṁ sarvami' ti śrutau jaḍavarga abhedasya avibhāgādirūpasyaiva vaktavyatayā jīvabhedasyāpi avibhāgādi rūpasiddheśca, anyathā ardhajaratīya nyāyāyāpatteḥ*. See, VAB 1.1.2, p.25. '"The eternal Lord being everywhere stands here in my form,' says *Viṣṇupurāṇa*. Also scriptures, when they talk of oneness, teach identity as being non-separation. The identity of the world being described in terms of non-separation, the identity of the soul also on the basis of non-separation, is established by the scripture like: 'This whole world has that for its self' (CU 6.8.7). If this were not so, then the maxim of half the age of an old woman would apply." See, Borelli, "The Philosophy of Vijñānabhikṣu," 51.

[94] For more details on the purpose of *śūdra's* exclusion by Śaṅkara, refer Jaison Vadakkan, *Exclusion of Śūdras from Brahmajijñāsā: Re-Reading Apaśūdrādhikaraṇam of Brahmasūtra Śāṅkara Bhāṣya* (Delhi: Motilal Banarasidass Publications, 2019).

[95] This view called *Viśiṣṭaśivādvaitavāda*. *Viśiṣṭaśivādvaita,* the Śaivite qualified non-dualism of Śrīkanṭha is similar to the *Viśiṣṭādvaita* of Rāmānuja. The former believes in Viṣṇu (*Vaiṣṇava-sampradāya*) as the Supreme Being and for the latter He is Śiva (*Śaivasampradāya*).

Chapter Three

SOCIO-CULTURAL AND HISTORICO-PHILOSOPHICAL BACKGROUND OF VIJÑĀNABHIKṢU

Having studied the historical overview of *Bhedābheda* both in *śruti* and *smṛti* literature and the *Vedāntic* tradition itself, this chapter explores the socio-political and cultural background of Vijñānabhikṣu.

At the turn of the sixteenth century CE, the situation of India was quite different from the medieval period in terms of culture, philosophy, politics and spirituality. Hence, before studying the *Avibhāga-Bhedābheda* of Vijñānabhikṣu, it is proper to understand his background, biography and presuppositions.

3.1 *Sitz-im-Leben* of Vijñānabhikṣu

One cannot scrutinize a concept or a philosophy without having deliberated upon its how, what and why. Several factors, such as what was known, how was known, the challenges faced and socio-politico-religious colouring impact the fact of an author's writing with its equivalent forces on the society. For example, the *Vedic* prayer of 'peace' (*śānti*) should be understood in contrast with the non-violent (*ahiṁsā*) behaviour exhibited by the society. *Ahiṁsā* was originally applied to the relationship between humans and animals, to prevent any injury or ill-treatment to the sacrificer, the sacrificer's offspring and their livestock (RV

10.22.13). Years later, the idea was applied to human beings. Even in the well-acclaimed scripture, the *Gītā* justified violence; just like creatures live on creatures, mongoose on mice, cat on mongoose, dog on cat, wild beast on dogs, so too the ascetics cannot live without killing (BG 12:15-24). In this background, one should make a re-reading of the texts on peace and non-violence.

Similarly, when we interact with the theistic non-dualism of Vijñānabhikṣu, one must enroot oneself deeply in the socio-cultural and political life situation of the author. Ideas neither crop up in a vacuum nor are they a mere continuation of previous ones. Individuals have unique ideas which could be quite different from or similar to the ideas of others in time and space. Often something superior to one's comprehension is communicated by the very mode of its verbalization. Before getting into the biographical details and actual philosophy of Vijñānabhikṣu, we highlight *sitz-im-leben* of the thinker.

3.1.1 Ritualism and *Brāhmaṇic* Hegemony

There existed two trends of thoughts during the *Vedic* time: ritualistic and speculative. Jamison and Witzel in a research paper published by Harvard University identify these two opposing trends as "elaborate, expensive, and specialized system of rituals" and "abstraction and internalization of the principles underlying ritual and cosmic speculation on them."[1] Both these trends had a greater bearing on Buddhism, Jainism and the formation of Hinduism as a religion.[2] From its initiation till its settlement in the

Indian peninsula the *Vedic* Hinduism had to encounter several cultures and traditions. Obviously, in terms of technology, culture and agriculture, it had the upper hand over the original inhabitants (or aboriginals). For this reason, they called themselves '*ārya*,' the noble ones. Likewise, in the post-settlement period due to the link between the forces of acculturation, ritualism and the superiority of certain classes within the society became vivid. The 'superior classes' looked down upon the mistreated masses of the society both pragmatically and theoretically. It is at this juncture, that religions like Buddhism and Jainism came to light as a reaction against *Vedic* ritualism and the hegemony of Brāhmins.[3] When a prominent section of the society is revolted against, it is compelled to assuage the unpleasant feelings of the lesser privileged rebels by reinventing and accommodating the acceptable inclusive ideologies. To incorporate suitable ideologies, several stories, myths and deities were either composed or inserted in the traditional texts.

When Buddhism and Jainism were advancing rapidly across the country under the patronage of several kings, they threatened the existence of Hinduism. In opposition, they rebuffed *Vedic* ritualism and class systems and alternatively pioneered in carrying out civilizational influences into culturally backward areas to establish a caste-less egalitarian society.[4] This created a polemic atmosphere. To defy this, Buddha and Jina have designated the incarnations of Viṣṇu and devotion or *bhakti* was introduced.[5] The *Vedāntic* culture is nothing but the rejoinder of Hinduism against the then-popular religions (Buddhism and Jainism). The gradual result is the emerging *Bhakti Movement*. The invasion of Turks resulted in Islamification,[6] and the missionary works of Christians further provoked Hinduism as the former renounced polytheism and idol worship, and the latter inculcated the ideals of social equality and justice.

3.2.2 *Bhakti* as an Emerging Trend

The terse *Vedic* knowledge is made intelligible by various *smṛti* literatures in particular *Upaniṣads* and *Purāṇic* writings. Nevertheless, it was still unreachable for the common people, ensuing emergence of the requisite for devotion or *bhakti*. These devotional renderings were presented through the ideology of *Vedāntic* teachings in the language of everyone's understandability. Even so, it took a long time from Bādarāyaṇa to Śaṅkara to effect these changes.

Śaṅkara conformed to the traditional *brāhmiṇical* way of establishing the *Vedic* religion. He laid the foundation for *bhakti* in *Vedāntic* tradition, emphasizing knowledge as the supreme means of salvation. Still, it is *Viśiṣṭādvaita* which facilitated the way for devotion as the source of *mukti.* Rāmānuja (1017-1113 CE) reflects on *bhakti* as an epistemic state, specifically, comprehension of Brahman consists in directly perceiving it. *Bhakti* is a direct awareness of the nature of *Brahman*, and so constituting a type of knowledge (*jñāna*). Even the perceptual character of devotion is characterized as meditation or worship (*upāsana*).[7] Vallabhācārya in the 15th century (1473-1531 CE) emerged as one of the prominent personalities in the *Advaitic* tradition to propagate the nourishment of souls as means of devotion called, '*puṣṭi mārga*' through the philosophy of *Śuddhādvaita*. The period and place of his propagation of *puṣṭi mārga* is especially noteworthy since it is at the same plateau Vijñānabhikṣu latter appears. Though Vallabha from the South Indian Tamil *Vaiṣṇava* tradition arrives at the present Uttar Pradesh, particularly at to Banaras[8] to get rooted in the place, latter moves towards the Western region for his missionary pursuit.

The devotional means or *bhakti* propagated by the six famous *Vedāntic* thinkers—Śaṅkarācārya, Rāmānujācārya, Vallabhācārya, Madhvācarya, Nimbārkācārya and Caitnaya Mahāprabhu—ushered the rise of Hindu religion in the medieval period. Besides these, several others complemented a great deal to the growth and propagation of *bhakti*. Some of them are: Kabīr Dās (1398-1448 ? He is almost a contemporary to Caitanya), Guru Nānak (1469-1539), Dādu Dayāl (1554-1603), Mīra Bāi (1498-1546), Tulsīdās (1532-1623), Sūrdas (1478-1584 ?), Maluk Dās (1574-1682), Sundardās (1596-1689), and the list goes endless.[9] The notable features here are the place of their missionary work, the period and the content of their charisma. Most of these zealots were either born or hailed from elsewhere and voiced themselves in the North Indian soil. Secondly, the common period is from the 11th to 17th century, and in particular the 15th to 16th century CE. Their main contention was the love of God should be seen as an end in itself and not as means to something else.[10] Some of their works later turned out to be either social movements or religions like Kabīr-Panth, Sūfism, Nānak Panth or Sikhism.

Vijñānabhikṣu did not strictly advocate *bhakti* as a path of liberation like yhe various proponents mentioned above. However, there is a strong thread of *bhakti* throughout the commentary on the *Brahmasūtras* and in his other writings. This may be due to his belief in God. It is his faith in God that makes him to convert the *nirīśvara Sāṅkhya* into *seśvara Sāṅkhya*. Consequently, his commentary on the *Brahmasūtras* is one of the unique commentaries in the whole of *Vedāntic* traditions. He comments on it from the theistic *Sāṅkhya* perspective.

3.2.3 Political Situation of the Time

The Islam religion founded by Muhammad (570-632 CE) sets foot on the North-West of India through Arab invasion in the early seventh century and the North India proper through Mohammad Ghazni (979-1030 CE). The subsequent Islam kings spread their religion and its tenets. As certain sections of the peoples were already facing the brunt of casteism, several of them embraced Islam, denounced the caste system and idol worship. Later, the Islamic blend with the regional creed resulted in Sūfism and other religious movements.

In 1526, Zahir-ud-din Muhammad, otherwise known as Babur became the first Mughal emperor. After his death, Humayun (1530-1556) and then Akbar (1556-1605) became the emperors who were succeeded by Jahangir (1605-1627), Shaj Jahan (1627-1658), Aurangazeb (1658-1707), and

Farrukhsiyar (1713-1719). Some Mughal kings valued Hinduism very highly, while others abhorred it. Some viewed their religious practices not merely as 'erroneous' but downright blasphemy. Wendy Doniger writes regarding their relationship to Hinduism:

> Some were religious zealots; some didn't care much about religion; some loved Islam but didn't believe that they should impose it on anyone else. Some (notoriously Aurangzeb) were quite (though not unambiguously) horrid; some (most notably Akbar) were quite (though not unambiguous) wonderful; and most of them were a bit of both.[11]

The reign of Akbar and his religious pluralism is an immediate socio-politico-religious setting to the philosophy of Vijñānabhikṣu since our subject of research is composed during this period. Though there were several inter-religious dialogues before him, the credit for organizing a systematic endeavor goes to Akbar for convening a series of inter-religious dialogues in 1564,[12] for which he even constructed a room for religious discourse in the palace. Different religious leaders belonging to different faiths like Śia, Sunni, Sūfi, Kabīrpanth (disciples of Kabīr), Nānakpanth (later called Sikhism), Jains, Jews, Christians (Jesuits from Goa), Śaiva and Vaiṣṇava *bhakts* were invited to share their religious belief and heritage.[13] To promote religious tolerance in his kingdom, Akbar established a new religion, called *Din-i-Ilahi, The Divine Faith.* Sadly, the new religion of Akbar died along with his empire.

Akbar had a great admiration for all the religious people, especially the Hindus. His noteworthy army leader, Birbal was a Hindu. Another leading general, finance and the prime minister–all in all–was also a Hindu, Todar Mall (Todaramalla). There were scholars in Sanskrit, Persian and Arab languages deeply engaged in translation and composition of religious and secular literatures: *Toḍarānanda* (*Todar's Bliss*, a Sanskrit compendium of Hindu culture and learning), *Akbarnāmā* (a composition of Akbar's reign), translation of the *Mahābhārata* and the *Rāmāyaṇa* (by Abu'l Fazal), the *Harivaṁśa*, the *Yogavasiṣṭa, the Pañcatantra, the Quran* (for the first time) in Persian languages. Akbar abolished *jizyah* (religious tax) and pilgrim taxes (to take baths in Prayāg, Banaras, etc.) which the non-Muslims were required to pay in a Muslim state.[14] Despite these, he disapproved of certain social immoral practices: *sati* was allowed on condition that the widow consented out of her free will but never a widow of tender age. He also legalized widow re-marriage.

3.2.4 Time of Syncretism

The era of Akbar witnessed a greater understanding between Hindus and Muslims in promoting religious and secular literature. There was a greater tolerance and liberal policy in the governance. This is also the period of a remarkable series of popular saints who accentuated the essential unity of Islam, Hinduism and other cultures. The point in time stresses a religion or tradition based on love and devotion rather than rituals or a literal interpretation of revealed books. An ambiance is being created in which liberal sentiments and views could prosper and religious narrowness began to be despised.

The 16th century also witnessed a great mutual transfusion of *Hindu bhakti* and *Sūfi mysticism*. The transfusion was such that it was difficult to identify which tradition was the original one. The local mystical songs and stories were used to arouse devotion. As a result, several syncretic pieces of literatures and fusions emerged. *The ocean of the Nectar of Bhakti* written by Rupagoswamin relates the life of Kṛṣṇa modelled on Sūfi romance; many Muslim pilgrims attended the Hindu shrine festivals; several Muslim disciples had Hindu disciples, at Sūfi centres low-caste Hindus and Pariahs were present and even they shared meals with Muslims; many were Hindus by culture and Muslims by religion and vice versa; Urdu became a syncretic language, etc.[15] In short, the community was an accommodative one.

3.2.5 Liberalism *vis-à-vis* Traditionalism

Though the Mughal kings, in general, were liberalists, their primary religious affiliation was Islam. But they did not proscribe Hinduism since the purpose of Mughal was not to establish an Islamic kingdom. The first Panipat war, fought between two politically motivated Muslim kings, Lodhi and Babur in 1526 (which established Mughal rule) testified this. In order to establish their kingdom, they had to be compassionate towards the majority culture of the land.

However, there were several occasions Hindus retracted

into more conservative practices. This was obviously to shield their religion from the risk of cultural fusion. Wujastyk demonstrates this stance, quoting K.M. Panikkar:

> The egalitarian conception of Islam and its proselytising activity had created for Hinduism special problems which could not be overlooked. The reaction of Hindu lawgivers to this challenge was in general to make Hinduism more rigid and re-interpret the rules in such a way as to resist the encroachment of Islam. It is perhaps this defensive attitude toward society that is responsible for the orthodoxy of views which is characteristic of the *Dharma Śāstra* literature of this period.[16]

There were several rejoinders from orthodox *brāhmins* towards the vernacularization of the story of the Rāmāyaṇa by Tulsidās (1532/1543-1623). Tulsidās was sympathetic towards Pariahs and tribals and periodically challenged caste system in his poem *Rāmacaritamānasa*.

The heart of the matter cropping up from the setting are: dominant *bhakti* cult, sympathetic Mughal rule and favourable socio-cultural tradition of Hinduism overshadow Vijñānabhikṣu's entry. Therefore, an obvious question to be probed is the rationale for Vijñānabhikṣu's philosophical stand. Scrutinizing in the corpus of his writings, two characteristics, namely, his literary style and embedded content become clear.

The style of Vijñānabhikṣu is doxography. Doxography is a term used especially for the works of classical historians, describing the points of view of past philosophers and scientists. Literally, it means the writing of tenets, views or opinions. Greek *doxa* (δόξα) means "an opinion," "a point of view" and *graphein* (γράφειν) means "to write," "to describe." The word is a product of the modern scholarship. Vijñānabhikṣu in his exposition on the *Brahmasūtras,* extensively quotes both *śruti* and *smṛti* texts. To bloster his views, he uses several influential examples, metaphors and concepts used by prominent people over the time. What's more, he employs numerous people's views on a particular issue. Secondly, though he critiques *Kevala Advaita* vehemently, neither manipulates the name of the system nor of the founder, instead uses the word *'ādhunikā'* (the moderns). Thirdly, wherever appropriate, he incorporates the elements of *bhakti*, plurality, inter-relationship, inter-religiosity, monotheism and accommodation.

All these indicate Vijñānabhikṣu's attempt to address a common concern of the time. The common interest could be the revival of Hinduism from its threatened existence. The risk for Hinduism was both internal and external. The internal perils were due to various streams of thoughts, divarication into sects and religious ideologies within. The external vulnerabilities were due to the advent of Turks, establishing their dynasty and Islamic religion through proselytizing activity and in addition the beginning of the spread of Christianity with its mission in North India. Together with this, the sweeping *bhaktism* was also intimidating to establish a casteless society.

If the casteless society is established, the social stability or the order created by hierarchy will be in jeopardy. This would depose the popularity and advantages of the people of the higher rung. Further, *varṇāśrama* was deemed 'the tradition' of the Hindus sanctioned since the *Vedic* time will be questioned. Hence, Vijñānabhikṣu cannot spurn the *varṇāśrama dharma*. He has to endorse without barring untouchables (*śūdras* and *mlecchas*) and people of other creeds. The exclusion will anger the ruling people of the time, and resentment hatred from the people who embraced *bhakti* tradition. The commentary on the *Apaśūdrādhikaraṇa* (VAB 1.3.33-38) proves this point. [17] He defines *śūdra* as those people whose actions are like śūdra. *Śūdra* word is not about the *śūdra* caste. The text does not speak about the right to education or the equality of *śūdra* with other castes. But it informs about the worthiness of the person to humble oneself in front of a learned person. Therefore, Vijñānabhikṣu does not deny *śūdra* the right to know Brahman.

Another critical strategy before Vijñānabhikṣu is to espouse the materialistic well-being as taught by the *Vedas* and the spiritual well-being as propagated by *Vedāntic* culture beginning from the *Upaniṣads*. The materialistic welfare of the *Vedic* period denotes the well-being of the social organization of the primitive civilization. The polytheistic and 'gods as the cause of everything and therefore they need propitiation' philosophy is well-known in *Vedic* literature. The basic contention of the good of the empirical world (*dṛṣṭaloka*) is the good of the transcendental world (*adṛṣṭaloka*). The necessity for defending the existing system together with the prevalent understanding of the *Vedic* religion as polytheistic has to be resolved with an appropriate scriptural foundation for a monotheistic, cultural and accommodative understanding. Otherwise, the *Vedāntic* spiritualistic tradition drawn from *Vedic* culture tracing the social welfare through various trades, moral precepts, art, literature, etc. as the divine ritualistic work is to be reinstated. Vijñānabhikṣu tries to rediscover these elements in his philosophical endeavor.

Amidst these concerns, Vijñānabhikṣu proposes the *Vedic* Hinduism as a primitive all-encompassing superior religion which accommodates every culture and tradition in its fold, through the concept, *the theistic non-dualism*, the *Avibhāga-Bhedābheda*. Only *Bhedābheda* tradition could enfold his agenda and therefore, chose this system as his platform.

3.2 Biography and the Works of Vijñānabhikṣu

Vijñānabhikṣu is a unique philosopher who beautifully encapsulates the divergent views of *Vedāntic* philosophy through *Avibhāga-Bhedābheda.* This is substantiated in his work, *Vijñānāmṛtabhāṣyam, the Commentary of the Nectar of Wisdom,* which is the cornerstone of his entire corpus of writing and teaching.

3.2.1 Biography

Vijñānabhikṣu also known as Vijñānācārya, Vijñānendrabhikṣu, Jñānendrabhikṣu, Vijñānārka, Vijñānayati or Bhikṣu[18] is generally understood to have prospered in the 16th century CE.[19] In his commentary on the *Brahmasūtras* two names can be found—Vijñānārka and

Vijñānayati. Thus it is said, "*vedāntanagarī mārge* ***vijñānārkeṇa*** *darśitaḥ*" (VAB 1.1.5, p.75). At the end of every chapter, he signs off as "*iti brahmamīmāṁsāyāṁ* ***vijñānayati*** *kṛte vijñānāmṛtākhya ṛujubhāṣye....*" The terms *yati, yativara, yatīndra* and *bhikṣu* suggest that Vijñānabhikṣu must have been an ascetic.

Ramakrishna Acharya thinks that Vijñānabhikṣu thrived at the beginning of the 17th century.[20] Hayavadana Rao situates Vijñānabhikṣu about the middle of the 17th century. However, he does not decipher any reasons for it.[21] Goswami Prahlad Giri records the date mentioned at the end of the early manuscripts of *Vijñānāmṛtabhāṣyam*, "*iti brahmamīmāṁsāyāṁ śrīvijñānabhikṣukṛte vijñānāmṛtabhāṣyasya ṛjubhāṣye caturthādhyāyasya caturthapādaḥ. śubhamastu. saṁvat 1775 miti pauṣaśukla paurṇamāsyāṁ śukravāsare likhitaṁ.*"[22] However, the exact date and year are doubtful. We are uncertain to ascertain whether "*saṁvat 1775*" is in fact written by him or not. Presumably, it is the work of the editor. Hence, the modern scholars of *Sāṅkhya* presume a date around 1600 CE.

Though Vijñānabhikṣu has composed several works, they were unheard of till the 19th century. The most highly commented and edited works are on the *Sāṅkhya* (1852) and the *Yoga* (1883-84). The first dissertation, "*Ācārya Vijñānabhikṣu Aur Bhāratīya Darśan Me Unkā Sthān*" [*A Study of Vijñānabhikṣu and His Place in Indian Philosophy*] published in 1969 by Sureścandra Śrīvāstava in Hindi is the first authentic secondary source on Vijñānabhikṣu.[23] This is followed by several other works. It is at this juncture, Vijñānabhikṣu came into the limelight, not for his *bhāṣya* on the *Brahmasūtras* which is the foundation for his philosophy, but for the irreplaceable contribution to the world of philosophy on *Sāṅkhya* and *Yoga* traditions.

Among the several available manuscripts together with its linguistic analysis, Śrīvāstava dates one of the last compilations of Vijñānabhikṣu's *Sāṅkhyasāra* to 1623 CE. Prominent thinkers who endorse this view are A.B. Kieth, F.E. Hall, Richardson, Winternitz, N.N. Dasgupta, and S. Radhakrishnan. Hayavadana Rao reckons that Vijñānabhikṣu belonged to *Gauḍa* community, corresponding to the Modern Northern Bengal from *Karnākārnika* caste (a *kāyastha brāhmin*).[24] But there is no clinching evidence to deem it so. It may be possible that he belonged to *Gauḍīya brāhmin* community as he sanctions caste system in the *apaśūdradhikaraṇa* (though he defines it etymologically).

Though he lived in the near modern era, we are neither able to trace his parents nor has he mentioned about his time and place. He has used several expressions proper to Hindi. Tripāṭhi lists few of them: *ghoṭaka* (horse), *vilambasiddhi* (the act of being late), *milana* (meeting), *rātridina* (night and day), *dhāna* (to mean rice), *nārāyaṇa* (to mean sun), etc.[25] For that reason, surely he resided in North India. Unlike the olden days, he may not have received any kingly patronage due to the independent and rational thinking he had, and because of which his biographical details are not available. Therefore, the only way to find out is by re-reading the available literature. In fact his rational and independent thinking is very clear from his commentary on the first aphorism of VAB itself.

Mention of several Hindi words in other manuscripts, the style of writings, references to the places such as *Prayāga* (VAB 1.3.26, p.111), *Bhāratavarṣa, Triveṇi* designate the probable *terminus ad quem* of Vijñānabhikṣu as 1583-1623. Thus it can be noted in his works, "*syādevaṁ* ***prayāgādau*** *brahmādīnāṁ yāgādi śravaṇāt*" (VAB 1.3.26, p.111), "*nirīśvara vāde tu* ***triveṇīvad*** *anyonya avibhaktatayā*" (SPB 161), "*svagiṇāṁ bhāratavarṣamāgatya...****prayāgadau***" (*Yogavārttika*, 34). From these data, the credible place of his origin and mission, perhaps, is either the city of Allahabad (Prayāgrāj) or Varanasi of the present Uttar Pradesh.[26]

Vijñānabhikṣu lived at a time when *bhakti* was at its zenith both from the prospect of religion and from the notion of philosophy in North India. Unlike Rāmānuja and other thinkers, he did not very much advocate *bhakti* as the path of liberation. All the same, he did prescribe knowledge and actions (meditation, yogic practice, etc.) as sure the paths of liberation. The *ācāryas* starting from Rāmānuja in the 11th century till Baladeva Upādhyāya in the 18th century wrote commentaries that had *bhakti* as the highest means of liberation. As a staunch believer, Vijñānabhikṣu uncovers divine thread in all the philosophical systems of the *Vedānta*. He, being a *sannyāsi* added theistic flavor to his writings.

3.2.2 List of Works

Vijñānabhikṣu is mainly known for his works on the

Sāṅkhya and *Yoga*. They are written after his *Vedāntic* works. He regards three texts as *prasthānatrayī*: the *Brahmasūtras,* the *Upaniṣads* and the *Kūrma Purāṇa*. Authors vary in accepting the number of works Vijñānabhikṣu has compiled. Aufrecht adds two more works: *Vedāntāloka* and *Sāṅkyakārikabhāṣya.* Gopīnātha Kavirāja includes *Pāṣaṇḍamatakhaṇḍana* with the criticism on Śaṅkara. However, the authors like T. S. Rukmani, Srivastava, Kanshi Ram and Nicholson acknowledge only sixteen, as it lacks conclusive evidence for additions.[27]

By and large, the standard sixteen works are enlisted below according to the chronological order. As some of the works are extant now and the contents of them cannot be exactly predicted.

1. *Upadeśaratnamāla*: It is a work on the *Vedānta.* Though the actual contents of this work are unknown, the context mentioned of this book in his *Vijñānāmṛtabhāṣya* (*adhikaṁ tu upadeśaratnamālākhyaprakaraṇe dṛṣṭavyam.* VAB 1.1.2, p.32) suggests that it precedes the commentary on the BS, and deals with the relationship between Brahman and *ātman*.[28]

2. *Brahmasūtrabhāṣyam* or *Vijñānāmṛtabhāṣyam*: The Commentary on the *Brahmasūtras* of Bādarāyaṇa. He exposes in this work his philosophy of *Avibhāga-Bhedābheda.*

3. *Kaṭhavallyopaniṣadāloka*: Commentary on the *Kaṭha Upaniṣad.*

4. *Kaivalyopaniṣadāloka*: Commentary on the *Kaivalya Upaniṣad.*

5. *Maitreyyopaniṣadāloka*: Commentary on the *Maitrī Upaniṣad.*

6. *Māṇḍūkyopaniṣadāloka:* Commentary on the *Māṇḍūkya Upaniṣad.*

7. *Muṇḍakopaniṣadāloka*: on the *Muṇḍaka Upaniṣad.*

8. *Praśnopaniṣadāloka*: Commentary on the *Praśna Upaniṣad.*

9. *Taittirīyopaniṣadāloka*: Commentary on the *Taittirīya Upaniṣad.*

10. *Śvetāśvataropaniṣadāloka*: Commentary on the *Śvetāśvatara Upaniṣad.*

11. *Īśvaragītābhāṣya*: Treatise on the *Kūrma Purāṇa* (This is 'the *Gītā'* for Vijñānabhikṣu as he deems it to be one of the authoritative texts).

12. *Brahmādarśaḥ*: Work on *Vedānta*

13. *Yogavārttikam*: Treatise on *Yogasūtra* of Pātañjali

14. *Sāṅkhyapravacanabhāṣyam*: Treatise on *Sāṅkyasūtra*

15. *Sāṅkhyasāram*: Quintessence of *Sāṅkhya*

16. *Yogasārasaṅgrahaḥ*: Quintessence of *Yoga of Vyāsabhāṣya*

Subsequently, Vijñānabhikṣu has composed two works each on *Sāṅkhya* and *Yoga,* and one on the *Brahmamīmāṁsā* or the *Brahmasūtras*. These are well-known works published with or without translations. Eleven other works are either partly known and published or still unknown and partly published writes Kedāranātha Tripāṭhī.[29] Among the sixteen works cataloged above, the numbers 2, 13, 14, 15 and 16 are the only published works accessible today, and other works are unavailable to the researcher.

3.2.3 *Vijñānāmṛtabhāṣyam*

The *Vijñānāmṛtabhāṣyam* or *Brahmamīmāṁsābhāṣyam* is appraised to be the maiden work of Vijñānabhikṣu more due to its unevincing maturity than the works on the *Sāṅkhya* and *Yoga*.[30] This does not signify that the *Vijñānāmṛtabhāṣyam* lacks coherence. This work is the groundwork for the integral non-dualism or *avibhāgādvaita*. The prime objective of this work is to "provide a 'genuine' metaphysics and ethics... so that it might 'really' help the aspirants to attain liberation,"[31] says Kanshi Ram. This is the reason that the work condemns *māyāvāda* vehemently to rescue the *Vedānta* from the clutches of the '*wrong teachers*.'[32] In the *Sāṅkhyapravacanabhāṣya*, he states that there is not a single *sūtra* in which bondage is declared to be a mere deception. As to the novel theory of *māyā* propounded by *vedāntabrūva* (those who claim to be *Vedāntists*), it is only another type of Buddhist of the *Vijñānavāda* school. This theory has nothing to do with the *Vedānta* but to be understood by the doctrine of these new Buddhists, who assert the theory of *māyā* and reduce our bondage to mere illusion. In this way, this theory is challenged,[33] argues Richard Garb.

Another apparent and realistic reason for composing this work would be to rediscover the essence of the *Vedas* and the *Upaniṣads* and thereby to bring unity in the *Vedānta*, though explicitly does not declare it. Despite this, he tries to graft theism in the atheistic *Sāṅkhya* and weds it to *Yoga*.

The *Vijñānāmṛtabhāṣyam* or *the Commentary on the Elixir of Wisdom,* as literally translated, is a commentary on the *Brahmasūtras* of Bādarāyaṇa. Vijñānabhikṣu has a long commentary on the first five *sūtras* (*pañcasūtri*)[34] which are very crucial to determine the metaphysics.

The saddest factor of such a monumental work which gives ample space for every religious tradition, social unity and integration is not yet known to the general public due to the unavailability of the translation. John W. Borelli made a conscious effort in 1976 to translate one of the *sūtras* of the first section, that is, VAB 1.1.2 in his Doctoral Dissertation entitled, "*The Theology of Vijñānabhikṣu: A Translation of His Commentary on Brahma Sūtras 1.1.2 and an Exposition of His Difference-in-Identity Theology,*" submitted to Fordham University in New York. This opened up the possibility of delving deeper into the significance of Vijñānabhikṣu's writings. The same year Jadunath Sinha published the *Philosophy of Vijñānabhikṣu* in India. The third publication is *Integral Non-Dualism: A Critical Exposition of Vijñānabhikṣu's System of Philosophy*, by Kanshi Ram in 1995. This is the first book published on the key-concepts of Vijñānabhikṣu, *Avibhāga-Bhedābheda.* The misleading title is due to the English rendering of it. These books authenticate Vijñānabhikṣu's *Avibhāgādvaita* through certain concepts like the Absolute, Self, *prakṛti*, epistemology and ethics. But, this too is in line with the second one. As a result, a clear picture of the *Brahmasūtras* cannot be attained from this work. The fourth publication is by Andrew J. Nicholson in 2001 titled, *Unifying Hinduism: Philosophy and Identity in*

Indian Intellectual History. Then again, this book dedicates only one chapter for the *Avibhāga-Bhedābheda* to propose this concept as a viable solution to the integrity of the culture and traditions of India.

Apart from these, directly and indirectly, composed works on the *Vijñānāmṛtabhāṣyam*, we have dearth of resources for our research in any language other than the original Sanskrit text. There are two versions of the edited Sanskrit texts on the *Vijñānāmṛtabhāṣyam.* The first one is entitled, the *Brahmasūtrabhāṣyam,* edited by Mukunda Shastri in 1901 and published by Chowkhamba Publishers, under its *Sanskrit Series.* The second one is titled, *Brahmasūtra Vijñānāmṛtabhāṣyam,* edited by Kedāranatha Tripāṭhī and published by Kashi Hindu Vishvavidyalaya or Banaras Hindu University, Varanasi as the first issue of *Prācyavidyā Series* in 1979.[35]

3.2.4 Works on *Sāṅkhya*

There are two works on *Sāṅkhya*: *Sāṅkhyapravacanabhāṣyam,* a treatise on *Sāṅkyasūtra* of Kapila and *Sāṅkhyasāram,* the quintessence of *Sāṅkhya.* These works are available with English translations. Shiv Kumar has edited with its translation of *Sāṅkhyasāram* titled, *Sāmkhyasāra of Vijñānabhikṣu* and published by the Eastern Books Linkers of Delhi in 1988.[36] Earlier, Richard Garb has abridged the *Sāṅkhyapravacanabhāṣyam* named, *Sāṅkhya-Pravacana-Bhāṣya* and published by Harvard University in 1895.[37] Fitz-Edward Hall has written a separate introduction to this work.[38] Besides these, the Sānkhya work has also been translated by Nandalal Sinha along with other *Sāṅkhya* commentaries.[39] Recently, Anima Sen Gupta, a renowned *Sāṅkhya* scholar has written several works basing on the *Sāṅkhya* of Kapila[40] as commented by Vijñānabhikṣu in these works.[41]

3.2.5 Works on *Yoga*

There are two works on *Yoga*: *Yogavārttika,* a treatise on *Yogasūtras* of Pātāñjali and *Yogasārasaṅgraha*, the collection of the quintessence of *Yogabhāṣya of Vyāsa.* The first and only complete English translation of *Yogavārttika* with critical notes along with original *Yogasūtras* of Pātāñjali is made by T.S. Rukmani in four volumes titled, *Yogavārttika of Vijñānabhikṣu,* published by Mushiram Manoharlal Publishers in 1981.[42] This work assembles the *sūtras, bhāṣyas* and *vārttika* and proffers a great help for the research scholars in *Yoga* philosophy. The English translation of *Yogasārasaṅgraha*, a lucid explanation of the *Vyāsabhāṣya* is prepared by Ganganath Jha in 1894. Its Hindi translation is also available with two publishers.[43]

3.2.6 Tradition of Vijñānabhikṣu

Vijñānabhikṣu belongs to the *Vedāntic* tradition, in particular the *Bhedābheda* tradition. Within the *Bhedābheda* tradition, he advocates *Avibhāga-Bhedābheda*. However, he is a *Sāṅkhya* philosopher. Therefore, he comments on the *Brahmasūtras* from *Sāṅkhya* perspective. As far as his *ācāryatva*[44] is concerned, he belongs to *Purāṇic* tradition. Quoting the *Mahābhārata,* he articulates, "Vedas must be analysed with the help of *itihāsa* and *purāṇas.* If not, there is a fear of Vedas being misinterpreted."[45] That's why he has used *purāṇas* extensively in his commentary especially *Viṣṇu Purāṇa, Mārkaṇḍeya Purāṇa, Liṅga Purāṇa, Skanda Purāṇa, Padma Purāṇa,* etc. His concept of *Īśvaravāda* comes from these *purāṇas.* Among the epics, the *Mahābhārata,* particularly the *Mokṣadharmaparva* has been used very much.

What could be the reasons Vijñānabhikṣu uses epics and several *purāṇic* texts? Plausibly they are the easy gateways for theism. Theism is as old as the *Vedas* themselves. *Vedas* testify a kind of devotion, piety and reverence to certain divine powers. *Vedānta* is the rediscovery of that truth. It may be viable because of the impersonal aspect coupled with speculation of the highest reality, termed as Brahman or '*Puruṣa,*' a theistic blend is brought in the later Vedic traditions. Still, in the later period, popular devotion and personal devotion must have become part and parcel of life. This may be the reason epic demonstrated Brahman as the matter of experiential reality and termed it in terms of *trimūtri*: Brahmā, Viṣṇu and Maheśvara. The *Gītā* is the climax of these *para* and *apara* aspects. But this seemed lost when heterodox traditions and later *Advaitic* influence reigned. Therefore, these personal aspects had to be rediscovered with the help of *purāṇic* ideals. These may be the reasons why Vijñānabhikṣu is using lots of *purāṇic* texts.

Vijñānabhikṣu's philosophical views can be best comprehended from the first five *sūtras* of *Brahmasūtra,* which he labels '*pañcasūtrī*' in contrast to *catuḥsūtri* of

Advaitins. Vijñānabhikṣu himself puts across this, "Through the path of *Vedānta* Vijñānārka [Vijñānabhikṣu] has shown what was assembled in the first five aphorisms what the former teacher has enforced."[46]

3.2.7 Presuppositions of Vijñānabhikṣu in the *Vijñānāmṛtabhāṣyam*

Before we investigate *Vijñānāmṛtabhāṣyam* and its chief doctrine, let's try to ascertain the basic stand taken by Vijñānabhikṣu. The purpose of the *Brahmasūtra* according to Vijñānabhikṣu is to propose a *Brahmamīmāṁsā siddhānta*. This can be achieved by *brahmajñāna*. In fact, *brahmajñāna* is the main element to realize *paramapuruṣārtha*. To achieve *brahmajñāna,* one needs *jijñāsā*, an intense desire to know. The *vidhi* prescribed by the scriptures declare that Brahman should be meditated upon in the form of *Ātman*. Therefore, there is a need to know the nature, state, conception, knowledge, realization, etc. of Brahman. Already *Pūrvamīmāṁsā* has spelled out the *Brahmajijñāsā*. The entire *Vedānta* teaches the means to attain *brahmajñāna*. *Sāṅkhya* enlightens *jīvacaitanya siddhānta*. But to know *caitanya* and its form, we need to study *Brahmamīmāṁsā* (VAB 1.1.1, p.1-2).

However, the *Brahmasūtras* are not composed to give a detailed analysis of *jīva-Brahmaikya* or the understanding of *jīva*, rather the truth about it. The *Bhagavadgīta* confirms this: "*brahmasūtrapadaiścaiva hetumadbhrviniścitaiḥ*"[47] (BG 13.5, VAB 1.1.1, p.16), "with sound logic and conclusive evidence the *Brahmasūtras* and the hymns explain the truth about the field and the knower of the field." The *Brahmasūtras* give an account of *Brahmasāmīpya* and *Brahmaikya*. It is not that *jīvatatva* is not explained. They are sufficiently clarified in the *sūtras* concerning *jīva*. The truth is, both *jīvā* and Brahman look similar, but they are not the same. This is because of the principle of *arthaikyata* (*ātmabrahmaśabdayor arthaikyaṁ vā*), that Brahman is declared to be *ātman, ātman* being spoken in terms of Brahman or *ātman* is equalled to Brahman. Therefore, the first presupposition of Vijñānabhikṣu is that *there is sāmyata between jīva and Brahman*. According to Apte *sāmīpya* is 'vicinity, nearness, proximity'; and *sāmya* is the resemblance, likeness, similarity.'[48] Since they resemble, it is said to be closer. *Brahmasāmīpya,* explicitly, *jīva's* closeness with Brahman and not total one-ness with Brahman is presupposed here. BS 1.1.1 does not distinctly articulate about the *akhaṇḍa aikya* between *jīva* and Brahman, but clearly states that *jīva* is one with Brahman. At the same time, BS 2.1.22 (*adhikaṁ tu bhedanirdeśāt*) clearly indicates both these are radically different. Vijñānabhikṣu's part-whole relation or *aṁśa-aṁśī sambandha* and explanation of *tattvamasi* substantiate it further.

The second presupposition is *the acceptance of the duality*. When the *jīva* loses the sense of ego (*ahambuddhiyādi nivartitobhavati*), then it recognizes the nature of Brahman (*brahmasvarūpa*), attaining knowledge (*jñāna*). At this state, *jīva* perceives itself in front of Brahman and realizes it as the *Ātman* of Brahman. The realization of *ātmatva* by *jīva* is *mokṣa* in *Sāṅkhya*. It is only *Sāṅkhya* that provides the theory of *jīvatatva*. This knowledge will enable one to understand *Pūrva Mīmāṁsā* better. *Sāṅkhya* treats knowledge, or the liberation of *puruṣa* (*jīva*), whereas *Pūrva Mīmāṁsā* deliberates about *karma*. Both are complementary to each other. At the *mokṣa*, the person accomplishes *brahmasvarūpa* and not *brahmaikya*. Thus, *Brahma-śabda* is rooted in *Sāṅkhya*. Even within the *Sāṅkhya,* the two principles—*puruṣa* (representing *jīvā*) and *prakṛti*—though eternally fused to form one, there is *bheda*, by the fact of difference.[49] Another reason for *via Sāṅkhya* is that it works very well with the *Vedānta*. According to Dasgupta, "Bhikṣu [Vijñānabhikṣu] thinks that since we do not find in the *Brahma-sūtras* any account of the origin and growth of knowledge, the *Sāṅkhya-Yoga* account of knowledge may well be accepted on account of the general affinity of the *Sāṅkhya-Yoga* ideas with the *Vedānta*."[50] Further, *Sāṅkhya* system offers a great rational explanation to various facts very satisfactorily. This can be very well seen in his commentary, for example, his explanation of *athātho* in *athāthobrahmajijñāsā* (VAB 1.1.1). While all other *ācāryas* explain it as 'what precedes and thus what succeeds,' Vijñānabhikṣu clarifies it as the authority and auspiciousness of what is going to come, the account of the knowledge of Brahman. Thus, he handles the whole *Brahmasūtras* as one complete unit (*upakramaupasaṁhāra aikya*).

The third presupposition is *the divine prerogative of inter-penetration of Brahman in the creation* by bringing *puruṣa* to the vicinity of *prakṛti*[51] as *saṁyoga* that takes place in the case of husband and wife in their sexual congress or like a magnet that attracts metal (*ayaskāntena lohavat*, VAB 1.1.2, p.18). When both these *tatvas* of *Sāṅkhya* come closer, they form an intimate union, maximum possible absorption into the divine essence (*sāyujya*) like a magnet with iron. However, they don't become one complete essence. The amalgamation is such that they appear as one, in other words, 'a complete inter-penetration.' This is shown even by different scriptural statements like *Śvetāśvatara Upaniṣad* 6.5, Kūrma Purāṇa 4.13, *Viṣṇu Purāṇa* 1.2.27, etc.[52] Thus, though Brahman and *jīva* inter-penetrate each other, they do keep the distinction between them, leading to a *Bhedābheda* relation.

Summary

Three things seem to have had a great impact on the philosophical thinking of Vijñānabhikṣu: his religious convictions, the impact of *bhakti* tradition in society, and the political situation of the time. This was also the time society saw syncretism in literature and socio-religious practices. A lot of social awareness against the unjust structures was part of the general conscience of learned people. Surely, these things have influenced in shaping the tradition and philosophy Vijñānabhikṣu, which will be seen in the next chapter.

The reaction towards the over-emphasis of ritualism and social structures existed during the *Upaniṣadic* time. The emergence of Buddhism and Jainism is part of that reaction. However, the growing conscientization and search for the divine in communion with society resulted in *bhakti* movement in the medieval period. Later, the interruption of new socio-religious thinking and at times over-turning certain religious set-patterns threatened the organic unity of Hinduism. In this background, Vijñānabhikṣu makes his novel contribution that Hinduism known from ancient times is an accommodating religion and need for another creed or tradition not an answer for the problem. Vijñānabhikṣu's presuppositions in the *Vijñāmṛtabhāṣyam* establish this fact. *Brahmamīmāṁsā* establishes the truth about "the field and the knower of the field," the sacred and secular in terms of part and whole relation. Plurality is part of reality. But it has to be understood that divine interpenetration in the creation is that which organically binds into one single whole. This will be further clarified in the next chapter.

---

[1] S.W. Jamison and M. Witzel, "Vedic Hinduism" (Harward: Harvard University, 1992). Book online, available on http://www.people.fas.harvard.edu/~witzel/vedica.pdf, accessed on 10 October, 2018.

[2] Geoffrey Samuel, *The Origins of Yoga and Tantra: Indic Religions to the Thirteenth Century* (Cambridge: Cambridge University Press, 2008), 113.

[3] Vijay Nath, "From 'Brahmanism' to 'Hinduism': Negotiating the Myth of the Great Tradition," *Social Scientist* 29, no. 3-4 (March-April 2001): 26-28. For more detailed discussions on these issues, see, Vijay Nath, "From 'Brahmanism' to 'Hinduism': Negotiating the Myth of the Great Tradition," in *Proceedings of the Indian History Congress* (New Delhi: Indian History Congress, 2001); Bhairabi Prasad Sahu, "Brahmanical Ideology, Regional Identities and the Construction of Early India," *Social Scientist* 29, no. 7-8 (July-August 2001); Wendy Doniger, *The Hindus: An Alternative History*, 2015 ed. (New Delhi: Speaking Tiger Publishing Private Limited, 2009).

[4] One of the reasons for the decline of Buddhism is the militant

missionary zeal of *Vedāntic* thinkers of the medieval period. For more details read, K.T.S. Sarao, *The Decline of Buddhism in India: A Fresh Perspective* (New Delhi: Munshiram Manoharlal Publishers, 2012).

[5] Varan Vardhan, "Buddhist Compassion Towards Other Religions," in *Melodies from the Flute: Dialogue among Religions and Cultures: Memorial Volume for Indian Christian Philosopher Rev. Noel Sheth S.J*, edited by Kuruvilla Pandikattu and Thomas Karimundackal, JDV Philosophy Series (Pune: Jnana-Deepa Vidyapeeth and Christian World Imprints, 2018), 299-301.

[6] *Islamification* is a process where the society is reshuffling towards Islam as found in the countries like Pakistan, Iran, Malaysia, Algeria, etc. In the present context, it can refer to a perceived imposition of Islamic ideals on the society.

[7] *Vedārthasaṅgraha,* 238. Also see, *Śri Bhāṣya* 1.1.1.

[8] The city is also called Vāraṇāsi probably due to two rivers: Varuna and Assi, the tributaries of the river Ganga. The people of ancient India knew it by the popular name, Kāśī. Word *kāśī* is referred mainly to emphasize the traditional aspects of the city. Scholars trace the earliest description of the city to the late Vedic times (1400-1000 BCE), and regard it as one of the first Aryan settlements in the middle Gangetic Valley. Several texts refer to this city. Some of them are: *Jābalo'paniṣad, Skandha Smṛti, Parasara Smṛti, Mahābhārata, Rāmāyaṇa, Devī Bhāgavata, Sanatkumāra Purāṇa, Liṅga Purāṇa, Matsya Purāṇa*, etc. Surender Mohan Bhardwaj, *Hindu Places of Pilgrimage in India: A Study in Cultural Geography* (Berkeley: University of California Press, 1973), 5-6.

[9] Equally, the South India soil is rich in Bhakti. The Ālvars, the Nāyanārs, Basavaṇṇa, Allama Prabhu, Akka Mahādevī, Purandara Dāsa, Kanaka Dāsa, Tukārām, etc. saints had a great deal of impact in the society.

[10] Emilia Bachrach, "In the Seat of Authority: Debating Temple Spaces and Community Identity in a Vaiṣṇava Sampradāy of Contemporary Gujarat," *Journal of Hindu Studies* 10, no. 1 (2017): 20.

[11] Doniger, *The Hindus: An Alternative History*, 528. Original parenthesis.

[12] John Keay, *India, a History* (New York: Grove Publications, 2000), 316-17.

[13] Doniger, *The Hindus: An Alternative History*, 532.

[14] Satish Chandra, *History of Medieval India*, 2018 ed. (Hyderabad: Orient Blackswan Private Limited, 2007), 251-54.

[15] Doniger, *The Hindus: An Alternative History*, 548-49.

[16] Dominik Wujastyk, "Change and Creativity in Early Modern Indian Medical Thought," *Journal of Indian Philosophy* 33, no. 1 (February 2005): 110-11.

[17] *"śūdraśabdo atra śūdra jātiparo na bhavati, kintu śūdrakāryakāritvād upacarati iti. sūtrayojanāt evaṁ kāryā – hi śabdo'atrāvadhāraṇe.... yasmāt asya adhikāriṇo jānaśruteḥ svasya anādaraśravaṇāt yā śuk śoka utpannaḥ sa eva raikvena sūcyate. arthāt śūdraśabdena śūdrasya eva mānāvamānayorharṣaviṣādau jāyate na brāhmaṇasya samadṛṣṭer iti."* VAB 1.3.34, p.122. *"śrutyantare "taṁ hopaninya" ityādinā na śūdraśabdo atra mukhyaḥ."* VAB 1.3.36, p.123. *"śrutyantare ca śiṣyasya śūdratva abhāva avadhāraṇo satya eva upadeṣārtham guroḥ pravṛtti darśanāccet iti arthaḥ."* VAB 1.3.37, p.123.

[18] Śrīvāstava, *Ācārya Vijñānabhikṣu Aur Bhāratīya Darśan Me Unkā Sthān*, 21.

[19] Jadunath Sinha, *The Philosophy of Vijnanabhikshu* (Calcutta: Sinha Publishing House, 1976), 1.

[20] Ramakrishna Acharya, *Brahmasūtron Ke Vaiṣṇav-Bhāṣyon Kā Tulanātmak Adhyayan* (Agra: Vinod Pustak Mandir, 1960), 24.

[21] Rao, *The Śrīkara Bhāṣya*, 153.

[22] Vijñānabhikṣu, *Yogasārasaṅgraha of Vijñānabhikṣu*, 10.

[23] Borelli, "The Theology of Vijñānabhikṣu," 3.

[24] Rao, *The Śrīkara Bhāṣya*, 154.

[25] Vijñānabhikṣu, *Brahmasūtra Vijñānāmṛtabhāṣyam*, 12.

[26] For the complete discussion see, Śrīvāstava, *Ācārya Vijñānabhikṣu Aur Bhāratīya Darśan Me Unkā Sthān*, 22-45. Also see the preface of Tripāṭhi, *Brahmasūtra Vijñānāmṛtabhāṣyam*, 13.; P.K. Gode, "The Chronology of Vijñānabhikṣu and His Disciple Bhāvāgaṇeśa, the Leader of the Citpāvan Brahmins of Benaras," *Adyar Library Bulletin* 7 (February, 1944).; Ram, *Integral Non-Dualism*, 2-14.

[27] See, Śrīvāstava, *Ācārya Vijñānabhikṣu Aur Bhāratīya Darśan Me Unkā Sthān*.; Gode, "Chronology of Vijñānabhikṣu."; Ram, *Integral*

Non-Dualism.; Vijñānabhikṣu, *Yogavārttika of Vijñānabhikṣu*, translated by T.S. Rukmani, vol.1 (Munshiram Manoharlal Publishers: New Delhi, 1981), Introduction, 4-14.; T.S. Rukmani, "Vijñānabhikṣu: A Maverick Philosopher," *Journal of Indian Council of Philosophical Research* 24, no. 4 (October-December 2007): 131-132.

[28] Here, the context refers to the secondary meaning of the term '*brahman*.' He goes on explaining *tattvamasi* in detail by means of the relationship between supporter and supported as *tat* and *tvam*. And finally he testifies that, "Further discussion on this can be seen in my book the *Upadeśaratnamāla*." *adhikaṁ tu upadeśaratnamālākhyaprakaraṇe dṛṣṭavyam*. VAB 1.1.2, p.32. "More on this will be discussed in the *upadeśaratnamāla*."

[29] See the introduction, Vijñānabhikṣu, *Brahmasūtra Vijñānāmṛtabhāṣyam*, 13.

[30] Narayana Kumar Chattopadhyay, *Indian Philosophy – Its Exposition in the Light of Vijñānabhikṣu's Bhāṣya and Yogavārttika* (Sanskrit Pustak Bhandar: Calcutta, 1979), iii.

[31] Ram, *Integral Non-Dualism*, 13.

[32] Here, the wrong teachers meant the traditional Advaitins and the proponents of Heterodox systems of Indology.

[33] *brahma-mīmāṁsāyām kenā'pi sūtreṇa'vidyā-mātrato bandhasyā'nuktatvāt; "avibhāgo vacanād ityādi sūtrair brahma-mīmāṁsāyā. abhipretasayā'vibhāgalakṣaṇā'dvāitasyā'vidyādi vāstavatve api avirodhāc ca. yat tu vedānta-brūvāṇām ādhunikasya māyāvādasyā'tra liṅgaṁ dṛṣyate tat teṣāma api vijñānavādyeka-deṣitayā yuktameva.* Vijñānabhikṣu, *Sāṅkhya Pravacanabhāṣya*, edited by Richard Garbe, Harward Oriental Series, vol. 2 (Cambridge: Harward University Press, 1895), 16.

[34] However, the other *Vedāntic* thinkers form first four *sūtras* and call them *catuḥsūtrī*.

[35] Mukunda Shastri, (ed.), *Vijñānāmṛtabhāṣyam*, Chowkhmaba Sanskrit Series (Banaras: Chowkhamba Publishers, 1901). Kedāranātha Tripāṭhī. (ed.), *Brahmasūtra Vijñānāmṛtabhāṣyam*, Prācyavidyā Series (Varanasi: Banaras Hindu University, 1979). I have made use of the second book in my research for all the quotes and text, though the first one is also consulted.

[36] Vijñānabhikṣu, *Sāṁkhyasāra*, translated by Shiv Kumar (Delhi:

Eastern Book Linkers, 1988).

[37] Vijñānabhikṣu, *Sāṅkhya Pravacanabhāṣya*, edited by Richard Garbe, 2 Vols. Harward Oriental Series (Cambridge: Harward University Press, 1895).

[38] Fitz-Edward Hall, *Sāṅkhyasāra: A Treatise of Sāṅkhya Philosophy* (Calcutta: Asiatic Society of Bengal, 1862). Fitz-Edward Hall, *An Introduction to Sāṅkhya-Pravacana-Bhāṣya: A Commentary on the Aphorisms of the Hindu Atheistic Philosophy*, 1979 ed. (Delhi: Bharatiya Book Corporation, 1855).

[39] Nandalal Sinha (trans.), *The Sāṃkhya Philosophy: Containing Sāṃkhya-Pravacanasūtram, with the Vṛitti of Aniruddha, and the Bhāṣya of Vijñānabhikṣu and Extracts from the Vṛittisāra of Mahādeva Vedāntin; Tatvasamāsa; Sāṃkhyakārikā; Pañchaśikhāsūtram*. 1979 ed. (Delhi: Munshiram Manoharlal Publishers, 1862). I have retained the original spelling in the title.

[40] The Sāṅkhya has great impact in Indian philosophy. Among its classical treatise only few have survived censure by the various theistic schools. Other treatise are either extinct or have survived only in few fragments. They are *Sāṅkhyapravacanasūtram* with two commentaries by Vijñānabhikṣu and Aniruddha, *Kapila Sūtram*, *Saṅkhyakārika* of Īśvarakṛṣṇa and *Pañcasikha Sūtram*. The object of this philosophy is to differentiate between soul and non-soul. It starts with the primordial cause, unconscious *prakṛti* or *pradhāna* and *puruṣa*, the conscious principle, resulting in effect this world and beings. It explains the theory of evolution of both animate and inanimate objects and the world as an infinite number of permutations and combinations of three *guṇas* – *sattva*, *tamas* and *rajas*. It opposes *Vedic* sacrifice but not *Vedas*, therefore this is placed under *āstika darśana*, the orthodox systems of Indian philosophy. Though it does not deny God, it accepts the inability to prove His existence.

For more details on the evolution in *Sāṅkhya*, see the Appendix 1.

[41] Anima Sen-Gupta, *The Evolution of the Samkhya School of Thought* (Patna: Anima Sen-Gupta, 1953). Anima Sen-Gupta, *Essays on Sāṁkhya and Other Systems of Indian Philosophy: Part 1 and 2* (New Delhi: Munshiram Manoharlal Publishers, 1977). Anima Sen Gupta, *Classical Samkhya: A Critical Study* (Patna: Anima Sen Gupta, 1969). Besides these, there are number of articles published in national and

international journals.

[42] T.S. Rukmani, *Yogavārttika of Vijñānabhikṣu*, 4 vols. (New Delhi: Munshiram Manoharlal Publishers 1981).

[43] Vijñānabhikṣu, *Yogasārasaṅgraha of Vijñānabhikṣu*, translated by Ganganath Jha (Bombay: Bombay theosophical Publication, 1894). Vijñānabhikṣu, *Yogasārasaṅgraha of Vijñānabhikṣu: Edited and Revised Edition with Sanskrit Text and English Translation*, translated by Ganganath Jha, revised ed. (Delhi: Parimal Publications, 1995). Vijñānabhikṣu, *Yogasārasaṅgraha: Mūla Hindi Anuvāda Evaṁ Vistṛta Vyākhyā Sahita*, translated by Pavana Kumari (Delhi: Eastern Book Ltd., 1981). Vijñānabhikṣu, *Yogasārasaṅgraha: Hindi Vyākhyā Sahita*, translated by Sudhāṃśu Kumāra Saḍhaṅgī (Delhi: Bharatiya Vidya Prakashan, 2010). Vijñānabhikṣu, *Yogasārasaṅgraha of Vijñānabhikṣu*.

[44] To be an *ācārya,* one has to write a commentary each on *prasthānatrayī*: one each on Bādarāyaṇa's *Brahmasūtra*, any one of the *Upaniṣads* and the *Bhagavad Gītā*. For Vijñānabhikṣu *Avadhūta Gīta* is the '*Bhagavad Gītā*.'

[45] *"itihāsapurāṇābhyāṁ vedaṁ samupabṛṁhayet. bibhetyalpaśrutād vedo māmayaṁ prahariṣyati"* (MB, 1.1.267, 1.1.204). VAB 2.1.1, p.142.

[46] *"pañcasūtryāṁ samāsena pūrvācāryeiḥ pravartitaḥ. vedāntanagarī mārge vijñānārkeṇa darśitaḥ."* VAB 1.1.5, p.75.

[47] *asya śāstrasya jīvabrahmaikyaṁ viṣayaḥ, tajjñānasya can a karmaśeṣatvamiti tadapi na, asya śāstrasya jīvabrahmaikyaviṣayatve liṅgādhyabhāvāt: "brahmasūtra padaiścaiva hetu madbhihi viniścitai" riti gītāvākyena sūtrāṇāṁ brahmaviṣayatā mātra avagamāt, tathā satya "thāto jīvabrahmaikyajijñāse" tyeva sūtraṇaucityāt ca*. (BG 13.5), VAB 1.1.1, p.16. That knowledge (of the field of activities and of the knower of activities) is described by various sages in various Vedic writings, "especially in the *Brahmasūtra* and is presented with all reasoning as to cause and effect." Thus, through the words of *Gītā*, only matter concerning Brahman is understood. The truth that "that the desire for *jīva-brahman* union" is not necessarily according to *śruti*, says Vijñānabhikṣu.

[48] Apte, *The Student's Sanskrit-English Dictionary,* s.v. "sāmīpya."; Monier-Williams, *A Sanskrit English Dictionary*, s.v. "sāmīpya."

[49] *nityasaṁyukterapi vaidharmyāt jīva tad upādhidṛṣṭāntena bhedasiddhir iti.* VAB 1.1.2, p.19.

[50] Surendranath Dasgupta, *A History of Indian Philosophy*, vol. 1 (Delhi: Motilal Banarsidass, 1973), 61.

[51] *asmābhistu prakṛtipuruṣasaṁyoga īśvareṇa kriyata iti abhyupagamyate*. VAB 1.1.2, p.18.

[52] *"ādiḥ sa saṁyoganimittahetuḥ parastrikālādkalo'pi dṛṣṭaḥ."* ŚU 6.5. "He is the primordial being, the cause for the union (of matter and spirit), beyond the three periods of time and also devoid of parts. *"prakṛtiṁ puruṣaṁ caiva praviśya ātmecchayā hariḥ kṣobhayāmāsa samprāpte sargakāle vyayāvyayau."* KP 4.13; VP 1.2.29. "The Lord Viṣṇu by his own desire, having entered *puruṣa* and *prakṛti* (matter and spirit), at the time of creation agitates the eternal and the non-eternal." VAB 1.1.2, p.18.

Chapter Four

THE *AVIBHĀGA-BHEDĀBHEDA* OF VIJÑĀNABHIKṢU

īśāvāsyamidaṁsarvaṁ yatkiñca jagatyāṁ jagat, tena tyaktena bhuñjīthā mā gṛdhaḥ kasyasviddhanam (*Īśa Upaniṣad*, 1).

The Lord pervades in all things whatsoever exist in this universe and the universe itself. So one requires to savour one's life by abandonment without coveting anybody's wealth. The *Amṛtabindu Upaniṣad* too echoes this in the same manner, "I am That on which is the abode of all beings and also who lives in all beings by being gracious to all. I am that Vāsudeva—one residing in all, I am that Vāsudeva—one residing in all" (AbU 22).[1] Divinity is the linking element in every being. The potentiality to discover and realize lies in every sentient. Thus, there is an inseparable Oneness (*avibhāgādvaita*) in the reality.

Vijñānabhikṣu through his erudite style and coherent reasoning formulates his philosophical world-view in his commentary on the *Brahmasūtras*. Unique to its kind and nature, the concept of *Avibhāga-Bhedābheda* opens up the closed gates of unification of nature, culture and tradition under one canopy. This chapter deals with his philosophy as put forth in the *Vijñānāmṛtabhāṣyam*.

4.1 The Concept of *Bhedābheda* According to the *Vijñānāmṛtabhāṣyam*

Bhedābheda is a theory of reality that distinction and unity can co-exist in an intimate relationship with each other. Substance and its attribute, part and whole, universal and particular may seem incompatible with each other, yet they can co-exist in unity.[2] Though there is a seeming contradiction and may be rejected as a fallacy, yet there is a novelty, truth and integral unity (*avibhāga*) in it.

4.1.1 Meaning of *Bhedābheda*

The term *Bhedābheda* is a composite word: *bheda* and *abheda*. The root word for *bheda* is '*bhid*' meaning 'to split, to cut into parts, to divide and to separate.' Therefore, *bheda* means 'dividing,' 'separating,' or 'breaking apart.'[3] Vijñānabhikṣu himself comments about the splitting of the word according to the root described in Pāṇini's *sūtra*: "*bhidirvidāraṇe iti vibhāge'pi bhididhātoranuśāsanāt.*"[4] Elsewhere, while explaining the two-fold characteristics of Brahman and its relationship with *jagat* and *jīva*, he underscores that the *vibhāga* and *avibhāga* should be understood from their root.[5] *Abheda* is opposite to *bheda*, distinctively, non-separation or non-division, implying unity.

Grammatically, *Bhedābheda* is a *dvandva* word wherein both *pūrvapada* and *uttarapada* are important.[6] This denotes the compound referring to an issue it signifies: both *separateness and non-separateness* as one unit. This word can be looked at in two more ways. Firstly, as *madhyamapadalopin*, a compound in which the middle term has been omitted: *non-separation (which does not exclude) separation*. Secondly, it can be known in *tatpuruṣa* which means '*identity in difference*' or '*difference in identity*.' Even if one separates the words by a hyphen, the meaning would change substantially. Therefore, the right way to comprehend the compound is as *dvandva samāsa*: *difference and non-difference*. This would preserve the meaning the *Vijñānāmṛtabhāṣyam* has intended.

According to Vijñānabhikṣu, the statements of *bheda* and *abheda* can be grasped in two ways:

i. As *tādātmya* and *anyonyābhāva*: identity and mutual absence from Nyāya perspective.

ii. As *vibhāga* and *Avibhāga*: separation and non-separation (divisible and indivisible).

Quoting the *Viṣṇupurāṇa* (VP 6.4.44), Vijñānabhikṣu unravels the *avibhāga* in terms of *avibhakta* (*abheda*) and *vibhakta* (*bheda*). Before the creation, *puruṣa* was in *avibhakta* state, during the existence it is in *vibhakta* state.[7]

By adopting this interpretation, it is possible to spell out the statements of *bheda* and *abheda*, appearing in the *Vedas* without subordinating one another. The problem with the *modernists*[8] is that they understand these terms as *univocally* and not as *equivocally*.[9] They have (referring to *Kevala Advaitins*) identified *avibhāga* to be only *tādātmya* at the conscious level or the subtle level (*cinmātra*) or the level of knowledge (*jīvasya brahmatvaṁ jñānakalpitam* VAB 1.2.2, p.20). The distinction between *avibhāga* and *tādātmya* lies in the fact that the former exists even in the stage of dissolution whereas the latter exists only when cause and effect are explicitly manifested and strictly determined. Vijñānabhikṣu discerns *Bhedābheda* in equivocal terms. Therefore, the word *avibhāga* imparts a *viśeṣaṇa sambandha* for it.

He establishes this fact basing on the scriptural statements. There are statements speaking *akhaṇḍatva* and *vibhāgatva*. If through *abhedavākya* one can establish the *aupādhika bhedaparatva* of *bhedavākya*, why not establish *avibhāga bhedābheda* through both *bheda* and *abheda śruti*? Therefore, it is possible to prove both *bheda* and *abheda* (VAB 1.1.2, p.21), argues Vijñānabhikṣu. But Vijñānabhikṣu does not explain how to resolve *aupādhika bhedaparatva* in *bhedavākyas*.

4.1.2 Nuances of the Translation

Bhedābheda has been translated differently by different people. John W. Borelli and Jose Pereira translate it as 'difference-in-identity,' while Jadunath Sinha as difference-cum-non-difference and Andrew F. Nicholson as 'difference and non-difference.'[10]

Translation of Borelli and Pereira is influenced by the thinkers like Bonaventure, Spinoza and Hegel. Echoing Bonaventurian tone, Pereira quotes, "for, the indivision is unity; however, unity exists in the originating and in the originated, in universals and in particulars in the will and in the nature. Unity in the originating is simplicity; in the opposite or in the originated it is wholeness or fullness... in the will it is unanimity; and in nature it is separability." At this instant, he testifies, that "already the language of

Difference-in-Identity is reconcilable."[11] The rendition of Borelli and Pereira is substantial enough to show the organic unity (*akhaṇḍatva*) of the reality. Secondly, this translation considers the *Bhedābheda* word as a *saptami tatpuruṣa* compound. But the fact is, they somehow show importance to one approach, either difference or identity, and not both. Thus it lacks the spirit with which Vijñānabhikṣu understands. Jadunath Sinha's and Nicholson's translations offer us an equivocal approach to demonstrate the importance of different meanings co-existing in a common system giving credence to both polarities. Further, it goes along with the grammatical nuances that we have seen earlier. Therefore, the latter pair is preferred over the former.

But one thing is obvious from both the translations that the concept denotes complexity of the reality: *absolutely one and absolutely many*. The absolute has a self-differentiating unity in itself and at the same time self-manifesting unity. The subject is objectified (*tvameva tat*) and the object is subjectified (*tat tvameva*). The object and subject become non-self to others and are inter-related. In other words, a true absolute is immanent in the finite and is at home in itself with its other. The finite as a finite is contingent and it becomes real due to the presence of infinite in the finite.

4.1.3 Non-Contradiction of the Contradictory Term

At the outset, the concept *Bhedābheda* seems to be an oxymoron.[12] In fact, Richard Garb has accused Vijñānabhikṣu as a syncretist. To put it in his words, "Vijñānabhikṣu mixes up many [other] heterogeneous matters, and even quite often effaces the individuality of the several philosophical systems. Indeed, he maintains that all the six orthodox systems contain *in their principal dogmas* the absolute truth."[13] This could be a drawback in understanding the original meaning. Srinivasachari indicates, "to some a direct violation of the law of contradiction and is to be rejected as a fallacy... to others the theory, helped probably by its paradoxical character makes an irresistible appeal."[14]

Generally, difference and non-difference appear to be equivalent to the philosophical position, 'p and not-p.' Applying the law of contradiction (*vyāghāt niyam*), an object cannot be at the same time 'p and not p,' i.e., an object cannot be both difference and non-difference simultaneously in a locus. Understanding in this way is nothing but understanding it in the Jain epistemological way, *anekāntavāda*. In fact, Vedānta Deśika has already labeled Bhāskara to be so, "Vedāntin who smells like Jaina."[15] Once again, this is a wrong understanding of Jaina philosophy. Jainism never claims that reality is contradictory; rather it articulates that reality can be apprehended in several ways.

The expression *Bhedābheda* generally appeals to both 'distinction' and 'unity' which can co-exist and be in intimate relation with each other. When one observes the Reality, one can find that substance and attribute, universal and particular, whole and parts may seem different from or even opposed to each other, but there is no incompatibility between them. This is because unity pervades the difference and is its very being.

Bhedābheda not only bridges the apparent illogical terminologies but also brings together the contradictory philosophical positions. Nicholson says that the *Bhedābheda* is "bridging the apparently unbridgeable disagreements between philosophers who subscribe to the theory of difference (or dualism, *dvaita*) and complete, unqualified non-difference (non-dualism, *Advaita*)."[16] Nicholson is in search of a unifying tradition in Hinduism. And this statement comes as a result of his research. The bridging feature becomes clear when one reads Vijñānabhikṣu's works on the *Sāṅkhya*, the *Yoga* and the *Brahmasūtras.*

The terms *bheda* and *abheda* are not contradictory rather they are complementary. Light gets its significance in the reality of its opposition, the darkness. Similarly, the reality of Brahman becomes meaningful only when the non-Brahman entity is assumed. Therefore, the relational aspect is vital to the Reality. Here in *Bhedābheda,* the words may appear or connote *vijātīyatva,* but in their essence, they do have something common to present them *sajātīya,* like *tat* and *tvam* in *tattvamasi,* and yet remain distinct. Contradiction takes place between two things when the same meaning is juxtaposed in the same locus at the same time. In the word '*bhedābheda*' they may appear contradictory, but not semiotically. Therefore, contradiction is apparent and not real.

4.1.4 Vijñānabhikṣu's Answer to the Critiques

The *Brahma-Mīmāṁsā* or the *Uttara-Mīmāṁsā* concerns

the nature of Brahman, and it distinguishes itself from the *Pūrva-Mīmāṁsā,* pertaining to the performance of rituals. The prime interest of both is the interpretation of the *Vedas.* Both the schools accept a basic principle of interpretation—*ekavākyata—Vedas* as *one complex sentence having a single message*. Going further, Vijñānabhikṣu claims that the scriptures, both *smṛti* and *śruti* are interwoven into one complex whole. Therefore, when one reads scripture, one should read the divine thread flowing in all, "*śrutismṛti eka vākyatvāt,*" namely, "*śruti* and *smṛti* form one complex sentence." "*Śrutismṛti eka vākyatvāt*" (VAB 1.1.4, p.59). Of course, the discussion here in the VAB is to show that the *Brahmasūtras* are in fact proposing an *Avibhāga-Bhedābheda* tradition. Therefore, Vijñānabhikṣu is showing *śruti-smṛti aikyata* . Vijñānabhikṣu quoting *śruti* text enunciates, "Knowing Brahman is all, knowing self is all, what was is all He, what was in the past is He, verily not many in any."[17] Thus, whatever the material world does, having the divine within, proclaims the unity of Brahman. Further, he validates that the same thing is true of *smṛti* as well.

The knowledge of this *one-ness* arrives from the *śabda* as the primary source of knowledge, "*śāstraṁ yonirmūlapramāṇam*" (VAB 1.1.3, p.36). Given this, one cannot insist on the message of the Veda as only *bheda* or *abheda*. If so, one is against the *śruti* itself. The *Vedas* as *śruti* ought to be preferred over *smṛti.*[18] "*Śruti* is the basis of the valid source of knowledge."[19] Only the *Bhedābheda* executes the above task. Therefore, there is no contradiction in the concept.

For the Advaitins, only those sentences are real which exhibit *tādātmya* between *ātman* and *Brahman*. For them, the space inside the pot and the space outside the pot are the same, due to uniformity. That is, "The soul to be Brahman because of the uniformity of pure consciousness." Vijñānabhikṣu accuses Śaṅkara who considers only those statements as true which show the *Jīva-Brahman* relation: "You are that, I am Brahman, having entered by means of this, the soul, name and form are differentiated, there is no perceiver other than He." Majesty and bondage are two qualities which serve as conditions, says Vijñānabhikṣu.[20]

But there are also other statements that suggest *jīva* is not identical with Brahman. Vijñānabhikṣu furnishes the following *Upaniṣadic* statements: two birds like friends sitting on a tree (MuU 3.1.1); of all eternals, there is only one who is the Chief Eternal. Of all conscious living entities, there is only one who is the chief conscious entity. That supreme living entity, the personality of Godhead, preserves the others, gratifying their desires according to their merits (KaU 2.2.13); the wise who perceive Him seated within their self, to them belongs eternal bliss and not to others (KaU 5.13); he who resides in the self, but other than the self, soul like living in three worlds as enjoyment, an enjoyer and enjoyment, as pure consciousness, I as witness to ever living. Thus, we have several statements of logical inherences and so, one is obliged to accept the *upādhis*,[21] insists Vijñānabhikṣu.

The opponents argue, 'the statements of *bheda* contradict the statements of *abheda* due to *upādhis*, the artificial conditions.' Vijñānabhikṣu questions the claim itself, 'why they don't claim that the statements of *abheda* contradict the statements of *bheda* only is because they refer to *abheda* in the form of non-separation?' Therefore, he conveys, 'Non-contradiction is possible.'[22]

Vijñānabhikṣu now puts forward some texts from both *śruti* and *smṛti* to demonstrate the existence of both *bheda* and *abheda* at different times and not simultaneously. The difference and non-difference of part and whole, in the form of separation and non-separation, is not contradiction since it refers to differences at different times. But the mutual non-existence of the self and the Brahman is permanent, and the non-separation of the power and the power-possessor is permanent.[23] Therefore, there is no contradiction at all.

Avibhāga can be explained in the form of *abheda*. It is like the pure water poured into water, so is the *ātman* of the learned seer. It is neither a second nor is it different from that which is divided or undivided within. That which is existing, stands as divided, whether manifestingly or unmanifestingly is the Supreme Being.[24]

Advaitins are busy authenticating only the expression of *tādātyma* between *ātman* and *Brahman* and all other statements as false. In reality, Vijñānabhikṣu does not consider it so. *Vibhāga* is the primary meaning of *bheda,* and not its figurative meaning. Therefore, *vibhāga* can be understood as *anonyābhāva* from *Nyāyā* perspective. Separation is only a transitory state. The fundamental state between *Brahman* and *ātman* is *avibhāga*.

4.1.5 *Tattvamasi* According to Vijñānabhikṣu

According to Vijñānabhikṣu, the *Advaitins* reckon that Brahman and *ātman* as principle referents by differently equating the power of God (*māyā*) with *avidyā* (ignorance) in order to explain the absolute unity (*akhaṇḍa aikya*) like the space outside the pot and inside being the space as same (VAB 1.1.2, p.20) because the perceivable objects of the phenomenal world are not real. The *Catuḥsūtrī* of Śaṅkara thus relays, "The real nature of the Self [*ātman*], as revealed in the *Upaniṣad* is being one with the Brahman constitute the subject matter of *brahma-jijñāsā*."[25] Consequently, for them, *ātman* or *tvam* of *tattvamasi* is Brahman or *tat* (VAB 1.1.2, p.20). Therefore, *tattvamasi* is 'Thou **art** that' (*tat-tvam-asi*). Conversely, for the *Bhedavādins* like Madhva who propose mutual exclusiveness as the supreme truth and *bheda* and *abheda* having no basis in *śruti*,[26] consider *ātman* (*tvam*) cannot be Brahman (*tat*), and therefore, 'Thou art **not** that' (***a***-*tat-tvam-asi*). We have dealt with this in the first chapter, under the title *tattvamasi*. Now, let us see how Vijñānabhikṣu understands *tattvamasi*.

Vijñānabhikṣu writes that "The purport of the *mahāvākya* is neither to teach *Brahma-ātma* or *Brahma-jīva aikya*, nor to denote the words '*tvam*' and '*aham*' as *ātman*. Basically, the *mahāvākyas* '*tattvamasi*,' '*ahaṁ brahmāsmi*,' '*so'yam*,' etc. teach the divine essence or the spiritual nature of the Supreme Being."[27] This requires to be understood from the context (*prakaraṇa saṅgati*). This is the teaching of the *Vedānta*. If the context is not taken into consideration, then the texts will appear contradictory.[28] Only *aṁśa-aṁśī sambandha* can give the purport of the *Vedānta*. This does not indicate that Vijñānabhikṣu is not explaining *tattvamasi*. He defines it as 'Thou art **in** That.'

This claim comes closer to Rāmānuja's Viśiṣṭādvaita and Vallabha's *Śuddhādvaitic* interpretation of *tattvamasi*. If Rāmānuja interprets it as 'You are His part' or 'You are God's part,' Vallabha interprets it as 'you are in essence God' or 'Soul is an essence of Brahman.' This is because Vallabha splits *tattvamasi* into two parts: *tattvam* and *asi*, where *tattva* refers to the essence or state of *tat* (*Brahmanhood*). *Tvam* in *tattvamasi* does not refer to the second person singular form but a termination conveying the sense of state added to *tat*. The meaning, therefore, is that the soul is an essence of Brahman as its part or *aṁśa*.[29]

According to Vijñānabhikṣu, Brahman is not the same as *ātman* in the primary meaning. The primary meaning of the word '*brahman*' refers only to Supreme Being. However, it can also refer to *Ātman*, but only in the secondary sense (*gauṇārtha*). Just as the word '*paṅkaja*' popularly refers to lotus, and in the secondary sense from its etymology, that is, that which is mud-born; so too, Brahman can mean something specific as well as something general.[30] Generally, the word *brahman* alludes to the Highest Being. He is qualified positively by his attributes of greatness and negatively by without imperfections. Even in the primary meaning, there is a distinction between primary[31] and secondary meaning regarding the word '*brahman*.' The former refers to the Supreme Being (*Parabrahman*) and the latter to the Lower Being (*Aparabrahman*). The secondary sense also can imply to the beings like *hiraṇyagarbha, puruṣa, ātman, jīva*, creator, individual soul, and so on (VAB p.20,35,36). Therefore, when *tat* is referred to *tvam*, it means *tat* finds its proximity to *tvam* only in the secondary sense. Even though *ātman* is understood to be equal to Brahman, yet they cannot become one ultimate reality, just as butter and milk cannot be one. Butter in essence is from milk, yet they aren't the same.

What would happen if Brahman were to have only one meaning? Brahman is tranquility, without passions, without any conditioned activity, not like perceiving nothing someone in deep sleep, omniscient, qualityless, and eternal. It is free of contact with any qualities or the qualities are totally dissolved, distinct from any *jīvas* and all-knowing.[32] Quite the opposite, *jīva* and *jagat* are tainted by the impurities of *karma* and stained by modifications. If *Ātman* and Brahman were to be the same, then Brahman should be the cause of misery, pain and joy in the world. This cannot be the case. All the *kleśakarmavipākāśaya* (the impurities) are the characteristics of *prakṛti,* caused due to the union of *puruṣa* with *prakṛti*. The qualityless being (*nirguṇa Brahman*) cannot be the cause of misery. Therefore, Brahman cannot be *Ātman*. Though they cannot be totally one, there is something common to both because of which they are known to be one.

As a result, the question emerges at once, "why do we say

there is *Brahmanhood* in *Ātman?*"[33] The answer to this question leads us to view *tat* as *tvam*. *Parabrahman* cannot be *ātman, jīva* or *jagat*. Brahman is the *adhiṣṭhānakāraṇa*, the supporting cause of everything or the *mūlakaraṇa*, the root cause[34] (like *pradhāna* in *nirīśvara* Sāṅkhya). As having the nature of witness, it sustains *prakṛti*. However, it is not separate from Brahman as it is a part or *aṁśa* of Brahman. *Prakṛti* and *puruṣa* are powers of Brahman. Owing to the power of Brahman (*śakti*), *prakṛti* evolves and the *sṛṣṭi* emerges.[35] Hence, deep down in the *sṛṣṭi* Brahman's penetration is always there. Since Brahman is indwelling and immortal (*ātmāntaryāmyamṛtaḥ,* BU 3.7.3), all this is verily Brahman (*etadātmyamidaṁsarvam* CU 6.8.7); and in this way, *ātman* is considered to be Brahman. Since the indwelling, immortal essence within you (*tvam*) is of Brahman and it is He (*tat*) who created you upon His base (*mūla*) by His power, that (*tat*) essence you are (*tvamasi*).

There is *brahmanhood* deeply engraved in all the *abheda mahāvākya śruti* texts. The *brahmanhood* is nothing but the divine essence or the "Spiritual nature."[36] Vijñānabhikṣu asserts the *abhedavākyas* in *mahāvākyas* as acclaimed due to their characteristics of removing ignorance. That is the general rule of such statements also. The first part of the verse containing the word *tattvamasi* in the *Chāndogya Upaniṣad* epitomizes *abheda* between a whole and its part which can lead to knowledge of the spiritual nature of Brahman. It is not that the first part of the sentence only speaks about the essence of Brahman and the latter part doesn't, rather the whole sentence speaks primarily about it.

That is the reason, Vijñānabhikṣu reminds the commentators to view the whole scripture as a unit from the "beginning till end," "*upakrama-upasaṁhāra-aikya*" (VAB 1.1.1, p.3). It is the nature of Brahman to be one with the world in its quintessence, just as the pot in essence is clay. This does not mean that pot is clay, similarly, *Ātman* and Brahman are not absolutely one. There is an *avibhāga* relationship with them. In the same way, *abhedavākyas* which give *brahmātma aikya* should be understood according to propriety and context.

How and when is this relationship understood? He posits,

> The difference and identity between souls and God, which is composed of separation and non-separation, is established through the relationship between a whole and its parts. Only non-separation, because it is co-incident, essential, and eternal, is true at the beginning and at the end. Separation, on the other hand, in the middle through a limitation of parts is temporary and of a purely nominal existence. This is the distinction.[37]

In this manner, in the beginning and end (at the *sṛṣṭi* and *praḷaya*), there is *avibhāga* between Brahman and *ātman*; and during the course of its existence in the world (*sthiti*), there is *vibhāga* as understood by *aṁśa-aṁśī sambandha*.

Vijñānabhikṣu, using this *sambandha*, explains the *mahāvākya tattvamasi* once again. *Jīvā* and Brahman differ so far as to be divided as *aṁśa* and *aṁśī*. These two cannot be called the same. Being *aṁśa* and *aṁśī* in their true forms, the *tat* and *tvam* remain different from each other,[38] yet they are mutually related. If the *ātman* is totally different from Brahman, then it will be unconscious like pot.[39] The *Bhagavad Gītā* also recounts about *avibhāga* between *aṁśī* and *aṁśa* (*tat* and *tvam*), "know that I am the conscious principle" (BG 13.2).

Tat cannot be understood without *tvam*, or a part can be understood as a part of the whole like the son is a part of the father. The question is, when do we assert Brahman and *ātman* are one? As far as divine essence is concerned (*brahmātmatāvagatiphalatvāt*) between part and whole (*tvam* and *tat*) they are one. In other words, the divine nature of the world in its essential form, before the creation and after the dissolution, is the same as that of Brahman through the relation of *avaibhāga*. That's why it is said, *ātman* is Brahman or Brahman is *ātman*, i.e., *tat* is *tvam* and *tvam* is *tat.* In short, *tat tvameva* and *tvameva tat*. This is the reason, *ātman* is considered to be the witness, chief coordinator and consciousness. In fact, these qualities are of Brahman. Since the *ātman* in essence is the divine, it acts as chief coordinator and exhibits in *tvam* and *aham* words. These words are related to each other like master-slave (*sva-svāmi bhāva avagamāt*, VAB 1.1.2, p.31). *Yama Purāṇa* discloses this in terms of the master-slave relationship between Lord Hari and his devotees respectively. They are joined together by the will of that same Lord of souls.[40]

In the perception of *ātman*, Brahman is understood. Put it differently, in the perception of *tvam*, *tat* is realized in the secondary sense of the term *brahman* (*Aparabrahman*). The

Aparabrahman is figured out to be the energy of the *Parabrahman*. This understanding is possible only through the part-whole relationship. We enunciate, consciousness (*caitanya*) is the substance of *Aparabrahman*. In the same way, *caitanya* is the very substance (*dravya*) of *ātman* and not its quality (*guṇa*). Therefore, when *ātman* is perceived, Brahman is perceived because both have the same thing as their substance (*adhiṣṭhāna*). It is like seeing fire or light, one sees simultaneously light and that which lights (VAB, p.33). Along these lines, unity is inferred.

The words 'I' and 'mine' exhibit the relationship between the possessor and possessed. At this point, they mean *ātman* and *aham* (ego) respectively, as the *Sāṅkhya* philosophy depicts. When *ātman* identifies itself with ego, it is called *jīva*. Yet again, we detect *Avibhāga Bhedābheda* here. To put it in a pictorial sense, the blackness of a crow is possessed by the crow. One can also synonymously say upon looking at 'a black crow like bird' as the crow. Once again, the relationship between *ātman* and *jīva* is something similar to this, but beyond it.

The important point to note here is the relationship represented by the word '*asi*.' Only when there is coordination between the two (for example, I and Thou or *aham* and *tvam*), it is said that I am thou or *aham* is *tvam* or *tvam* is *aham*. The activities of *ātman* are realized through speech and senses. That's the reason *prāṇa* is thought to be *ātman*. In the same way, the activities of Brahman are realized through *ātman*. *Tattvamasi* statement elucidates this fact—the coordination between *tat* and *tvam*. In the statement, *asi* represents this coordination. In the statement of *tattvamasi*, *tat* elucidates the specific sense and *tvam*, the general sense of agent and acts as a coordinator.[41]

Thus, Vijñānabhikṣu neither concurs with Śaṅkara's way of understanding *tattvamasi* nor Madhva's way. If Śaṅkara's way is taken, he has to accept the unreality of the phenomenal world which is not acceptable to Vijñānabhikṣu. Conversely, if Madhva's way is accepted, unbridled duality becomes the fact. Nevertheless, both have something unique to offer, divinity and dependence despite independence. Vijñānabhikṣu is closer to Rāmānuja. However, if his view is taken without a critique, then Vijñānabhikṣu has to accept *jīva* and *jagat* (*cit* and *acit*) as *viśeṣaṇa* (qualifying adjuncts) of Brahman, resulting in *Brahmapariṇāmavāda.* For Vijñānabhikṣu, *ātman* and *jagat* (*puruṣa* and *prakṛti*) are not the qualifying principles of Brahman, rather they are powers of it. Brahman's essential divinity is manifested in these *tatvas.* Therefore, Vijñānabhikṣu's causality is *Brahmaśaktiprakṛtipariṇāmavāda.*

4.2 The Epistemological Rendering of *Avibhāga-Bhedābheda*

If something is to be called knowledge (*jñāna*), it must be true, uncontradicted, unfalsified and eternal (*anādigata abādhitaratavişayaḥ jñānam*) and free from false knowledge (*mithyajñānam*). This is called *pramā*. Thus, *pramā* is a definite and assured knowledge (*yathārtha anubhava*) of an object which is the true representation in nature and not in similarity or semblance. *Jñāna* can be valid or invalid. The sources of *jñāna* are called *pramāṇa*. Western Philosophy generally accepts knowledge as valid whereas invalid cognition is not knowledge at all. The Indian Philosophy makes a distinction between '*jñāna'* and '*pramā*. *Jñāna* stands for all kinds of cognition or 'knowledge' either true or false in the ordinary sense of the term. It may be open to further scrutiny. But '*pramā'* is a kind of knowledge necessarily true. It is said to be true because it is obtained through some 'valid' sources of knowledge. Apart from truth, it has also the quality of novelty (*abādhitatva* or *yathārthatva* and *anādhigatatva*). But the meaning of truth varies according to different schools. Many regard truth as the harmony of experience (*saṁvāditatva*). For *Advaita*, truth of knowledge consists in its non-contradictedness (*abādhitatva*). It is not enough that knowledge should be true, but it should be new or previously not acquired (*anadhigata*). A *pramā* or knowledge is cognition, the object of which is neither contradicted nor already known as an object (*anādhigatā-bādhitā-rata-viṣayaṁ jñānam*). The special sources of a particular *pramā* or knowledge are called *pramāṇa*. Thus, *pramāṇa* is the *kāraṇa* of *pramā*. *Kāraṇa* means the unique cause and through its function, a particular effect is produced. The object known through *pramāṇa* is described *prameya* and the knower is called *pramāta*. A *prāmāṇika* is the one who bases his conclusion on *pramāṇas* and generally, he is called a philosopher.

Vijñānabhikṣu acknowledges three *pramāṇas* (sources of knowledge) that can lead to the *pramā* (the true cognition):

pratyakṣa (perception), *anumāna* (inference) and *śabda* (sacred tradition).[42] The word 'sacred tradition' may lead to confusion as '*śabda*' is understood to be the 'verbal testimony.' The reason for my translation as 'sacred tradition' is to include both scriptures and the tradition, namely, *śruti* and *smṛti* literature (*śāstra*) along with tradition proper (*aitihya*). This is my conclusion after reading *Vijñānāmṛtabhāṣyam*. Vijñānabhikṣu uses the *śabda pramāṇa* in this sense. There seems to be a hidden purpose why Vijñānabhikṣu is coupling tradition and testimony in one *śabda pramāṇa*. It seems to me that this serves his purpose of emphasizing the tradition and traditional values of Hinduism followed over the years. Therefore, no outside forces can dictate the traditional practices such as varṇa-āśrama systems, certain ritual practices, worship patterns and other customs.

In the *Sāṅkhyapravacanabhāṣya* Vijñānabhikṣu testifies that the *pramāṇas* are the "immediate means of discriminative knowledge" (SPB 1.88). Further, he affixes (also in VAB), "Knowledge of the Self is acquired using threefold *pramāṇas*—this we learn verily from such texts of the Veda as *ātmā va are dṛṣṭavyaḥ śrotavyo mantavyaḥ*, that is, verily the self is to be seen, to be heard about, to be reasoned about."[43] Along these lines, *pratyakṣa* is "the determination of distant objects" through one's senses, *anumāna* as "inferential or verbal cognition" through *vṛtti*, and scriptural testimony as *śabda*. These three include every other *pramāṇas* like *upamāna* (comparison), *anupalabdhi* (non-existence), *arthāpatti* (comprehension) and *aitihya* (tradition), and it follows, one does not need any other *pramāṇas* to be expounded. The *Sāṅkhyasūtra* says, "On the establishment of that [that three *pramāṇas*] no more proof is essential."[44] Quoting Manu, Vijñānabhikṣu clarifies, "*pratyakṣa, anumāna* and *śāstra* [*śabda*] are the means of getting at the objects."[45] Further, he illuminates that *upamāna* and *aitihya*, etc. come under *anumāna* and *śabda* respectively, and *anupalabdhi*, etc. come under *pratyakṣa*.[46]

Pratyakṣa is defined as "*yat sambaddhaṁ sat tat ākāro'llekhi vijñānaṁ tat pratyakṣam*" that is, "the knowledge arising from the relation or connection and thus portraying the form" (SPB 1.89). According to Vijñānabhikṣu *pratyakṣa* is "that cognition which, coming into relation to the thing cognized."[47] The knowledge "produced by relation" (*sambandha-siddham*)[48] can be internal or external. In the case of empirical objects, the perception is an external one (*laukika-jñāna*) and in the case of *yogic* practitioner's cognition (*yaugika-pratyakṣa-jñāna* or *alukika-jñāna*), it is an internal relation. Apart from internal or external forms, Vijñānabhikṣu accentuates the relational aspect in knowing a thing.

Among all the *pramāṇas*, *śabda* or the *śāstra* is the root source of the knowledge of Brahman, "*śāstraṁ hi brahmaṇi mūlaṁ pramāṇam*" (VAB 1.1.3, p.36), and therefore, scripture is a vital source of knowledge before *pratyakṣa* and *anumāna*. Quoting the *Kaṭha Upaniṣad* Vijñānabhikṣu says, "*sarve vedā yat padamāmananti, vedeiśca sarveir ahameva vedhyaḥ*," namely, "all the Vedas thus proclaim that supreme goal which says that I exist in all that is known."[49] All that is known through perception and inference is through *manas* through intellect (*buddhi*). This is intellectual knowledge. The intellectual work is born of secondary perception like the action of origin of the pot. Here, the act of the cause of secondary perception is to be noted not as a consciously done thing. Even then, the cause for the birth of the desire of secondary perception in the intellect is for the sake of the enjoyment of the other, expressly, the *jīva* and its enjoyer, the *Īśvara*. So, any knowledge claim is referred back to the divine.[50]

4.2.1 The Single Reflection Theory

The question often asked in epistemology is about the knower, "Who knows?" It is the *ātman* who knows, however, it is through *manas*, the internal sense or the sixth perceptible sense after *pañcendriyas*. *Manas* acts as a window through which data collected from the *indriyas* is reflected upon in the soul. This is called the single reflection theory.

Vācaspatimiśra explains this theory in his *Sāṅkhyatattvakaumudī*, a commentary on the *Sāṅkhyakārika*. He articulates, "The self on the other hand is conscious and admits of no contact with knowledge, pleasure, etc. That *ātman*, having been reflected in the mind and identifies with it, appears to possess knowledge, pleasure, etc. which subsists in the mind."[51] Further, he justifies this through the imagery of the reflection of the moon in the water in the following way:

> The image of the moon in water appears to take on the characteristics of water. If there is a movement in the water on account of a draft of air, the image of the moon also appears to be moving and if there is red colour in the water, so appears the moon. In the same manner, the self [*ātman*] appears to take on the characteristics of the mind in which it has been reflected. It is only due to the real mode of the mind that the self seems to feel serene, sad, indolent, etc.[52]

This implies that the reflections of the *ātman* are the modes of mind and the agent of experience is the reflected *ātman*. Thus, the *ātman* is understood to be "the substance and knowledge as its adventitious quality."[53] This is called single reflection theory in a traditional *Nyāya-Vaiśeṣika* sense. This suggests that every knowledge is an object and even the *ātman,* and therefore, as an object the *ātman* is knowable.

For the Bhāṭṭa school of *Pūrvamīmāṁsā*, knowledge is a mode of the *ātman*. Knowledge is revealed not directly (as in *Nyāya*) but through inference. Hence, the *ātman* is knowable. But for the Prābhākara School, *ātman* is not knowable and employs the *kartṛkarmavirodha* theory or the contradiction of the subject and the object being the same in any act.[54] Vijñānabhikṣu applies Prābhākara's view to reject the idea of the *ātman* as knowable.

Vijñānabhikṣu borrows his epistemology from *Sāṅkhy-Yoga* School. This system has a close affinity with *Advaita* concerning epistemology, which Vijñānabhikṣu makes use of it though he criticizes it (*Advaita*) vehemently. For Śaṅkara, *ātman* is pure *cit* or pure consciousness itself. In its pure state, *ātman* is never the knower. The one who knows is its lower form, the *jīva*. *Jīva* is the identification of *ātman* with *manas*, in other words, the mode of *ātman*. Thus, *jīva* has both objective contents as *antaḥkaraṇa* and subjective content as *sākṣin*. This aspect of *jīva* can be compared or equalled with the *puruṣa* aspect of *Sāṅkhya* which Vijñānabhikṣu is comfortable with. Thus, *ātman* is not knowable, but being self-luminous (*svayamprakāṣa*), its presence itself is its revelation.[55]

4.2.2 The Double Reflection Theory

Vijñānabhikṣu acknowledges the theory of knowledge according to *Sāṅkhya-Yoga* that the reflection of *puruṣa*,[56] the conscious principle in the unconscious *prakṛti* begets the knowledge. However, here, it is the reflection of *puruṣa* in the modification of the intellect (*buddhi-vṛtti*) that sets in motion the knowledge possible. Therefore, the knowledge—in general—belongs to *puruṣa* due to its reflection in the *buddhi*. In *Sāṅkhyapravacanabhāṣyam* he asserts this, "right cognition is lodged in *Puruṣa*."[57] How does it occur? He furnishes the process here.

In the first place, there is a reflection of the *puruṣa* in the modified *buddhi* (*buddhivṛtti*). Then, the *buddhi* in turn reflects it back to *puruṣa*. This is the second reflection resulting in knowledge. This knowledge is the 'knowledge as,' that it is, 'I know *that* pot.' If this is not accepted, then one falls back to *kartṛkarmavirodha*, that is "Contradiction of oneself knowing oneself directly."[58] The first reflection intelligizes the content of *buddhi* and the second reflection makes *puruṣa* the agent of particular knowledge. Thus, the *jaḍa buddhi* appears as if it is conscious and the inactive *puruṣa* appears as if it is the doer. In the words of Kanshi Ram, the theory of double reflections holds that "not only does the self gets reflected in the mind, but the modes of the mind [*buddhivṛtti*] which take shape when the inner senses through outer senses come in contact with the objects of experience, also are reflected in the self. The latter reflection phenomenalizes the self and seems to confer experienceship on it."[59] K.C. Bhattacharyya offers an amended version of Vijñānabhikṣu's double reflection theory. The dual function comprises of both the reflecting and manifesting aspects of the mind itself. While reflecting the object, the mind functions causally, for, during the process of reflection, it gets modalised into a substantial vṛtti similar to the object. On the other hand, while manifesting the object, the mind functions non-causally, as it does not undergo any transformation as in the case of substantial mode.[60]

While the *puruṣa* is the experiencer, consciousness, knowledge and feeling or sensation, the *parkṛti* is the object of knowledge, insentient, *tamas* and ignorance.[61] Just as the light shows the objects placed in the dark, so too, through contact, with the object of experience, the consciousness becomes the knower of the objects.[62]

Following the *Sāṅkhya-Yoga* in the *Vijñānāmṛtabhāṣyam,* Vijñānabhikṣu explains the process of knowing in the following way:

> After the *Tamas* of the mind is removed by the senses coming in contact with objects like the dirt of clothes, the pure *Sattva* of the mind takes on the form of objects through sense-contact just as the clean cloth takes on the form of the Kusumbha flower, i.e., takes on its colour, coming in contact with it. This state of the mind which has taken the form of objects is called *Buddhivṛtti* (mode of the mind). This mode of the mind is immediately followed by an experience of the self because the mode is the direct means of experience for the self as a chariot becomes a means for the charioteer to reach the village. The mode of the mind thus being generated gets reflected in the self. This reflected mode of the mind which is coloured by the object is manifested by the self, the seat of reflection, just as the cloth dyed in the Kusumbha, which is reflected in the crystal wall, gets illuminated by the latter. In this manner the modes of the mind along with their contents when reflected in the consciousness (self) are cognized by the self in exactly the same fashion as the water superimposed on the rays of the sun in a desert is made illusory manifest by them (rays).[63]

This is again expounded in the *Sāṅkhyapravacanasūtram* in the following way:

> Now, the process of knowing rightly is as follows: By means of the contact with objects, through the

channels of the Senses, or by means of the knowledge of the (inferential) mark etc., is at first produced a modification of *Buddhi* in the form of the objects (to be cognized). Of these, the perceptual modification produced from the contact of the senses, is dependent upon *Buddhi* together with or affected by the Senses, seeing that modifications in the form of the bile, etc., arise in consequence of the depravity of the bile, etc., appertaining to the eye, etc.; this is the difference. And the same modification, tinged with the object, enters upon (the field of vision) of *Puruṣa* by the form of a reflection, and shines there, inasmuch as *Puruṣa*, since he is not liable and capable of transformation, cannot possibly be modified into the form of the object. And it is only modification into the form of the object that can apprehend objects; it is difficult to say this in respect of other things. This the author will declare later on by the aphorism: *japāsphaṭikayoriva noparāgaḥ kintvabhimānaḥ* (6.28), as between the China rose and crystal, (there is) no *uparāga* or actual transference of 'colour' (from *Buddhi* to *Puruṣa*), but (only) *abhimāna* or an assumption (of such transference).[64]

The neutrality or the motionlessness of *ātman* does not affect the reflection of the modes of the mind, just as a red rose is placed near a crystal; the crystal will look red but will not have any substantial change in the crystal. An example from *Yogāvasiṣṭa* is very apt here, "just as the trees on the bank are reflected in the lake so also are reflected in the clear mirror of conscious self all the mental modes of the form of objects."[65] Accordingly, the *ātman* may appear to be perceiving, experiencing, etc., but may not undergo any substantial change. The *ātman* intimately connected to *buddhivṛtti*, without getting veiled by it, remains as a witness in knowing an object (VAB 1.1.3, p.40-41). Therefore, *ātman* is not veiled by ignorance (as *Advaita* would say). If *ātman* were to be shrouded by ignorance, then one needs to accept the nature of *ātman* as ignorance. But this is not the case. Ignorance and knowledge cannot co-exist. The mental modes or the *buddhivṛtti* delimits the nature of knowledge reflected in the *ātman*. Thus, the *avibhāga* is maintained.

Here, the theory of causality comes to salvage Vijñānabhikṣu. According to *Sāṅkhya*, the effect is identical with the cause. The modified *ātman* is the effect of the original *ātman* (*cidātman*). Therefore, every action of modified *ātman* is the action of the original *ātman*.

The process of knowing the Brahman or the *ātman* (in that sense any divine or transcendental objects) is the same as that of knowing any external objects.[66] What differs in knowing the external objects and internal or transcendental objects is the *abhimāna svabhāva* (ego nature). In the knowledge of the external objects the ego is not annihilated whereas in knowing internal objects, the ego is annihilated. When the ego is annihilated by means of the study of scriptures or *yogic* practice such as meditation, the mind is modalized in the form of Brahman. It is here one call oneself, *ahaṁ brahmāsmi.* This is the valid means of knowledge (*pramāṇa*) which gets reflected in the self.[67] The resulting knowledge is the knowledge of Brahman or soul. This definition of "I am Brahman" is slightly different from the *Advaitic* notion. In the *Advaitic* understanding, upon liberation, *ātman* totally identifies itself with the Brahman. It takes place when ignorance is removed from the soul. In Vijñānabhikṣu's understanding, the soul is as pure as Brahman. Ignorance is attached to the *buddhi*, in the form of *buddhivṛtti*. Since the *sattva* form of *prakṛti* is the *buddhi*, it becomes easier for the *ātman* to identify itself with the *buddhi.*

In the process of knowing the self, there is no *karmakartṛvirodha*, doer-knower difference, that is, there is no *ātman* and *buddhivṛtti* difference. *Ātman* as a knower itself is reflected, just as "sun gives light and the same sun becomes the object of light in the form of reflection."[68] Thus, there is no contradiction in the subject itself becoming the object. Vijñānabhikṣu quotes the *Mokṣadharmakāṇḍa* of the *Mahābhārata*, "like the light enlightens the lamp present in front of the lamp, so too the light of knowledge enlightens the tree of senses."[69]

Further, when the self is identified with *prakṛti*, it is understood as the whole self interpenetrating in the whole of creation, to say, when Brahman is illuminating, it illuminates everything. Specifically, there is a vivid *avibhāga* between Brahman and *ātman* on the one side, and Brahman and *prakṛti* on the other side. K.C. Bhattacharya confirms, "The dual function of the mind is illusorily referred to self. The self appears to take the reflection (*pratibimba*) of *buddhivṛtti* which reflects the object and to be itself reflected in *buddhibhāva* which projects the object."[70] So, there is no contradiction within the *Bhedābheda*.

The fundamental difference between the single and double reflection is the reflection in the pure conscious *ātman*. In the first case, the reflection is in the modified *prakṛti,* while in the latter case, it is in the *puruṣa*. The application of this is more than what one can think of. If followed the single reflection, then it appears that the effort of purgation of the self or the liberative efforts seems to be redundant or futile, because the knowledge belongs to the unconscious *prakṛti*. If accepted the double reflection, then it is easy to give meaning to the liberative efforts of the individuals, because the knowledge is reflected in the conscious *puruṣa*. As a consequence, if the experience is with the reflected self, then the liberation and bondage become useless and in such cases assuming original sense is meaningless.

4.3 The Metaphysical Rendering of *Avibhāga-Bhedābheda*

Vijñānabhikṣu comments extensively on the metaphysical stand of his philosophy. To put it in a capsule form, *Avibhāga-Bhedābheda* is an integral vision of the Ultimate Reality where individual selves or *puruṣa* and *prakṛti* are essentially inseparable as its powers like sugar in milk, salt in water, wave in the sea and river emptying in the sea.[71] *Puruṣa* and *prakṛti* as the power of Brahman is not a new concept in Vijñānabhikṣu's thought. In the *Vedānta Kaustubha,*

Śrīnivāsācārya (belongs to the *Nimbārka Sampradāya*) considers *prakṛti* as the power of Brahman. There, the author does not insist on any distinction between *śakti* of Brahman and *prakṛti*. Perhaps, it is equated with the lower form of Brahman (*Apara Brahman*).[72] The chief contention in all this is that whatever we perceive and experience is a divine interpenetrated reality, i.e., Brahman from its subtle form becomes gross form, and effectuate to various animate and inanimate objects in the universe. To go still deeper, Jainism considers every animate and inanimate object as the embodiment of '*ātman*.' This leads us to consider the world as sacred.

The *śrutis* portray very well the existence of truth of divine integration (*brahmādvaita*) in the *ātman* of every person in the nature, as follows, "This everything verily is Brahman, This everything is *Ātman*, He alone is all as what was and is existing from the eternal, and this is not plural whatsoever."[73] This is very much corroborated by *smṛtis*, "I am Hari, all this is Janārdana, and there is no other born cause-effect. Perceptible, and He alone is imperceptible, He alone is the absolute being, Vāsudeva that I am all."[74] Therefore, the *Upaniṣadic* statement makes sense, "*sarvaṁ khalvidaṁ Brahman*" (CU 3.14.1). The seen reality is not separate from the unseen reality, and the unseen is very much made manifest in the seen. Their mutual interpenetration is like "sugar mixed in milk."[75] The obvious manifestation of divine in all the time in the world or in the person can be understood very much by means of one's intellect (*buddhi*) and the quality of a person (*guṇa*). Neither the quality is separate from the person, nor is the intellect apart from the person. They are intimately united in a special relation of *saṁyoga*,[76] in the likeness (*svarūpa*) and knowledge (*viveka*) as the sugar dissolved in milk.[77] Therefore, it is the same Brahman manifested in every being at every place and at all times.

Intellect and quality or virtues are indispensable for harmonious existence in society. A balanced person should exhibit both in one's life. If intellect leads to right reasoning, the virtues give an ethical foundation for the way one behaves. Both are complementary to each other. If there is a lack of reasoning, the belief may turn into superstition. If the virtuous life is sans reasoning, then the person might turn out to be a puppet in the hands of a puppeteer. Therefore, one should not blindly believe and accept whatever is being offered.

Vijñānabhikṣu further expresses this *bheda-abheda* relation quoting the *Kūrma* and *Nārada Purāṇa*, "The difference (*abheda*) between one energy and the other energy is only seen in the empirical world. At the metaphysical level, this difference is not seen. The one who resides within is of the form of world and is spotless witness. Brahman exhibits himself in various forms."[78] As the *Vedic* seer assumed, "*ekaṁ sadviprā bahudhā vadanti*" "truth is one known it in many ways." This leads us to probe into the nature of the Brahman, *Ātman*, *jagat*, and their inter-intra relationship.

4.3.1 The Concept of Brahman

Brahman is the cause of everything (*janmādyasyayataḥ* BS 1.1.2). However, this cause cannot be seen through our naked eyes, nor imagination can reshape it. It has to be understood through one's relationship with the effect of His creation. Giving the example of *paṅkaja,* Vijñānabhikṣu instructs that Brahman has to be understood through *yogarūḍhi* (VAB 1.1.2, p.19). That which is born in mud is understood to be lotus. There is a close affinity between two seemingly different entities. Due to this relationship, a third thing is understood. Therefore, when the relationship between the two seemingly different entities is unearthed, one can find their pristine pure state and origin.

Let us try to understand this concept this way. There exists a necessary relation between *paṅka* (mud) and *kamala* (lotus). It is a real relation. On the other hand, there is a relation between *nabha* (sky) and *kamala* (lotus). But this relation in the *nabhakamala* (sky-lotus) is imaginary and therefore an illusory or unreal relation. Similarly, between Brahman and *Ātman* there is a necessary and real relation, so too between Brahman and *jagat* or *puruṣa* and *prakṛti.*

Unlike other traditional *Vedāntic* thinkers, Vijñānabhikṣu does not carp on the materialistic *Sāṅkhya* system. He perceives a divine thread around which the whole system is constructed. In as much as *puruṣa* is part of the divine, so too *prakṛti* is a manifestation of it. Even the blending of *puruṣa* and *prakṛti* is divine willed (VAB 1.1.2, p.18). Therefore, there is a requirement to understand the characteristics of

Brahman and its relationship with *puruṣa* and *prakṛti*.

4.3.1.1 The General Characteristics

Brahman is the foundation (*sarvādhāratvam)* of all that exists. He is the supreme great soul, the great abode of all, smaller than small, eternal principle (KU 16).[79] He is the absolute, eternal, unborn, indestructible, of one mind and form (*ekasvarūpa*), pure, guileless, all-pervader (Viṣṇu),[80] and omnipresent. He is eternal among the transient, conscious among the conscious, the original seed of all existences, the intelligence of the intelligent, and the prowess or lustre of all-powerful men, the separate soul, moving force or the controller, and immortal, greater than the self and the unmanifest, ruler of all.[81]

Further, Vijñānabhikṣu responds, "In which, from which, at which time, by which, of which, due to which, whatever, in whatever manner creates or cause to create, that is Brahman" (BP 7.9.20). He is the highest of things, high and low, and the self-existent before all things. It is the cause, the unique, and the One. This dual causality is exemplified by potter and spider. Therefore, all forms of causality of the world can be uttered as Brahman.[82]

4.3.1.2 Brahman as *Saguṇa* and *Nirguṇa* or *Saviśeṣa* and *Nirviśeṣa*

Vijñānabhikṣu envisages Brahman as both *saguṇa* and *nirguṇa* or *saviśeṣa* and *nirviśeṣa*, contrary to Śaṅkara's *nirguṇa* or *nirviśeṣa* Brahman. He is formless (*arūpavad*). The argument of the *pūrvapakṣin* is that Brahman is inexpressible and incomprehensible by both words and mind (*manas*),[83] that is, Brahman is *nirguṇa* or *nirviśeṣa*. Responding to this Vijñānabhikṣu asserts that the words uttered by people cannot express Brahman completely. In an ordinary sense, scriptures cannot convey the knowledge about Brahman totally (VAB, p.37-38). It is also true that the scriptures do not deny, on the other hand, that the purified *yogin's* mind through meditation immediately apprehends Brahman. The scriptures give knowledge about Brahman in a general way. Brahman is known gradually and not instantaneously. Otherwise, scriptures will contradict themselves. There cannot be contradictions within the scriptures. Scriptures have testified that the meditative mind has inconceivable power. A *yogin* can experience Brahman instantaneously, but an ordinary person may not be able to achieve this or may resort to some other ways. This is another way of knowing Brahman in the world. Therefore, Brahman is both *saguṇa* and *nirguṇa*.[84]

In VAB 4.4.22 Vijñānabhikṣu distinguishes two forms of Brahman: *kāraṇabrahman* and *kāryabrahman*. The former is the foundational cause. No one totally merges unto it.[85] It is also called *Parabrahman*. The latter one is called Brahman. It is in this form the *mumukṣus* attain their union. This would be *saguṇa Brahman*. Those who realize the *kāryabrahman*, achieve temporary bliss, whereas those who arrive at *kāraṇabrahman* do not return.[86] The *jīvas* attain *Brahmatva* but not *Parabrahmatva*.

4.3.1.3 Proof for the Existence of Brahman

The principal means of valid knowledge of Brahman is

scripture, "*śāstraṁ hi brahmāṇi mūlaṁ pramāṇam*" (VAB 1.1.3, p.36). So, the scriptures are the attestations for the existence of Brahman. Additionally, Vijñānabhikṣu quotes the *Taittirīya Upaniṣad* to substantiate the scripture as the root source of knowledge. All that is generated in the world are known through the great scriptural roots, "That from which the entire universe is created, that which is responsible for the entire universe to sustain, that into which the entire universe merges into at the end is Brahman."[87] "The seat and goal that all the Vedas glorify that all the Vedas contain I am [Hari] only."[88]

This directs us to a second proof for the existence of Brahman. The ongoing creation or/and the empirical world is the proof for the existence of Brahman. *Prakṛti* is active and there is a continuous creation as long as *puruṣa* is in its proximity. However, *puruṣa* is only a *upādhi*. It is the Lord who freely chooses to enter into *puruṣa* and *prakṛti* as the *Viṣṇu Purāṇa* imparts, "*prakṛtim puruṣam ca eva praviśya ātmecchayā*" (VP 1.2.29).[89] Therefore, the activities of *prakṛti* remind the divine ruling in the creation.[90]

4.3.1.4 The Nature of Brahman: *Sat* and *Cit*

Śaṅkara's understanding of Brahman is *saccidānanda*: *sat*, *cit* and *ānanda*—existence (truth), consciousness and bliss respectively. Vijñānabhikṣu differs from this. According to him, many scriptural statements assert this variedly: "Brahman is understood to be bliss" (TU 3.6.1), "Brahman is both knowledge and bliss" (BU 3.9.28), "From this bliss all beings are born" (TU 3.6.1). These statements are for the sake of argument. But, Brahman is *sat* and *cit*. He is devoid of bliss. The *bhedaśruti* elucidates thus: "Brahman is neither bliss nor non-bliss, a self-knowing Brahman discards joy and grief, Brahman is devoid of pleasure and pain."[91]

Ānanda not being the part of Brahman seems to be contradicting *śruti* and *smṛti*. Vijñānabhikṣu is aware of it. This way of understanding comes from his affinity towards *Sāṅkhya*. He attributes *ānanda* to the *prakṛti*. *Prakṛti* already embodies the divine. On the contrary, if *ānanda* were to be the characteristic of Brahman, (and *prakṛti* sans bliss) then the bliss emerging from the *puruṣa-prakṛtiaikya* will have to be sacrificed.

Brahman is devoid of desire, volition and bliss. *Sat* and *cit* are his essential natures. However, for Śaṅkara, Brahman is of the nature of pure bliss. Vijñānabhikṣu contests this as wrong. Brahman's attribute of supreme bliss as the attribute of Brahman is due to the *prakṛti upādhi*. This is only meant for the worship of Brahman (VAB 3.3.11, p.260). Bliss is actually one of the natures of *prakṛti* along with desire (*kāma*) and creation (*kṛti*). The *Taittirīya Upaniṣad* is alluded to, "*ānando brahmeti vyajanāt*" (He realized that bliss is Brahman, TU 3.6.1) to convey Brahman created having recourse to this bliss. If Brahman were already bliss, then Brahman does not need to realize that he is so. Therefore, *ānanda* is not the real nature of Brahman. Instead, *prakṛti* is the divine power of Brahman, just like Pārvati is the power of Śiva as supposed in the *Kūrma Purāṇa*,[92] and so bliss is an attribute of *prakṛti*. The words employed in the scripture,

'Brahman as bliss' signify the relation of '*dharma-dharmya bhedaparatva*.'[93] This clearly demonstrates the relationship between Brahman and *prakṛti* as *Avibhāga-Bhedābheda*.

Secondly (Vijñānabhikṣu's argument for establishing bliss to be the nature of *prakṛti*), Brahman cannot have varying degrees of knowledge, pleasure, pain, bliss, etc. in its parts, as the *Taittirīya Upaniṣad* affirms, "His head is lovable, right is pleasure, the wing is joy, the soul is bliss, the tail is Brahman, etc." (TU 2.5.2). The varying degrees of bliss, knowledge, joy, happiness, sadness, etc. are the nature of *prakṛti*. Because of *upādhi*, they seem to be part of the nature of Brahman.[94] In the *Sāṅkhyapravacanabhāṣyam* Vijñānabhikṣu insists on, "*puruṣārthameva pradhānasya pravṛtti svabhāvo na tu sāmānyena*,"[95] meaning, "that it is the nature of *prakṛti* to act for the sake of *puruṣa*, but not in a general way." Therefore, there is a teleological reason why pleasure, pain, etc. is said to be the nature of Brahman.

This necessitates that Brahman of Vijñānabhikṣu should be regarded as a personal God or a self in contrast to the impersonal nature in Advaita. In this respect, *Avibhāga-Bhedābheda* is something similar to *Viśiṣṭādvaita* tradition. Brahman is the highest Person having excellent qualities. He is the ruler of all, omniscient, omnipotent, from whom creation, subsistence and reabsorption of the world take place. He is the cause of evolution, maintenance, dissolution. He is boundless, unsurpassable, known under various names in the Vedas—Supreme Brahman, Supreme Glory, Supreme Principle, Supreme Spirit and Real Being.[96] He is the inner soul of the entire visible and invisible reality. He is the ground of all existence, the cause. In the traditional sense, he is *satyam, jñānam* and *anantam*. This immanent aspect resembles a general word used for God in Tamil Language, '*Kaḍavuḷ*.' *Kaḍa* = crossing or moving and *vuḷ* = inside. That is, the one who moves/crosses inside everything is God. In the deepest of the deep, there is an unseen reality causing everthing to move ahead.

This may resonate that the God of Vijñānabhikṣu is an admixture of personal and anthropomorphic image. It is true because it is the human way of speaking. In reality, Vijñānabhikṣu endeavours to reconcile the God of philosophy with the God of religion. Through former, he establishes Him as Brahman and by way of later, as *Puruṣa* or as *Īśvara*. As long as *puruṣa* and *prakṛti* remain as the body and powers of Brahman, he sticks faithfully with the God of philosophy. But when he deviates from here, expressing the divine in terms of anthropic images, he seems to go off the track. But it is not so. Expressing the divine in terms of anthropic images does not reduce God having physical body, but a being that is self-existent, self-conscious endowed with perfect freedom and will.

4.3.1.5 The Inter-intra Relationship Between *Brahman*, *Ātman* and *Jagat*

There is a close affinity between Brahman, and *ātman* and *jagat*. Brahman is like the bridge. There is no absolute non-difference of Brahman with others. Brahman, because of its eternal substance, is different. Quoting the *Upaniṣadic* texts,

Vijñānabhikṣu concludes that Brahman is like the boundary for the world and souls, the supreme bridge of immortality like a fire that burns without fuel (SU 6.19), the bridge for those who perform sacrifices, the highest immortal one, fearless and the other shore for those who wish to cross the ocean of *saṁsāra* (KaU 1.3.2). What we experience is only a minuscule, and everything is His glory (*Puruṣasūkta* 1.3). Thus, all things are related in Brahman and Brahman rules over all the objects of the world.[97] Consequently, Brahman is everywhere, can experience only minuscule reality, but His presence has to be inferred through His essential modes like *puruṣa, ātman, jīva, prakṛti*, etc.

4.3.2 The Concept of *Ātman*

Every *ātman* is like a luminous spark erupting out of the luminous fire of Brahman. Each member has the nature of the source fire. In the same way, souls emerging from Brahman too have the same nature of Brahman, the pure consciousness. The form of Brahman can also be equated to light, so too is *ātman* in sentient beings. Just as Brahman is of the consciousness nature (*Brahmaḥ caitanya svarūpa ātmaḥ*), so too, is every *ātman* or *jīva*. However, Brahman's consciousness nature cannot be seen in isolation. It is like the imaginary head of Rāhu. One cannot pinpoint it in a particular place. Brahman's consciousness is manifested in the universe, just like the sun has no attribute of light, but its light reveals all things. Thus, Brahman's consciousness discloses his existence in the world.[98] Light, be it of the sun or the moon, illumine every object. It is the light that facilitates us to spot the objects of our apprehension. Similarly, every *ātman* aids us to perceive Brahman, since in its essence the former is non-different from the latter. So, *ātman* is mirroring the consciousness of Brahman. In this sense, every being is a mirror image of Brahman, *pratibimba of bimba*. In other words, every *ātman* is the *pratima* of *pramā*.

In our ordinary understanding, according to Vijñānabhikṣu, everyone is equal in the eyes of God. The equality comes from the very fact of foundational existence (*adhiṣṭānakāraṇa*). But, the manner of understanding and paying obeisance may be different. Therefore, one cannot consider the pattern and tradition of the other as superior or inferior. Being in one's circumference one can accommodate the other.

The relation between Brahman and *ātman* is that of *samavāya* (inherence). However, though *ātman* is the *aṁśa* of Brahman, like spark and fire, there is *Bhedābheda* relation between them. Just like there are hundreds of the same kinds of sparks in a bright fire, so too is the relation between Brahman and *ātman* and Brahman and *jīva*.[99] Likewise, pure water is added to pure water, so too is the nature of the knowledge of *ātman* and Brahman. Pleasure, pain and delusion are effects of *sattva*, *tamas* and *rajas* respectively. They are all attributes of *prakṛti* and not the *guṇas* of Brahman. Vijñānabhikṣu says that he has explained in the *Pañcasūtras,* the first five *sūtras* of VAB, that bliss is not His characteristic,[100] contrary to the *Advaitin's* stand. Inspite of that, Vijñānabhikṣu does not deny bliss in Brahman.[101] If he were to deny this, then he would go against the scriptures since several statements communicate the blissful nature, like: "Brahman is knowledge and bliss, these creatures are born of bliss, sustained by bliss and merge in bliss, Brahman is bliss, the *ātman* requires bliss from Brahman and *ātman* becomes bliss."[102] Bliss is an attribute of *prakṛti*. This attribute is superfluous in Brahman. Further, Brahman cannot have degrees of pleasure and bliss, as He is partless. Increase and decrease in joy and bliss is the nature of *prakṛti*. Consciousness is the real attribute of Brahman.

Vijñānabhikṣu articulates three kinds of *puruṣas* in his *bhāṣya*: Supreme *Puruṣa* (Brahman), *Īṣvara* and other ordinary *puruṣas*. All exhibit similar relations as acknowledged above. The latter is subordinate to the former and one is meant for the other.[103] The supreme *puruṣa* is Brahman. The nature of Brahman as understood from its etymology is 'expanding.'[104] This Brahman is understood in its subordinate sense with secondary meanings. In this sense, even *jīva* can be called 'Brahman.' There are also *puruṣas* of lower-order exhibiting the nature of Brahman in their different modes. They are *Brahamā*, *Viṣṇu* and *Maheśvara* in its *sattva*, *tamas* and *rajas* prominence respectively creating, maintaining and annihilating the creation.[105] These lower deities, called the *trimūrtis*, are born of *guṇas* in their *kṣobha* state. "Brahman created himself," entails, Brahman is the source of all, He is the impregnator and making possible all things.[106] This indicates that every soul finds its existence in Brahman.

Ātman is part of Brahman. The relation between them is akin to part and whole. Brahman's nature of all-pervading manifested in the *ātman's* pervading nature. This is very much supported by Bādarāyaṇa, *ātman* is part of Brahman because it is affirmed to be many by *śruti,* and yet they are non-separate.[107] Brahman is infinite conscious spirit, while *ātman* is conscious spirit. In their manifested attributes both possess different characteristics. In the end, *ātman* merges in Brahman along with *prakṛti* (VAB 2.1.22). With Brahman's desire to become "many," "*ātman* becomes a son." Merging doesn't mean that *ātman* becomes *Parabrahman*. More accurately, there is identity or non-separateness between soul and Brahman, like father and son. For this reason, even in the liberated state, *Avibhāga-Bhedābheda* is maintained.

4.3.3 The Concept of *Prakṛti*

Brahman as the cause of the *jagat* is the creator. Consequently, the world is a real manifestation of Brahman. The world is not a false appearance. *Māyā* is one of the adjuncts (*upādhi*) of Brahman. The world is created, maintained and destroyed by Brahman. As a substratum cause (*adhiṣṭhānakāraṇa*), Brahman is the witness and supervisor. Through *māyā upādhi,* He is the efficient cause; and as the *prakṛti upādhi,* He is the material cause.

Both *puruṣa* and *prakṛti* are the separate powers of Brahman,[108] but it doesn't mean that Brahman's power is divided. He is all-powerful. Just as by seeing through eyes, we dared to say that we own the truth, so too, these conscious and unconscious realities are known to be the powers of

Brahman. A clear *Bhedābheda* can be observed here. However, Vijñānabhikṣu does not elucidate why and how they become powers of Brahman in the *Vijñāmṛtabhāṣyam*. He assumes that it is not the scope of the *Brahmasūtras*. But, it needs a detailed articulation. Therefore, he outlines commentaries on Sāṅkhya and Yoga to support what has been said in the *Vijñāmṛtabhāṣyam.* The *Yogavārttika* latter clarifies this fact, that "the *prakṛti* is the power of Brahman."[109] Brahman cannot be modified as it is, noticeably, He cannot be reduced to mere material objects. But Brahman, as the cause for every power and effect of the *prakṛti* and just as eyes are the cause for the knowledge of viewed objects for the soul,[110] becomes the cause for the multiplicity of beings in the world. Therefore, we don't declare everything is God, but God in everything (*tvameva tat*).

The *prakṛti's* nature of freely becoming many for the sake of *puruṣārtha* is effected due to the union of *puruṣa* with it. Once again, this union is its very nature, like iron and magnet. Just by their own action, the disturbance in the image of *puruṣa* and *prakṛti* is not possible. However, the disturbance is possible in the changing equilibrium of *guṇa* in the *prakṛti*, and for *puruṣa* in its *upādhi* (like ether in the air). But, this does not happen by itself. Divine interpenetration in the *puruṣa* and *prakṛti* brings change. Therefore, the union is a part of the action of the divine (VAB 1.1.2, p.18-19). The divine by its desire intervenes in the *prakṛti* and thus at the creation both manifest and unmanifest are set to motion.[111] Accordingly, we discern

Vijñānabhikṣu's admission of three *tattvas*: *puruṣa, prakṛti* and Brahman or divine, just like Rāmānuja who admits *cit, acit* and Brahman. It is the divine that brings together the static conscious *puruṣa* and dynamic unconscious *prakṛti* in the depth of nature as a result of a creative disturbance in the three *guṇas*.

Brahman, effecting the creation through *puruṣa* and *prakṛti*, does neither get modified Himself entirely nor partially. If so, that would be making His parts. Brahman as partless creates diverse modifications without undergoing any change in Himself. This is because *puruṣa* and *prakṛti* are its power. In the adjunct of Brahman, the *guṇas sattva, tamas* and *rajas* are unmixed, while in the adjuncts of *puruṣa* or *prakṛti,* they are mixed. This makes Brahman greater than *ātman*. He is non-different from the modifications of *puruṣa* and *prakṛti,* as the conscious snake is non-different from its coil produced by it through particular conjunction of the parts of its power (VAB 3.2.27). Brahman, as a conscious principle by its will and desire, produces modifications in *prakṛti*. Therefore, *prakṛti* is said to be 'the abode of Brahman' in other words, "*sarvam khalvidam brahman*."[112]

The *Avibhāga* relation between Brahman and *jīva-jagat,* like the rays of the sun and the body of the sun, are non-different. Just as sparks emanate from a fire, so too, conscious souls originate from conscious Brahman. This does not assert total identity. God is non-different from *jīva-jagat* as whole and parts. When *avidyā* initiates thew difference between soul and Brahman and when it is removed totally, one finds non-separateness, but not identity.[113]

4.4 Models of Metaphysical Relationships in the *Vijñānāmṛtabhāṣyam*

Vijñānabhikṣu elucidates the *Bhedābheda* relationship in the *Vijñānāmṛtabhāṣyam* employing various models. This is his hermeneutical strategy as well. Predominantly, five kinds of relationships have been explored here. All these relationships demonstrate a mysterious and indubitable difference and non-difference in the reality. This in itself is a proof of the existence of theistic[114] non-dualism.

4.4.1 *Aṁśāṁśī Sambandha*

The relationship between *ātman* and *Brahman* is that of *aṁśa* and *aṁśī,* part and whole. Vijñānabhikṣu associates the relationship into that of the spark and fire, intimately united. The *ātman* exhibits the image of the latter,[115] but it is not the image proper, in the sense of *tādātmya*. It is like the fact of only one sky with its space, both within the pot and outside and even after the pot is destroyed (*Yājñavālkya Smṛti* 3.144).[116] *Ātman* is primarily a part (*aṁśa*) of Brahman (*aṁśī*), just like the hair in the body is part of the body or the son is the part of the father.

Jīva is the part of Brahman as son is the part of the father or spark is the part of the fire.[117] However, *jīva* is not a reflection (*pratibimba*) of *Īśvara*, rather it is *aṁśa* of *paramātman*. Scripture contains both *bhedaśruti* and *abhedaśruti*. There is neither an absolute one-ness (*akhaṇḍatābodhatva*) in the *abhedaśruti*, nor there an absolute difference in the *bhedaśruti*. This difference and non-difference (*bhedābheda*) is beautifully explained in VAB 2.3.43, "*aṁśo nānāvyapadeśādanyathā cāpi dāśa kitavaādītvam adhīyata eke*," "Part on account of difference being declared and otherwise also, for is spoken of as being fisherman, knaves, etc." *Abhedatva* is to be understood from *kāryakāraṇa avibhāgalakṣaṇā* view (from inseparable cause-effect relation). This purports that the *abheda* is from the fact of pervasion (*vibhūtibhiḥ*) or immanence. *Bhedatva* is to be comprehended in the sense of *anyonyābhāva,* mutual absence. *Abheda* cannot be acknowledged from a secondary sense, but should be from primary sense as mentioned in the etymology, "*bhidir vidārane iti anuśānāt ca*." The famous examples support this, "*lavaṇaṁ jalambhūt, dugdhaṁ jalambhūt*" "*yatra tvasya sarvamātmaivabhūta, āpa evedamagra āsuḥ, vāyurbhūtvā dhūmo bhavati.*"[118] However, the *Advaitins* grasp the *abheda* from a secondary sense.[119] Therefore, whether it is through difference or non-difference, in all the situations between *jīva* and Brahman, there is *avibhāga* relation. *Smṛti* confirms this, '*paramātman* exists everywhere in the world. He subsists in *bhinna* and *abhinna* forms.'[120] It is through this *jīva* and *jagat,* the Brahman expands His energy, keeps this cosmic manifestation visible and again sometimes renders it invisible. He is both the supreme cause and the supreme result, the observer and the witness, in all circumstances.

Every *jīva* is an *ātman* and every *ātman* is a part of Brahman. However, the consciousness of *jīva* comes from the *ātman*[121] due to the will and desire of the Brahman. Therefore, *jīva* can be duly called *aṁśa* of Brahman.[122] Thus, *jīva* is just an instrument of Brahman in the world.

Vijñānabhikṣu gives further reasons. The relation between *ātman* and Brahman is that of *bhedābheda*. It is intimately united and simultaneously exhibited as different. *Ātman* is anything from which something issues forth and then having stayed there for a while again merges into it like a wave in the sea.[123] In this way, *ātman* is the *aṁśa* of Brahman.[124] The *bheda* relationship between them is related with the *ātman* gaining consciousness at the supervision of Brahman, the *aṁśī* and thus is able to perceive, see, hear and cognize things. In this way, they are distinct, yet inseparable and exhibit the nature of *avibhāga*, like rays of the sun. The sun has got light from its many rays, but they are all of one *sun* and each *ray* is non-separate from it. So is the relation between *amśā* and *aṁśī*.[125]

The question which remains now is the multiplicity of beings. Vijñānabhikṣu answers this through the *śruti* text, just as the air upon penetrating different spheres of existence, assumes different forms, similarly, the souls of living beings, upon entering different bodies, assume different forms. So also is fire.[126] In VAB 2.3.43, he articulates *aṁśatva* is possible because of similar nature (*aṁśatvaṁ hi sajātiyatve sati*). *Abhedatva* between the *jīva* and Brahman is possible when both do share a similar nature like the hand is part of the body. But it does not mean that hand is a complete body. Then again, Brahman cannot have limbs as the living beings possess. If that were so, the consciousness of son should have been the consciousness of the father. Thus, is the *bheda* and *abheda* exhibited between *jīva* and *Brahman*.

There is a difference as well as non-difference between *ātman* and Brahman as part and whole in the forms of separateness and non-separateness at different times, which does not involve self-contradiction as shown elsewhere. A part (*aṁśa*) is a *pratiyogin* of non-separateness from the homogenous whole. A whole is an *anuyogin* of non-separateness from a part. A *pratiyogin* is one of two things connected by a relation to rest on the other, and an *anuyogin* is that thing upon which it rests. The part rests on a whole, and the whole is the abode of the part, both being homogenous and non-separate from each other. The soul is a part of Brahman as a conscious spirit, and so has homogeneity with Brahman, infinite conscious spirit, or separateness consists in possessing different characteristics or different manifested attributes, and non-separateness consists in not possessing them. Or, non-separateness is a particular conjunction, a unique or essential relation, like content in a substrate. *Prakṛti* and *puruṣa* both merge in Brahman at the time of *praḷaya*, as the *śruti* pronounces, "Separate and distinct things at dissolution are concealed," and "They will know that what constitutes this will be something else and will be manifested in different forms."[127]

4.4.2 *Avibhāga Sambandha*

This is a novel concept of Vijñānabhikṣu. Nicholson expresses *avibhāga* or the non-separation in this way, "non-separation refers to a state in which two entities are perceptually indistinguishable from one another, while nonetheless not having the relationship of identity (*tādātmya*)."[128] According to Vijñānabhikṣu *avibhāga* is defined as "an intrinsic relation and is constituted of total fusion"[129] as the mixture of water and milk. In other words, non-distinction or non-separation is like a drop of water obtained by the mixture of two droplets, 'A' and 'B.' Upon mixing, both droplets lose their individuality and at the same time cannot negate their presence in the single resulting droplet. Thus, there is an inherent relationship in the *avibhāga* concept.[130]

In a modifiable cause, there is *avibhāga sambandha* through a relationship of constituents. In the supporting cause, there is *avibhāga sambandha* through cause and effect, for, there is *avibhāga* between both cause and effect. Thus, it is an inherent relationship between two objects of similar natures and qualities of similar type (*sajātīya vastu*). Objects may seemingly differ like sugar and water, but both have certain internal qualities and natures that go along with them. Yet, there exists a distinction between them even though both have seemingly become one body. This special relationship is called *avibhāga sambandha*.

There is no *tādātmya* at all between the *jīva* and Brahman. Whatever the differences uttered in the scripture refer only to 'non-separation.' Therefore, one needs to understand the difference as 'mutual absence' or *anyonyābhava*.[131] *Anonya abhāva* can be explained as 'A is not B' or 'pot is not the cloth.' This does not imply that there is the mutual absence of any qualities in each other; rather the relationship of identity is absent mutually. At the foundational level, there is something common to both. In other words, non-separation or *avibhga* is the special quality of union.[132]

The *avibhāga sambandha* is further explained through examples—*water in the milk* and *salt in the sea*.[133] In both these examples, the objects mixed become one, yet remain distinct. Another way of explicating it is the relation between a *power* and *power possessor,* or between *a property* and *property possessor,* or *blueness* and *cloth* in blue-cloth. The separation cannot be applied spatially to *jīva* and *Brahman* but in the property. However, it is impossible to explain exactly the state of non-separation, says Vijñānabhikṣu. Further, he gives scriptural foundation to establish the fact of non-separation, "But it is not a second thing, other than himself and different" (BU 4.3.23-30); "Even though they reach Being, they do not know 'We have reached Being'" (CU 6.9.2); "Both Matter and Spirit dissolve in the highest Self"; 'Fulfilment,' 'Absorption' and 'Combination' mean non-separation from this injunction: "Indicatory marks, syntactical connection" (*Pūrva Mīmāṁsā Sūtras* 3.3.14); "Non-separation according to the statement of scripture" (BS 4.2.16), etc.[134]

The *avibhāga sambandha* between Brahman, and *prakṛti-puruṣa* is also explained by means of *samavāya* and *saṁyoga*. *Samavāya sambandha* or inherent relationship is a perpetual co-inherence, inner or intimate relation, constant and intimate union, inseparable concomitance. It is the sixth category for the *Vaiśeṣika*[135] where it expresses a relation between a substance and its qualities, between whole and part. *Saṁyoga* is a mutual absorption or union as in the case of sexual congress. Brahman is ever united in the *prakṛti* and there is an *abheda* relation with the *prapañca*. They are intimately or inseparably united like sugar and milk.[136] This relation is termed as *svarūpa-sambandha-viśeṣa* or *saṁyogādi-viśeṣaḥ*.[137]

Another quality of *avibhāga sambandha* is the temporality of the relation. *Avibhāga sambandha* occurs in time. Vijñānabhikṣu cites the example of *sea and waves* to demonstrate how the part and whole are related in time. Waves are neither permanent in the sea, nor are they separate from it. They are part, but transient in nature. Similarly is the relation between *jīva* and Brahman.[138] Under certain conditions, self and Brahman get separated like water is evaporated from the salt or colour gets bleached from the cloth, or waves merge in the seawater.

In the above example, the wave is a part of the sea, whereas the sea is not part of the wave. The former is an inter-penetrated reality with the latter. "God desires to enter into *puruṣa* and *prakṛti* at the time of creation"[139] as the *smṛti* declares. Individual self cannot be the cause of the world. Reason and intellect may not be able to answer this, but one-pointed devotion (*ekāgracitta dhyāna*) or meditation can reveal the hidden qualities of the Lord who presides in evert individual selves.[140]

4.4.3 *Aupādhika Sambandha*

Vijñānabhikṣu uses some frequent analogies to portray

the relation between Brahman and *jīva* in terms of sun and its reflection in the water, space and space delimited by pot, moon and its reflection in the water, fire and spark, shadow and heat, and male and female.[141] What is to be noted here is the accompanying images in the pair act as a delimiting factor which is called *upādhi*. *Upādhi* is artificial conditioning or a property pertaining to attributes because of which an effect is produced differently.[142] In the example of *ghaṭākāśa*, "the pot is an artificial condition which limits the space,"[143] that is, the presence of the pot makes one feel the space outside as different from the space inside the pot (*ghaṭākāśa* as different from *maṭhākāśa*). Therefore, Vijñānabhikṣu's effort here is to abolish the artificial condition through the concept of *aṁśavāda* to observe the relation between *jīva* and Brahman in its pristine pure state.

Śaṅkara cannot uphold *aṁśavāda,* the mutual appreciation and organic relationship. This is because there is no room for the acceptance of the plurality of souls, but only *ekamevātman*, one solid entity. Contrary to this, Vijñānabhikṣu's *aṁśavāda* recognizes the unassailable individuality and the reality of the manifold finite souls and matter, i.e., *puruṣas* and *prakṛti*. In fact, this is the core of *aṁśavāda*. Further, Vijñānabhikṣu assigns an appropriate place, function and value to *puruṣa* and *prakṛti* in the all-embracing unity without sacrificing the supreme perfection of the Absolute. In the process, the Absolute though manifests itself as *prakṛti* and *puruṣa*,[144] yet does not identify itself completely with them, resulting in preserving its original purity, the transcendence. Alternatively, *puruṣa* and *prakṛti* too enjoy the company of the Absolute without getting themselves annihilated in the all-embracing unity, discharge their functions as a community. Thus, they exhibit a triangular relationship where each end meets each other in support of the other, simultaneously retaining their individuality.

Vijñānabhikṣu neither accepts a mere plurality nor a pure unity, rather the plurality is an expression of the Supreme Being. In this way, Brahman is a concrete existential reality that desires to be plural. It is a whole, which does not deny part. It is a ground (*adhiṣṭhāna*) of being but does not deny its consequence. It is complete (*pūrṇa*), but does not prefer to remain so.

For Bhāskara, the *One* becomes *Many* finite beings by means of *upādhis,* like a pure diamond appears to be red when it is placed next to a red flower. As long as there is a limiting condition, the transformation is real and finite. Since it is finite, it is subjected to suffering and bondage. However, this condition is only a temporary state. In reality, Brahman is *One* and not *Many*. The ultimate aim of all *jīvas* is to undergo realization, specifically, to realize the absolute state. Liberation is the removal of this artificial condition.[145] Nonetheless, for Nimbārka, the *Bhedābheda* is not effected by *upādhis*, but it is the nature (*svabhāva*) of reality itself, and hence, it is called *Svābhāvika-Bhedābheda.*

Vijñānabhikṣu attempts to demolish the *upādhi* for the sake of the liberation of the *jīvas.* If the Brahman were to be *one partless whole* (*akhaṇḍaikātmya*), then there would have been souls previously liberated from one *antaḥkaraṇa* level that would look for union with other *antaḥkaraṇa*. This means that the space limited by one pot, even when the pot is broken, eventually comes back into relation with another pot.[146] Every time one is liberated, one discovers another liberated. Two liberated merges together, finding a third and the process goes on. This model delays the possibility of liberation *ad infinitum*. Therefore, there is a need for *aṁśāvāda*[147] to rectify the *jīva*-Brahman relation, "a part, due to being stated as different."[148] For the liberation of the soul, one needs to remove all *upādhis*. It is in the removal of *upādhi* one encounters one's *ātman* united (*abheda*) with Brahman as the *mahāvākya tattvamasi* speaks about *akhaṇḍatva*. Untill the *upādhi* is removed there is *bheda* relationship between *tat* and *tvam*, thinks Vijñānabhikṣu (VAB 1.1.2, p.23).

This directs us to another insight. As long as barriers are intact one will not be able to unite oneself completely with the divine. To take a step further, when the barriers are demolished one can enter into an abiding relationship with the other. These barriers could be relieved by practicing *ṣaḍsampatti:*[149]*śama, dama, uparati, titikṣa, śraddha* and *samādhi* (*śamadamādhyupetaḥ syāttathāpi tu tadvidhestadaṅgatayā teṣām-avaśyānuṣṭheyatvāt* VAB 3.4.27, p.294). The seeker of *Brahmavidyā* must practice the control of one's passions, sensations and actions and the like. They are the key to success. Vijñānabhikṣu quotes the *Bṛhadāraṇyaka Upaniṣad*, "Therefore a seeker of Brahman, having conquered the internal and external indriyas, and being withdrawn within himself, patient and concentrated, finds the Self in his own self" (BU 4.4.23).[150]

To begin with *ṣaḍsampatti,* one needs to have *Brahmajijñāsā*. *Brahmajijñāsā* is *dharma* being established due to a characteristic of *codanā* (VAB 1.1.1, p.1; VAB 3.3.1, p.256). It is the highest *dharma* by which one attains self-realization. There is a curiosity within the word *'jijñāsā'* in *Brahmajijñāsā* word. It is the curiosity that directs to deliberation, '*vicāra.*' This is nothing but *mīmāṁsā*. Here, the deliberation is of 'the sacred tradition' (*śāstra*). Thus, *śāstra* fosters one to know the divine, to further in practicing *śamadamādi,* and finally to achieve *samādhi* or liberation.[151]

There seems be to another indistinct motive in the abolition of *upādhi*. The basic need for the abolition of *upādhi* is to recognize the reality in its pristine pure state as said above, especially, to see oneself as an embodiment of the divine. However, a yonder reality is to instruct people not to limit themselves with idols, rather go beyond the symbols and symbolics. Idols should guide to the Real without limiting one's search for the divine. They are only pointers to begin the journey. This understanding can be corroborated with the teachings of the abolition of idolatry by the ruling king of the time (Moghul rule). In other words, Vijñānabhikṣu emphasizes a monotheistic culture deeply rooted in Hindu tradition. What is being seen as the polytheistic practice is only adventitious conditioning (*upādhi*).

4.4.4 *Aṁśa-Avayava Sambandha*

To show the logical coherence of *bheda* and *abheda* in his philosophy, Vijñānabhikṣu differentiates between *aṁśa* and *avayava*. In ordinary understanding, both mean the same—*part*. But in reality, there is a subtle difference—*jīva* is *aṁśa* of Brahman while it is not the *avayava* of Brahman. *Avayava* has to be understood as *part* in the everyday sense, but *part* has a technical meaning. Secondly, *avayava* is related to the whole as 'relation,' and the absence of it diminishes the whole; whereas the *aṁśa* is not responsible for the diminishing of the whole.[152] Every *aṁśa* has in its minuscule the essence of the whole.

According to Vijñānabhikṣu, to be an *aṁśa* must satisfy two conditions. It must be of the same class (*sajātīya*) as the whole (*aṁśin*) and must be the adjunct of the non-separation (*avibhāgapratiyogin*). Vijñānabhikṣu clarifies *aṁśa* as "always of the same class and ever *avibhakta* in nature."[153] Then, the whole becomes subjunct of non-separation or becomes (*anuyogin*). When referring the part to the whole as the same class, one must keep consistency regarding the property under discussion. For example, when discussing part as *ātman*, it should be maintained that it falls under the class of *ātma-hood* (*ātmatva*). Similarly, the part as existence must be regarded as the class of existence.[154]

Another reason why Vijñānabhikṣu does not wish to use *avayava* metaphor is, the diminishing aspect of the whole when one or more *avayavas* cease to exist. This is not so with *aṁśa*. In the example of fire and spark, fire can exist even when the spark is separated from the former, and the same thing is true for the father-son metaphor. This is the reason, why he prefers *aṁśa* over *avayava*.

Brahman is *niravayava*, devoid of any limbs.[155] If so, how could one speak of the *jīvā* is *aṁśa* of Brahman and therefore, Brahman possesses *aṁśa*? Vijñānabhikṣu clarifies this objection by giving three metaphors: hair is the *aṁśa* of body, part is the *aṁśa* of a group, the son is the *aṁśa* of father, and so, all the *jīvās* are the *aṁśa* of Brahman. This is expounded even by *śruti* as, "*ātmā vai jāyate putraḥ*," "*bahusyāṁ prajāyate*." At the time of dissolution, *aṁśa* relinquishes its characteristic of illumination and unites with the illumination of Brahman, the pure consciousness. At the time of creation, *ātman* attains effective consciousness and manifests as *aṁśa*, as the *śruti* affirms it, "he himself is manifested as the son," "let me manifest as many" (C.U. 6.2.3, VAB 1.1.2, p.27). This brings us to the issue of causality, how the *One* manifests itself into *Many*.

The *aṁśa-avayava* metaphor displays yet another circumstantial influence of Vijñānabhikṣu of the time. Just as an *avayava* is a part of the body, *aṁśa* too is part of the whole. In other words, *avayava* can also be called *aṁśa*. Both can intimately co-exist without destroying the other.[156] In this concept, we can see the social background on which Vijñānabhikṣu is influenced. Essentially, everyone is part of the greater reality.

4.4.5 *Kārya-Kāraṇa Sambandha*

According to *Advaita Vedānta*, the whole visible world is a mere illusion—unreal and illusory appearance—while Brahman is the only real entity. *Sarpa* is a *vivarta* of *rajju*, so is the world a *vivarta* of the real entity of Brahman, and the *vivarta* is removed by *vidyā*. This doctrine is called *vivartavāda*. The *Bhedābhedavādins* cannot uphold this for two reasons: i.) it gives only one way of looking at the reality, ii.) the illusion cannot be accounted for the reality of multiplicity of *jīvas*. Therefore, Vijñānabhikṣu upholds the contrary view—the world is real, so also all the objects of the phenomenal world.[157] Here the issue, therefore, is how does the *nirguṇa, niravayava, aṁśīn, ekaṁ* and *sat* Brahman change and become many in the universe? In other words, how does He become the *jagatkāraṇa*?

Brahman is the *kāraṇa* of both *jīva* and *jagat* or *cit* and *acit*. The latter is related to Brahman in the form of *kāryakāraṇabhāva, aṁśa-aṁśī bhāva* and *śaktiśaktimadbhāva* (VAB 3.2.25, p.248). Thus, there is a clear difference and non-difference between the cause and effect. They are to be understood as the snake and its coil (VAB 3.2.27, p.248). The coil is part of the snake, but snake doesn't need to exist only with the coil. Even without coil, the snake can exist. Similarly, the world and the sentient beings are contingent on the existence of Brahman, but without Brahman, the latter cannot exist.

A *Vedāntin* cannot reject Brahman as the cause of the *jagat*. If one rejects, it is against the *śruti* as the *Brahmasūtras* claim, "*from which proceeds the origin*."[158] The most basic way to accept this is through the metaphor of *clay and pot*, the potter transforms the clay into various forms. The forms although have changed, the essence (*svarūpa*) of clay, the *clay-ness* remains.[159] The potter is only an instrumental cause or *nimitta kāraṇa* and the clay is a material cause or *upādāna kāraṇa*.[160] Brahman is the material cause of the *jagat*, as the clay is the material cause of various utensils.

Bhedābhedavādins deem *jagat* as the real transformation (*pariṇāma*) of Brahman, as the clay has transformed itself into a pot, though the *clay-ne*ss did not change. Brahman undergoes a real transformation in form (*rūpa*) in the phenomenal world. Thus, the material cause and effect are different and non-different—different with regard to *rūpa* and non-different with regard to *svarūpa*. Now, the issue to be resolved is the 'unchanging becoming changing' for which Vijñānabhikṣu introduces a concept called, "*adhiṣṭhānakāraṇa*."[161]

Adhiśṭhānakāraṇa is that which joins and supports the material cause with its effect. Technically, it is "that from which the material cause is not separated, and by which the material cause is fully supported."[162] *Adhiṣṭhāna* is the "locus cause"[163] or *the ground of being* in the primary meaning of material cause. Vijñānabhikṣu defines the material cause as, "that which is a substratum, non-separate from its effect."[164] This implies that the locus or *adhiṣṭhāna* does not change in its *svarūpa*, the '*is-ness*' even when the clay becomes a pot or any other utensil. To the understanding of the ordinary people, it is like, water is considered to be the locus cause of the universe which was filled with water along with gross elements.[165]

Here, the *adhiṣṭhānakāraṇa* is distinguished in three

levels: as unchangeable locus cause (is-ness), as the changeable cause (that-ness) and effect. The changeable cause is both non-separate with the effect and also inheres in the effect.[166] This points out that both Brahman and the *jīvas* share the same material stuff. Brahman does not inhere what the *jīvas* have—the changeable form and effect. It is only the *jīvas* inhere the changeable *rūpa* and *svarūpa* of Brahman.

There is something fundamental, unchanging and common for all religions. It is divinity. God is the creator and sustainer. He is the one in whom one finds meaning. He is the cause of both living and non-living, and sentient and non-sentient. It is the *prakṛti* that changes and not the ontic reality. Humans try to deify and immortalize certain aspects of their mortal existence by erecting monuments, shrines, monolithic structures and even by spiritual hypocrisy. All these are transient and unreal. One should identify the divine in each one's soul and build a lasting and eternal monument by relating oneself with Brahman as the *Mokṣadharmakhanḍa* of the *Mahābhārata* pronounces, "*paśyatyātmānamātmānā*" (MB 12.242.10, seeing the Self through the self).

4.5 Soteriological Rendering of *Avibhāga-Bhedābheda*

Vijñānabhikṣu zeroes down the existence of every aspect of the reality to Brahman. It is from Him that beings have their origin, existence and finality. Thus, in all three states, one can see *Avibhāga-Bhedābheda sambandha*.

4.5.1 The Theory of Causality

The causality of Vijñānabhikṣu seems to be based on two

assumptions: consciousness (*citta*) and witness (*sākṣi*). Both these are imported from (the *seśvara*) *Sāṅkhya*. *Puruṣa* is the conscious and witnessing principle and *prakṛti* is the dynamic and creative principle.[167] That is, *prakṛti* is perceived as bringing or seizing and exciting in bringing the creation (*be-ing* of it) and *puruṣa* as witnessing and enabling the process of creation (enabling the *be-ing* of it).

According to Borelli, importing the *seśvara Sāṅkhya* doctrine seems to achieve a serious goal – to answer the problem of evil and suffering in the world. Suffering and evil is a reality in the world. Can a good, loving God cause this? Surely, He cannot. However, *upādhi* of Brahman as *puruṣa* and *prakṛti* under various circumstances can cause it. Such cause of evil cannot be accounted for by Brahman. The first evolute of *prakṛti* is *mahat* and then *buddhi*. Both in their *aupādhika* state can be accounted for evil. This paves the way for disproving the evil emanating from God. Secondly, no imperfect being can emerge from a perfect being. The imperfect beings come from imperfect *tattva*, the *prakṛti*.[168]

It is not possible to have any other witness for the cause of the world other than Brahman in its *prakṛti-puruṣa* form. Brahman cannot be modified into any modifiable cause. He remains non-separate (*avibhāga*) from the cause and its effect. Brahman as supporting and root cause retain any transformation in the cause. On the contrary, *prakṛti* as a material cause is also non-separate from Brahman, but it is a modifiable cause and therefore, can transform itself into various objects of existence.

The *Taittirīya Upaniṣad* enunciates, "That from which the entire universe is created, that which is responsible for the entire universe to sustain, that into which the entire universe merges in the end, is Brahman."[169] To corroborate this, the *Kaivalya Upaniṣad* echoes in the same tone, "He [Brahman] is the substratum [*ādhāram*], bliss [*ānandam*] and unbroken consciousness [*akhaṇḍabodham*] and in Him alone, the three cities go back into dissolution." Further, it spells out, "From Him [Brahman] are born the vital breath, the mind, all the sense organs, the sky, the wind, the fire, the water, the earth and everything of the earth [*pṛthvī viśvasya dhāriṇī*] that it supports."[170] From the *Upaniṣadic* statement, often Brahman is understood to be the material cause (*upādāna kāraṇa*) and efficient cause (*nimitta kāraṇa*) or both causes of the *jagat*. However, Vijñānabhikṣu goes a step further to communicate that Brahman is the supporting cause (*adhiṣṭhāna kāraṇa*) and root cause (*mūlakāraṇatvam*) of the *jagat*, on account of His unseen nature alone (*adṛśa kāraṇatvameva*).[171] In VAB 2.2.39 (*adhiṣṭānānupatteśca*, because supporting cause cannot be established), he supports his claim that "without cause it is not possible to have the author of the performer."[172] Another reason Brahman being *adhiṣṭāna kāraṇa* is the "pervading nature of its relationship" (*sambandho vyāptiḥ*, VAB 1.2.38, p.173). However, he did not negate Brahman as *nimitta* and *upādāna kāraṇa*.

According to *Sāṅkhya,* the sentient *puruṣa* and non-sentient *prakṛti* are independent due to their natures. The appearance of the pot is for the consciousness and not for its own (pot's) nature; similarly, the omnipresence of the divine is for the sake of others. The experience of Brahman is more important than the way He brings in creation.[173] For Vijñānabhikṣu, *puruṣa* and *prakṛti* are brought together by the divine creative intervention, "*asmābhistu prakṛtipuruṣasaṁyoga īśvareṇa kriyate*" (VAB 1.1.2, p.18).[174] Brahman is the uniting factor in the world. He unites matter with *ātman*, the various causes with each other and with their effects, the action with the result, the doer of the action with the enjoyer of the result, one thought with another and so on. There is a purpose for bringing these two together by a common substratum. As a substratum, Brahman exists in all the existence, "*vedaiśca sarvair ahaṁ eva vedhyaḥ*" (VAB 1.1.3, p.36). This substratum is Brahman and the purpose is to bring a divine order (*ṛta*).

Brahman is the *adhiṣṭhāna kāraṇa* (supporting cause) of the *jīva-jagat*. *Adhiṣṭhāna kāraṇa* is the *kāraṇa* from which the *upādāna kāraṇa* (material cause) is not separate from the *adhiṣṭhāna*, but *upādāna* supports and transforms into effect.[175] This conveys, Brahman without undergoing change, supports the creation. And the creation, in turn, creates the creation (new creation) without Brahman's changing in the effected new creation, simultaneously remaining intact in it. As non-separate from the effect, Brahman is the *sākṣi* of *jagat*.

Before the creation, only Brahman existed and after creation too, He continues to exist in the same way. Vijñānabhikṣu offers the example of the formation of *pṛthvi*. The tradition informs us that water is the supporting cause of the earth. It is because, at the time of creation, a molecule of earth, being supported by water, got transformed into earth. But water remained the same without getting transformed into anything. This is how water is being called the supporting cause of the earth.

Thus, Vijñānabhikṣu primarily upholds *satkāryavāda*. This is something contrary to *Nyāya-Vaiśeṣika*'s *asatkāryavāda*. Further, as the *Sāṅkhya* proponents, he upholds *prakṛti pariṇāmavāda*, that is, he believes in the modification of *prakṛti*. However, he differs from *Sāṅkhya*. In *Sāṅkhya*, *prakṛti* is an independent material cause. But for Vijñānabhikṣu, *prakṛti* is permanent (*śāśvata*) yet it is the power of Brahman. The power of Brahman pervades or dissolves (*antarlīna*) in it, just as curd liquefies in the milk. Due to Brahman's foundational cause (*adhiṣṭhānakāraṇatva*), the *māyā* power pervades in the *prakṛti* which brings in the creation of *mahat*. The *mahat* generates *ahaṅkāra* and from it *manas*, then *indriya*, *tanmātras*, three *guṇas*, etc., and thus the whole creation. In this way, the effect which is borne out of *prakṛti* is said to be the effect of Brahman. Therefore, it is also *brahmapariṇāmavāda*. But it is not the *brahmapariṇāmavāda* like *Viśīṣṭādvaita*. Brahman is ever unchangeable, world is permanent. The world is always an effect. Thus, assembling all these things, we can assert the causality of Vijñānabhikṣu as *brahmaśaktiprakṛtipariṇāmavāda*.

4.5.2 The Theory of *Karma*

Vijñānabhikṣu accepts the theory of *karma*.[176] According

to him, *karma* as an obstacle prevents the person from attaining *samādhi* and at the same time becomes the cause of knowledge. *Karma* established through the love of God, guides the way to *naiṣkarmya* by causing *samādhi*. Thus *karma* should be inferred as a cause of liberation through the destruction of sins.[177]

In *Sāṅkhyapravacanabhāṣyam,* Vijñānabhikṣu exposes that one particular aspect of *buddhi* acts for the benefit of one particular aspect of *puruṣa* due to its purchase by the *karma* of that particular *puruṣa* (SPB 2.46). Therefore, one may inquire about the proprietorship of *karma*. Since *puruṣa* is immobile and immutable, it has no taint of the last act, *karma*. However, *puruṣa* is said to be the experiencer (*bhogtṛ*) just as victory is achieved by the army and the owner of that victory or the victor is the king. *Karma* is not reflected by the *puruṣa* or self on *buddhi*, but *buddhi* on the self. Therefore, in principle, *prakṛti* is the owner of *karma*. That's why *prakṛti* is called '*prādhānyam*'[178] just like pre-eminence belongs to the prime minister alone among the governors of the villages and the rest, says Vijñānabhikṣu.

The accumulation of *karma* is due to the multiplication of individuals. It is the *svabhāva* (nature) of the *prakṛti*. In the *Sāṅkhyapravacanabhāṣya,* Vijñānabhikṣu recounts that from one single body (*liṅga-śarīra*) several *karmas* can emerge or arise due to '*karmabheda karmaviśeṣa*' (SPB 3.10), explicitly, differentiation of individuals proceed from the distinction of *karmas*. It is like from one single *liṅga-śarīra* of father several children are begotten, or from a single golden embryo (*hiraṇyagrbha*) many-fold divisions into individuals arise, so too, from one *karma* several *karmas* can emerge.

Further, Vijñānabhikṣu classifies three kinds of bodies based on *karmas*: *kārmic* body, *bhogic* body and dual body (SPB 5.124). *Kārmic* bodies are dispassionate due to their performance of the acts. They are great sages. *Bhogic* bodies have beasty bodies. They are people like Indra. *Kārmic-bhogic* bodies or dual bodies are people of experience or competence. They are the royal sages. The diversity of *karma* in the creation is due to the diversity of *karmas*.

4.5.3 The Bondage and Liberation

Vijñānabhikṣu, following *Sāṅkhya,* thinks that pure conscious *ātman* cannot be in bondage. Moreover, *buddhi* reflects the action in *ātman* by means of a process called 'double reflection.' If so, who is the experiencer of bondage? What is the cause of bondage? And what is liberation?

In reality, the action takes place in the same locus where the cause resides, that is, where the cause resides, the action should occur. The cause of bondage is in the *upādhi* or *vikāras* of *buddhi. Vikāras* of *buddhi* is *avidyā* or *aviveka, duḥkha*, etc. which reside in *buddhi. Puruṣa* gives only "echo-like reflection" or *prati-saṁvādi* as Nandalal Sinha translates. *Prati-saṁvādi* can be translated as "re-cogniser," plainly, it is the seat of reflection.[179] Therefore, bondage, suffering, pain, etc. takes place in *prakṛti* and its evolutes.

At the same time, *prakṛti* is not the direct cause of bondage as the *Sāṅkhyasūtra* asserts, "*prakṛtinibandhanāccenna tasyā api pāratantryam,*" "Nor is bondage due to *prakṛti*" (*Sāṅkhyapravacanasūtra* 1.18).[180] However, Vijñānabhikṣu says that though *prakṛti* cannot be the direct cause of bondage, it (bondage) can follow from *prakṛti* as its cause from its particular *upādhi*, just like the hotness of water is from the *upādhi* of fire (SPB 1.19). Thus, the association of *upādhi* of *prakṛti* with *puruṣa* constitutes bondage.

If the bondage is experienced *only* in the mind, why is a need for liberation or emancipation, or why do we need various ways of liberation at all? Added to this, the scriptural statements speaking *ātman's* emancipation would be contradictory. To answer these queries, Vijñānabhikṣu's double reflection theory is very important. The *buddhi vikāras* are reflected in the *ātman*. Upon reflection, the reflected objects act as if they are original objects, just like trees standing on the bank are reflected in the lake, so too, in the mirror of consciousness all the mental modes are reflected.[181] The reason for the reflection in the *ātman* is to accept the plurality of worldly experiences. A particular experience is particular to an individual self and therefore, one's pain cannot be the same as of the other.[182] At the same time, one can go along with scriptural injunctions that give space for freedom from pain.

The cause of bondage is *aviveka*, the non-discriminatory knowledge. *Aviveka* occurs in *buddhi*. When this happens, it remains there as *vāsanā* in the form of latent impression[183] and later enters into individual self. *Vāsanā* is "a tendency or a residual potency of the modification experienced by the subject itself."[184] *Aviveka* is not an entity of absence as the word *'a-viveka'*[185] itself suggests but a concrete reality. If it were so, it would not have been bringing bondage. However, it does lack transcendental or ultimate reality in the form of immutability and eternality. But it does possess as much reality as water-pot. Therefore, *a-viveka jñāna* as an empirically real cognition, it is the cause of bondage and suffering, advocates Vijñānabhikṣu in his *Sāṅkhyapravacanabhāṣya*.[186]

However, *avidyā* or *aviveka* cannot be the direct cause of bondage. If so, then there would not have been any possibility of experiencing *prārabdha* after annihilating *avidyā* by *vidyā*, because by then suffering, pain, etc., would have been annihilated. *Avidyā, karma* or moral conduct, and the like become causes of bondage by way of establishing *upādhi* of *ātman* with the body. These *upādhis* do not pass away except on the termination of *prārabdha* or *āgāmi karma*.[187]

In this way, *bandhana* or bondage is due to the *ātman's* contact with pain through the reflection in the intellect. Because of this association, the intellect gets modified. The release or *mukti* is nothing but *ātman*'s cessation or stoppage of link with the modified intellect. The contact remains as long as the change in the intellect (*vikāras*) remains. As the modification of the intellect stops (*cittavṛttinirodha*), reflection too stops, resulting in the total separation of the *manas* with *ātman*. Thus, liberation or *mukti* is the complete cessation of the modification of the mind.

This does not mean that *ātman* has no contact whatsoever with *prakṛtitatvas*. As far as bondage is concerned, the contact is annihilated. But it can continue to remain liberated state independently till one's life is intact and thus the progression of occuring. For that reason, even in the liberated state *avibhāga* is maintained.

Prakṛti has a greater role in the liberation. *Prakṛti* has the nature of getting into action and stopping the change, just like there is a dance in the dancer, and only in the *dance-ing* the dance emerges from the dancer. When the audience disappear, the dancer stops the dance and is no more a *dance-ing* dancer. Similarly, modification ensues at the close affinity of *puruṣa* with the *prakṛti*.

Vijñānabhikṣu advocates *videha-mukti* as the ideal liberation. He prefers *sālokya* and *sāmīpya* as the state of liberation (*kaivalya* or *mukti*) than *sāyujya.*[188] At this point, Vijñānabhikṣu rules against *Advaitins* (*Kevala Advaita* and *Viśiṣṭādvaita* traditions) who claim that after liberation the *ātman* becomes totally united with Brahman (*aikya*), and becomes '*ekam*' (*tādātmya*). Vijñānabhikṣu in BS 4.4.22 (*anāvṛttiḥ śabdādanāvṛttiḥ śabdāt,* there is no return as it is understood from the scripture), quotes the *Bhagavad Gītā*, "From the highest planet in the material world down to the lowest, all are the places of misery wherein repeated birth and death take place. But one who attains to My abode [*māmupetya*], O son of Kunti, never takes birth again."[189] From there, 'there is no return' (*anāvṛttiḥ*) implies that once the *ātman* reaches the *kāryabrahman* (effective Brahman) it may take a return, but not when it reaches the *kāraṇabrahman* (causal Brahman).

Vijñānabhikṣu cites the *Skanda Purāṇa* about bondage and liberation, and ignorance and knowledge of the *ātman* depending upon the will of God. The absolute power of binding or revealing is with Brahman. In Vijñānabhikṣu's words, "Brahman *binds* the souls with the ropes of birth and death. He *unties* the ropes of birth and death that bind the souls. The supreme Brahman, eternal Lord Viṣṇu alone (*viṣṇureva*) is the bestower of *mukti* (*kaivalya*)."[190] Brahman alone is the *bandhaka* and *mocaka*. This implies that the grace of God is essential for liberation.[191] It is by His will, liberation and bondage materialize. In the liberation, the *ātman* gets united with Brahman, and manifests the same transcendental conscious nature as that of the latter, like pure water added to pure water remains only pure water, so too is the soul of the human being and Supreme Being. In short, in the liberation, one will find both *parajyoti* and *brahmajyoti* as the same *jyoti*.[192] Instantaneously, we distinguish deep theistic patronage in Vijñānabhikṣu's philosophy.

This does not mean that in *mukti,* there is *tādātmya* between *ātman* and Brahman. Though both are said to have similar transcendental nature, there is an indeterminate consciousness expressed in terms of *upādhis*. When the *upādhis* are removed–like the river upon meeting the sea discards its name, form and taste – *ātman* identifies itself *with* Brahman. Identifying itself '*with*' Brahman refers to identifying itself '*in*' Brahman. Vijñānabhikṣu substantiates this as follows. There is an *avibhāga* relation, as the word '*evam*' expresses in BS 4.4.7, "*evamapi upanyāsāt pūrvabhāvāt avirodham bādarāyaṇaḥ*," owing to the representation of the released soul as pure consciousness in scriptures (*upanyāsāt*), and owing to the attribution of the properties mentioned before (*pūrvabhāvāt*), there is no contradiction (*avirodham*), says Bādarāyaṇa. That is, though the released soul is said to be of pure consciousness by Auḍulomi, Vyāsa, Bādari and others stated in previous *sūtras* (VAB 4.4.5,6, p.332),[193] Bādarāyaṇa affirms that it must be accepted as having consciousness and other such properties. Therefore, there is a difference of opinion among those above-said people. Therefore, *jīva's* consciousness is due to its being *upādhi* and Brahman's consciousness is due to its very nature (VAB 4.4.5, 7, p.333). Then, even in the released state, there is the distinction between *ātman* and Brahman in certain aspects. This amounts to *avibhāga*.

The freed soul is in a pure conscious state as Brahman, but to reach that state the soul has to shed its adventitious attributes incurred due to *buddhi upādhi*. Once the final release takes place, the soul enjoys or freely moves in Brahman's sovereignty. Vijñānabhikṣu conveys the released soul unites in Brahman with a subtle body as decomposed body (*vilayarūpa*, like everything decomposes during great *praḷaya*) in one way, and enjoys freely moving and relating with *Brahmaloka* (*gaganapakṣi*, like a bird, freely flies in the sky) on the other hand,[194] deriving benefit from its subtle body made of *pure sattva*. Hence, the released soul being with Brahman, without obstructing the will of Brahman, becomes a self-governed (*svarājya*) principle, as the BS declares, "There is no lord for the souls emancipated" (VAB 4.4.9, p.334), expressly, in the words of Vijñānabhikṣu, "It becomes wise and independent as it is said in the scripture 'whatever the soul does, become the part of the musical chord,'" that is, the liberated soul lives a Self-Soverign, is able to live freely moving in all the worlds. In the words of the *Bhagavad Gītā* and *Manusmṛti* such a person sees the divine in all, and also sees every being in divine. Indeed, the self-realized man sees the divine everywhere including oneself.[195] There is a yonder reality, one can reread from Vijñānabhikṣu's liberation concept. Any action, of a truly liberated person becomes an accommodating act, that is, any key of the musical instrument played becomes the part of the music piece. For this to happen, one needs to be of pure *citta* and heart. Centring both the mind and heart is the *Yoga*. One can easily see the back of the mind of Vijñānabhikṣu. He is proposing an accommodative theology for the times.

Mukti is entering into Brahman, enjoying Him, and abiding in Him inseparably. Using the metaphor of sun from the *Bṛhadāraṇyaka Upaniṣad,* Vijñānabhikṣu formulates, "That person situated within the sun, who is not the sun-god, whom the sun-god does not know, who manifests the sun-planet as His own body, who controls the sun-planet from within, that person is the immortal Supreme Personality of Godhead, who is present within the heart of every living entity as the Super-soul."[196] The soul which gets intimately united in Brahman enjoys the very nature and form of the latter, but with the quality of service (*seva*) and worship. The scriptures support this, "He (the liberated *ātman*) enjoys all desires simultaneously" (TU 2.1), "so do all beings take care of him" (BU 1.5.20), "through Brahman, the *ātman* attains identity with It (Brahman) or lives in the same world" (BU 1.5.23).[197] Once the *ātman* reaches this state, it will not take a second birth (*punarjanma*).[198]

The *Upaniṣadic* statements, "the one who knows Brahman becomes Brahman" (MU 3.2.9), "He is all this" (BU 1.4.10) and "You are all-pervading and everything" (BG 11.40)[199] should be understood like this, 'once the *ātman* achieves *brahmasānnidhya*, it becomes Brahman, that is, *ātman* is being pervaded by the all-pervasive Brahman and is being supervised by Him.'[200] The return of *ātman* from the abode of Brahman does not take place unless the *ātman* has detached all its adjuncts.

A completely liberated soul (which has reached its *sālokya* or *sāmīpya* state) does not have the nature of *ānanda*. It appears that *ātman* is filled with *ānanda* in its liberated state. This is not so. Just as when one views a bright object of light from far looks as if it is a firebrand of light and when observed from its proximity, one can detect very well what it is,[201] so too, is the consciousness and bliss of *ātman* in the company of *Brahman*. Both *ātman* and *Brahman* have the same substance and therefore, they look alike.

Secondly, if Brahman is devoid of *ānanda*, then obviously, *ātman* too is devoid of *ānanda*,[202] as both are of the same nature. However, *ātman* is blissful (*ānandamaya*) in the sense that it treasures the graciousness of *brahmasānnidhya* in *Brahmaloka*. In its pure state, *ātman* does not undergo pleasure or pain (so too the Brahman). What is said about the *ātman* experiencing pleasure and pain is due to the adventitious attachment of *buddhi-upādhi*. Since *buddhi* is the cause of this, it is its prerogative to terminate pleasure and pain (VAB 1.1.2, p.34-35). Thus, *mukti* sets free *puruṣa* from its *vikāras,* finding its original conscious state.[203]

4.5.4 *Jñānakarmasamuccaya*, a Path for Liberation

Vijñānabhikṣu advocates *jñānakarmasamuccaya* as the path for liberation. It is a doctrine that envisages both knowledge and action together producing the highest destination. Along these lines, Vijñānabhikṣu abides by any other *Bhedābhedavādins* expressed in the first chapter.

Knowledge also is a path for liberation. After having *tattvajñāna,* one achieves *samprajñāta samādhi* in the liberated state. Just as the knowledge of Brahman (*brahmatattvajñāna*) is a path of liberation, so too is *jīvatattvajñāna*. The former is a higher state than the latter. Sometimes and for some people, knowledge can be an effective path; and for others, it may be a combination of knowledge and action (*jñānakarmasamuccaya*) or action guided by knowledge.

Jñānakarmasamuccaya is a cornerstone in the development of *Bhedābheda* ethics. Here two different ideologies are clashing with each other. They are Jaimini and Bādarāyaṇa regarding the nature of scriptures aiming at the *puruṣārthas*. Jaimini advocates 'the performance of rituals' while Bādarāyaṇa settles for 'the final release.' Jaimini goes along with Aryan's performance of rituals since the *Vedic* time and holds *vidyā* as subordinate to *karma.* Śaṅkara reverses it, '*jñāmevahī mokṣamārgam.*' But for Bādarāyaṇa *vidyā* is an independent cause of liberation along with *karma.* The *Bhagavad Gītā* also advocates this, "It is only the lesser intelligent (*bālāḥ*) say that the analytical study of the material world (*sāṅkhya*) and work in devotional service (*yogaḥ*) are separate and not the learned,"[204] and so too is the opinion of Vijñānabhikṣu. Therefore, both knowledge and actions (here we mean, the rituals) are similar, nor are they arbitrarily different. One supports the other. Śaṅkara is against this claim, "the conclusion, therefore, of the *Bhagavad Gītā* is that salvation is attained by knowledge alone, not by knowledge conjoined with works,"[205] reiterates the *Advaitin,* Alladi Mahadeva Sastry.

In the *jñānakarmasamuccaya, jñāna* (knowledge) is understood as, '*jñāyate anena,*' i.e., it is that knowledge through which the whole *jaḍa prakṛti* is realized as *brahmamaya*. And *karma* is that action by which the nature of *puruṣa* is realized. By knowing the creation, we know the whole creation as divine; and by our creative engagement in the creation, we realize the divine in the creation. Further, knowledge has two-fold meanings: knowledge and remembrance (worship). Knowledge is about the content of the scripture and also the worship (*upāsana,* i.e., *karma*) being part of it. But, for Bādarāyaṇa, scriptural injunctions and actions (*karmāṇi*) should go hand-in-hand which will accompany the person till death. The clear knowledge of

Brahman (*vidyā*) is not subordinate to rituals; it is independent of the rituals. In order to attain clear knowledge of Brahman one needs to practice all good and shun all evil *karmas* brought by previous life. The person who has attained the clear knowledge of Brahman does not need any ritual practices. He forsakes all desires and becomes a mendicant (*sannyāsi, mumukṣu*).[206]

Everyone has the right to worship or meditate on Brahman, suggests Vijñānabhikṣu. Worship is not just a prerogative of one section of society. Divine is in the worship and not in the rituals of the worship (*upāsanāvidhi*).[207] Rituals or actions are secondary and worship is primary.

The path-breaking issue here regarding the ritual performers (*Brāhmaṇas*, the priestly class or the people of hierarchy in caste structure) who have been the performers so far in the culture and society for the sake of the welfare of the house-holders, is now differed. They consider the performance of rituals as their prime duty. Contrary to this, the priests are termed not to be free from bondage. Secondly, house-holders are the ones supporting financially the higher castes (VAB 1.3.33-36). Now, the ideal is portrayed as desire-less wandering mendicants (VAB 1.1.1). This is certainly a debunking approach of Vijñānabhikṣu and must have been the effect of the influence of the changing social milieu.

Bādarāyaṇa does neither negate equal authority to a house-holder and mendicants nor does he adduce any definite texts of authority. He merely expresses that there are verses to command one to abandon the practice of rituals, but here the contrary theories are also equally valid. Thus, scriptures have both mutually contradictory and non-contradictory statements. That is the reason the different schools of thought can co-exist without cancelling anyone or can live in harmony. This is the strength and beauty of Indian culture and heritage. The same thing applies to other cultures and traditions of other places.

Thaibaut refers to the theory advocated by Auḍulomi as *satyabhedavāda*. The finite self is different from Brahman; but in *mukti*, it passes out of the body to become one with Brahman. Auḍulomi, Nimbārka and Bhāskara seem to represent three different traditions. There is an absolute difference between the finite self and the infinite for Auḍulomi. But for Nimbārka like Vijñānabhikṣu, there cannot be absolute identity as well as the difference between Brahman and *jīva-jagat*, if so, it will be opposed to the *Upaniṣadic* ideals. The *Upaniṣads* uphold reality to be both equally different and non-different.[208]

Another important aspect of 'this-worldly liberation' (*aihikamukti*) is a continuous practice of knowledge till one reaches the *asamprajñāta samādhi*.[209] This denotes, that i.) there is no end for learning, and ii.) only a right knowledge can lead to the *mukti*. Vijñānabhikṣu furnishes the scriptural basis for his stand: "He who sees the Viṣṇu ever sees the sun, the enjoyer, the object enjoyed and the ruler, when known, is known Brahman himself."[210] That's the reason the person who desires to be liberated must follow the one-pointed practice. The kind of practice spoken here is the control of senses, mind and their modifications as in the case of *Yoga*. "When five senses and mind are in rest, the intellect ceases to function. That is the highest state" (KaU 6.10-11). Further, Vijñānabhikṣu appends, "Therefore, a firm control of senses is called *Yoga*."[211] Without regular practice, one cannot remove the modifications of the mind.

Vijñānabhikṣu's concept is against the Advaitin's claim of *jñānamevahī mokṣamārgam,* and *karma* as merely purifying and facilitating *jñāna*. Śaṅkara thinks that *yajñādi* produce perishable fruits whereas *jñāna* results in imperishable fruits. Therefore, control of senses and enduring heat and cold, etc., is preferred for *Brahmajijñāsā.* But, Vijñānabhikṣu considers both are essential for *mumukṣutva* or *kaivalya*. It is said that for the monks, abandoning all works is not according to the scriptures.[212] In conformity with Bādarāyaṇa, Vijñānabhikṣu discusses that the *sūtrakāra* does not abandon the work, but rather prescribes abandonment of works motivated by *kāma* (desire) for fruits. What is essential is internal means or inner disposition of sense-control which facilitates one to meditate and to achieve *Brahmajñāna.*[213] Even Manu does not suggest abandonment of works, but prescribes both pieces of knowledge and work to act together. For him, the one who performs sacrifices to the one who resides deeper into one's being (Brahman) attains *svarājya*, because the one who does such a sacrifice sees all creation within oneself and one's self in all.[214]

In *Sāṅkhyapravacanabhāṣya,* Vijñānabhikṣu advocates *svakarma anuṣṭhāna* as means of accomplishing knowledge in one's stage of life. This applies to all human beings who fall under *karma*. By the word *'sva-karma,'* he alludes to the performance of the *aṣṭāṅgamārgayoga* where one needs to apprehend *yama*, restraints; *niyama*, observances; *āsana*, posture, *prāṇāyāma*, regulation of breath; *pratyāhāra*, abstractions; *dhāraṇā*, concentration; *dhyāna*, meditation; and *samādhi*, contemplation (SPB 3.35).

There are two kinds of works prescribed by the *Vedas*: external works and internal works. External works are performing the rituals, uttering *mantras*, taking food and so on. Internal works are carried out by mind and speech.[215] Internal sacrifice is offering all good acts to God. Further, Vijñānabhikṣu states that if the actions performed are a hindrance to achieve Brahman, even if they are well-known religious rituals like *agnihotra*, should be abandoned even by the monks (VAB 1.1.1, p.4-6). If they do not hinder, then they should be performed. Therefore, every act should be performed without attachment to the fruit, as the *Bhagavad Gītā* instructs, "The renunciation of necessary appropriate activities, is not proper. Such relinquishment is due to delusion and is declared to be from the quality of inertia"[216] (BG 18.7).

Anybody can have *mukti* by performing one's action. Till one holds on to a physical form, one should abide by the rules of *varṇāśramadharma* without which one cannot attain *karmamukti*. Else, the person will be termed *karmabhraśṭa*. Scriptures prescribe certain rules and regulations and actions to certain *varṇa* or *āśrama* to be fulfilled. Abandoning them is immoral. *Karmaphalatyāga* is a true renunciation or asceticism. The *Kūrma Purāṇa* stipulates, "not only through *yoga* one receives supreme place [*mumukṣutva*], but also knowledge leads to its appropriate fruit [liberation]."[217] And the liberated person is the one who exults in the illumined and fully satisfied self. And for such people, there is no duty, "*tasya kāryaṁ na vidhyate.*"[218] Such liberated people do not inherit any demerits if they abandon their external duties, for they are in the refuge of the Lord.[219] Thus, even a complete surrender to God despite enduring all the grievances will also direct to liberation. *Niṣkāmakarmayoga* (work performed without any desire for fruits) is another form of asceticism, leading one to liberation.[220] The *Bhagavad Gītā* regards this kind of abandonment as the supreme act, citing Janaka and Vasiṣṭa's examples. It is in this sense of renunciation the '*karmatyāga*' in the *Upaniṣadic* statement, "*na karmaṇa na prajayā na dhanena*"[221] to be understood. The most profound renunciation (*pareṇa nākam* or heavenly bliss) within (*nihitaṁ guhāyām*, in the deepest cave of the being) is achieved by the combination of gnosis and work. Therefore, the word '*eka'* (alone) is important.

It is not that once a person achieves liberation should stop all the duties, rather should continue to perform meritorious actions. What is to be abandoned here is all that which dehumanizes the individuals, such as hatred, desire, indifference, etc. (*rāgadveṣādityāgam*). The meritorious actions are sacrifices, charities and penances. They must be performed in a sense of duty without attachment and expectation for rewards.[222] Giving up actions or bodily functions is impossible for any living being (BG 18.11), but it is possible to give up the dehumanizing acts. This applies to all, even to a learned twice-born (*dvija*), except when one is incapacitated by serious sickness. But still, even in sickness, person should focus one's life on Brahman.[223] May be for the beginners (*āruruksạḥ*) abandonment of work is the key to union with the divine, but for the advanced people (*yogarūḍhaḥ*) tranquility of mind is essential (BG 6.3).[224] This entails that everyone is bound to perform their duty, depending on their seriousness of approaching the divine. This is the hallmark of Vijñānabhikṣu's *jñānakarmasamuccaya*.

'Everyone should perform their duties.' Here, the 'everyone' refers to people of all walks of life. The person who aspires to achieve liberation, no matter the person's rank of *varṇāśrama*, the person is provided with, i) the peace of mind from performing the duty, ii) faith in God, and iii) respect for the teacher and the guidance of the path. A teacher has to hold mastery over the entire scripture with a complete personal experience of the divine, specifically, the teacher must be a person who is well integrated with the knowledge and work. Vijñānabhikṣu issues a statutory warning here, 'let the teacher not teach, if the aspirant is not performing one's duty.'[225] The prime duty of any aspirant – be it a student or anyone who renounced the worldly life – is to procure knowledge of Brahman (*Brahmajñāna*). If one does not perform one's duty, the *worlds* would perish. The aspirant is held responsible for the pandemonium prevailing it.[226] The work becomes more fruitful if it is performed without sin; and if performed with sin, then will hinder their liberation.

But an objection may be raised on the co-existence of *jñāna* and *karma* as contradictory. Against this allegation, Vijñānabhikṣu expresses that if *jñāna* is understood to be *samādhi* state in Brahman, then it cannot co-exist with work. But a *yogin* obliges to get out from the *samādhi* to empirical consciousness to perform an internal sacrifice (*ātmatyāga*), wander and beg food for sustenance, and work for the welfare of the worlds (*lokasaṅgrahārtha*). The *yogis* let go of the attachments to perform the internal and external actions for purification.[227] In this sense, anyone who selflessly serves society or the people in need can achieve liberation.

To reach the stage of *samādhi*, both *śravaṇa* and *manana* are essential: *śravaṇa* leads to *manana*. Unless the *indriya*s grasp, the mind cannot process. Grasping necessarily involves *jñāna*. Upon reflection, the knowledge is processed and the *sat* is understood. That which is processed in the mind has to lead to *nidhidhyāsana*. This is nothing but consciously performing (*yajña*) sacrifice for the welfare. Welfare could be of self or others. When one works for one's liberation, it is the welfare of the self (*svasaṅgraha*), and when it is for others, it is *lokasaṅgraha*. Therefore, the *jñānakarmasamuccaya* is a blend of both knowledge and work.

Thus, Vijñānabhikṣu situates both work and knowledge on an equal pedestal. To support this, the *Chāndogya Upaniṣad* intimates, "What indeed one performs with knowledge, with attentive faith, with awareness of its mystery [or backed by meditation], is more powerful and effective."[228] In the words of Vijñānabhikṣu, the conflict of knowledge with work is not substantiated by valid evidence in the scripture. If works become superior to knowledge, then abandonment of them is not right.

Summary

The material well-being expounded by *Vedic* culture points to a social organization of a primitive culture, while the *Upaniṣadic* ethos is a spiritual one. Broader scrutiny of them demonstrates them not as a gobbling up culture but as an accommodative one. *Advaitic* propaganda disregarded material well-being. Therefore, Vijñānabhikṣu opposed it to accept a phenomenal reality as a divine sanction. His idea of wedding theism to *Sāṅkhya* has to be recognized in this perspective. On the contrary, *Dvaita* polemics did not sufficiently explain the theanthropocosmic inter-relations. Once again, therefore, Vijñānabhikṣu had to bring a special relation to retain plurality and at the same time to preserve unity in the theistic continuum. Did Vijñānabhikṣu succeed to explain sufficiently this inter-religiosity, inter-relationship, unity-in-plurality, monotheism and accommodation? At the cursory glance, he did achieve the target to a certain extent, but in doing so, fell into a *dvaita* trap.

Vijñānabhikṣu's concern seems to establish a 'metaphysics and ethics' to help the seeker achieve liberation. But the metaphysics explained by him appears to be ambiguous due to the nature of its explanation. He has inter-mixed the understanding of Brahman with *puruṣa*. However, his acceptance of Brahman as both *saguṇa* and *nirguṇa* is not without reason. Though at the core, he deliberates Brahman to be *nirguṇa,* it is an attempt to answer the Islamic allegations of idolatry and polytheism. Hence, he has given a synthetic approach that takes into consideration very much the changing time and milieu.

Vijñānabhikṣu neither accepts a mere plurality nor a mere unity. Rather his plurality is an expression of the Supreme Being. This is a landmark insight into the philosophical thought of the time. For Bhāskara, it is a temporary state (*upādhi*), while for Nimbārka, it is nature (*svabhāva*) of the One. For Vijñānabhikṣu, *abheda* is possible only when the temporary states of differences are demolished.

There is a recurring issue discussed among the non-Hindus that Hinduism is a polytheistic religion due to several *devi-devatas* and their worship. The plurality of 'gods' is addressed as '33 *koṭi devas'*. This is a wrong reading of this expression. The *Bṛhadāraṇyaka Upaniṣad* explains different aspects of One Brahman through various philosophical dialogues. The Sanskrit word, '*koṭi*' means 'type' or 'kinds'. Therefore, 33 *koṭi* means 33 types or kinds or expressions of One Supreme Being. They are,

- Eight *Vasus* (sustaining material elements) – *Dyauṣ* (sky), *Pṛthivī* (earth), *Vāyu* (wind), *Agni* (fire), *Nakṣatra* (star), *Varuna* (water), *Sūrya* (sun), *Chandra* (moon).
- Eleven Rudras or the vital forces in human beings upon their termination people weep (rudra). They are *prāṇa,*

apāna, vyāna, samāna, udāna, nāga, kūrma, krikal, devadatta and *dhanañjaya* and *atman.* They are also called *pañcaprāṇa, pañca-upaprāṇa* and *ātman.*

- Twelve Ādityas (suns) representing twelve months of the year, causing the lapse of the term of existence.
- And the remaining two are Indra (the all-pervading) and *Prajāpati* (the purificatory aspect as in sacrifice). In some accounts, they are replaced by *Aśvinikumars* (twin solar deities).

Understanding from this viewpoint, these names refer qualities of an *ekameva Sat,* Brahman. Therefore, Vijñānabhikṣu affirms *Parabrahman* is "*samastakalyāṇaguṇaika rāśitvam.*" Brahman encompasses the material aspects, the personified transcendentals, the abstractions, the divine qualities like revealing and concealing grance, dissolution, preservation, self and guardians.

Vijñānabhikṣu's philosophical strategy of 'part-whole relation' is also not a new feature in *Vedānta* either. Various other *bhedāvādins* have used it and commented upon it. In spite of various *vijātīya tattvas*, there is a deep-down *sajātīya tattvas* to make the *abheda* relation possible. Even if a certain amount of *sajātīya tattvas* diminish, yet an *akhaṇḍattva* is possible to establish. This is proved by the very fact of certain unchanging things in the creation. One may call it the foundational things or locus cause.

Another important element to be noted is the path of liberation expounded through *jñānakarmasamuccaya* by

Vijñānabhikṣu. At a time, when knowledge is contrasted either with action in the mid centuries or later with devotion, his synthesis of all three in one capsule expressed through the *Vedānta* highlights the superior quality of ethics. This gives a boost to any type of seeker to experience divine with their respective *modus operandi.*

Having documented his philosophical stand and salient features, the next chapter will attempt a critique and appropriate them to the concrete situation of today's time and place.

---

[1] *"sarvabhūtādhivāsaṁ yat bhūteṣu ca vasatyapi, sarvānugrāhakatvena tadasmyahaṁ vāsudevaḥ tadasmyahaṁ vāsudeva iti."* AbU 22. As translated by Swami Tejomayananda, *Amṛtabindu Upaniṣad: A Drop of Immortality* (Mumbai: Central Chinmaya Mission Trust, 2012), 76.

[2] Srinivasachari, *The Philosophy of Bhedābheda*, v.

[3] Apte, *The Student's Sanskrit-English Dictionary,* s.v. "bheda." Also see, Whitney, *The Roots, Verb-Forms*, s.v. "bheda."

[4] *"na ca abvibhāgaparatve satyabhedaśabde lakṣaṇā asti, bhidirvidāraṇe iti vibhāge'pi bhidi-dhātor anuśāsanāt."* That is, not that *avibhāgaparatva* in its true sense of the word is known to be in secondary sense, but it has to be understood from its primary sense. VAB 1.1.2, p.21.

[5] *vibhedo vibhāgaḥ 'bhidir vidāraṇa' ityanuśāsanāt.* VAB 3.2.28, p.249.

[6] *prāyeṇa ubhaya padārtha pradānaḥ dvandvaḥ.* Apte defines *dvandva* as 'a couple of any two things, opposite conditions or qualities like *sukha* and *duḥkha*, *śīta* and *uṣṇa.*' Apte, *The Student's Sanskrit-English Dictionary,* s.v. "dvandva."

[7] *"avibhaktaṁ ca bhūteṣu vibhaktamiva ca sthitam. vyaktaṁ sa eva vā avyaktaṁ sa eva puruṣaḥ paraḥ."* VP 6.4.44. "The non-separate stands nonseparate in all things, He is the Supreme Spirit, be he manifest or not." VAB 1.1.2, p.21. As translated by Borelli, *The*

Theology of Vijñānabhikṣu, 39.

[8] Advaitins and Dvaitins are known as the modernists or *"ādhunikāstu"* according to Vijñānabhikṣu. See, Vijñānabhikṣu, *Brahmasūtra Vijñānāmṛtabhāṣyam*, 20.

[9] Nicholson, *Unifying Hinduism*, 43. Also see, Andrew J. Nicholson, "Reconciling Dualism and Non-Dualism: Three Arguments in Vijñānabhiskṣu's Bhedābheda Vedānta," *Journal of Indian Philosophy* 35 (2007): 379.

Univocal means, the word has only one idea or meaning. Equivocal means the word has multiple distinct meanings. A nut, for example, refers to the food, the mechanical tool and a foolish or insane person.

[10] Borelli, "The Theology of Vijñānabhikṣu." Also see, Jose Pereira, *Hindu Theology: A Reader* (New York: Image Books, 1976).; Jadunath Sinha, *The Philosophy of Vijnanabhikshu*.; Nicholson, *Unifying Hinduism*.

[11] Pereira, *Hindu Theology: A Reader*, 141.

[12] An oxymoron is a figure of speech in which two apparently contradictory terms appear together, like a *deafening silence*, a *serious joke, and a bitter sweet issue.*

[13] Vijñānabhikṣu, *Sāṅkhya Pravacanabhāṣya*, xiii-xiv. Also see, Nicholson, *Unifying Hinduism*, 68. The stress is original.

[14] Srinivasachari, *The Philosophy of Bhedābheda*, xi.

[15] *jainagandhivedāntin.* See, Nicholson, "Reconciling Dualism and Non-Dualism," 375.

[16] Nicholson, *Unifying Hinduism*, 39. Also see, Nicholson, "Reconciling Dualism and Non-Dualism," 375.

[17] *"brahmaivedaṁ sarvam* (BU 2.5.1)*, ātmaivedaṁ sarvam* (CU 7.25.2), *sa eva sarve yadbhūtaṁ yacca bhavyaṁ sanātanam* (KU 9)*, neha nānāsti kiṅcane* (KaU 2.1.11)" *tyādhyāḥ śrutayaḥ prakṛtitatkāryayoḥ puruṣāntarasya sattāmpratiṣidhyāpi brahmādvaitam bhodayanti*. VAB 1.1.4, p.59.

[18] Vijñānabhikśu regards *śruti* and *smṛtis* as the chief *pramāṇas*. In the case of doubt arising from the conflict between *śrutis,* and between *śruti* and *smṛti*, he resorts to inference in harmony with *śruti* to resolve it. VAB 1.1.3, p.37-38. Also see, Jadunath Sinha, *The Philosophy of Vijnanabhikshu*, 4.

---

[19] *"śāstraṁ hi brahmaṇi mūlaṁ pramāṇam."* VAB 1.1.3, p.36. Scripture is the source of knowledge of Brahman.

[20] *ādhunikāstu jīvabrahmaṇorakhaṇḍatayā jīve'pi brahmaśabdo mukhya eva ākāśaśabda iva ghaṭākāśe. jīvasyābrahmatvaṁ tvajñānakalpitam. tathāhi "tattvamasi* (CU 6.8.7), *ahaṁ brahmāsmi* (BU 1.4.10), *anena jīvenātmanā'nupraviśya nāmarūpe vyākaravāṇi* (CU 6.3.2), *nānyadato'sti dṛṣṭā* (BU 3.7.23)" *ityādhyabhedaśrutiśatebhyo jīvo'pi brahmaiva cinmātratvāviśeṣāt.* VAB 1.1.2, p.20.

[21] *na ca "dvā suparṇā sayujā sakhāyā samānaṁ vṛkṣaṁ pariṣasvajāte* (MU 3.1.1), *nityo nityānāṁ cetanaśca tanānāmekā bahūnāṁ ya vidadhāti kāmān* (MuU 3.1.1, SU 4.6). *tamātmasthaṁ ye'nupaśyanti dhīrāsteṣāṁ śāntiḥ śāśvatā natareṣām, ātmani tiṣṭan ātmāno'ntaraḥ sa ma ātmeti vidhyāt* (KaU 5.13, SU 6.13), *triṣu dhāmasu yad bhāgya bhoktā bhogaśca yadbhavet. tebhyo vilakṣaṇaḥ sākṣī cinmātrāhaṁ sadāśivaḥ* (KU 18)." *ityādi bhedaśrutiśatānupapattiriti vācyam, aupādhikabheda anuvādakatvena tādṛśavākyopapatteḥ.* VAB 1.1.2, p.20; 2.3.43, p.195. Also see, VAB 3.2.31, p.251.

[22] *tatrocyate–abhedavākya anurodhena bhedavākyānām aupādhikabhedaparatvaṁ yathā kalpyate, tathā bhedavākya anurodhena abhedavākyānam avibhāgādilakṣaṇābhedaparatvaṁ kathaṁ na kalpyate? avirodhasya ubhayathaiva sambhāvat.* VAB 1.1.2, p.21.

[23] *aṁśāṁśinośca bhedābhedau vibhāga avibhāgarūpau kālabhedena aviruddhau. anyonyābhavaśca jīva-brahmaṇor atyantika eva, tathā śaktiśaktimadavibhāgo'pi nitya eveti mantavyam.* VAB 1.1.2, p.26.

[24] *śrūyate ca avibhāgādirūpa abhedo api, "yathā udakaṁ śuddhe śuddhamḥkṣiptaṁ tādṛgeva bhavati evaṁ munervijānata ātmā bhavati gautama* (Kau 4.15), *na tu tad dvitīyamasti tato'anyad vibhaktaṁ* (BU 4.3.23)" *ityādi śrutiṣu. smṛtiṣu ca – avibhaktam ca bhūteṣu vibhaktamiva ca sthitam* (BG 13.7), *vyaktaṁ sa eva va avyaktaṁ sa eva puruṣaḥ paraḥ* (VP 6.4.45). VAB 1.1.2, p.21.

[25] S. Sankaranarayanan, ed., *Brahmasūtracatuḥsūtrī Śāṅkarabhāṣyam: Śrī Śaṅkarācārya's Commentary on the Catusūtrī of Brahmasūtra with Sanskrit Text, Transliteration, Word for Word Meaning, English Translation and Annotation*, 2 vols., vol. 1

(Ernakulam: Chinmaya International Foundation, 2015), 54.

[26] Vijñānabhikṣu also uses the word *'tārkikā'* (logician) for *Dvaitins*. Though he did not explicitly take the name, from the meaning of the text, reference to *Dvaita* is clear. *"ye tu tārkikā avibhāgalakṣaṇābhedamapi tyatktvā upāsanāmātraparatvena eva abhedavākyāni nayanti, tanmate bhedanindāśrutiyanupapattiḥ, anyonya abhāvasya pāramārthikatvād vibhāga-avibhāga rūpayośca bheda-abhedayoḥ śrutyarthatvānabhyupamād iti."* VAB, 1.1.2, p.32. "And these logicians or *dvaitins* having rejected identity described as non-separation consider the identity statements as useful only for the sake of worship. And in their thinking the scriptural statements condemning difference have no force due to the mutual exclusiveness is a supreme truth. Difference and identity as constituted of separation and non-separation have no basis in revelation."

[27] *""tattvamasi ahaṁ brahmāsmi" ityevaṁvidhānyeva vedānta mahāvākyāni ca na jīvabrahmābhedaṁ bodhayanti. nāpyetaṣu vākyeṣu tvamahaṁ śabdārtho jīvaḥ, kintu sandhānāntargasya ṣaḍviṁṣati tattvasya madhye ko'ahaṁśabdātha ityākāṅkṣāyām pravṛttatayā 'tattvamasyādi' vākyāni brahmoddiśya tvamahaṁ śabdārthatvaṁ vidaghati, ko ghaṭaḥ? kambugrīvādimān ghaṭa ityādivākyavat."* VAB 1.1.2, p.35.

[28] This view is something similar to Caitanya's understanding of *mahāvākya*. Thus, for both Caitanya and Vijñānabhikṣu the purport has to come from the context.

[29] Shah, *Shri Vallabhacharya: His Philosophy and Religion*, 133-135.

[30] *etaśca jagajjanmādikāraṇatvaṁ brahmaśabdapravṛttinimittam api bodhyam. mūlakāraṇasya eva niratiśaya bṛhattvāt. brahmaśabdaśca paṅkajādivad yogarūḍhaḥ. ato na jīvādirmukhyo brahma-śabdārthaḥ*. VAB 1.1.2, p.19.

[31] This should be understood as super-primary meaning or *paramamukhyavṛttiḥ*. For more details on this notion read, Ivan D'Souza, "*Paramamukhyavṛtti* (Super-Primary Meaning) in *Dvaita Vedānta* of Madhva: A Hermeneutical Probe into Its Scriptural Application and Significance" (Unpublished PhD Dissertation, Pune: Jnana-Deepa Vidyapeeth, 2017).

[32] *śāntaṁ, rāgādirahitam, aupādhikyavyāpāraśūnyaṁ ca, na tu suṣuptavad viṣaya saṁvedana-rahitaṁ, sarvajñam iti uttarāt.*

nirguṇaṁ nityam eva guṇānābhimānena guṇasaṅgena ca guṇātītaṁ, gurṇānāṁ vilayādva nirguṇatvam. VAB 1.1.2, p.19.

[33] *kathamasya brahmatāparatvam avadhāraṇīyam iti cet*? VAB 1.1.2, p.30.

[34] *etādṛśakāraṇatvam eva adhiṣṭhānakāraṇatvam iti mūlakāraṇattvam iti ca ucyate*. VAB 1.1.2, p.17.

[35] *evañca jagataḥ sarvaprakārakāraṇatvam api brahmalakṣaṇaṁ kartuṁ śakyate*. VAB 1.1.2, p.18.

[36] *"brahmatāparatvam."* VAB 1.1.2, p.30. Borelli, "The Theology of Vijñānabhikṣu," 63.

[37] *"tasmāt siddau jīveśvarayor aṁśāṁśibhāvena bhedābhedau vibhāgāvibhāgarūpau. tatrāpyavibhāga eva ādhyantayor anugatatvāt svābhāvikatvāt nityatvācca satyaḥ. vibhāgāstu madhe svalpa avacchedena naimittiko vikārāntaravad vācārambhaṇamātram iti viśeṣaḥ."* VAB 1.1.2, p.32. Translation by Borelli, "The Theology of Vijñānabhikṣu," 32.

[38] *etena "eṣā ta ātmāntaryāmyamṛtaḥ* (BU 3.7.3) *sa ma ātmeti vidhyāt* (KauU 3.9), *tattvamasi* (CU 6.8.7)*" ityadi śrutayo vyākhyātāḥ jīvabhede'pīti mantavyam*. VAB 1.1.2, p.30. "He is your self, inner-controller, immortal," "He is my self, one should know," "Thou art That," etc. scriptural statements can be interpreted from difference (*jīva-bheda*) point of view.

[39] Vijñānabhikṣu quotes *Gautamīyatantram*, *"yadi jīvaḥ parād bhinnaḥ kāryatāmeti suvrata, acittvaṁ ca prasajyeta ghaṭavat paṇḍitottama*." Exact reference to *Gautamīyatantram* is untraceable. VAB 1.1.2, p.32. If the soul were separate from the supreme, then it would be an effect, holy man, and as a consequence it would be unconscious, most learned sir. Borelli, "The Philosophy of Vijñānabhikṣu," 65.

[40] *"paramātmā hariḥ svāmī dāso'ham tasya sarvadā. svecchayā viniyoktātastasyaivātmeśvarasya hi*." VAB 1.1.2, p.30. "The highest self is my Lord Viṣṇu and I am always his slave. They are joined together through the will of that same Lord of souls." Translation, Borelli, "The Theology of Vijñānabhikṣu," 62.

[41] *ahaṁ śabdārthatvena prayoktṛsaṅghāta adhyakṣatvādinā sāmānyarūpeṇaivā kāṅkṣāyām tat ityādi viśesa rūpeṇa upadeṣa iti*. VAB 1.1.2, p.30.

[42] SPB 1.55, 45. Also see, Kapila, *The Sāṃkhya Philosophy*, 137-138. Borelli, "The Theology of Vijñānabhikṣu," 22.

[43] *"dvayorekatarasya vāpyasannikṛṣṭārthaparicchittiḥ pramā tatsādhakaṁ yat tat trividham pramāṇam."* BU 2.4.5; 4.5.6. Also, SPS 1.87. See, Kapila, *The Sāṃkhya Philosophy*, 132-33. Also see, VAB 1.1.3, p.37.

[44] *"tat siddhau sarvasiddhernādhikayāsiddhiḥ."* SPB 1.88, p.45.

[45] *"pratyakṣamanumānam ca śāstram ca viṣayāgamam, trayaṁ suviditam kāryam dharma-śuddhim abhīpsate iti."* *Manu Saṁhitā* 12.105. Also, SPB 1.88, p.45.

[46] *"upamāna aitihya ādināṁ ca anumāna śabdayoḥ praveścaḥ, anupalabdhi ādināṁ ca pratyakṣe praveśca iti."* SPB 1.88, p.45.

[47] Kapila, *The Sāṃkhya Philosophy*, 138. For Aniruddha, *pratyakṣa* is that cognition being produced by means of relation to the thing cognized.

[48] This is how Aniruddha would read and define *pratyakṣa,* but for Vijñānabhikṣu, it is *sambaddham*, that is, connected or relation. See, Kapila, *The Sāṃkhya Philosophy*, 138.

[49] VAB 1.1.3, p.36; KaU 1.2.15.

[50] *buddhiprabhṛtikāryaṁ upādānagocarapratyakṣajanyaṁ kāryatvād ghaṭādivat iti. atra ca upādāna gocara pratyakṣavṛttereva kārye hetutvaṁ lāghavāt na tu caitanyasyāpi gauravāt. tadā buddhyādīnaṁ upādānagocaravṛtīcchākṛtimajjanyatvena kāraṇasattvasya siddhyanantaraṁ, tat kāraṇasattvaṁ parasya bhogyam icchādimattvājjīvopādhivat iti kāraṇasattvabhoktṛtayeśvaro'numeya iti*. VAB 1.1.3, p.37.

[51] *"puruṣastu sukhādhyananuṣaṅgī cetanaḥ, so'yaṁ buddhitattvavartinā jñānasukhādinā tatpratibimbita tat cchāyāpattyā jñānasukhādimāniva bhavati." Sāṅkhyatattvakaumudī* on *Sāṅkhyakārika,* 5. For the translation see, Kanshi Ram, "Vijñānabhikṣu's Theory of Double Reflection," *Annals of the Bhandarkar Oriental Research Institute* 69, no. 1/4 (1988): 77.

[52] *"śāntaghoramūḍharūpāyā buddheścaitanya bimbodgrāheṇa caitanyasya śāntādhyākāra adhyāropaḥ candramasa iva sacchasalila pratibimbitasya tatkampanāropaḥ." Tattvavaiśāradī* of Vācaspatimiśra. As quoted by Ram, "Vijñānabhikṣu's Theory of Double Reflection," 78.

[53] T.S. Rukmani, "Vijñānabhikṣu's Double Reflection Theory of Knowledge in the Yoga System," *Journal of Indian Philosophy* 16, no. 4 (December 1988): 367.

[54] Rukmani, "Vijñānabhikṣu's Double Reflection Theory," 367.

[55] Rukmani, "Vijñānabhikṣu's Double Reflection Theory," 368.

[56] Here the puruṣa is synonymously understood to be ātman.

[57] Kapila, *The Sāṃkhya Philosophy*, 139.

[58] Rukmani, "Vijñānabhikṣu's Double Reflection Theory," 371.

[59] Ram, "Vijñānabhikṣu's Theory of Double Reflection," 81.; Ram, *Integral Non-Dualism*, 114.

[60] Krishnachandra Bhattacharyya, *Studies in Philosophy*, vol. I (Calcutta: Progressive Publishers, 1956), 190-91.

[61] Sāṅkhyasāra 3.2. see, Vijñānabhikṣu, *Sāṁkhyasāra*, 128-29.

[62] Sāṅkhyasāra 3.3, p.129.

[63] *"sāṅkhyayogayoścetthaṁ jñānotpattiprakriyā - viṣeya indriyasaṁyogādīnā vastramālinyasya eva bauddha tamo dravyasa apasāraṇe sati yathā nirmalavastre kusumbhasaṁyogāttu kusumbhākāratā bhavati, tattaiva nirmale buddhissattve viṣayasaṁyogād viṣayākāratā bhavati. sā buddhyavasthā viṣayākārā buddhivṛttir ucyate... vṛteśca pramāṇatvamamubhavākhyaphalāyoga-vyavacchinnatvāt, rathārūḍhasya grāmasambandhe rathasyeva cetanasya viṣaya sambandhe dvārattvat ca... sā ca vṛttir jāyamāneva cetane pratibimbitā bhavati "vṛttisārūpyamitaratre"iti yogasūtrāt. tataśca svapratibimbitāṁ viṣayoparaktāṁ tām buddhivṛttiṁ sa eva pratibimbādhiṣṭhāna cetano avabhāsayati, yathā svapratibimbita kusumbha raktavastraṁ sphaṭikabhittiḥ... tathā ca cetane pratibimbanād eva buddhivṛttitadviṣayayor-bhānam marumarīcikādhyasta jalsya eva marīcinā prakāśanam it."* VAB 1.1.3, p.39-40. For the translation see, Ram, "Vijñānabhikṣu's Theory of Double Reflection," 87.

[64] Vijñānabhikṣu, *Sāṅkhya Pravacanabhāṣya*, 1.87. The translation is taken from, Kapila, *The Sāṃkhya Philosophy*, 134. Original parenthesis.

[65] *"tasmiṁściddarpaṇe sphāre samastā vastuṣṭayaḥ, imāstāḥ pratibimbanti sarasīva taṭadrumāḥ."* VAB 1.1.3, p.39. Also *Yogavasiṣṭa* 91.113. Translation is taken from Ram, "Vijñānabhikṣu's Theory of Double Reflection," 83.

[66] VAB 1.1.3, p.41, Kanshi Ram, 83.

[67] *ya ceyaṁ jñānotpatti prakriyā bahirviṣayeṣvavadhāritā eṣaivātmanyapi pratyetavyā, ekarūpa-kalpanāyāḥ sarvathaucityāt. tathāhi, śāstrādinā yogajadharmeṇa vā buddhestamo'bhibhave sati nirmalāyāṁ buddhāvātmākārā vṛttirjāyate "ahaṁ brahmāsmī" tyadirūpā. sā pramāṇam. sā ca vṛttivātmānaiva cetane pratibimbitā sati bhāsate. tadetad puruṣaniṣṭhaṁ phalamātmajñānamucyate. ghaṭādijñānāccātmajñānasyāyaṁ viśeṣo yad ātma tattvākāra vṛttyā abhimāno nivartyate, ghaṭādhyākārabuddhivṛttibhistu mithyājñānaṁ na niyamena nivartyata iti. cetanapratibimbita buddivṛttivyāpyatvameva bāhyābhyantarasādhāraṇaṁ jñeyatvam bodhyam*. VAB 1.1.3, p.41.

[68] *yathā sūryo bimbarūpeṇa prakāśakaḥ pratibimbarūpeṇa ca prakāśya iti na karmakartṛvirodhaḥ*. VAB 1.1.3, p.42.

[69] *"yathā pradīpaḥ purataḥ pradīptaḥ prakāśamanyasya karoti dīpyan, tathendriyaṁ ca indriyadīpavṛkṣāḥ jñānapradīptāḥ paravanta eva."* VAB 1.1.3, p.42.

[70] Bhattacharyya, *Studies in Philosophy*, 190. Original parenthesis.

[71] See for example different pages of VAB, pp.21,50,51,57,58,59, etc.

[72] *avyākṛtā sūkṣmarūpā brahmaśaktiḥ prakṛtirbrahmaśaktitvād brahmavannitrājetucyate, saiva śaktimatā visṛṣṭā kāryātmana sthitā sati brahmopakrametyucyate*. *Vedānta Kaustubha* 1.4.10, p.125.

[73] *brahmaivedaṁ sarvaṁ, ātmaivedaṁ sarvaṁ, sa eva sarvaṁ yadbhūtaṁ yaśca bhavyaṁ sanātanam, neha nānāsti kiñcane*. VAB 1.1.4, p.59.

[74] *ahaṁ hariḥ sarvamidaṁ janārdano, nānyattataḥ kāraṇakāryajātakam. vyaktaṁ sa eva ca avyaktaṁ sa eva puruṣaḥ paraḥ. vāsudevaḥ sarvami*. VAB 1.1.4, p.59.

[75] *śarkarādugdhayorekībhāva vyavahārat.* VAB 1.1.4, p.59.

[76] Etymologically, *saṁyoga* is obtained adding the prefix *saṁ* (good) to the word *yoga* or *yuj* (union). However, the word *saṁyoga* or conjunction is defined differently by different schools of philosophy. In *Āyurveda,* it is a resulting connection of the combination of multiple substances. They can be temporary (*anitya*) or permanent (*nitya*). In the conjunction either amalgamation or co-incidence may happen. For *Vaiśeṣika* School, *saṁyoga* is one of the 7

guṇas or categories (*padārthas,* objects). *Sāṅkhya* understands it as a contact or a type of relationship. Mainly, it speaks about eight kinds of conjunctions: i. *anyatākarmaja saṁyoga* (unilateral contact), ii. *ubhayakarmaja saṁyoga* (bilateral contact), iii. *saṁyogaja saṁyoga* (contact generated by contact), iv. *svābhāvika saṁyoga* (natural contact), v. *śaktinimitta saṁyoga* (contact for potency), vi. *yogyatālakṣaṇa saṁyoga* (capability defined contact), vii. *yādṛccha saṁyoga* (accidental contact), and viii. *viṣaya-viṣayānimitta saṁyoga* (dependent-substratum based contact). In *Buddhism,* it is understood as bond, union or association, and in *Jainism,* it is combining two things.

[77] *ayaṁ ca sārvakālo brahmaṇi prapañcābhedo buddhipuruṣayoriva guṇapradhānabhāvena atyanta sammiśraṇarūpaḥ saṁyogādiviśeṣaḥ svarūpasambandhaviśeṣo va astu, vivekinām api śarkarādugdhayor ekībhāva vyavahārāt.* VAB 1.1.4, p.59.

[78] *śaktiśaktimatorbhedaṁ paśyanti paramārthataḥ. abhedaṁ va anupaśyanti yoginastattvacintakāḥ. antaryāmī jagadrūpi sarvasākśī niraṅjanaḥ. bhinnābhinnarūpeṇa sthito'sau parameśvaraḥ*. VAB 1.1.4, p.59.

[79] *brahmaṇaḥ sarvādhāratvamavadhārayati. evaṁ hi "yat paraṁ brahma sarvātmā sarvasya ayatanaṁ mahat. sūkṣmāt sūkṣmataraṁ nityaṁ tattvameva tad* (KU 16)." Introductory passage of VAB 1.3, p.110.

[80] Monier-Williams derives the probable root of *viṣṇu* as *viṣ* which means 'all pervader' or 'worker.' Viṣṇu is one of the principle deities of Hinduism. The later scriptures regard Viṣṇu as 'the preserver' along with other two members of the *Trimūrti* – the creator, Brahmā and the destroyer, the Śiva. See, Monier-Williams, *A Sanskrit English Dictionary,* s.v "viṣṇu." William D. Whitney derives the meaning to the same root as 'be active.' See, Whitney, *The Roots, Verb-Forms,* s.v. "viṣṇu."

[81] *nityo nityānāṁ cetanaścetanānāṁ* (KU 2.3.13), *bījaṁ māṁ sarva-bhūtānāṁ viddhi pārtha sanātanaṁ buddhir buddhimatām asmi tejas tejasvinām aham* (BG 7.10), *pṛthagātmānāṁ preritāraṁ ca matvā juṣṭaḥ tataḥ tena amṛtatvam yeti* (SU 1.6), *mahataḥ param avyaktamavyaktāt puruṣaḥ para* (KU 3.11), *brahma īśitavya sarvapadārthebhyaḥ param*. VAB 3.2.31, p.251.

[82] *"yasmin yato yarhi yena yasya yasmai yad yo yathā kurute kāryate va. parāvareṣām paraṁ prāk svasiddhaṁ tad brahma tadveturananyanekam"* (BP 7.9.20) *iti ca. asmiṁśca kāraṇatādvaye kulālo-ṛṇanābhau dṛṣṭāntāviti. evaṁ ca jagataḥ sarvaprakāra kāraṇatvam api brahmalakṣaṇaṁ kartuṁ śakyate*. VAB 1.1.2, p.18. Translation by Borelli, 31. Vijñānabhikṣu seems to have modified the quote from the *Bhāgavata Purāṇa*. The original quote goes like this, *"yasmin yato yarhi yena ca yasya yasmād yasmai yathā yaduta yastvaparaḥ paro vā bhāvaḥ karoti vikaroti pṛthak svabhāvaḥ sañcoditas tad akhilaṁ bhavataḥ svarūpam."*

[83] And therefore, Brahman cannot be known through scriptures. *"yato vāco nivartante aprāpya manasā sahe"* (TU 2.9.1). VAB 1.1.3, p.37.

[84] Therefore, one religion cannot uphold its truth as the ultimate one. Islamic influence of banning idolatry during the Moghul rule can be seen in upholding the *saguṇa* and *nirguṇa* aspect of the Supreme Being. Islamic understanding of God is *nirguṇa*. The deeper understanding of God in Hinduism is in fact *nirguṇa*. But *nirguṇa* is not amenable to the ordinary understanding. Therefore, *saguṇa* is accepted and is represented by certain deities and divine practices and rituals.

[85] It is at this point Vijñānabhikṣu smells *Dvaita,* which will be discussed in the next chapter.

[86] *atra ca ayaṁ viśeṣaḥ–kāryabrahmaṇi gatānāmapunarāvṛttirautsargikī kāraṇabrahmaṇi gatānāṁ cāpunarāvṛttirniyatā.* VAB 4.4.22, p.340.

[87] *"yato vā imāni bhūtāni jāyante yena jātāni jīvanti yat prayantyabhisaṁviśanti tad vijijñāsasva tad brahmet"* (TU 3.1.1). VAB 1.1.3, p.36.

[88] *"sarve vedā yat padamāmananti, vedeiśca sarveirahameva vedhyaḥ."* VAB 1.1.3, p.36.

[89] VAB 1.1.2, p.19.

[90] This is something similar to Teilhard de Chardin's view of creative transformation or revelation of God through cosmic and historical revelation.

[91] *Nanu "ānando brahmeti vyajānād* (TU 3.6.1), *vijñānamānandaṁ brahma* (BU 3.9.28), *ānandāddhyeva khalvimāni*

---

bhūtāni jāyanta" (TU 3.6.1) *ityādi śrutibalatvāt tarkasyāprayojakatvaṁ syāditi cenna, ānandādātmani bhedasya api śravaṇāt tarkasya evādartayatvāt... kiṁ bahunā, sākṣāt eva ānandarūpatva pratiṣedho api śrūyate "na ānandaṁ na nirānandaṁ, vidvān harṣaśokau jahāti."* VAB 1.1.2, p.33.

[92] VAB 1.1.2, p.34. *kūrmapurāṇe "śivasya paramā śaktirnitya ānandamayī hyaham" iti prakṛti-devatāyāḥ pārvatyā vākyam iti.*

[93] *brahmaṇa ānandarūpatābodhakaḥ śabdaḥ... śrutivad dharmadharmyabhedaparaḥ.* VAB 1.1.2, p.34.

[94] VAB 3.3.11,12, p.260-61. *taittirīyake ānandamayasya priyaśirastvādikaṁ pradarśitam "tasya priyameva śiraḥ modo dakṣiṇaḥ pakṣaḥ pramoda uttaraḥ pakṣaḥ ānanda ātmā brahma pucchaṁ pratiṣṭe"tyanen... upacaya apacayau hi bhede sambhavata iti śeṣaḥ... nānātve tasya brahmasvarūpa-ttvaṁ na sambhavati brahmaṇa ekatvānniravyavatvād iti arthaḥ* (TU 2.5.2). VAB 3.3.12, p.260-61.

[95] SPB 3.6, p.149.

[96] *sarvātma* (SU 3.21), *parama brahman* (TU 2.12), *parama jyotiḥ* (CU 8.3.4), *parama tattvam* (CU 6.2.1), *paramātmā* (BU 3.1.1), *sat* (CU 6.2.1).

[97] *atha ya ātmā sa seturvidhṛtireṣāṁ lokānāmasambhedāya, amṛtasya paraṁ setuṁ dadhendhanamivānalam* (SU 6.19), *yaḥ seturījānānām akṣaraṁ brahma tat param iti...* (KaU 1.3.2), *etāvānasya mahima ato jyāyāṁśca puruṣaḥ. pādo'sya viśvā bhūtāni tripādasya amṛtaṁ divī* (*Puruṣasūkta* 1.3)... *sarvavastūnāṁ brahmaṇi sambandhavyapadeśāt ca... brahma īśitavya sarva padārthebhaḥ.* VAB 3.2.31, p.251. To prove the divine presence he further quotes from MuU 3.11; KaU 2.2.13, SU 1.6; KaU 3.11, etc. VAB 3.2.31, p.251. Also see, VAB 1.1.2, p.20.

[98] *tad brahma svarūpataḥ prakāśatulyaṁ ca pratyetavyam. yathā sūryādiprakāśe prakāśākhyaṁ dharmāntaraṁ nāsti. sūryādiprakāśo ghaṭādikaṁ prakāśayatīti dharmadharmivyavahārāstu rāhoḥ śira itivad vikalpamātraḥ. tatraiva paramātmāpi caitanyamāto na caitanyadharmakaḥ.* VAB. 3.2.15, p.243.

The existence of the phenomenal world itself is a viable proof for the existence of God.

[99] *"yathā sudīptāt pāvakād vispulliṅgā sahasraśḥ prabhavate (nte)*

sarūpāḥ" (MU 2.1.1). VAB 3.2.16, p.243. "As from the flaming fire thousands of sparks similar to its form or nature issue forth," so is the relationship between the beings that arise from the immortal Brahman and Brahman itself.

[100] "*nānandam.*" Further it is said, "*aduḥkhaṁ asukhaṁ brahma bhūtabhavyabhāvātmakam.*" VAB 3.2.16, p.243-44. Also see, VAB 1.1.2, p.33. "*na ānandaṁ na nirānandaṁ, vidvān harṣaśokau jahati,*" that is, "Brahman is neither bliss nor non-bliss."

[101] In the previous section it is said that Brahman is devoid of bliss. At this juncture, he gives another reason why he differs.

[102] BU 3.9.28, TU 3.6.1. VAB 1.1.2, p.33.

[103] *puruṣākhyaḥ sa vijñeyo bhoktṛbhāvaḥ sa uccyate.... parameśvare ca puruṣaśabdaḥ upādhi saṁbandhamatreṇa gauṇaḥ*. VAB 1.1.2, p.18.

[104] The root word of Brahman is *bṛh*. The derivative is interchangeably used as *vṛh* or *bṛh*. *Bṛh* or *vṛh* has the meaning of '*tearing apart, to grow, to increase, to cause to grow, to nourish, expand.*' The confusion of *b* and *v* goes back to the oldest time. See, Apte, *Sanskrit-Hindi-English Dictionary*, s.v. "brahman." Whitney, *The Roots, Verb-Forms,* s.v. "bṛh." However, the origin of the word *brahman* is controversial. The etymological meaning is ambiguous. That may be the reason why the word is traced to *vṛh* or *bṛh.* Śaṅkara traces it to *bṛh,* meaning *to depart.* Another meaning would be *to burn*. In this sense, *Brahman* has something to do with fire and heat and so to sacrifice. For more details on this issue, see, K. Luke, "The Term Brahman in Modern Research," *Indian Theological Studies* 30, no. 2 (June 1993): 145-170.

[105] *sṛṣṭisthitisaṁhareṣvadhikāriṇastu sattvādi kārya upādhikāra trayo deva brahmaviṣṇu-maheśvarāḥ mahad akhyā avāntara īśvarā eva*. VAB 1.1.5, p.70.

[106] "*yo yoniṁ yonimadhitiṣṭhatyeko yasminniddaṁ saṁ ca vi caiti sarvam.*" "By realizing the one Lord who resides over every womb in whom everything exists and merges." SU 4.11. "*mama yonir mahad brahma tasmin garbham dadhāmyaham. sambhavaḥ sarvabhūtānāṁ tato bhavati bhārata.*" "The total material substance, called Brahman, is the source of birth, and it is that Brahman that I impregnate, making possible the births of all living beings, O son of Bharata." BG 14.3. See, VAB 1.4.27, p.140. "*īśvaraḥ sarvabhūtānāṁ hṛddeśe arjuna tiṣṭati.*"

BG18.61. The Supreme Lord is indwelling in everyone's heart, O Arjuna. VAB 4.2.15, p.319.

[107] *"aṁśo nānāvyapadeśāt anyathā cāpi dāśakitavāditvam adhīyata eke."* VAB 2.3.42, p.195. From the statement of variety or difference, the *ātman* is known by scriptures as part of Brahman, and even otherwise, *śrutis* decipher that even a fisherman and a knave are no other than Brahman. In VAB 4.2.15 he says, *"avibhāgo vacanāt," Avibhāga* is the declaration of *śrutis*.

[108] *prakṛti-puruṣādiṣu śaktiṣu pratyekaṁ upādānatva ādi rūpeṇa pratiniyatam eva kāraṇatvam*. VAB 1.1.2, p.18. Also see, VAB 3.2.27, p.248.

[109] *"pradhānā brahmaśaktayaḥ."* YVV 1.25. Vijñānabhikṣu, *Yogavārttika of Vijñānabhikṣu*, translated by T.S. Rukmani, 1981 ed., vol. 1 (New Delhi: Munshiram Manoharlal Publishers), 150.

[110] VAB 1.1.2. p.18. Mind acts only as a window to gather the piece of knowledge. Ultimately, it is the soul which knows the object.

[111] *asmābhistu prakṛtipuruṣasaṁyoga īśvareṇa kriyata iti abhyupagamyate... "prakṛtiṁ puruṣaṁ caiva praviśya ātma iccyayā hariḥ kṣobhayām āsa samprāpte sargakāle vyaya avyayau"* (KP 4.13; VP 1.2.29). VAB 1.1.2, p.18.

[112] VAB 3.2.27, p.248-49.

[113] See, VAB 3.2.28, p.249; YVV 1.26. Vijñānabhikṣu, *Yogavārttika of Vijñānabhikṣu*, vol.1, 154.

[114] Rāmānuja and Vijñānabhikṣu concur as far as theism is concerned. Both emphasize on the immanence and transcendental aspects of Brahman in *jīva-jagat*. Both accept *apṛthaksiddhi*, though there is subtle difference. For both, *apṛthaksiddhi* is a special kind of irreplaceable relation. Vijñānabhikṣu retains *avibhāga* even after merging in Brahman, while for Rāmānuja, after merging they become one, that is, *advaita*.

[115] *kiraṇasūryādivad aṁśāṁśinor jīvabrahmaṇor ekapiṇḍībhāvena tasya jīvarūpair aṁśair avaccheda vādasya api pratibimbavādavadevopapatteḥ*. VAB 1.1.2, p.25.

[116] *ākāsam ekaṁ hi yathā ghaṭādiṣu pṛthagbhavedi*. Space is only one as in the pot and and outside. VAB 1.1.2, p.25. Also see YV 1.24, p.141.

[117] *nanu niravayavasya brahmaṇaḥ kathaṁ mukhyoṁ'śaḥ syāditi*

cenna, yathokta lakṣaṇāṁśatvasya avayavatva abhāve'pi darśanāt. yathā śarīrasya keśādiraṁśo, raśeścaikadeśoṁ'śaḥ, pituśca putra iti. VAB 1.1.2, p.27. *jīvo brahmaṇo aṁśaḥ pituriva putraḥ. tathā ca pitāputrayor iva agnivisphulliṅgayor iva.* VAB 2.3.43, p.195.

[118] "Salt dissolved in water, milk dissolved in water, everything has become one's own self, waters alone was in the beginning (*Śatapatha Brāhmaṇa* 14.8.61), smoke in the air." VAB 12.3.43, p.196.

[119] *ādhunikāstu ghaṭākāśavad aṁśatvam vadanti, tatra aṁśaśabdasya gauṇatvāpatteḥ*. VAB, 2.3.43, p.198.

[120] *paramātmā jagadrūpī sarvasākṣī nirañjanaḥ. bhinnābhinnasvarūpeṇa sthito'sau parameśvaraḥ*. VAB 2.3.43, p.196. Original *śruti* is untraceable. The Lord is spotless witness in the world. He exists in different forms.

[121] *Sāṅkhyapravacanasūtra* and *Sāṅkhyasāra* explain *ātman* as the *Īśvara* and *jīva* as part of *prakṛti*. *Jīva* gains consciousness because of *puruṣa* which is equivalent to *Īśvara*.

[122] *ato jīvā brahmāṁśā bhavanti. "ātma vai jāyate putraḥ"* (KauU 2.11) *iti śrutyā putre pituravibhāga lakṣaṇābhedavajjīve'pi brahmaṇe avibhāgalakṣanābhedasya "bahusyāṁ prajāyeye" ityādi śrutyā siddheriti. ato, jīvā brahmāṁśā mukhyā eva bhavanti*. VAB 1.1.2, p.27. Thus soul is part of Brahman. The statements like "the self appears as the son" (Kau 2.11), "let me many let me reproduce" (CU 6.2.3) the non-differnce of Brahman and the souls, defined as non-separation, is established to be like the non-difference between a father a son which is defined as non-sparation.

[123] *nanvaṁśāṣi bhāvajñānāt kathaṁ brahmātmajnānaṁ syāt? uccyate – yo'yata āgatya yadadhiṣṭitaṁ yatra jīvitvā yatra līyate samudratarangādivat jīvāt tadbudddyādivaśca sa tasyātmā bhavati.* VAB 1.1.2, p.28. How can the knowledge of the relationship between a whole and its parts lead to the knowledge of Brahman and the Self? That is the Self, from which anything comes, by which it is supported, which constitutes its life, and where in it is dissolved like the waves of the ocean, that is to say, the soul, its instinct, and the rest. As translated by Borelli, "The Philosophy of Vijñānabhikṣu," 59.

[124] T.S. Rukmani, "Vijñānabhikṣu: The Sāṅkhya-Yoga-Vedāntācārya," *Journal of Indian Council of Philosophical Research* 27, no. 3 (July-September 2010): 24.

[125] *sūryakiraṇavad aṁśānām aṁśinya vibhāgādi ityarthaḥ*. VAB

1.1.4. p.58.

[126] "*vāyuryathaiko bhuvanaṁ praviṣṭo rūpaṁ rūpaṁ pratirūpo babhūva* (KaU 5.10). *ekastathā sarva-bhūtāntarātmā rūpaṁ rūpaṁ pratirūpo bahiśca." "agniryathaiko bhuvanaṁ praviṣṭa"* (KaU 5.9) *ityādiḥ sakhaṇḍatādṛṣṭānaḥ.* VAB 1.1.2, p.26. Just as air, after it has entered the world, though One, assumes different form, accoding to the shape it enters (KaU 5.10), eternal soul, though One, takes a form according to each shape it enters and also in itself exists beyond them (KaU 5.9b), just as fire, after it has entred the world, though One, assumes different forms according to the shape it enters (KaU 5.9a), etc. are few examples. For translation see Chinmayananda, *Kaṭhopaniṣad,* 246-49.

[127] *pṛthag vibhaktā praḷaye ca gopte'ti, tadātmakaṁ tadanyat syādyadrūpaṁ bhāsakam viduri'iti cet.* VAB 1.1.2, p.26. As translated by Borelli, "The Theology of Vijñānabhikṣu," 53.

[128] Nicholson, *Unifying Hinduism*, 47. Original parenthesis. Also see, Nicholson, "Reconciling Dualism and Non-Dualism," 382.

[129] As translated by, Borelli, "The Theology of Vijñānabhikṣu," 30. *avibhāgaścādhāratāvat svarūpasambandhaviśeṣo'tyanta saṁiśraṇarūpo dugdhajalādhi ekatā pratyaya niyāmakaḥ*. VAB 1.1.2, p.17.

[130] *avibhāśca ādhāratāvat svarūpasambandha viśeṣo atyanta sammiśraṇa rūpo dugdhajalād ekatāpratyatya niyāmakaḥ.* VAB 1.1.2, p.17. Also see, *jalasya dadhi, lavaṇasya samudre avibhāga vyavahārasya apalipitum śakytvāt.* VAB 1.1.2, p.26. The speciality of the nature of non-different relationship is in its root is like total dissolution of milk in the water, water in the curd, salt in the sea. The English equivalents are 'inseparable' and 'indistinct.'

[131] *anyonya abhāvaśca jīvabrahmaṇor ātyantika eva, tathā śaktiśaktimad avibhāgo'pi nitya eva iti mantavyam.* VAB 1.1.2, p.26. Non-separation is eternal just as there is mutual non-existence between *jīva* and Brahman is great, so too between power and power-possessor, is to be understood.

[132] *avibhāgaḥ saṁyogaviśeṣāḥ*. VAB 1.1.2, p.26.

[133] VAB 1.1.2, p.26. also see, VAB 2.3.43, p.196.

[134] *"na tu tadvitīyamasti tato'nyad vibhaktimo"ti śrutyā "sati sampadya ten a viduḥ sati sampadyāmaha" ityādiśrutyā ca jīvasyāpi*

brahmaṇyavibhāgaśravaṇāt. "yā prakṛtiḥ puruṣaścobhau līyate paramātmanī" ityādi smṛteśca. "padagatau, liṅgaśleṣaṇa" ityādyanuśāsanebhyaḥ sampatti laya apyayādiśabdānām avibhāgārthatvāt. tathā "avibhāgo vā vacanādi" tyāgāmisūtrācceti. VAB 1.1.2, p.26-27. As translated by Borelli, "Theology of Vijñānabhikṣu," p.54.

135 Originally, the *Vaiśeṣika darśana* classified the objects of experience into six categories, called *padārtha*. *Padārtha* literally means an object can be thought (*jñeya*) and named (*abhidheya*). They are: substance (*dravya*); quality (*guṇa*); action (*karma*); generality (*sāmānya*); particularity (*viśeṣa*) and inherence (*samavāya*). The later *Vaiśeṣikas*, namely Śrīdhara, Udayana and Śivāditya included the seventh category called non-being (*abhāvā*) when it became more epistemological. Kaṇāda defined *samavāya* as the relation between the cause and the effect. Praśastapāda defined it as the relationship between the substances that are inseparable, standing one to another in the relation of the container and the contained. The relation of *samavāya* is not perceivable but only inferrable from the inseparable connection of the substances. See, S. Radhakrishnan, *Indian Philosophy*, vol. 2 (New Delhi: Oxford University Press, 2006), 216-19.

136 *ayaṁ ca sarvakālo brahmāṇi prapañcabhedo buddhi puruṣayoriva guṇapradhāna bhāvenātyanta sammiśraṇa rūpaḥ saṁyogādiviśeṣaḥ svarūpasambandhaviśeṣovā'stu, vivekināmapi śarkarādugdhayor ekībhāva vyavahārāt*. VAB 1.1.4, p.59.

137 *avibhāgaḥ saṁyogaviśeṣaḥ, svarūpasambandho vā ādheyatvādivat.* VAB 1.1.2, p.26. *Avibhāga* is a special relation, a particular relation and attributive nature.

138 *aṁśa amśinośca bhedābhedau vibhāga avibhāga svarūpau kālabhedena aviruddau. anyonya abhāvaśca jīvabrahmaṇor atyantikam eva, tathā śaktiśaktimadavibāgo api nitya eva iti mantavyam*. VAB 1.1.2, p.26. *Avibhāga* is applied only in time. This is because time is an effect and not an ultimate cause, though time seems to be eternal, since everything happens in time. The awareness of the sequence of events which is called *karma saṁvit* gives rise to the concept of time. Hence, time is not independent. Effect cannot be the cause.

139 *prakṛtiṁ puruṣaṁ ca api praviśyātmecchayā hariḥ, kśobhayāmāsa samprāpte sargakāle vyayāvyayau.* VAB 1.1.2, p.25.

140 *"te dhyānayogānugatā apaśyan devātmaśaktiṁ svaguṇairnigūḍhāṁ, yaḥ kāraṇāni nikhilāni tāni kālātmayuktānyadhitiṣṭatyekaḥ"* (SU 1.3). VAB 1.1.2, p.25. Following the path of meditation, saw the power of the Lord, hidden in its own inherent qualities, the Lord who alone presides over all causes, from time to the individual self.

141 *candrajalacandrākāśaghaṭākāśāgnivisphuliñgacchāyātapastrīpuruṣādi dṛṣṭānteiḥ pratibimba avaccheda aṁśādi vādaḥ paraspara virodhena sarve na sambhavantītyeka eva vāda āśrayaṇīyaḥ*. VAB 1.1.2, p.26. For Vijñānabhikṣu, the theory of *pratibimbavāda* (theory of reflection) doesn't hold good because what is reflected is not real. In this theory, Brahman is the real and what is reflected in the world as *jīva* is not real. *Jīva* has the nature reflection. See, Rukmani, *Yogavārttika of Vijñānabhikṣu*, vol.1, 145.

142 Apte, *The Student's Sanskrit-English Dictionary,* s.v. "upādhi."

143 Nicholson, *Unifying Hinduism*, 51.

144 This may be termed as hierophany. *Hierophany* (from Greek "*hiero*," "sacred," and "*phainein*," "to show") is the manifestation of divine, not necessarily in a particular way. It can take place in any form: psychological, social, cultural or economic. There is no particular object to it. The sacredness of any object can be termed as hierophany. In this sense, manifestation of *prakṛti* and *puruṣa* can also be termed as hierophany because of which world of sentient and non-sentient are made sacred. On the other hand, the appearance of God to human beings either visibly or through certain symbols is called Theophany or Epiphany. *Encyclopedia of Religion* (Encyclopedia.com, April 20, 2019), s.v. "Hierophany." Also see, "Hierophany," in Encyclopedia of Religion. Encyclopedia online. Available on https://www.encyclopedia. com/environment/ encyclopedias-almanacs-transcripts-and-maps/hiero-phany, accessed on April 30, 2019.

145 Nicholson, *Internet Encyclopedia of Philosophy*, s.v. "Bhedābheda."

146 *yathaikaghṭa avacchinna ākāśasya tadghaṭabhaṅge'pi ghaṭāntareṇa punaḥ sambandho bhavati.* VAB 1.1.2, p.23.

147 *tathā ca sati aṁśāvāda evāśrayituṁ yuktaḥ "aṁśo nānāvyapadeśāt" ityādisūtreṇācāryeir aṁśatvasya eva nyāyayato*

mīmāṁsyatvāt. VAB 1.1.2, p.26. The part doctrine is the only acceptable one because it was logically examined by the teacher with aphorism, "A part on account of a declaration of difference" (BS 2.3.43).

[148] *aṁśo nānāvyapadeśāt*. VAB 2.3.43, p.195.

[149] 1) Tranquility (*śama*): Intentional cultivating of an inner attitude of tranquility, peace of mind, or contentment is a foundation on which the other practices can rest.

2) Training (*dama*): Training of the senses (*indriyas*) means the responsible use of the senses in positive, useful directions, both in our actions in the world and the nature of inner thoughts we cultivate.

3) Withdrawal (*uparati*): With a proper inner attitude of tranquility, and the training of the senses, there also comes a sense of satiety, or natural sense of completeness, as if no more of the sensory experience need be sought.

4) Forbearance (*titikṣa*): Forbearance and tolerance of external situations allow one to be free from the onslaught of the sensory stimuli and pressures from others to participate in actions, speech, or thoughts that one knows to be going on in a not-useful direction.

5) Faith (*śraddha*): An intense sense of certainty about the direction one is going keeps one going in the right direction, persisting in following the teachings and practices that have been examined and seen to be productive, useful, and fruit bearing.

6) Focus (*samādhāna*): Resolute focus towards harmonizing and balancing of mind, its thoughts, and emotions, along with the other virtues, brings a freedom to pursue the depth of inner exploration and realization.

[150] *"tasmādevaṁ vicchānto dānta uparatastitikśuḥ samāhito bhūtvātmanyevātmānaṁ paśyati"* BU 4.4.23. VAB 3.4.27, p.294.

[151] VAB 3.4.27, p.294; VAB 1.1.1, p.3-4.

[152] Nicholson, *Unifying Hinduism*, 55. *Aṁśa* in the modern terminology can be understood as a hologram. When a hologram is broken into thousands of pieces, each hologram piece portrays the whole.

[153] *aṁśatvaṁ ca sajātīyatve sati kadācit avibhaktatvam eva vācyam*. VAB 2.3.43, p.197.

[154] *aṁśatvaṁ ca sajātīyatve sati avibhāgapratiyogitvaṁ,*

tadanuyogitvaṁ ca aṁśitvam. yena ca rūpeṇāṁśatā yatra vivakṣyate tenaiva rūpeṇa sājātyaṁ tatra grāhyaṁ, yathā ātma aṁśalakṣaṇe ātmatvenaiva sājātyaṁ sat aṁśādilakśaṇeṣu ca sattvādirūpeṇaivetyato nātiprasañgaḥ. athavā dravytva sākṣād vyāpyajātyā sājātyaṁ grāhyaṁ. VAB 1.1.2, p.26.

[155] *brahmaṇaḥ niravayavaḥ āsīt*. VAB 1.1.2, p.27.

[156] This is very much true about social traditions and cultures. One religion may find the other as different, but both have a fundamental unity in divinity, spirituality and the purpose of existence. Therefore, one cannot and should not consider the other as different, but should treat as part of the whole reality. Both can co-exist without cancelling each other. Neither is superior nor the other inferior, rather equally important to become the part of the One Whole.

[157] For the *Kevala Advaitins*, the world is real only at the conventional or *vyāvahārika* level. The real is only Brahman and is *nirguṇa*. At the *vyāvahārika* level, Brahman is seen as *saguṇa*.

[158] *janmādhyasya yataḥ*. VAB 1.1.2. Also see, VAB 3.2.25, p.248.

[159] This is the dialogue between Śvetaketu and Āruṇi in CU 6.1.4-5.

[160] If we consider the pre-existance of the effect in the cause, then it is *satkāryavāda*.

[161] *yata iti pañcamīcātrādhiṣṭānakāraṇatve*. VAB 1.1.2, p.17. '*janmādi*' word (from which) is ablative case (fifth case) which gives the root cause.

[162] *kiṁ punarādhiṣṭānakāraṇatvam? ucyate—tadeva adhiṣṭhānakārṇaṁ yatra avibhaktaṁ yenopaṣṭabdhaṁ ca sadupādānakāraṇaṁ kāryākāreṇa pariṇamate*. VAB 1.1.2, p.17.

[163] Nicholson, *Unifying Hinduism*, 59.

[164] *kārya avibhāga ādhāratvasya eva upādāna sāmānya lakṣaṇatvāt*. VAB 1.1.2, p.17.

[165] *sargādau jalāvibhaktāḥ pārthivasūkṣmāṁśāstanmātrākhyāḥ jalena eva upaṣṭambhāt pṛthivyākāreṇa pariṇamanta ityato jalaṁ mahāpṛthivyā adhiṣṭhānakāraṇam iti*. VAB 1.1.2, p.17.

[166] Nicholson, *Unifying Hinduism*, 59.

[167] MuU 3.1.2,3,8; SU 4.6-7; KaU 1.3.1, 12; SU I.9; 4.6,7; TU 2.4; RV 1.164.20.

[168] Borelli, Theology of Vijñānabhikṣu, 28.

---

[169] *"yato vā imāni bhūtāni jāyante; yena jātāni jīvanti; yat prayanti abhisaṁviśanti; tad vijijñāsasva; tad brahmeti."* TU 3.1.1. As translated by Swami Muni Narayana Prasad.

[170] *"ādhāram ānandam akhaṇḍabodhaṁ yasmin layaṁ yāti puratrayaṁ ca. etasmājjāyate prāṇo manaḥ sarvendriyāṇi ca, khaṁ vāyujjyortirāpaḥ pṛthvī vivśvasya dhāriṇī."* Kai.U 14,15; VAB 1.1.2, p.17.

[171] *yasya yat kāraṇaṁ proktaṁ tasya sākṣānmaheśvaraḥ, adhiṣṭhānatayā stithvā sadaiva upakaroti hi. iti. tathā cet adṛśa kāraṇatvam eva adhiṣṭhāna kāraṇatvam iti mūlakāraṇatvam iti ca ucyate.* VAB 1.1.2, p.17. Verily Maheśvara is that cause of that which is spoken, being as the supporting cause ever favours. And in the same way this unseen cause is the only supporting cause and thus the root cause, thus it is said.

[172] *kāraṇaṁ vinā kartṛtvāsambhavāccetyarthaḥ*. VAB 1.2.39, p.173.

[173] *brahmaṇo anubhavavyāpyatvānaṅgīkāre viduṣāṁ brahmaṇi vyavahāro na syād iti*. VAB 1.1.3, p.38.

[174] *prakṛtisvātantryavādibhyāṁ sāṅkhyayogibhyāṁ puruṣaprayuktā pravṛttiḥ (prakṛtiḥ) svayam eva puruṣeṇa ādhya jīvena saṁyujyata iti abhyupagamyate ayaskāntena lohavat. asmābhistu prakṛti-puruṣasaṁyoga īśvareṇa kriyata iti abhyupagamyate, "ādiḥ sa saṁyoganimittahetuḥ parastri-kālādakalo api dṛṣṭa"* (SU 6.5) *iti śruteḥ, "prakṛtiṁ puruṣaṁ ca eva praviśyātmecchayā hariḥ, kṣobhayāmāsa samprāpte sargakāle vyayāvyayau"* (VP 1.2.29) *iti smṛteśceti.* VAB 1.1.3, p.18. Sānkhya and Yoga thinkers believe in the independence of matter, and they all agree that matter, acting for the benefit of Spirit, is joined with the primeval soul, Spirit, like iron to a magnet. Now I maintain that the joining of matter and Spirit is effected by God because of this scripture, "He is the beginning, the source of the cause of joining; he is seen as higher than time and without parts." There is also this text from tradition, "The Lord Viṣṇu by his own desire, having entered Matter and Spirit, at the time of creation agitates the eternal and noneternal," thus says the *smṛti*. As translated by Borelli, *The Theology of Vijñānabhikṣu*, 32.

[175] *kiṁ punarādhiṣṭānakāraṇatvam? ucyate—tadeva adhiṣṭhānakārṇaṁ yatra avibhaktaṁ yenopaṣṭabdhaṁ ca sadupādānakāraṇaṁ kāryākāreṇa pariṇamate. yathā sargādau*

jalāvibhaktāḥ pārthiva sūkṣmāṁśa astanmātrākhyāḥ jalenaiva upaṣṭhambhāt pṛthvyākāreṇa pariñmanta ityato jalaṁ mahāpṛthvyā adhiṣṭhānakāraṇam iti. VAB 1.1.2, p.17. "What then is the supporting causality? I reply that the supporting cause that one from which the material cause is not separate and by which the latter, being supported, is transformed into the mode of an effect. Just as the molecule of earth, called subtle elements, at the time of creation, not being separate from water because they are supported by it, are transformed in appearance into the earth, so water is the supporting cause of the great earth." As translated by Borelli, *The Theology of Vijñānabhikṣu*, 29.

[176] *Karma* or merits and demerits are divided as past and future. The past *karma* is the consequence of action already acquired. They are divided into *sañcita karma* (stored up) and *prārabdha karma* (operative). *Sañcita karma* is the experience which has not yet begun. *Prārabdha karma* is for the experience of the consequence whereof the present birth has taken place. The future or *āgāmi karma* will be acquired afterwards.

[177] VAB 1.1.1, p.7.

[178] *"samānakarmayoge buddheḥ prādhānyaṁ lokavallokavat."* *Sāṅkhyasūtra* 2.47. "Admitting that they (the various instruments of soul, all) equally act, the preeminence belongs to intellect, just as in the world, just as in the world. As translated by Ballantyne, *The Sāṅkhya Aphorisms of Kapila,* 222.

[179] *"buddheḥ pratisaṁvedī puruṣaḥ."* "'Re-cogniser' (*prati-saṁvedi*), that is, the seat of *prati-saṁvedi* or echo-like reflection of cognition." See under the *sūtra* of SPB 1.87. For translation see, Nandalal Sinha, *The Sāmkhya Philosophy*, 134.

[180] "Does bondage result from *prakṛti* as its cause? No, because *prakṛti* herself is not autonomous." SPB 1.18. Nandalal Sinha, *The Sāmkhya Philosophy*, p.37.

[181] *tasmiṁ ciddarpaṇe sphāre samastā vastudṛṣṭayaḥ, imāstā pratibimbanti sarasīva taṭadrumāḥ. Yogavasiṣṭa* 91.113, 123. See, VAB 1.1.3, p.39.

[182] *ato bhogavaicitryopapataye bhoganiyāmakatayā duḥkhādiyogarūpo bandhaḥ puruṣo'pi svīkāryaḥ... pratibimbaḥ ca upādhivṛtter eva bhavatīti na sarvapuṁsāṁ sarvaduḥkhabhoga it bāvaḥ*. See under the *sūtra* of SPB 1.17. Nandalal Sinha, *The Sāmkhya*

Philosophy, 36. Also see, Ram, 137.

[183] "*vāsanarūpasya eva avivekasya saṁyogajanmahetutayā.*" See under the *sūtra* SPB 1.55. Ram, *Integral Non-Dualism*, 130.

[184] Nandalal Sinha, *The Sāmkhya Philosophy*, 136.

[185] The word '*aviveka*' is a *nañ-tatpuruṣa* (*vyāñjana tatpuruṣa*) compound where something is negated what has been said in the *pūrvapada* of the main word. Here, the prefix 'a' represents a *nañ* (negation), the *pūrvapada* '*vi*' means to sift or to extend from the root '*vic*' or '*vyac*' respectively. Therefore, *viveka* is that knowledge obtained after sifting (i.e., wisdom) and *a-viveka* is that knowledge which is not sifted. Ram, *Integral Non-Dualism*, 130.

[186] For the *advaitins*, incidence of bondage cannot be satisfactorily accounted for. *advaitavādināṁ teṣām avidyāyā api avastutvena tayā bandhānaucityāt. na hi svāpnarajjuvā bandhanaṁ dṛṣṭim iti arthaḥ... anayaiva rītyā navīnānām api pracchannabaudhānāṁ māyāvādinām avidyāmātrasya tucchasya bandhahetutvaṁ nirākṛtaṁ veditavyam. asmanmate tu avidyāyā kūṭastha nityatā-rūpaparamārthatva abhāve api ghaṭādivad vāstatvena vakśyamāṇa saṁyogadvārā bandhahetutve yathoktabādhānavakāśaḥ.* See under the *sūtra* SPB 1.20, 22. For translation see, Nandalal Sinha, *The Sāmkhya Philosophy*, 45-47.

Vijñānabhikṣu even discards doctrine of *māyā* in the stricter sense. He says, it is not the tenet of the *Vedānta* system, "that great system, the doctrine of *māyā*, containing the truths of the Veda, but not supported by the Veda." Nandalal Sinha, *The Sāmkhya Philosophy*, 46-47.

[187] SPB 1.24. See Nandalal Sinha, *The Sāmkhya Philosophy*, 48.

[188] *Sāyujya* is "an intimate union, identification or absorption." Apte, *Sanskrit-English Dictionary*, s.v. "sāyujya." *Vaiṣṇavas* advocate four kinds of *muktis*: *sālokya, sāmīpya, sārūpya* and *sāyujya. Sālokya* refers to the sharing by the devotee of the same sphere as is occupied by the deity. *Sāmīpya* is the proximity to the goal of liberation won by those who perform the duties of their respective stations in life. *Sārūpya* is to acquire the bodily features of the deity. *Sāyujya* aims at the unity of devotee with the deity worshipped. It is a complete absorption or identification. Vaishali Sunil Karnik, *Concept of Mokṣa: In Advaita Vedānta with Special Reference to Jivanmuktiviveka of Sri Vidyārañyaswāmī* (Delhi: Bharatiya Kala Prakashan, 2012), 12. Madhva and Caitanya add *sārṣṭi mukti*. It means attaining opulences like those

of the Supreme Lord.

[189] *"ābrahmabhuvanāllokāt punarāvartito'rjuna māmupetya tu kaunteya punarjanma na vidyate."* BG 8.16; VAB 4.4.22, p.340. As translated by Prabhupāda, 377.

[190] *yasmāt tataḥ parameśvarābhidhyānādevāsya jīvasya manovikārair bandhaḥ, tadviparyayo vikāravilayena cinmātrarūpatayā'vasthānam mokṣaśca bhavati. "bandhako bhavapāśena bhava-pāśācca mocakaḥ. kaivalyadaḥ paraṁ brahma viṣṇur eva sanātanaḥ"* (*Skanda Purāṇa*). VAB 3.2.5, p.237. Original *śruti* is untraceable.

[191] In this sense, he is very close to Vallabhācārya's *purṣṭi mārga*.

[192] *yathodakaṁ śudde śuddaṁkśiptaṁ tādṛgeva bhavati evaṁ munervijānata ātmā bhavati* (KaU 2.15), *paraṁ jyotiḥ paraṁ brahma jyotiṣām api tat jyoti*. VAB 4.4.1, p.331. As pure water poured into pure water becomes the same only, so becomes the ātman of the sage who knows this unity of ātman (KaU 2.15), the supreme light is the source of light of all luminous objects (BG 13.8).

[193] *brāhmeṇa jaiminirūpanyāsādibhyaḥ,* the released soul emerges from bondage as endowed with the properties belonging to the Supreme BeIng Himself. VAB 4.4.5, p.332. *"citi tanmātrena tadātmakatvāt iti auḍulomiḥ,"* the released soul manifests himself solely as pure consciousness, thinks Auḍulomi. VAB 4.4.6, p.332.

[194] *paraṁ jyotirūpasampadhyasvena rūpeṇa abhisampadhyata ityavyadhānena paṭhitatvāt, "sa tatra paryeti jakṣan krīdin ramamāṇa"* (CU 8.12.3) *iti vākyāt parabrahmaṇo api bhogasiddher iti... prabhrahmaṇi dvividhā gatiḥ: ekā vilayarūpā, sa ca prākṛta praḷaya ātyantika praḷayayor eva bhavati. dvitīyā ca gagana pakṣiṇām iva sarva āvaraṇād bahiṣṭe māyāśabala brahmaṇi liṅgadehasya sanghamātram*. VAB 4.4.8, p.333.

[195] *"ata evā* (*eva cā*) *na anya adhipatiḥ."* VAB 4.4.9, p.334. *viduṣāṁ svārājyaṁ ca "sa svarāṅbhavati tasya sarveṣu kāmacāro bhavati iti" śruteḥ* (CU 7.25.2). *"sarvabhūtastham ātmānaṁ sarvabhūtani cātmani, samaṁ paśyannātmayājī svarājyamadhigacchati"* (Manu 2.12; 43.2, also BG 6.29). VAB 4.4.9, p.334.

[196] *"ya āditye tiṣṭhann ādityād antaro yam ādityo na veda yasyādityaḥ śarīram ya ādityam antaro yamayati eṣa ta ātma antaryāmi amṛtaḥ"* (BU 3.7.9). VAB 4.4.20, p.339. The *Kaivalya*

Upaniṣad also speaks this in the same sense, "That which is the supreme Brahman, the Self in all, the ample support of the universe, subtler than the subtle and eternal—That alone Thou art, That alone art That" (Kai.U 1.16). For the translation see, Swami Chinmayananda, *Kaivalya Upaniṣad*, 2015 ed., Upaniṣad Series (Mumbai: Central Chinmaya Mission Trust, 1952), 80.

[197] *"so aśnute sarvān kāmān saha brahmaṇā vipaścite iti"* (TU 2.1), *"sa yathaitāṁ devatāṁ sarvāṇi bhūtānyavanti evaṁ hainaṁ sarvāṇi bhūtānyavanti"* (BU 1.5.20), *"tena etasyai devatāyei sāyujyaṁ salokatāṁ jayati"* (BU 1.5.22), *iti ādi śrutau parameśvareṇa saha tadviduṣāṁ bhogamātraṁ samānaṁ śrūyate... avantu (avanti) sevakarūpā layantīsarthaḥ (laṣantī iti arthaḥ). sāyujyaṁ ca upāsye praviśya tena saha ekīrbhāvena eka rūpo bhoga iti.* VAB 4.4.21, p.340.

[198] *"māmupetya tu kaunteya punarjanma na vidhyate"* (BG 8.15), that is, having reached Brahman, there is not rebirth, O Arjuna. VAB 4.4.22, p.340.

[199] *"brahma veda brahmaiva bhavati* (MU 3.2.9), *sa idaṁ sarvaṁ bhavati* (BU 1.4.10), *sarvaṁ samāpnoṣi tato'si sarvaḥ"* (BG 11.40). VAB 4.4.21, p.340.

[200] VAB 4.4.20-21, p.339-40. See 3.5.1 of this thesis, *tattvamasi* as 'Thou art in That.'

[201] *caitanyaṁ ca ātmano na guṇaḥ, kintu dravyaviśeṣa eva dharmadharmivibhāgaśūnyaścetana iti caitanyaṁ iti ca uccyate caitanyadharmakatva pratiṣedhāya. yathā tejo dravyaṁ prakāśakaṁ prakāśa iti ca uccyate, sadā saha upalambhena lāghavād ekatvasya eva nyāyayyatvāt.* VAB 1.1.2, p.33. Consciousness is not an attribute of the Self, but it is its very substance. What is called consciousness is a conscious being in whom the division into substance and attribute is absent. This is said in order to exclude the character of attribute from consciousness. Just as fire is always said to be a luminous substance or luminousness because the two are simultaneously perceived, for reasons of logic and economy, and because oneness is deduced.

The same thing applies to a person who is a really united with God. He cannot get credit for himself, the credit goes to the scripture.

[202] *"etena Brahmaṇa ānandarūpatvamapāstaṁ "neikasyānandacidrūpatve virodhādi" iti sāṅkhya-sūtroktanyāyācca."* VAB 1.1.2, p.33.

[203] *vikāravilyadvārā cinmātrarūpeṇa purṣasya avasthāmeva*

mokṣāḥ. Liberation is a complete release of impurities of *puruṣa* in the form of consciousness.

[204] *"sāṅkhyayogau pṛthag bālāḥ pravadanti na paṇḍitāḥ, ekam apy āsthitaḥ samyug ubhayor vindate phalam."* BG 5.4.

[205] Alladi Mahadeva Sastry, *The Bhagavad Gita with the Commentary of Sri Sankaracharya* (Madras: Samata Books, 1979), 28-29. *tasmād gītāsu kevalād eva tattvajñānād mokṣa prāptiḥ na karma samuccitād it niścitaḥ arthaḥ*.

[206] Nakamura, *A History of Early Vedānta Philosophy*, 414-24.

[207] *upāsanāt cetanatve na upāsanāvidhānāt iti yāvat.* VAB 1.3.32, p.121. Consciousnessness is in the worship and not in the worship pattern ever.

[208] *kāryasya kāraṇānanyatvamasti, natvatyanta bhinnatvam. Vedānta Pārijāta Kaustubha* 2.1.14, p.61. See, Goswami, *Śrī Nimbārka Vedānta*. Also see, Satyanand, *Nimbārka: A Pre-Śaṅkara Vedāntin and His Philosophy*, 296.

[209] *vidhyāyā asakṛdāvṛtiḥ kartavyā asamprajñāta samādhiparyantaṁ yathā vighnena na abhibhūyate.* VAB 4.1.1, p.304. For the knowledge gain, constant repetition should follow till one becomes unconscious and not till the obstacles are removed.

[210] *"tadviṣṇorvedaṁ sadā paśyanti sūrayaḥ, etad jñeyaṁ nityamevātmasaṁsthaṁ nātaḥ paraṁ veditavyaṁ hi kiṅcit, tamevaikaṁ jānathātmanaṁ tameva dhīro vijñāya prajñām kurvīta brāhmanaḥ"* (SU 1.2; BG 6.10). VAB 4.1.1, p.304.

[211] *āvṛtteśca vighnotsārakatvaṁ pātañjale sūtritam, "tatpratiṣedhārthakatattvābhāsaḥ" iti.* VAB 4.1.1, p.304.

[212] *etena sannyāsināṁ sarvakarmatyāga aśāstrārthaḥ.* VAB 1.1.1, p.4

[213] VAB 1.1.1, p.3. Spirit of performance is more important than ritual performance.

[214] *"paramātma ātmanor ekatve vijñānena tayorbheda eva vibhagnaḥ sāndhyaṁ sandhyeti. tathā manau, "sarvabhūtsthaṁ ātmānaṁ sarvabhūtāni ca ātmani, samaṁ paśyannātmayājī svarājyaṁ adhigacchati."* VAB 1.1.1, p.8 of Mukunda Shāstri. Vijñānabhikṣu, *Vijñānāmṛtabhāṣyam*. There is a difference in the text edited by both editors. For better flow of thoughts, I have used Mukunda Shastri's version here.

[215] The *Manusmṛti* speaks of three kinds of actions of mind as bad: desiring for other's things, nurturing evil thoughts and telling lies. "*paradravyeṣvabhidhyānaṁ mansaniṣṭacintanam. vitathābhiniveśaśca trividhaṁ karma mānasam.*" *Manusmṛti* 12.5. Referring to this, Vijñānabhikṣu says, "*mānasakarmavidhānāt,*" "performing action of the mind." VAB 1.1.1, p.5.

[216] "*niyatasya tu sannyāsaḥ karmaṇo nopapadhyate, mohāttasya parityāgastāmasaḥ parikīrtitaḥ*" (BG 18.7). VAB 1.1.1, p.5.

[217] One who is, however, taking pleasure in the self, who is illumined in the self, who rejoices in and is satisfied with the self only, fully satiated—for him there is no duty (BG 3.17). "*na kevalena yogena prāpyate paraṁ padam, jñānaṁ tu kevalaṁ samyagapavarga phalapradam.*" VAB 1.1.1, p.6.

[218] "*yastvātmaratireva syād ātmatṛptaśca mānavaḥ, ātmanyeva ca santuṣṭaḥ tasya kāryam na vidyate*" (BG 3.17). VAB 1.1.1, p.7.

[219] *sarvadharmān parityajya māmekaṁ śaraṇaṁ vraja, ahaṁ tvā sarva pāpebhyo mokṣayiṣyāmi mā śucaḥ* (BG 18.66). VAB 1.1.1, p.6. Having abandoned all your actions, come to my abode alone. I will forgive you from all your sins, do not be afraid.

[220] *asaktabuddhiḥ sarvatra jītatma vigata-spṛhaḥ naiṣkarmyasiddhiṁ paramāṁ sannyāsena adhigacchati* (BG 18.49). VAB 1.1.1, p.7. One can obtain the results of renunciation simply by self-control and by becoming unattached to material things and disregarding material enjoyments. That is the highest stage of renunciation.

[221] *na karmaṇa na prajayā [na] dhanena tyāgenaike amṛtatvam ānaśuḥ, pareṇa nākaṁ nihitaṁ guhāyāṁ vibhrājate yat yatayaḥ viśanti* (KU 1.3; MnU 12.3.4). VAB 1.1.1, p.8. Not by actions, not by progeny and not by wealth one attains liberation, but only through renunciation it is achieved.

[222] "*etānyapi tu karmāṇi saṅgam tyaktvā phalāni ca kartavyānīti*" *me pārtha niścitaṁ matauttamam* (BG 18.7). VAB 1.1.1, p.8. All these activities should be performed without any expectation of result. They should be performed as a matter of duty, O son of Pṛtha. That is my final opinion.

[223] *tatra hi karmatyāgo na vidhīyate, kintu rogād aśaktyā karmabhāve prasakte vidvān ātmajñānāditatparo bhaved iti eva vidhīyate.* VAB 1.1.1, p.7.

[224] *"āruruksormuneryogaṁ karma kāraṇamucyate, yogārūḍhasya tasyaiva śamaḥ kāraṇamucyate"* (BG 6.3). VAB 1.1.1, p.9. *Āruruksus* are those *sādhaks* who aspire for union with God but have just begun their path to liberation whereas the *yogārūḍhas* are those who have already elevated to liberation. But still both need to have some kind of *tyāga*.

[225] *parīkṣya lokān karmacitān brāhmaṇo nirvedam āyāt na asti ākṛtaḥ kṛtena tat vijñānārthaṁ sa gurumeva abhigacchet samitpāṇiḥ śrotriyaṁ brahmaniṣṭaṁ tasmai sa vidvānupasannāya samyak praśāntacittāya śamānvitāya yena akṣaraṁ puruṣaṁ veda satyaṁ provāca tāṁ tattvato brahmavidhyām* (MuU 1.2.12-13). VAB 1.1.1, p.8. Let a *Brāhmaṇa* (an aspirant), after his examination of the worlds gained by *karma*, acquires freedom from all desires, reflecting that nothing eternal can be gained by *karma*. Let him in order to obtain the knowledge of the eternal by taking sacrificial fuel (*samit*) in his hands and approach the preceptor alone who is well versed in the Vedas and established in Brahman. To that pupil who thus approached the preceptor in a proper manner with the mind at rest and the senses are subdued, let the wise teacher truly teach the *Brahmavidyā* (science of Brahman) by which the true immortal *Puruṣa* is known. Appropriated from the translation of Swami Chinmayananda, *Muṇḍakopaniṣad: Tale of Two Birds: Jīva and Īśvara*, 2016 ed. (Mumbai: Central Chinmaya Mission Trust, 1953), 55,60. *"kṛīyāvantaḥ śrotriyā brahmaniṣṭhā svayaṁ juhvanta eka ṛṣīṁ śraddhayantaḥ teśāmevaitāṁ brahmavidhyāṁ vadet."* VAB 1.1.1, p.8.

[226] *"utsīdeyurime lokā na kuryāṁ karma ced ahaṁ, saṅkarasya ca kartā syāṁ upahanyām imāḥ prajāḥ"* (BG 3.24). VAB 1.1.1, p.10. The word 'world' should be highlighted here. It involves not only the empirical world one experiences, but also the transcendental or unseen world as well. This can be proved by the expression *lokasaṅgraha*. For more details see, Raju Felix Crasta, "Lokasaṅgraha, the Welfare of the Worlds: A Hermeneutical and Exegetical Exploration" (Unpublished MPh Dissertation, Pune: Jnanadeepa Vidyapeeth, 2013).

[227] *kāyena manasā buddhyā, kevalair indriyair api yoginaḥ karma kurvanti saṅgaṁ tyaktvā ātmaśuddhaye* (BG 5.11). VAB 1.1.1, p.9-10. The yogis, abandoning attachment, act with body, mind, intelligence, and even with the senses, only for the purpose of purification.

[228] Vijñānabhikṣu has slightly modified the quote from the

Chāndogya Upaniṣad as "*yadeva vidyayā karoti, vidyāṁ ca avidyayāṁ ca yastad vedobhayaṁ saha.*" The original quote is, "*yadeva vidyayā karoti śraddhayopaniṣadā tadeva vīryavattaraṁ bhavati*" (CU 1.1.10).
VAB 3.4.8, p.284. As translated by *Prasad, Chāndogya Upaniṣad*, 39.
VAB 3.4.8,10, pp.284, 286.

CHAPTER FIVE
A CRITICAL APPROPRIATION AND RELEVANCE OF THE *AVIBHĀGA- BHEDĀBHEDA*

Vijñānabhikṣu embarks upon his philosophical endeavor where his precursors concluded to further it with his scholarly insights. Having learnt the *Bhedābheda* tradition of the former teachers, socio-political and cultural background, and the tradition of Vijñānabhikṣu proper, this chapter attempts to critique and appropriate his philosophical perspicacity.

5.1 Appreciation of Vijñānabhikṣu and His Thought

Regarding the educational background of Vijñānabhikṣu, we neither have ample evidence nor has he spoken anything about his teachers. Surely, he must have had a great *Vaiṣṇava* background together with a pluralistic social milieu. Though we cannot verify with evidence of his affiliation to any particular sect, we do have some indications from his familiarity with the *Pañcarātra* text, different *Bhedābhedā* traditions, other rival schools and their proponents. This leads us to presume that he is strongly rooted in the *Vaiṣṇava* faith.

Does Vijñānabhikṣu follow the *Vedāntic* tradition of antiquity in toto? At the cursory glance, it appears to be so by the fact of his traditional commentary style. On a stricter note, Vijñānabhikṣu debunks this tendency. That is the reason, instead of the *Bhagavad Gītā,* he settles for the

Avadhūta Gītā as one of the *prasthānatrayī*. Secondly, when all the *Vedāntic* teachers deliberate the first four aphorisms of BS (*catuḥsūtrī*) as the basis for *samanvaya*, Vijñānabhikṣu adds one more, calling it, *pañcasūtrī* (VAB 1.1.1-5). While the other commentators are known to be the *Vedāntic* teachers, he is recognized as the *Sāṅkhya-Vedāntic* teacher.

Dasgupta succinctly sums up the salient features of Vijñānabhikṣu's philosophical thought. It is very much in line with various *Vedāntins* and *Vedāntic* thoughts, *Sāṅkhya* and other allied schools. He enunciates,

> Bhikṣu's [Vijñānabhikṣu's] philosophy is a type of *bhedābheda* which has shown itself in various forms of Bhartṛprapañca, Bhāskara, Rāmānuja, Nimbārka and others. The general viewpoint of this *bhedā-bheda* philosophy is that it believes in the reality of the universe as well as in its spirituality, the distinctiveness of the individual souls as well as in their being centres of the manifestation of God, moral freedom and responsibility as well as a spiritual determination, a personal God as well as an impersonal reality, the ultimate spirit in which matter and pre-matter are dissolved into spirituality, an immanent teleology pervading through matter and souls both in their origin and mutual intercourse as well as in the holiness of the divine will, omnipotence and omniscience, in the superior value of knowledge as well as of love, in the compulsoriness of moral and social duties as well as in their abnegation.[1]

Thus, Vijñānabhikṣu understands God, soul and world to be real. They can be substantially identified with God, but at the same time, they are distinct. Soul and world have a spiritual origin that ultimately will return to the place of their origins.

Bhedābheda has a long-standing history. He winnows out such proponents and addresses their standpoints in his *bhāṣya*. We have enlisted and discussed them earlier. Therefore, Vijñānabhikṣu's commentary and interpretation is neither an altogether new thing in the history nor does it betray any non-*Vedāntic* influence. In fact, his philosophy is a faithful interpretation of the *Vedāntic* teaching based on *prasthānatrayī*.

Vijñānabhikṣu's interpretation of BS is more satisfactory than other commentaries. *Abeda* and *bheda* commentaries are unidirectional whereas the *Bhedābheda* commentaries are multi-directional *per-se*. Multi-directional because they break orthodoxy to render a creative synthesis. They are a combination of the former ones. His interpretation of *tattvamasi* corroborates this.

He has left ample space for the readers to interact with the text. For example, as we have discussed in the previous chapters, *abheda* and *bheda* traditions exclude the *śūdras* from the reach of scriptures whereas the *Bhedābhedavādins,* though do not reject outright, are more sympathetic towards them. As a result, they point out the text having recourse to its primary and secondary derivatives.

It is also fitting because Vijñānabhikṣu's system is more

logical and systematic with rationality in its explanations. It is a healthy admixture of faith and reason, *tattva* and *śraddha,* keeping in mind the changing times. His interpretation of the first *sūtra* (*athāto brahmajijñāsā*) is an example for this fact. Further, he is more balanced, organismic and comprehensive in his outlook which meets both intellect and feelings.

Probably, this balanced approach is due to the very nature of the *Vedic* and the *Upaniṣadic* texts themselves. They speak in double voice: identity and difference. The *Gītā,* the *Upaniṣads* and the BS do not explicitly speak about complete identity of *ātman* and Brahman or matter and spirit. Furthermore, the *Vedānta* or the *Upaniṣads* present a gradual development of theism, devotion and accommodative tendencies. Even the BS indicates the existence of such philosophies through various people like Ātreya, Āśmarathya, Auḍulomi, Kārśnājinī, Bādari, Jaimini, etc. with divergent views (BS 1.4.20-22; 3.4.7; 4.4.5-7, etc). Further, he was more comfortable with the *sūtras* and their style of writing. If the previous thinkers have harped more on the *śruti* texts, Vijñānabhikṣu has added several *smṛti* texts. His use of *purāṇic* and other lesser-known texts is noteworthy. Thus, he had a wide variety of canons available at his disposal. Their different point of view gave him a wider approach to his standpoint. Due to these reasons, he was successful in his reasoning and demonstration.

Another noteworthy feature of Vijñānabhikṣu is his effort to safeguard the unity and difference as one whole without compromising the sacredness of the Absolute simultaneously raising the matter to the divine rank. If the Advaitins claimed the phenomenal reality to be unreal, the *Avibhāga-Bhedābhedavāda* considers it real in as much as the Absolute is real. On the contrary, if *Dvaitins* reasoned matter and spirit to be dependent on the Absolute, then Vijñānabhikṣu endorses it adding *avibhāga* dimension to it and thus making it independent as well as dependent. This was made possible by the fact of his theistic stance, *everything as an embodiment of the divine* (*īśavāsyam idaṁ sarvam*). For this purpose, he chose a school of *darśana* which was an *anathema* for most of the *Vedāntic* thinkers of the past due to its atheistic blend. However, Vijñānabhikṣu reads it from the theistic 'viewpoint.' Thus, the credit goes to him for bringing theism in *Sānkhya* with his ingenuity and also removing the stigma of 'untouchability' from it. Ever since this effort, *Sāṅkhya* has been looked upon with salutary glances by the later thinkers.

5.2 Critique of *Avibhāga-Bhedābheda*

5.2.1 *Bhedābheda* as the Hermeneutical Strategy of Vijñānabhikṣu

Distinct yet *one, bheda* yet *abheda* and *different* yet *non-different* are the common terms by which *Bhedābheda* is spoken of. For the Advaitins, this is contradictory and necessarily to be rejected as a fallacy.[2] They claim that it is not in the spirit of *Vedāntic* philosophy. If one looks from this spectacle, *Sāṅkhya* and *Yoga* do not qualify to be so. *Sāṅkhya* advocates reality in terms of unity in totality to end up in the dualism of *prakṛti* and *puruṣa*, leaving aside the *ātman*. *Yoga* delimits itself on *ātman*. Also, the *Mīmāṁsā* School having two branches opposes each other. With the same observation, there are *Vedāntins* who accept the reality of *bheda* or reject it and vice-versa. This paradox is the strength of Eastern philosophy and not its weakness.

However, discrepancies somehow have to be explained. The easiest way to do this is the *Bhedābheda* way, that the ultimate reality is neither the pure *Advaita* nor *Dvaita* but a synthesis of both. Vijñānabhikṣu tries to bring this unity in the *Vedāntic* tradition. Nicholson acknowledges, "He [Vijñānabhikṣu] hopes to show the viability of a philosophical tradition that by the late medieval period had been savaged by *Advaita, Viśiṣṭādvaita,* and *Dvaita* polemics."[3] We can boldly testify that to a certain extent he has succeeded in fulfilling his vision.

5.2.2 A Critique on the Hermeneutical Presuppositions and Strategies

One of the prominent hermeneutical presuppositions of Vijñānabhikṣu is the integral non-dualism or the non-duality of inseparables (*avibhāgādvaita*). *Avibhāga-Bhedābheda* of Vijñānabhikṣu integrates both *bheda* and *abheda tattvas* in a single concept. The *ekameva advitīya* reality expressed by the *Vedas* and the *Upaniṣads* is meticulously understood by the *Vedāntin*. The reality is complex and integral. It can neither be limited to dualism nor non-dualism only.

This has been very well articulated in the *Vijñānāmṛtabhāṣyam* by employing several hermeneutical strategies such as *aṁśa-aṁśī sambandha, aṁśa-avayava sambandha, kārya-kāraṇa sambandha, viśeṣa-viśeṣaṇa sambandha,* etc. These are not altogether new tools, but the continuation of other *Vedāntic* thinkers like Rāmānuja, Bhāskara, Madhva, etc. The intriguing novelty in this *bhāṣya* is the integration of all the strategies in a single capsule called '*avibhāga*.' *Avibhāga* includes 'incomprehensibility' (*acintya*) of Caitanya and 'nature' (*svabhāva*) of Nimbārka. In this way, the concept expounds '*akhaṇḍatva*.'

A question can be raised here regarding the authenticity of Vijñānabhikṣu's hermeneutical strategy. The basic presupposition is *avibhāga* explained by means of various hermeneutical strategies as cited in the previous chapters. But what lacks here is the originality as expected. For example, his *avibhāga* sounds more like *apṛthaksiddhi* of Rāmānuja. The inseparable relation existing between Brahman and the world with its souls (its modes) is *apṛthaksiddhi.* The attribute which cannot be apprehended apart from the subject, of which it is the distinguishable attribute, is called *apṛthaksiddha viśeṣaṇa* like flower and its fragrance or luminosity from its light.[4] The *mahāvākya tattvamasi* has to be understood as *viśiṣṭa aikya*[5] between Brahman and soul (*tat* and *tvam*), therefore it is not absolute identity. Vijñānabhikṣu's *avibhāga* though smells like this, goes beyond this. For him, the purpose of *mahāvākyas* in the scripture is neither to explain the *brahmajīvāikya* nor to equate *tvam* and *aham* to *ātman* and eventually to Brahman. They are there to edify divine essence rooted in creation.[6] The primary meaning of those words refers to this essence only, and only the secondary meanings explain their inter-intra relationships.

Vijñānabhikṣu finds a place for *prakṛti* or nature and *puruṣa* within Brahman in an inseparable special relation which he calls *svarūpa-sambandha-viśeṣa* or a *saṁyogādi-viśeṣa*.[7] There is no rigorous discussion on the nature of this *avibhāga* relation. All that it gives is only a description of it. Is it different from related or relation, and non-different from the relation itself or both? He speaks about identity-relationship (*svarūpa-sambandha*), but remains silent thereafter,[8] thinks T.S. Rukmani. Consequently, he allows the reader to dialogue with the text. The allegation sounds valid. True, a detailed explanation is not given in the commentary. But in that matter, most of the commentators too are in the same boat including Vijñānabhikṣu without exception. He tends to repeat the same thing said on different occasions. This is the reason, the same quotation is found in different places. This tendency is very much present in his other works as well. And whenever they are repeated, he comes up with a different explanation with a logical conclusion.[9] The reader must gather these arguments for the lucid presentation. Probably, this must be the reason a detailed explanation of *avibhāga* is not given in one place.

The nature of *prakṛti* of Vijñānabhikṣu is not something different from the *Kevala Advaita*. Like Śankara, *prakṛti* is *triguṇātmika* (*sattva, tamas* and *rajas*) and having 24 *tattvas.* During the *praḷaya, prakṛti* and *puruṣa* lie submerged in the absolute, like a coiled snake in a pit.[10] This means that both *puruṣa* and *prakṛti* are either inactive or different from

Brahman. In addition to this, *puruṣa* is considered to be Brahman (Absolute) in the *Yogavārttika*. So, there is inadequacy in reasoning out the strategies. However, this does not delimit the significance of *Avibhāgādvaita* of Vijñānabhikṣu.

5.2.3 A Critique on *Tattvamasi* Concept

The nature of identity is, in fact, a perplexing one. The way Vijñānabhikṣu understands *tattvamasi*, naturally raises a question, whether there is a tautology in it? Wittgenstein has said, "Roughly speaking, to say of two things that they are identical is non-sense, and to say of one thing that it is identical with itself is to say nothing at all."[11] The identity statements question the very proposition itself, "What is it being claimed to be identical in a true identity statement?"[12]

At the outset, *tat* and *tvam* seem to be identical either formally or materially. It cannot be formally, because in its form both are different. Secondly, *tat* and *tvam* is not just a logical truth (for example, a = a) but much more than that. It cannot be materially, as the material identity deals with numerical identity (for example, a = b). Material identity pertains to two different entities or objects: it will be true, if and only if the objects are the same entity; and it will be false if one is different from the other or it is not an entity at all (object). In *tattvamasi*, the identity sought is beyond formal or material one, a metaphysical one. If one considers *tat* and *tvam* to be inter-definable or one of the concepts contained in the other, then, it would be tautology in the first sense.[13]

For the Advaitins, *tat* and *tvam* are identical entities,

whereas for the *bhedavādins*, it is the contra view and for the *Bhedābhedavādins*, it is both. For the non-*advaitins*, the oneness of *tattvamasi* is "neither intended nor implied."[14] If *tat* refers to Brahman and *tvam* the embodied *jīva,* then one cannot talk about identity for the former is an unqualified, unlimited and unconditioned entity and the latter qualified, limited and conditioned entity in its primary meaning. And therefore, it would be a tautology. But, if one considers *tat* to be pure consciousness and *tvam* to be embodied pure consciousness as the *Advaita* refers, then the entities can be deemed identical. Therefore, the secondary meaning is important while interpreting the text. At this point, as *jahadajahallakṣaṇā* understands, the primary meaning is defunct and the secondary meaning is active. Thus, the *Advaitin*'s understanding, 'the Reality is One and Pure Consciousness,' is insufficient.

The point regarded here is not the tautology or identity issues, but the subject-object intricacy. There is something unchanging and permanent essence in every individual. *The person whom I saw ten years ago and behold now is the same* though there is a remarkable change in him/her. *Ghaṭākāśa* (space inside the pot) and *bahirākāśa* (space outside) have something unchanging and permanent thing. Individual soul and Supreme Soul have something identical. Śaṅkara teaches us this unique mystical union.

This guides us to interpret the issue from a different angle. The hermeneutics exposed here distinguishes two kinds of relationships: i. Brahman is immanent in the *jīva* and *jagat,* expressed as *abheda* or identity, ii. Absolute transcendence of Brahman enunciated as the distinction between finite and infinite.

Absolute transcendence is dangerous at least for two reasons – danger of leading towards mechanical deism and pantheism. Mechanical deism creates an unbridled gulf between Supreme Being and *jīva-jagat,* undermining unity or harmony of things. Dualism and pluralism are the necessary outcomes of transcendence. The *Kevala Advaita* notion of *tattvamasi* regards the reality belonging to the Real and all the phenomenal existence as unreal with no human reason daring to touch and contaminate.

The immanence of Brahman comes to rescue the transcendental approach. But an undue emphasis on immanence will lead to identifying Brahman with the world of experience. If this is the case, then the finite objects will be the shadows of the Brahman depriving them of their independent existence. Rāmānuja's *Viśiṣṭādvaita* somehow falls into this category. The objects of the phenomenal world are *viśeṣaṇa* of the *viśeṣa.* Worldly becoming is necessary through which the divine can become self-conscious. But the peril is that it might lead to materialism. Brahman's self-subsistence depends on the existence of *jīva-jagat* where unity is sought.

Śaṅkara errs in accepting the absolute transcendence and independent existence of Brahman, thus ushering us to pantheism. Instead of explaining the relation between Brahman and *jīva-jagat,* he nullifies the thing to be related, branding it as unreal. Further, he superimposes the related as *upādhi* (illusion). Even after counterbalancing unreality, the appearance of the finite world cannot be negated.

Neither the *bhedavāda* nor the *abhedavāda,* neither immanence nor transcendence independently defines *tattvamasi* adequately. Especially, both *bheda* and *abheda* alone are inadequate to describe the nature of Brahman and the *jīva-jagat.* Accepting one will lead to denying the other as an illusion or emphasizing the other will lead to the unbridgeable gulf between Brahman and the *jīva-jagat.* Even the logic fails in front of *the logic of infinity*, as the Bible declares, "*My ways are different from your ways*" (Isaiah 55:8).

Where then shall we find a solution or at least a balance? The only way is as Buddhism recommends, *the middle way*; a third possibility which embraces both – the *Bhedābheda* way of interpretation. Here, transcendence and immanence are reconciled to a higher synthesis. They are made associate aspects of an abiding unity in the Reality, be it proposed by *Bhedābhedavādins* like Bhāskara, Vallabha, Caitanya or Vijñānabhikṣu.

Bhedābhedavādins, in general, consider Brahman to be both *nirguṇa* and *saguṇa,* and real. Brahman as *nirguṇa* appears *saguṇa* for the practical purpose. To corroborate their view, the concept of *māyā* is brought in as the power (*śakti*) of Brahman to define it as *anirvacanīya,* describing neither real nor unreal. If there is an absolute identity, then the fault of one should be the fault of the other. In other words, can either real or unreal be the power of Brahman who is real? On the other hand, if the absolute differs, then immanence is not possible, it will end up in dualism or pluralism. Therefore, just like the case of the sun and its rays or sea and its waves which cannot be separated, the immanence of Brahman from its transcendence cannot be separated.

The interpretation given for *tat* and *tvam* as Brahman and *jīva-jagat* as denoted by *abhidhā* and *lakṣaṇā* are sound enough to accept without any complication. But the query is the copulating verb '*asi*' to describe the relationship between the two terms.

The *Nyāya-Vaiśeṣika* system points to *samavāya* relation between two objects. On the contrary, Rāmānuja acknowledges *apṛthaksiddhi* (inseparable) relations. The former is external relation and the latter is internal relation. The external relation pointed out is between two real objects, quite distinct from each other, for example, *gavaya* and *gau* (wild cow and domestic cow). But the existing relation between *tat* and *tvam* is not just external as material *gau* and *gavaya*, but a physico-transcendental one. In this respect, a well-accepted relation could be *apṛthaksiddhi* between Brahman and *jīva-jagat*. But again this relation is not conclusive. In other words, it is *avaktavyam*, (indescribable).[15]

What kind of difference-in-identity (*bhedābheda*), therefore, is to be envisaged: *aupādhika* (accidental), *svābhāvika* (natural), *acintya* (incomprehensible) or *avibhāga* (non-differentiable), or is it not sufficient to restrict oneself to *bhedābheda*?

Bhāskara's system is called *Aupādhika-Bhedābheda* where *abheda* is real and eternal, while *bheda* is unreal and accidental. *Bheda* is due to *upādhi* (accidental predicate). He gives an example of a diamond looking red due to a red object placed near it. Thus, *bheda* is unreal and unacceptable.

Nimbārka's *Svābhāvika-Bhedābheda* considers both *bheda* and *abheda* as real. They represent the very nature (*svabhāva*) of Brahman. Therefore, this system is preferred over Bhāskara, as it reconciles the apparent contradictory statements of the scriptures.

Caitanya encapsulates both the preceding views in his *Acintya-Bhedābheda* system. If both *bheda* and *abheda* are real, then they must necessarily be *svābhāvika*. The *bheda* and *abedha* is conceived between Brahman and *jīva-jagat* as whole and part, body and limb (*avayava-avayavi*) and cause and effect by Bhāskara and Nimbārka. To be precise, the cause or whole is both transcendent and immanent in the effect or in part. But they cannot both be one. Therefore, the reality is to be understood as incomprehensible, affirms Caitanya.

Yet, a better way of expressing it is *Avibhāga-Bhedābheda* way as Vijñānabhikṣu envisages. The reality is indescribable because it is *avibhāga, bheda, abheda,* and cannot be separated like spark and fire, or wave and sea.

Basing on the context of *tattvamasi*, Uddālaka's purpose of *upadeśa* to Śvetaketu was to remove his arrogance and pride to instill in him a sense of a power greater than everything. At the same time, this power is to be found within as *kastūri* in the *nābhi* of the *kastūrīmṛga*. Nine illustrations clearly illustrate the above purport. For example, just as honey collected from various flowers remains one unit, so also the transcendental Brahman is immanent in you and you in Him. Thus, you are inseparable from Him and He from you. That you are, *tat tvamasi*.

From the dynamics of the relationship between *tat, tvam* and *asi*, one can infer the Supreme Reality in three ways.

i. From *anubhava* (experience): One can begin the search for the Supreme from *anubhava*. From its etymological sense, *anubhava* comes after (*anu*) the empirical reality (*bhava*). The word '*tvam'* refers to the empirical reality. It is an epistemology that leads to ontology. The knowledge of the seen reality apart from bringing awe, leads one to a sense of mystery, to experiencing it as divine.

ii. From *śruti* (revelation): One can also advance the search for the Supreme from *śruti*. According to the *Mīmāṁsā*, scriptural injunctions are *codana śabda*s due to the inherent power (*śakti*) in them. The power of *sphoṭa* of the *śabda* guides one to have a mystical experience. This is the reason, the *Sāmavedic* hymns open with the meditation on AUM, as the symbol of Brahman (CU 1.1). The word '*tat*' refers to this revelation, of Supreme Reality.

iii. From *upadeśa* (denotation): Certain things cannot be learnt without the aid of a proper *guru*. The 'point of view' of the *ācāryas* impels the disciples to construe a particular system from that 'viewpoint.' The *Upaniṣad,* in this sense, is an instruction of the teacher to the student to understand the Reality. Śaṅkara's mystical experience of Viṣṇu initiates him to perceive everything as divine, thus to define *tattvamasi* as 'You are That.' Therefore, it is not indirect learning, but as a witness of the first-hand experience with its greater role to deepen one's faith-experience.

5.3 *'Advaita'* of Vijñānabhikṣu

Vijñānabhikṣu refers *advaitins* as *'ādhunikā,' 'māyāvādin,'* etc., and criticizes them vehemently. There is a concrete reason to critique Śaṅkara. The chief reason is that Śaṅkara is not true to the semantic autonomy of Bādarāyaṇa's *Brahmasūtras* as he manipulates with his examples and ideas opposing the textual meaning.[16] Swami Vireswarananda corroborates this fact of Śaṅkara's manipulation. "There is a strong opinion current among scholars today that whatever be the merit of Śaṅkara's metaphysical doctrines considered by themselves or even as doctrines elucidating the teaching of the Upaniṣads, he is not faithful to Bādarāyaṇa in his interpretation of the *Sūtras.*"[17] The second reason is that the *Brahmasūtras* are more empathetic towards pluralistic tendencies. George Thaibhaut agrees with this fact. "The system of Bādarāyaṇa has greater affinities with that of the Bhāgavatas and Rāmānuja than with the one of which the *Śaṅkara-bhāṣya* is the classical opponent."[18] It is already said that Bādarāyaṇa's *Sūtras* are in *Bhedābheda* tradition. *Bhāgavatas* and Rāmānuja's system too are in *Bhedābheda* tradition. Dasgupta argues that *Brahmasūtras* don't support

Śaṅkara's doctrine. He specifies, "Judging by the *sūtras* alone, it does not seem to me that the *Brahmasūtra* supports the philosophical doctrine of Śaṅkara."[19] De Smet too concurs with Dasgupta, "Even, commonly accepted interpretation of Śaṅkara's thought is being questioned today."[20] In this sense, Vijñānabhikṣu is in the right direction.

However, critiquing a rival school is a common practice in the Vedāntic tradition. And therefore, there is nothing wrong with it. This is also the commentarial methodology (*adhikaraṇa paddati*). The fact that one criticizes the other, does not mean that one is totally against the principle of the opponent. It is not a reasonable way as well. Vijñānabhikṣu's *Advaita* neither implies that there is an absolute non-difference between Brahman and *ātman*, nor does it assert the unreality of *jīva* and *jagat* (as Śaṅkara understands). But rather, he uses the word '*Advaita*' to mean '*avibhāga*,' or non-difference between Brahman and the individual self or soul and world.[21] If '*Advaita*' is not accepted, then *avibhāga* too cannot be accepted. At some point or the other, there must be a unity, if not absolute, at least an apparent one. Vijñānabhikṣu states clearly, "The object is the realization of the ultimate Self through the divinity of *ātman*,"[22] and to prove it quotes the *smṛti* text, "There is no other seer than He."[23] This indicates that Vijñānabhikṣu accepts *Advaita*, but with a new interpretation.

On the one hand, *Advaitins* claim the unreality of the world (*brahma satyā, jagat mithyā*); and *dvaitins,* on the other hand, claim the world as a *līla* of two *svatantra tattvas,* the *puruṣa* and the *prakṛti.* For Vijñānabhikṣu the *acitprakṛtitattva* cannot have a creative relation with pure *cit,* the *puruṣa.* In themselves, they have no teleology. Therefore, a third spiritual agent is necessary to unite these to bring out creation. This spiritual agent is Brahman. But then, there can be a contradiction between Brahman, the uniting spiritual power and Brahman whom people worship (*apara* and *para,* or *nirguṇa* and *saguṇa*). In other words, it is a tussle between the God of Philosophy and the God of Religion. They aren't two different realities, rather one. In an ordinary understanding, the God of Philosophy is the Absolute reality that Vijñānabhikṣu names as Brahman in its *apara* or *nirguṇa* form, and the God of Religion in *para* or *saguṇa* reality. But what binds all or what is common to all including *Advaita* and *Dvaita* is the divine essence, *Brahmātmatātattva.* This is also the foundation for all religions, cultures and traditions.

In the Sāṅkya way of understanding, at the time of dissolution, the *prakṛti* ceases to have any activity (*kriya*). It becomes subtle and indistinguishable from Brahman. This is called *prakṛtilaya.* Thus, *prakṛti* is never destroyed but acquires the same status as it was before it came to the proximity of the *puruṣa.* (This does not mean that *prakṛti* desires to come closer to *puruṣa* for evolution. It is the divine desires to be many as said earlier, *bahusyām prajāyajet*). Alternatively, *puruṣa* too does not cease to exist but withdraws all its epistemological activities. This indistinguishable and inseparable union of the three *tattvas* is '*advaita.*' However, the activity of liberation termed here is only of a particularly bound *ātman*. Upon its release, the *ātman* unites with Brahman, and *prakṛti* continues to exist for the liberation of other bound souls like upon the destruction of *ghaṭa, ghatākāśa* merges with *bahirākāśa*.

This brings to us a great insight that *God is the ultimate substratum of everything. The indistinguishable penetration of the divine in the world of matter and life, prior, during and after creation gives meaning and significance to every existence. One can neither separate these three tattvas nor can give prominence to any one or two tattvas as supreme. They together form one reality.* This is the *'advaita'* of Vijñānabhikṣu.

Further, for Śaṅkara the world is unreal, so too *jīva* as long as *avidya* envelops it. Only at the self-realization (*jñāna*), when *avidya* is removed, the *jīva* unites itself with Brahman. Therefore, the reality outside is only an illusion (*māya*). Conversely, Rāmānuja understands *Advaita* as 'qualified' as the Brahman qualifies the *jīva* and *jagat*. To remove the unreality of the world of Śaṅkara, Rāmānuja brings in a novel concept called *apṛthaksiddhi*, inseparableness to explain the organic unity between the three *tattvas – cit, acit* and *Īśvara*. In his opinion, all these three *tattvas* are identical and concurrently exhibit an inseparable relation as in the case of the body and soul of a living being. The unity between these three *tattvas* is also seen in the manifested and unmanifested conditions of the world. This continues even in the released state.

Vijñānabhikṣu accepts this view but with a difference. For

him the unity created by *avibhāga* exists only in the unmanifested condition, when Brahman alone is felt and the other two *tattvas–puruṣa* and *prakṛti*–remain merged in Brahman. In the manifested state, *avibhāga* relation continues to hold, not like a jar of water merging in water in a pond, but like the relation of the father and the son, or the body-hair and the body. Father and son are the two distinct entities, yet son is the continuation of the father, and both constitute one unit.[24] Thus, the *apṛthaksiddhi* of Vijñānabhikṣu treats the reality in the manifested state as *vibhāga* and in the unmanifested state as *avibhāga*.

This insinuates that there is diversity in the manifested state while there is no diversity in the unmanifested state. In other words, the manifested reality is like a salad – full of colours, traditions, cultures, diverse attitudes, manifestations of potentialities, etc. However, in the unmanifested state, that is in the core of a 'Being,' everything is *ekam*. Cultures, traditions, lifestyles, classes, creeds, castes, etc., lose their diversities just as the river upon mingling with sea loses its identity and one can no more say, 'this is seawater, and that is river water.' This paves a way for a new interpretation of integral wholeness. There is a need for a new interpretation of 'integral wholeness' or '*akhaṇḍattva'* due to the ambiguous understanding of unity-in-diversity in contemporary India. The present general ethos is taking away the essence of integrity, constitutional rights, moral values, dignity, freedom and the will of human being. *Akhaṇḍattva,* like a salad of different items, though have varying tastes, flavours and colours, together they nourish the one body without any discrimination.

5.4 '*Dvaita*' of Vijñānabhikṣu?

When we analyze the nature of Brahman, the question naturally arises, whether Vijñānabhikṣu is in fact a *Bhedābhedavādin*. We have two prominent reasons to doubt so. Firstly, Vijñānabhikṣu categorizes Brahman into higher (*parabhrahman*) and lower forms (*aparabrahman*). In other words, he categorizes Brahman into *kāryabrahman* and *kāraṇabrahman*. In VAB 1.1.2 and 4.3.12, he articulates that the primary meaning of the word '*brahman*' refers to the Higher Lord and the secondary meaning is only by conviction.[25] This word can have or denote two meanings: to the higher Brahman in the primary sense, and in the secondary meaning *Hiraṇyagarbha*, *Ātman*, *Puruṣa*, *Īśvara*, etc. to the lower Brahman. To prove this standpoint, he quotes *Manusmṛti* (1.11) under two different *sūtras* (VAB 1.1.2 and 4.3.9). Borelli translates this as follows, "in popular usage that Spirit is called Brahman, in the unmanifested and eternal cause, Being and non-being in essence when it has caused this."[26]

Secondly, most of his critique is levelled against *Advaitins*. For example, in VAB 1.1.2, he assesses two stands of *Advaitins*: *pratibimbavāda* and *avacchedavāda*. But his position on *Dvaita* is neither clear nor has he given any reason for not critiquing it. This is equally true about his stance on other *Bhedābhedavādins* who preceded him.

However, from the fact of his exposition of the BS, he comes across as a *Bhedābhedavādin*, but a deeper analysis reflects his *dvaita* approach too. Maybe because of his regard for *Dvaita Vedānta*, he reserved his critique. Hayavadana Rao already has censored him a *Dvaitin*. The accusation in his words, "Vignāna Bhikshu [sic] is thus a dualist: he postulates *jīva* and *Parabrahman*; he denounces *aikya*; he suggests that *moksha* [sic] is attaining *sālokya* and *sāmīpya*; and he limits the *import* of *sāyujya* to *sāmīpya* and not *aikya*."[27] Surely, this is a coloured reading about Vijñānabhikṣu.

Vijñānabhikṣu in VAB 4.4.22 quotes the *Bhagavad Gītā* in this way, "From the highest planet in the material world down to the lowest, all are the places of misery wherein repeated birth and death take place. But one who attains to My abode [*māmupetya*], O son of Kunti, never takes birth again."[28] It seems from the interpretation of the word "*māmupetya*," Vijñānabhikṣu understands it as 'that they are near me' and 'not united in Brahman.' *Māmupetya* would mean (*mām* = unto me, *upetya* = having arrived or *upa iti* = near thus) 'having approached near to me' or 'having reached me.'[29] This suggests that those who believe that they are near *Paramātman*, there is no return (*āvṛttiḥ*). If the statement were to say, 'having united,' then it would have referred to *sāyujya*. But he doesn't. Therefore, Vijñānabhikṣu refers either to *sālokya* or *sāmīpya*.

His understanding of *tattvamasi* confirms this fact. The expressions *aham* and *tvam* without contradicting (*na līyate*) each other, by its very nature, the meaning attached to them imply two different agencies but with a similar form (*sāmānyarūpeṇa eva*). This gives us the understanding of two different beings with their respective characteristics. This is also in accordance with the ordinary usage.[30] There is the absolute difference between *jīva* and Brahman,[31] and this is the conclusion. This connotes, that Vijñānabhikṣu somewhat lands up in *dvaita* category or at least passing through *dvaita* pathway.

Vijñānabhikṣu cannot say *sāyujya*. If he were to state that, then he will fall into *Advaita* category. However, he vehemently criticizes *Advaitins* and never accepts the soul's *tādātmya* or *aikya* with Brahman. If he were to speak *sālokya* or *sāmīpya*, then he falls under *dvaita* category.

For Madhva, the *Dvaita* proponent the *jīvā* is totally dependent on Brahman. By no means can both merge into one. In this sense, Vijñānabhikṣu is a *Dvaita* proponent at par with Madhva who also proposes a *sālokya* and *sāmīpya* in the state of *mokṣa*. Vijñānabhikṣu's non-subscription of *jīva-brahmaikya* in *Brahmamīmāṁsā* can be considered from this point of view.

Nowhere in the commentary has he accepted the fact of his being a *Dvaitavādin*. Probably, this allegation may not be right altogether. If he were to be so, he wouldn't have used *aśṁśāṁśī sambandha* to prove *tattvamasi*. He would have defined as '*attattvamasi*.' But he doesn't. This implies, the allegation of being *Dvaita* as only superficial. He adheres to *Bhedābhedavāda* with the view that Bādarāyaṇa's work is based on this *vāda*, which we have already commented on in the previous chapter. The very fact of converting *nirīśvara Sāṅkhya* into *seśvara Sāṅkhya* and based on it writing the commentary of *Bhedābheda* tradition, condemning the unreality and *māyāvāda* of *Advaitins,* and upholding theism is a commendable work. This may be the reason he smells *Dvaita*. But a deeper analysis of his *tattvamasi* informs us that *jīva* is in Brahman (*tattvamasi*), and not *jivā* is 'not Brahman' (*atattvamasi*). Thus, Vijñānabhikṣu is not a *Dvaitin*.

5.5 *Avibhāga-Bhedābheda* as a Tool to Unite Materialism and Theism

During the early *Vedāntic* period, many philosophical schools spent a great time critiquing their rival schools. The *nāstika* blend of any *dārśanic* school was the first *pūrvapakṣa* of any proponent than others who wanted to establish one's stand. Therefore, one can find the early *Vaiśeṣikas* and a part of *Nyāya* was refuted by many ācāryas. In addition to it, critiquing *Sāṅkhya* and *Yoga*, especially the concept of *prakṛti* was normal even if it were not the rival schools. The critical assessment of *Sāṅkhya* was mainly due to its insentient and uncreated nature of *prakṛti,* rejection of God and the three *guṇas.*[32] Thanks to Vijñānabhikṣu for unmasking *Sāṅkhya* from this allegation and grafting theism to its atheistic nature through his benign insight from the *Bhedābheda*. One of his purposes in writing a commentary on *Sāṅkhya* is to show the harmony between *Vedic* and *Vedāntic* writings, and to ascertain, that "*Puruṣa* is one and one only, as is the sky."[33]

Vijñānabhikṣu applies *Bhedābheda* first and foremost to the *Upaniṣadic mahāvākyas* and notifies us that there is no contradiction whatsoever in the *Brahmamīmāṁsā siddhānta*. There is neither contradiction whatsoever between *jīva* and

Brahman in any *Vedānta mahāvākya* like *tattvamasi, ahaṁ brahmāsmī,* etc., nor is there any contradiction between the meanings of *tvam* and *ahaṁ* as *jīva*. In his words, "The great statements of *Vedānta* and any other statements like "You are That," and "I am Brahman," do not signify the identity of Brahman and the souls, nor do the words "you" and "I" signify the souls in these statements: however, the meaning of the words "who am I" are significant in the context of the twenty-six principles."[34] The purpose of *Vedānta* therefore is, to show "essential consciousness" between Brahman and *jīva* (souls).

Of the 'twenty-six principles,' twenty-five are taken from the *Sānkhya* system and the twenty-sixth is the Brahman, typical for Vijñānabhikṣu. Further, he claims that it can be applied to the *Sāṅkhya* and other systems too. However, he differs from the *Sāṅkhya* too, "the primary object of Sānkhya is practical (pragmatic) self and the secondary is the texts of divine revelation, whereas for the *Vedānta* Ultimate Self is the primary object which is the spiritual nature of the soul."[35] Thus, bringing in the twenty-sixth principle, the *Sāṅkhya* system is made theistic.

This gives us a clue as to why he is called primarily the *Sāṅkhya* philosopher than a *Vedāntin*, though his first work is his commentary on the *Brahmasūtras*. When he commented on the *Vedāntic* text, relating every aspect of reality as interconnected and inter-penetrated with the divine essence, he needed a firm theistic foundation to answer both material insentient aspects as well as theistic sentient aspects of the reality. The theistic *Sāṅkhya* could only be that rescuing point and that's the reason his commentaries on the *Sāṅkhya* becomes pivotal.

5.5.1 *Bhedābheda* and *Sāṅkhya*

Until the 20th century, people had a different opinion about the *Sāṅkhya* School. Nicholson articulates it beautifully.

> "Often the position that there was an early school of purely atheistic Sāṅkhya is argued on philosophical grounds. Commentators [Anima Sen Gupta] frequently allege that God is logically superfluous in *Sāṅkhya* system. For God has nothing to do in *Sāṅkhya* cosmology. He is not needed to effect the union of *prakṛti* and *puruṣa*, since the attraction between the two is automatic, like the attraction between a magnet and iron. The *Sāṅkhya* system is purely a mechanistic one, and the superfluity of God is attested to by his uncomfortable situation in Patañjali's *Yogasūtras*. There the existence of God is taught, but as a God who has little positive role to play other than to be an object of devotion and meditative contemplation. Surely, proponents of this picture of the early *Sāṅkhya* suggest, the introduction of God in the *Sāṅkhya* of the *Upaniṣads* and Epics, and in the school of Yoga philosophy, is merely an attempt to appeal to popular prejudices and not supported philosophically in any way." [36]

Nicholson's observation is very much true. This is the reason why this school became a common ground of critique for both orthodox and heterodox proponents of the *Vedānta.* Richard Garb, one of the first English commentators and translators of certain aphorisms from *Sāṅkhyapravacanabhāṣya* and *Sāṅkhyasūtra,* considers Vijñānabhikṣu as a '*non-vedāntin,*' 'syncretist' and 'inauthentic' person.[37] According to Nicholson, this misconception of Garb is due to the wrong reading of *Sāṅkhya*, Vijñānabhikṣu and their cultural milieu. Further, he says, "This mixing up of heterogeneous matters, which is frequently given the name "syncretism," is ultimately what led Indologists to label Vijñānabhikṣu as an unreliable representative of his own cultural heritage."[38] This is very much true. Besides this, a coloured reading will only encolour the text.

In reality, it is Vijñānabhikṣu who rescued *Sāṅkhya* from this dogmatic slumber. Shiv Kumar deems it, "He [Vijñānabhikṣu] was not a believer in dogmatism and was always trying to reconcile the *Sāṅkhya*, *Yoga* and *Vedānta*."[39] Vijñānabhikṣu interprets it through the spectacles of *Upaniṣads* to avoid any contradictions with *śruti*. This is once again true. The way he reconciled the *Vedānta* and the *Sāṅkhya* proves this fact.

There is another reason for using the *Sāṅkhya* platform in his investigation. *Sāṅkhya* system provided such a rational explanation that even without divine intervention, it could explain most of the facts satisfactorily. For example, the evolution theory or the *triguṇātmic* nature of *prakṛti*, even without bringing *Īśvara*, it can explicate the evolution. If so, by bringing in divine it can remove the stigma associated with the School as well as appeal very well to the common people.

Sāṅkhya's Dual Principles

The central doctrine of *Sāṅkhya darśana* is the nature and relationship between the two eternal principles, *prakṛti* and *puruṣa*. The *Upaniṣadic* crux is the doctrine that the *Ātman* within is pure consciousness and the ground of all our experience. This pure *Ātman* is identical with the Supreme Reality, Brahman. The material reality has no existence apart from or independent of it. The *Upaniṣadic* teaching demonstrates the *sarga* and *praḷaya* of the *jagat* in relation to Brahman. But it doesn't speak about the existence of the world of multiplicity from the One reality.[40] This task is being explained by the *Sāṅkhya darśana* through *prakṛti* and *puruṣa* and their inter-intra relationship.

Prakṛti is *jaḍa*, unconscious, free, eternal, one and the mother of all *tattvas: buddhi, ahaṅkāra, guṇas, jñānendriya, karmendriya* and their *tanmātras*. It is the originator or impregnator[41] of all *karmas,* and yet, it is not originated. It is eternal. Due to its *jaḍatva* it is known to be '*māyā*.'[42] It is also called *avyakta* due to its hidden nature of action and works. Only through the inference, the cause can be understood and therefore, it is also called *anumāna*. *Prakṛti* is *triguṇātmik*[43] and has three *guṇas – sattva, tamas* and *rajas*. Though these three *guṇas* are contrary to each other, there exists an *anyonya sambandha* like an oil-wick-light relationship. This relationship is for the welfare of the world.

Puruṣa is *cetana* or consciousness. It is the principle of *Ātman*. It is the *viśayī, jñātā* and *anubhavakartā* or *sākṣī*. It is *nitya, satya* and *ananta*. It is pure consciousness. It is the *adhiṣṭhāna* of knowledge, existence and experience. It is *svataḥsiddha* and *svaprakāśa*. It is *nirguṇa* or *nistraiguṇya* (devoid of three *guṇas*). Since *puruṣa* is the conscious principle, it becomes the *dṛṣṭā* and *sākṣī* of every action of *prakṛti*.

Though by nature, both *prakṛti* and *puruṣa* are different, they always remain close to each other. The proximity of *puruṣa* makes the *prakṛti* active and thus effects creation, like *magnet and iron*. The remoteness of both brings *praḷaya*. Thus, the *puruṣa* is transcendental and immanent in the *prakṛti*. *Prakṛti* is *sāvayava* whereas *puruṣa* is *niravayava*, the former is *jaḍa* and the latter is inactive.

Grafting Theism in the 'Atheistic' *Sāṅkhya*

Sāṅkhya darśana of Īśvarakṛṣṇa accepts *svatantrapradhānakāraṇavāda* (the theory of the creation wrought about independently by the *prakṛti*). Refuting this independent material claim, Śaṅkarācārya had assumed the contact (*saṁyoga*) caused by *Īśvara* (Lord). Vijñānabhikṣu accepts this progress made by Śaṅkara to elucidate Īśvara as superior to *puruṣa* and *prakṛti* (*pradhāna*). To support this claim, he brings several *purāṇic* statements. In this way, Vijñānabhikṣu builds a bridge between atheism and theism, replacing *svatantrapradhānakāraṇavāda* with *Īśvarādhīnapradhānakāraṇavāda*. According to him, the cause of the world is from the body of Brahman and not independently by the *pradhāna.* He explains this in the *sūtra*, '*camasavadviśeṣāt*' (VAB 1.4.8). Just as in the case of the *Upaniṣadic* statement "Bowl that has its opening below and bulges at the top" (BU 2.2.3), the bowl represents the body of sacrifice with no independent significance, so also, the *prakṛti* (*pradhāna*) is the body of the causal Brahman of the world devoid of an independent reality.[44]

This gives us two-fold natures of the history of *Sāṅkhya*: atheistic *Sāṅkhya* of Īśvarakṛṣṇa which was under the influence of *svabhāvavāda* of Buddhism, and a moderate theistically blended *Sāṅkhya* of Vijñānabhikṣu equally supported by the *Purāṇas*. The influence of *svabhāvavāda* is understood from his interpretation of the *sūtra*, '*mahaddīrghavadvā hnsvaparimaṇḍlābhyām*' (VAB 2.2.11, p.165), as both concealed and unconcealed nature of *prakṛti*. Both these natures exist as part of *Īsvara* in the *pradhāna*.

Vijñānabhikṣu never claimed the *Sāṅkhya* as atheistic; instead, through his writing, he clarified the atheistic trends prevalent during his time. The *svabhāvavāda* or *yadṛcchavāda* of Lokāyata or the Cārvāka system of philosophy and the *upaniṣadic* teaching of the world as 'by chance' as said in *Śvetāsvatara Upaniṣad* proves this fact. Secondly, he claims that each school has its own purpose, "just as it is not the *Nyāya-Vaiśeṣika*'s project to teach ultimate truths about the nature of self, *Sāṅkhya* is unconcerned with the topic of the existence or nonexistence of God."[45] At the same time, there is no explicit rejection of God's existence in *Sāṅkhya* of Kapila. Śaṅkarācārya is called 'a pseudo-*Sāṅkhya*'[46] as he established the doctrine of *nirguṇabrahman* and revived the *Sāṅkhya* philosophy of *puruṣa* in his *Brahmasūtrabhāṣyam*.

Another reason why atheism is spoken of is to deviate evil people from the reach of knowledge or truth. Therefore, the atheism in *Sāṅkhya* is not to be taken seriously.[47] Vijñānabhikṣu considers Kapila, the author of *Sāṅkhya* as the sage, and *avatāra* of Nārāyaṇa:

> Now, the Lord, in the person of Kapila, taught by this *Viveka-Śāstra*, lessons on Discrimination between the Self and the Not-Self, consisting of Six Books, valid arguments, not conflicting with the Veda, in respect of *Puruṣa-artha*, Purpose of Life, *Jñāna*, knowledge, which is its source, *Ātma-svarūpa*, Nature of the Self, which is the object of knowledge and the like, as learnt from the Veda.[48]

If Vijñānabhikṣu were to accept *Sāṅkhya* to be an atheistic system, then he would neither have considered its proponent to be a sage nor to be an *avatāra* of Viṣṇu. Accordingly, with his belief in the existence of God, the author Kapila composes the *sūtras* to substantiate not the existence of God, but the existence of a plurality of *jīvas*. Otherwise, there are hundreds of scriptural statements to prove the existence of God. In the *Sāṅkhyapravacanabhāṣya*, Vijñānabhikṣu employs the word *brahman* sparingly, because that word is outside the scope of *Sāṅkhya*. However, he utilizes the word *puruṣa* and *ātman* inter-changeably, and *ātman* and *jīva* inter-changeably.[49]

According to Anima Sen-Gupta, the *Sāṅkhya* of Vijñānabhikṣu considers *ātman* and *prakṛti* as the modes of God. They depend on God. Already, it is noted that *pradhāna* is the body of Brahman. Their coming together is also due to God (VAB 1.1.2, p.18), and also by the will of God (VP 1.2.29, VAB 1.1.2, p.18). Now, this is again confirmed with *puruṣa* and *prakṛti* as very much parts of Brahman. Sen-Gupta testifies, "Both the individual self and *prakṛti* are modes of God and are, therefore, dependent on Him. It is this supreme spirit that gives the start to the process of creation and orders all things. Individual souls are nothing but the sparks of God and have, therefore, no existence apart from Him."[50]

They are the modes of God, because, their original cause is *Viṣṇu*. This is the reason, they are known to be eternal. "From whom are produced *Puruṣa* [sic] and *Prakṛti*, and from whom proceeds this creation, moveable and immovable, He **Viṣṇu** the cause of all this, may be pleased to us."[51]

Evolution is effected in the unconscious *prakṛti*. The unconscious becomes conscious at the immanent vicinity of the conscious *puruṣa*. This means, that *puruṣa*, who is known as Brahman in the form of *Ātman*, effects the evolutionary process.

The *Upaniṣads* describe Brahman as *saccidānanda: sat-cit-ānanda*. For Śaṅkara, *ānanda* (bliss) is Brahman, at par with *cit* (consciousness) and *sat* (existence). For Rāmānuja, *ānanda* is an attribute of Brahman. (VAB 1.1.2, p.33). Vijñānabhikṣu interprets them in the framework of *Sāṅkhya*. *Sat* has to be understood as *pāramārthika-sat*. *Prakṛti* is deprived of this Ultimate Real. This is the reason the *prakṛti* is unconscious. *Cit* has to be understood like the prism becoming red at the proximity of a red rose. Bliss is confined to the realm of *prakṛti* or the pure *sattva* adjunct as it possesses objectivity. Since it is in the realm of *prakṛti*, it is in the form of an unmanifested condition. *Puruṣa* is the *adhiṣṭhāna* or locus of *prakṛti* and immutable in nature and therefore, it is the cause or the *kāraṇa* of the *jagat*. Therefore, *sat-cit-ānanda* is not the nature of Brahman but may be an attribute, as *puruṣa* and *prakṛti* are the modes of Brahman.[52]

Brahman, apart from being the unmodifiable *adhiṣṭhāna kāraṇa* (supporting cause) of the world, is also the *upādāna kāraṇa* (the material cause). *Puruṣa* and *prakṛti* have identical natures with Brahman to a certain extent. The reason is both are with their *avibhāga* (non-separate) effects. This does not signify that the world directly comes from Brahman. If so, Brahman cannot be termed as Perfect Being. In that case, Brahman would be the originator of the evil. This is one of the distinguishing features of Vijñānabhikṣu among other *Bhedābhedavādins*.

Difference and Non-difference in *Sāṅkhya*

The *Puruṣa* is conscious and all-pervasive,[53] while the *prakṛti* is the unconscious aspect of Brahman in the world. By accepting *cit* and *acit* to be the attributes of Brahman, Vijñānabhikṣu falls into the *Viśiṣṭādvaita* tradition. *Puruṣa* is the Lord or the owner of the creation.[54] Since both are the modes of the Supreme Being, they are eternal.[55] This implies that there is a non-difference or *abheda* tone in the two basic divisions of the *Sāṅkhya* with Brahman. At the same time, they are not the same. There is the difference, *bheda*.

According to *Sāṅkhyasāra*, the all-pervasive conscious *puruṣa* does not know all the objects simultaneously, because it is not affected by the object on account of the lack of the instrumentality in the form of the external functioning.[56] If this is so, how does *puruṣa* know the objects, while the intellect is the property of *prakṛti*? To answer this, Vijñānabhikṣu employs a theory of *double reflection*.[57] According to this theory, *puruṣa* reflects on the *buddhi* (intellect) and the *buddhi* starts functioning like a sentient object. *Buddhi*, then having the reflection of the object of cognition, reflects back the *puruṣa*. Through this reflection, the *puruṣa* comes to know its own.

Bheda in Sāṅkhya

Puruṣa is said to be the experiencer of worldly experience such as pain and pleasure. It indeed experiences these.[58] In this sense, *puruṣa* is the same as the experiencer in the world as *ātman* or *jīva*.

A classic example given by Vijñānabhikṣu to substantiate the *bheda* nature of *puruṣa* and the evolutes of *prakṛti* is *a red rose placed near a crystal*. The colour of the crystal is only red because the rose kept at its proximity and the latter acts as a *upādhi*. In reality, crystal is white, so also is *puruṣa*.[59]

Abheda in Sāṅkhya

The release from *duḥkhatraya* is the liberation of *prakṛti*. Multiple *ātmans* in the *prakṛti* seem to be identical with the *prakṛti*. But it need not be so, since by nature *puruṣa* is free from all attachments as the *Bṛhadāraṇyaka Upaniṣad* asserts.[60] Though *puruṣa* is immanent in the *prakṛti,* it remains independent without undergoing any change like a lotus-leaf in the water. The immanence is explained in the *Sāṅkhya* as *dwelling in prakṛti* or *prakṛtisṭhaḥ.*[61]

A second reason is the action as the property of the *prakṛti*. Growth and development in the evolutionary process is only the action of release from the bondage. The *prakṛti* cannot be the *upādhi* of *puruṣa* on the contrary.

Abheda is also known as *avibhāga*. While explaining the non-contradiction of the reality of *avidyā*[62] Vijñānabhikṣu uses the word, *Avibhāga.* He cites the example of Brahman expressed as multiple souls which are declared in the Vedas as *avibhāga.*[63]

The *abhedā* is also explained in terms of eternally existing. Whatever is seen existing is not momentary, as the *Vedas* explain, "All this, O peaceful one, was verily existing at the beginning. How can that which exists proceed from that which exists not?"[64]

The effect was already present in the cause. Likewise, the world existed before it came to be. In this way, there is a non-difference between the world and Brahman. "The world is not a mere idea, on account of the intuition of objective reality."[65]

Sāṅkhyasāra, speaking about the existence of *jagat,* sheds light on the immanence of Brahman in the world. If the objects are sans Brahman, then such objects cannot be said to exist. "The universe is not existent, nor is it absolutely non-existent, (and hence) is of the nature of both existence and non-existence."[66]

5.5.2 *Bhedābheda* and *Yoga*

In the *Yogavārttika*, Vijñānabhikṣu differentiates Brahman between *nirguṇa* and *saguṇa* aspects, that is, a divine being devoid of any attributes and a divine being with attributes. This divine being is termed as '*puruṣa*.' The *saguṇa* reality of *puruṣa* is termed as *Īśvara*,[67] "*Īśvara* is a special *puruṣa* untouched by *kleṣa, karma, vipāka* and *āśaya*," like "the victory or defeat, though dependent on the soldiers, is attributed to their king." This special *puruṣa*, who is untouched by this kind of experience, is *Īśvara*.[68] *Īśvara* is equivalent to the *Ātman*. This implies two truths: Brahman as *puruṣa* with both difference and non-difference.

The non-difference of *puruṣa* has to be understood in relation to the bondage of a person. The soul is ever free and never under the bondage of *Īśvara*, "*sat tu sadaeiva muktaḥ sadeiveśvara iti*."[69] Thus, there is *abheda* relation between the *jīva* and *Īśvara*. At the same time, there is *bheda* relation between them. The latter is pre-eminent and superior to the other.

For the worldly understanding, *puruṣa*, associated with *buddhi* and other *prakṛti tattvas*, is called the *jīvātman* and devoid of these is called *Īśvara*. The *Puruṣa's* experiencing pain and pleasure means that the *puruṣa* only witnesses. Pleasure and pain are the properties of the intellect.

The *Yogasūtra* explains *bheda* in terms of the reason for the multiple objects as "his [Hari's] own desire." He supports it using *śruti*, "By entering through his [Brahman's] own desire, both *prakṛti* and *puruṣa* at the time of creation, disturbs both *prakṛti* and *puruṣa*... the disturbance which causes dissimilarity in '*prakṛti*,' is due only to the desire of *Īśvara*" (VP 1.2.29, KP 4.13).[70] *Bheda* is, further, substantiated by the *śruti*:

i. The *jīva* has a limitation of the nature, whereas *Īśvara* has a limitation of the nature of cause (SuU 3.12)

ii. He saw (CU 6.2.3)

iii. He desired (TU 2.6)

iv. That self was created by itself (TU 2.7)

v. That is the bliss of Brahman (TU 2.8)[71]

All these scriptural references point out Brahman as a witness and not an experiencer, because he is pure consciousness and devoid of any *guṇas*.

Bhedābheda can be spoken in terms of *Ātman*[72] and *jīva*. *Ātman* is known to be the pervader, *vyāpaka* and the *jīva* is said to be pervaded, *vyāpya*. The pervader is the whole and the pervaded is the part. Like space in a pot and a bowl, they are mutually exclusive. Therefore, it is assumed that there is a multiplicity of *jīvas*, but the *Ātman* is one. The multiplicity of *jīvās* needs to be accepted, otherwise birth and death cannot be explained by accepting one *Ātman*.

The examples such as space, sun and moon advocate *bheda* whereas the examples such as fire and spark, bubbles in water advocate *abheda* between *Brahamn* and *jīvas*. Since the *jīva* and Brahman are essentially of the nature of eternal consciousness, there is non-duality between them as they belong to the same class (*jāti*). But, because the limitations are of a different, they are also different. Thus, Vijñānabhikṣu strongly blosters reality as *Bhedābheda*.

Reaching the *samādhi* at the end of the practice of *yoga* means, realizing the eternity of what is being chanted (*praṇava mantra*) and the meaning. As the meaning of the latter two is eternal, so too realizing the eternal relation between *ātman* and *Brahman* is *samādhi*. Such a person is called a "*yogin*."[73] The absorption of *puruṣa* in Brahman is not identity. The absorption takes place when one dissolves all one's *prakṛtitattvas* and gets united in Brahman. Getting united is like *ghaṭākāśa* uniting with *bahirākāśa* upon breaking the *ghaṭa*. Or it is like fire placed in the fire, becoming similar to it, so too, a *yogi* is becoming similar to the Brahman. This does not mean that *puruṣas* will become *Ātman* and *Ātman* into *Brahman*. *Puruṣa* and *prakṛti* are just modes of *Brahman*.

Thus, there are two facets of divine realities in the *Sāṅkhya-Yoga* system of Vijñānabhikṣu: Brahman and *Īśvara*. They do not belong to two different levels. Both are equally real. *Prakṛti* and *puruṣa* are known to be the two energies (*māyāśakti*) of the Brahman, whose association and dissociation are due to the operation of Him. They bring about creation, preservation and destruction. Thus, this *Sāṅkhya* is known as theistic *Sāṅkhya*.

5.6 Reconciliation of Different Schools

Vijñānabhikṣu is probably the first thinker to reconcile

Sāṅkhya with *Yoga*. Further, he extended its scope to the *prasthānatrayī*, especially to the *Brahmasūtras*. His ingenuity of knitting the *āstika darśanas* with their use of rationality to explain the relationship between Brahman, *ātman* and *jagat* is noteworthy. For him, if the *Pūrva-Mīmāṁsā* explains the *Brahma-ātmaikyatva*, the *Uttara-Mīmāṁsā* through Bādarāyaṇa's *Brahmasūtra* should explain the *Brahmaikyata* (VAB 1.1.1, p.1). His concept of union (*sambandha*) is taken from the *Nyāya darśana*. John Borelli clarifies the attitude of reconciliation of Vijñānabhikṣu as follows:

> He based his principles of ecumenism upon this passage in the *Bṛhadāraṇyaka Upaniṣad*: "Verily the self should be seen, should be heard, should be reflected on, and should be meditated on." Seeing the self is the intuition which the liberated soul possesses, but hearing, reflecting, and meditating represent a triple teaching for attaining that intuition and indicate the salvific activities of *Vedānta, Sāṅkhya* and *Yoga* respectively. *Vedānta* examines the scriptures, which the Hindus believed were the transcriptions of those eternal sounds which the ancient sages heard. Thus, *Vedānta* interprets the correct hearing of revelation. *Sāṅkhya* through reflection upon Scriptures and the facts of the world offers its explanation that the two first principles, Matter and Spirit, are distinct. *Yoga* is the doctrine of the methods and result of meditation. Even though there are aspects of these three schools which are contradictory, in their principal doctrine they do not conflict with the double norm for

orthodoxy, Scripture and Tradition.[74]

Not only these three systems (*Vedānta*, *Sāṅkhya* and *Yoga*), but also Vijñānabhikṣu brings in the *Nyāya-Vaiśeṣika* systems. These two Schools consider the *ātman* as the enjoyer and sufferer as distinct from the body, but this is only a basic knowledge of the soul. *Sāṅkhya* too goes along with this, *ātman* as distinct from *prakṛti*, the matter.[75]

Over and above, Vijñānabhikṣu has used several *upaniṣads*, various *purāṇas* and other *smṛti* texts to prove his stand in the commentary. In all these things he has shown that scriptures by their very nature cannot be contradictory. Even if contradictory statements are found, they are only apparent contradictions and not the real ones. It may be a human error while scribing them in *sūtras*.

5.7 *Avibhāga-Bhedābheda* and the Theory of Causality

The *Nyāya* understanding of causality is *asatkāryavāda*, namely, the effect doesn't exist in the cause, as the curd was not present in the milk. Therefore, every effect is a new beginning. Contrary to this, *Sāṅkhya* and *Vedānta* in general, accept *satkāryavāda*, the effect was pre-existent in the cause as the curd was present in the milk. Thus, the effect is not altogether a new beginning, but a modification of the cause.

Vijñānabhikṣu admits the *Sāṅkhya* perspective of causality. But he is not comfortable with the *prakṛtipariṇāmavāda*. He does not endorse the view like *Sāṅkhya* that the effect is the modification of the primordial *prakṛti*. Vijñānabhikṣu accepts Brahman as the material causality of the universe (VAB 1.1.4, p.50). In this sense, he is similar to Vallabha. But Vijñānabhikṣu's material cause is different from Vallabha. Vallabha treats *Sāṅkhya* as part of the *Vedānta* whereas Vijñānabhikṣu treats the *Vedānta* at square with the rationalism of *Sāṅkhya*. Retaining the basic causality, Vijñānabhikṣu presents Brahman as the supporting material causality (*adhiṣṭhāna kāraṇa*) as well as *nimitta kāraṇa*. The outcome of this causality is the acceptance of Brahman as deeply engrossed in every aspect of reality in its ontological state. That's why Vijñānabhikṣu's causality can be termed as *Brahmaśaktiprakṛtipariṇāmavāda*. As a result, he proves a physico-transcendental relationship existing within and between every being.

In other words, there is physical and transcendental continuation between the originated and the originator, simultaneously physical and transcendental discontinuation. The son has a physical continuation of the father and at the same time, physical discontinuation. So too, Son has a transcendental continuation and discontinuation with the father. The same principle applies even to other beings and their relationship.

5.8 *Bhedābheda* in Other Philosophical Systems

Vijñānabhikṣu believes that the *Bhedābheda* is the superior philosophy and is the best way to explain reality. Bādarāyaṇa's *sūtras* are very close to this philosophy. Dasgupta says that "Bādarāyaṇa's philosophy was some kind of *Bhedābheda-vāda* or a theory of transcendence and immanence of God (Brahman) – even in the light of Śaṅkara's commentary. He believed that the world was the product of a real transformation of Brahman, or rather of His powers and energies (*śakti*)."[76] Several philosophical schools reiterate either partially or completely the *Bhedābhedavāda* though there are major differences. Bhāskarācārya holds, "*Bhedābheda* is the central truth of the *Vedānta*"[77] and it is the state of Brahman. Srinivasachari puts into words, "It [*Bhedābheda*] may generally be taken to indicate that *bheda* or 'distinction' and *abheda* or 'unity' can co-exist and be in intimate relation with each other."[78] Substance and attributes, universal and particular, part and whole may seem contradictory, but there is no incompatibility as such. This can be stated as *unity-in-diversity* or in the words of Vijñānabhikṣu, *Bhedābheda sambandha.*

The first part of the *Kevala Advaita*, 'as the reality being one and it is immanent in the world,' is nothing but the non-different aspect of the *Bhedābheda*. Vijñānabhikṣu doesn't refuse the *advaitic* aspect of Brahman, what he refutes is the 'unreality of the world,' like Rāmānuja or Madhva. The unreality of the world is already commented on and refuted vehemently by the *Viśiṣṭādvaita Vedānta.* Once again, Vijñānabhikṣu presupposes that the people of the time are aware of both these schools and their refutation of māyā of Advaita. The world is as real as Brahman. It is not an illusion. Reality consists of Brahman, *jīva* and *jagat*. *Jīva* and *jagat* are the modes of Brahman. Coupled with the *Kevalādvaita* and the *Viśiṣṭādvaita*, therefore, is nothing but the *abheda* aspect of Vijñānabhikṣu.

One of the important contributions of Vijñānabhikṣu is the

non-separateness or *avibhāga* of *jīva* with Brahman. For Rāmānuja, it is the *apṛthaksiddhi sambandha*[79] where both *jīva* and Brahman are in *avibhāga* relation and the former is an attribute of the latter.[80] Vijñānabhikṣu accepts the above view but not as an attribute. He believes in their entitative existence. For Vijñānabhikṣu what gives meaning to the reality is its non-differentiable (*avibhāga*) relationship that exists between two beings, be it divine or non-divine, spiritual or material.

The third major school of the *Vedānta* is the *Dvaita Vedānta*. The reality is *one* but expressed in eternal duality: *jagat* and *ātman*. According to Madhva, there are two orders of reality: *svatantra*, independent reality, the Brahman alone, and *paratantra*, dependent reality consisting of *jīva* (souls) and *jaḍa* (lifeless objects). Each entity is real and relates with the others. Although dependent reality would not exist apart from Brahman's will, this very dependence creates a fundamental distinction between Brahman and all else, implying a dualistic view. This view corresponds well with the *bhedavāda*.

Bhedābheda is not an entirely new inspiration to the world of philosophy. There are traces and elements of it spread both in the West and the East in different forms. In the first chapter, we have already surveyed its presence in the Eastern tradition. Let's ascertain now the Western equivalent.

5.9 *Avibhāga-Bhedābheda* and the Western Philosophy

There is neither a definitive stand nor clarity on

Bhedābheda in the Western thought as seen in the Eastern thought pattern. Srinivasachari enlists several Western thinkers who could be possible *Bhedābhedavādins*. The prominent scholars are Plotinus, Spinoza, Hegel, Bradley, Royce, Bosanquet, Fichte and Schelling.[81] Borelli assents with Srinivasachari's list. Further, he adds Bonaventure, Friedrich Engels, Alfred North Whitehead and John B. Cobb Jr., to the list without repeating detailed analysis made by Srinivasachari except that of Spinoza.[82] Affirming what has been expressed by these thinkers, we investigate further to acquire any pointers leaning towards Vijñānabhikṣu.

If the Neo-Platonic[83] or the Spinozian thought[84] patterns are more leaning towards the *Advaitic* trends due to their illusory nature of the world, Hegelian dialectics points to the *Dvaita* philosophy. But while in the Neo-Platonic thought 'One becomes the source of Many,' the Hegelian thought origins from the abstract language to concrete, bridging the gulf between One and Many. If Plotinus understands creation as not an altogether new beginning, but the manifestation of the perfection of God, then Hegelian understanding of the world is a contingent being.[85] Both the systems seek to bridge the gap between infinite and finite. Srinivasachari reckons that the purpose of Spinoza is "to trace the diversity of finite life to the infinity of God."[86]

Further, he speaks out for Spinoza, "The absolute is one self-conscious spirit realizing itself in and through finite directions. By its inner impulse, it goes forth from itself to objects foreign to it and then returns to itself. It is both self-differentiating and self-integrating."[87] One can recognize both immanence and transcendental nature of Brahman of Vijñānabhikṣu's theology here.

For Vijñānabhikṣu, there is a non-differentiable relationship between Brahman and other beings. It is this relationship that gives meaning to the whole reality. Jacques Derrida (1930-2004), the French philosopher introduces something similar, calling it *Différance,* to indicate an inexhaustible relationship between the text[88] and the meaning. He neither calls it a concept nor a theory, rather as a web of relationships. The meaning emerges by 'spacing' or 'gaping' between the signifier and signified.[89]

It is a way of *deconstructing* a text. *Deconstruction* is a method of decentering or a way of reading a text. It makes one aware of the centrality of the central term. Then it attempts to *subvert* the central term so that the marginalized term can become central.[90] The marginalized word[91] temporarily overthrows the hierarchy. In the process of making the marginalized central, the central becomes marginalized. Therefore, it is neither the central nor the marginalized that gives meaning but rather their relationship or the 'difference,' or 'gap' – the *différance*. Vijñānabhikṣu's understanding of *tattvamasi* also advances like this, it is *asi* in *tattvamasi* that defines *tat* and *tvam*. In other words, it is the kind of relationship between the signifier and the signified, or the subject and that which is subjectified that gives meaning to the enigmatic polarities.

However one strives to understand the reality, yet it

remains an enigma. Vijñānabhikṣu points this out through *avibhāga*. For Derrida, it is the deliberate misspelled 'a' in the *différance* that shows this axiom of incompleteness. *Différance* ruptures the ideology of identity, myth of clarity and communication. It bridges what is known and unknown and possibility and impossibility.[92]

Further, for Vijñānabhikṣu, the difference is an attribute of identity. This is true even for Bhāskara. Not only this, but also there is an element of co-existence of the absolute and particular inter-penetrating in the difference-in-identity (*Bhedābheda*). Though it can be expressed in many ways, truth is that there is a relationship existing between the polarities (where there is an absolute difference) or creative oppositions (as in the case of Hegelian dialectical oppositions) in Derridian language of *différance.*

Derrida critiques Western thought for its unidirectional approach–for being logocentric.[93] In the words of Vijñānabhikṣu, it is an *abhdedātmaka* methodology. According to Saussaure, there is a natural relationship between what is being said within (the inner meaning or *antaryāmin*) and the outer expression of it (the sound, *sphoṭa*). Again, in terms of Vijñānabhikṣu, what is being unexpressed or within is the *antaryāmin* and it is expressed in terms of *prakṛtitattva* or its manifestations. Therefore, the meaning of one's existence depends on the difference of being with the other.

This insight is not a unique insight of the modern or the post-modern Western world. During the medieval period, St.

Bonaventure (1217-1274) echoed his theological writings in *Bhedābheda* archetype. In his sermon, *Collationes in Hexaemeron* states that God is the origination, exemplification and termination.[94] This very much coincides with Vijñānabhikṣu's commentary on BS, "Brahman is the origin, preservation and destruction of the world" (VAB 1.1.2). Bonaventure understands these three-fold functions of the divine as generation and spiration in the Christian Trinitarian theology. Borelli, understanding both Bonaventure and Vijñānabhikṣu, asserts thus:

> A closer examination of the generation of the Son further elucidates the dual aspect of God and his relationship with the manifest world, because for Bonaventure Christ is the metaphysical medium and through him the three orders of being are related: emanation, exemplification, and return. From all eternity the Father begets the son, who is his like-ness and also expresses all that he can do. This total expression of his Being in the image of the Son is called divine art by Bonaventure. Therefore, the nature of God is the same, but the mission and manifestation of each Person is different. The Father sends the Son and expresses the totality of creation through him while the Son, being the Exemplar of everything, is the cause of the return of everything to God in the Spirit.[95]

To understand the relationship between God and creation, Bonaventure had used several imageries –as Vijñānabhikṣu too has employed– image, trace, likeness, shadow, echo, and representation. The Universe is like a book reflecting and representing the Trinity, all creatures are traces and shadows while the intellectual creatures are images, etc.[96] All these point to an intimate relationship (*avibhāga sambandha*). Thus, we see an *Avibhāga-Bhedābheda sambandha* in Western medieval thought as well. These are not exhaustive details rather a few pointers towards the philosophy. Therefore, there is ample scope for further research in this area.

5.10 *Avibhāga-Bhedābheda* in Contemporary India

There is not much literature written about *Bhedābheda* in recent years. Two prominent works, however, are Srinivasachari's *The Philosophy of Bhedābheda* and Hayavadana Rao's introductory volume to *The Śrīkara Bhāśya*. Apart from these, Dasgupta's third volume of *A History of Indian Philosophy* gives a detailed analysis of various *Bhedābheda* traditions of Indian Philosophy such as "The Bhāskara School of Philosophy," "The *Pañcarātra*," "The *Āḷvars*," "The *Viśiṣṭādvaita* School of Thought," "The Philosophy of Yāmunācārya," "The Nimbārka School of Thought," "The Philosophy of Vijñānabhikṣu," and "The Philosophical Speculations of some of the Selected *Purāṇas* like *Viṣṇu Puṛāṇa, Vāyu Puṛāṇa, Mārkaṇḍeya Puṛāṇa, Nāradīya Puṛāṇa* and *Kūrma Purāṇa*." But there is no literature so far from *the Avibhāga-Bhedābheda* view-point, either to appropriate the philosophy or to extend an inter-disciplinary flavour. The only available works are from Borelli and Nicholson. This part of the work is an attempt to appropriate the philosophy.

5.10.1 *Avibhāga-Bhedābheda*, a Relevant Made Irrelevant

A serious concern can be raised at the universal spread of *Bhedābheda* tradition. While *Advaita* came to its existence in the 8th century CE, understood to be *the philosophy* of Hinduism, and *Dvaita* philosophy is also not so badly accepted by common people today. However, *Bhedābheda* tradition was, in fact, *the real ethos of the Vedic Hinduism* which even the Bādarāyaṇa's *Brahmasūtras* mentions being the philosophy of several people has not become *the philosophy* of the majority. Caitanya's *Bhedābheda* tradition, though, strives by means of ISKON movement, people have misunderstood it to be the *Advaitic* tradition, largely. Therefore, the puzzle of evangelization of a particular thought pattern could be a matter of debate and research. Wendy Doniger in her book, *The Hindus: An Alternative History* beautifully conveys, "Often history can explain why some ideas take hold and spread while others do not; ideas take root only when they become important to people at a particular time, when they hitch on to something that those people care about."[97] Vijñānabhikṣu's theistic non-dualism was more appealing to the people and time who considered their language, tradition and religion as accommodating and tolerant. When the hierarchy considers each one as 'the person' endowed with dignity and freedom, it gives ample space to express and practice what one's convictions are, then *Avibhāga-Bhedābeda* is possible as was during the time of Akbar.

Hinduism, known in our contemporary time as the '*sanātana dharma*' has taken a U-turn from the *Vedic* understanding. Hinduism, from the *Vedic* time till the last few centuries was known for accommodation and religious tolerance is not so at present. The present Hindutvaization and 'one culture, one country, one language' meme cannot but reject accommodation and pluriculture. Vijñānabhikṣu's philosophy re-invents the *Vedic* culture, contrary to the culture of the majority today.

When one is threatened of one's existence, one feels the need to protect one's identity and therefore, putting a boundary or bracketing becomes inevitable. Hinduism was threatened of its existence in the fifteenth and sixteenth centuries by the advent and the spread of the Mughal rule, obviously by Islamic invaders on the one hand, and the advent of Christian evangelization in North India on the other. This is the time, the proponents of Hinduism wanted to uphold and show their inclusiveness that the need for another creed is not a desired one. This is the time, Hinduism as a religion is defined as an all-encompassing ancient religion. Vijñānabhikṣu with his erudite style and knowledge of scriptures redefines Hinduism as a staunch proponent of *Bhedābheda*. One may question, 'if this is so, why Vijñānabhikṣu did not critique Islam and Christianity?' This seems to be a relevant question here, but he did not even name *Advaita* or *Dvaita*, though he vehemently critiqued them. The oft word while critiquing is, '*ādhunikāstu*.' For him, the *ādhunikā* are anyone who upholds the principle other than his.

There must have been an invisible pressure or threat to name as to who these 'modernists' are. Had he mentioned clearly the Mughals or Muslims he would have been branded as 'antinational' as it was their rule. On the contrary, if he were to mention his opponents as the *Vedāntins* (either *Dvaita or Advaita*) or *nāstikavādis* (Buddhism and Jainism), then again he would be in trouble. The history is very clear. Śaṅkara has made several *digvijaya yātras* (tours of victories in all directions) to win over or destroy the people who do not endorse his views. This kind of enslaving fanatic attitude neither fosters a healthy theology nor philosophy. Naming one group of people is against the very nature of the philosophy of accommodation. A healthy critique is that which condemns the wrong teaching and not the person as the Gandhian dictum goes, "Hate the sin and not the sinner." This could be an added reason to settle for a neutral word. Again, it was not unusual for the *paṇḍits* to use such rhetorical language. One of the famous scholars (*navaratna*s) in Akbar's kingdom was ṭoḍāramalla (?-1589), an ardent follower of *puṣṭīmārga* of Vallabhācārya.[98] Though he was faithful to Akbar, in his encyclopedic writing on the textual assemblage of *smṛti* writings specially taken from *Dharmaśāstra, Jyotiśāstra* and *Āyurveda* called *ṭoḍārānanda* (*ṭoḍāra's Joy*) recounts one of the purposes of his work as, "to rescue the *Vedas* from the deluge of foreign culture." Further, he says, "In him was the sun of sovereignty that cleanses the world, which had been blotted out amongst royalty [*rājaneṣu*] by the cruel and dark age of Kali."[99] Dominik Wujastyk notices the expression '*rājaneṣu,*' (among the royalty) as a veiled reference to the royal family of the reigning emperor Akbar, as an incarnation of *Kaliyuga.*[100] Therefore, it is not surprising to perceive an imminent threat by the dominant Mughal culture towards Hinduism. The literature thus emerged from Hindus suggests a demystifying trend to preserve their cultural heritage. Therefore, Vijñānabhikṣu too must have used this technique to strengthen his claim.

5.10.2 *Avibhāga-Bhedābheda* as the Philosophy of Religious Pluralism

The word 'religion' derives from the Latin word, '*ligare*' meaning 'to connect' or 'to bind together' to which the prefix '*re*' meaning 'again' or 'back' is added.[101] Thus, religion is 'that which unites or binds again.' What binds human beings primarily is a sense of 'divinity' as the *Īśa Upaniṣad* declares in its opening *mantra, "īśavāsyam idaṁ sarvam."* This sense of divinity (*brahmātmata* as Vijñānabhikṣu states) is common to all the religions. In fact, Vijñānabhikṣu considers that the primary purpose of the *mahāvākyas* in the *Upaniṣads* is to perceive this hidden divine essence.

The *Cārvākas* or *Lokāyatas* may not agree with 'divinity' or 'god' being a common thread to bind everyone. But they do acquiesce a sense of *ṛta,* the orderliness, ethical or deontological[102] prerogatives as guiding principles in life. It can be termed as '*dharma.*' In its stricter note, *dharma* is not religion. The root word for *dharma* is '*dhṛ,*' 'to hold on.' What holds on is '*sat,*' 'that which is.' That's why customarily it is said in the Hindi language, *"jo dhāraṇ karein vah dharm hain,*" "that which holds on is religion." There is parallel Sanskrit saying, "*dhāraṇāt dharmaṁ ityāhuḥ*" or "*dhāratā iti dharmaḥ.*" 'That which is' is *nitya, ananta* and *sanātana*. The *Vānaprastha Khaṇḍa* of *Mahābhārata* asserts, "*ārambho nyāyayukto yaḥ sa dharma iti smṛtaḥ. anyāyayastu adharma iti etat śiṣṭānuśāsanam,*" that is, "whatever is being done justly is *dharma*. Unjust act is *adharma*, thus is the advice of the wise" (MBh 207.77). Added to this, *Manusmṛti* gives ten characteristics of *dharma*, "courage, forgiveness, self-control, non-stealing, purity, sense-control, right use of intellect, wisdom, truth and non-anger."[103] And those who study and practice these enter the highest state (*paramagati*). Goswāmi Tulsidās in the *Rāmacaritamānasa* echoes this in the similar style, that "There is no superior *dharma* apart from performing an act of welfare for others and there is no *adharma* superior to oppressing the other."[104] A *dharma* should embrace everyone and everything with *samadarśina,* equanimity (BG 5:18). Thus, *dharma* refers to a set of common rules and regulations, good behaviour, ethical principles, truth, non-violence, honesty, justice, etc. For that reason, the religion holds on to eternal truths and the truths that bind everyone under one common *sūtra* or 'a set of beliefs.' This in totality is termed in the words of Vijñānabhikṣu '*brahmātmata,*' the essence of divinity.

This is ably supported by Vijñānabhikṣu himself to elucidate the very purpose of his writing at the beginning of his commentary, "*brahmajñānasya ca dharmatvaṁ codanālakṣaṇātvāt siddham,*" "to prove the impelling meaning of *dharma* and *brahmajijñāsa*" (VAB 1.1.1, p.1). And more strongly, all the scriptural teachings are intended to establish this impelling force.[105] Therefore, there is an impelling meaning (*codana-lakṣaṇa*) to be established through his commentary. One of the impelling meanings is to prove that *dharma* unites everyone, irrespective of any class and creed. The darkness will only trigger darkness, "*tameva viditvāti mṛtyum*" and the knowledge of the divine will make you divine "*brahmaveda brahmaiva bhavati,*" and so, attain that supreme knowledge of Brahman "*brahmavid apnoti param*" which every religion advocates (VAB 1.1.1, p.1).

The setting in which Vijñānabhikṣu writes his commentary amply proves this point again. The Islamic contemporary literature at the time of Vijñānabhikṣu in Persian language, *A'in-I-Akbari*, the third volume of *Akbarnāma*, '*the Book of Akbar*' enlightens us in the following words:

O God in every temple I see people that see Thee, and in every language I hear spoken, people praise Thee! Polytheism and Islam feel after Thee. Each religion says, 'Thou art one, without equal.' If it be a mosque people murmur the holy prayer, and if it be a Christian Church, people ring the bell from love to Thee. Sometimes I frequent the Christian cloister, and sometimes the mosque. But it is Thou whom I search from temple to temple. Thy elect have no dealings with either heresy or orthodoxy; for neither of them stands behind the screen of Thy truth. Heresy to the heretic, and religion to the orthodox, but the dust of the rose petal belongs to the heart of the perfume seller.[106]

Vijñānabhikṣu composed his commentary at a time when Moghuls ruled, particularly Akbar who was known for his inter-religious affinity with Hinduism as an accommodative religion. Through his philosophy, he stresses that Hinduism does not disregard other religions, cultures, philosophies and traditions, and that the inclusiveness is the striking element in it.

Bhedābheda philosophy ponders the reality as unity-in-diversity, *ekam advitīyam* or in the *ṛgvedic* term, *ekam sadviprā bahudhā vadanti*. The Supreme Brahman is One without the second. Everything else is part and parcel of this cosmic One, like *bimba-pratibimba* (image and likeness) and *samānādhikaraṇyam* (part and whole). Even the material body or the *prakṛti* is the power of this Supreme. The divine inter-penetrates the whole reality, and at the same time, is both immanent and transcendent to a certain extent. The Human being is at once divine and non-divine. Both are so intimately connected like the wave in the sea. This is nothing but the essence of the 'divinity' found in every religion. The Christian theology, especially the Christology understands the dual nature of Jesus—Son of God and Son of Man— as a hypostatic unity. Hypostasis, the Greek term, literally means 'substance.' Therefore it is a substantial unity or subsistence in contrast to Platonic abstract categories. Kierkegaard in his philosophical fragments understands this concept as 'the Absolute Paradox.' According to him, God is understood as a perfectly good, perfectly wise, perfectly powerful being, fully became a human, in the Christian understanding of the term: burdened by sin, limited in goodness, knowledge, and understanding. To teach us the difference between God and human beings, God shared our human nature. This nature can also be termed as 'the Mystical Union.'[107]

The 'divinity' mentioned here is to be understood not just in a religious sense, but also in a Panikkerian sense of 'sacred-secular.'[108] Sacred and secular are not in opposition to each other, rather they are intimately connected or entwined (*jugalbandi*) as in the *Sāṅkhya* School which fascinates Vijñānabhikṣu. This *'Advaita'* of Vijñānabhikṣu allocates one to have a valid autonomy for the secular to know, see, and feel the presence of the divine (God or Brahman) in all. Therefore, this divinity is not the monopoly of a particular religion, but rather the *elixir of creative life* in the world. Then, there is a mutual *samadarśina,* generating a new creation. This is the *elixir* (*amṛta*) *of creative life.*

The elixir gives immortality. The divinity spoken here is that elixir to immortalize the person upon consuming or nurturing in life. Once one practices this divinity in life, one perceives everything and everyone as sacred and begins to pay what one owes (justice) to the other. We owe to others because we are indebted. The *Śatapatha Brāhmaṇa* presents four kinds of debts (*caturṛṇa*) a person inherits upon the birth, whosoever one may be: debt to gods, to sages, to the ancestors, and to men.[109] One must add a cosmic dimension to make it a *pañcarṛṇa,* since we are indebted to the world for what we are and will be. One cannot limit one's debt only towards the divine and human world. In as much as one is connected to these, one is very much part of the material world as well. That's why the *Atharvaveda* speaks of a metaphor called 'Indra's net' symbolizing "the universe as a web or connections and interdependencies among all its members, wherein every member is both manifestation of the whole and inseparable from the whole."[110] This net is like the dew-filled spider's web, spreading the whole of the universe. Each joint is woven with a jewel connecting each other, and one reflecting the other and simultaneously indivisible and one complex whole net. In the Mahāyāna School of Buddhism, this metaphor is used to depict the concept of the universe. Indra-jāla (Indra's Net) is refers to emptiness, dependent origination and interpenetration. Each bead in this net is the reflection of the other and in turn, reflects to the other. Thus, it describes the interconnectedness of the universe. Vijñānabhikṣu's concept of Brahman, *ātman* and *jagat* can be compared to this kind of network, more so like a triangle wherein all three corners are interconnected and independent, making it *avibhāga*.

The way of repaying the debt is nothing but *bhakti* or *upāsana*. It is at this point, the secular duties and observations become divine, as the dictum goes, "render to Caesar what is Caesar's and to God what is God's" (Mt. 22:21; Mk 12:17). This implies that the activities building the universe are more sacred and spiritual than many of the religious performances. The pain and physical labour involved in them is better acceptable than ritualistic penances. If one cannot find divine or God in one's working fields, families, in daily sweat and blood, better not to seek God in temples and religious customs. That would be an idolatrous practice. So the divine relation has to be translated into the dialogical relationship with the other. Thus, the dialogue becomes an authentic prayer.[111] Human existence is understood not as existence in isolation but as existence in relation with the divine, the others and the world. In the Encyclical on *Laudato Si'* Pope Francis stresses the unfolding of the divine in the universe, "There is a mystical meaning to be found in a leaf, in a mountain trail, in a dewdrop, on a poor person's face."[112] All the goodness present in these realities and experiences point to a sublime reality of the divine. This, in other words, makes the world into one family, "*vasudaiva kuṭumbakam*" (*Mahopaniṣad* 6.71), a vision of universal brotherhood.

One sect of religion or philosophy cannot claim supremacy over the other declaring that 'it is the truth' or 'it is the real one' or 'what it proclaims is the absolute' or 'other than that, others have no salvation'. Everyone is a partaker of the *dharma* and is in equal distance from the centre, the *Sat*. To put in terms of a metaphor, it is like a circle wherein every tradition, philosophy or religion is at equidistance from the centre, the Ultimage Reality. Considering multi-centres in this circle will aberrate not only its structure but also will create distance with the other traditions. In line with this, if one is avoiding one section of the people from the reach of the scripture, such structure cannot be called 'the religion' in a stricter sense. An umbrella has its existence upon a common point. Though the number of ribs may vary in an umbrella, each rib is at an equal distance from the centre. If any one of the ribs is broken or one utters that is not part of the whole, the umbrella cannot remain intact. Similarly, Hinduism (or any religion) to be intact has to accommodate every culture and tradition. Therefore, no religion is superior to the other. It depends on the person to accept a way of life that gives a better meaning to live by.

Thus, *Bhedabheda* can very well answer the juggernaut of secularism without getting involved in political tumult. It leads us to a dialogical power *kenosis*. There is a need for an honest dialogue between the religious world and the secular world.

5.10.3 *Avibhāga-Bhedābheda,* Invisible Made Visible

Vijñānabhikṣu recounts reality in duals: visible and invisible, part and whole, *Ātman* and Brahman, *jīva* and *jagat*, *saguṇa* and *nirguṇa*, etc. The invisible aspect is not amenable to ordinary perception. Therefore, the invisible has to be made palpable into visible forms. The Supreme *Puruṣa* is manifested in terms of *Īśvara*. This implies, that for human beings *nirguṇa* provides meaning in its *saguṇa* aspect. It is through *saguṇa* one has the access to *nirguṇa*.

Vijñānabhikṣu quotes the *Garuḍa Purāṇa* in the *Yogasārasaṅgraha,* "In the beginning of meditation (*yoga*), contemplate on the *saguṇa* image of God, after this on the *nirguṇa* image. When the mind is well gripped in gross objects it can easily lead to the subtle"[113] (GP 1.229.25). It is very much practical to move from the gross to subtle, i.e., to move from the image to the imagelessness or from the visible to the invisible. Once the person reaches the state of realization, the gross *saguṇa* perception ceases to exist as the

Chāndogya Upaniṣad declares, "*Ghaṭa* and the like are mere developments for the sake of the name and the beginning of language, the only earthly reality is the clay as the cause"[114] (CU 6.1.4). Thus, in the highest state, imageless awareness or devotion should reign.

In the same way, every human has two aspects: visible and invisible. The physical body, muscles, organs are the visible parts, while the intellect, spirituality, inter-personal relationship, trust, confidence, fidelity, concern, humanness, love, compassion, forgiveness, values, morality, concern, etc. are the invisible aspects. It is these foundational invisible parts that safeguard the visible part to make the existence on the earth humane and divine. This applies even to the nation as a body. People are contented mostly with visible parts without giving prominence to the invisible. One requires to recounting the invisible through the visible.

5.10.4 *Avibhāga-Bhedābheda* as the Key to Understand the Divine

Avibhāga-Bhedābheda is the key to understand the divine Revelation in a world dissected by religious pluralism. In the modern pluricultural world, the divine is limited to a particular culture and tradition. Certain belief systems or traditions stamp the trademark of a particular structure. But, can one reduce the divine revelation to a particular way? God reveals if not, that reality is not God.[115] If one curbs the divine to reveal 'in this way only,' the very purpose of religion is defeated. Religion should break the boundaries of 'this way only.' Caste-class division is not a divine will, but a human construct. If it enslaves instead of liberating, then it has to be abandoned. So too are the other unbecoming traditions and cultures to be dumped.

Patriarchy was understood to be good and correct, but that excluded the freedom of the other gender, yoking for power. When one affirms that the vulnerable are also entitled to an equal share in the divine banquet, the patriarchal nature of the society finds threatened of its existence. Similarly, when the divine is monopolized, one restrains the revelation of God. Theistic non-dualism rescues us: that the divine should be perceived as the thread to bind all culture and tradition; and that the same divine is discerned in everything, irrespective of name and form the human has fabricated to express, in everything.

5.10.5 *Avibhāga-Bhedābheda* as a Literary Ingenuity

Ingenuity is "an ability to think of clever new ways of doing something."[116] In literature, every section is independent and at the same time, a continuation of the whole. For example, a particular chapter in itself is a complete unit, and simultaneously, a part of the whole book. *Bhedābheda* writing is a typical literary genre, just like *Advaita* or *Dvaita*. However, this literature gathers together both *Dvaita* and *Advaita* traditions. Similarly, *Avibhāga-Bhedābheda* itself as a concept becomes a literary tool to express similarities, differences and the unity of thought patterns.

5.10.6 *Avibhāga-Bhedābheda* as a Leap from Individualism to Communitarianism

Vijñānabhikṣu attempts to re-invent and re-establish the lost meaning of the *Vedic* communitarian dimension of life through this concept. The introduction of certain concepts like *karma*, sacrifice, caste-creed difference, hierarchy by the *Brāhmiṇic* class in the tradition influenced the religion individualistic. The *vānaprastha* or the forest-dwelling for salvation (*vairāgya*) involved living an ascetic and individual life without having a touch with the society to strive for individual salvation. It is nothing but a movement away from social responsibilities, social interactions and community well-being. This may be an apparent reason why the Buddhist's *saṅgha* theory or Jain's community life became a great consequence. Wendy Doniger buttresses this view:

> The whole tradition was becoming individualistic, not just renunciation; we begin to see a transition from group to individual, a perceived need for personal ritual of transformation, forming certain sort of person, not just a member of the tribe. At the same time, collective rather than individual choices needed to be made in order to start and maintain alternative societies, such as Buddhism, and monastic communities, as well as to engage in the highly collective enterprise of growing rice.[117]

Perhaps, Vijñānabhikṣu witnesses a strong community bond or dimension between Muslims and Christians in their scriptural teaching and religious life, vis-à-vis Hindu way of life during his time. This may be perceived as a potential threat to Hinduism and its scriptures. To protect this or to do away with the belittling of Hinduism, Vijñānabhikṣu upholds the *Bhedābheda* tradition of Hinduism. And to show mutual respect, interaction, mutual penetration, he puts forward *avibhāga* in it to avoid superiority over other cultures and traditions of the *ādhunikā*.

Another way of looking at Vijñānabhikṣu's concept could be to re-invent and establish the lost communitarian culture in the wake of growing individualism. If this is so, or even otherwise, this concept appeals well to the present situation of the world, especially a country where globalization and cyber culture have hampered community life.

5.10.7 *Avibhāga-Bhedābheda* as an Integrity of Experience

Bhedābheda is a theory of integrity of the experience. The theory of *Bhedābheda* teaches that transcendence and empiricism can co-exist without any contradiction.[118] The world of experience and the Supreme Being is different, yet they are mutually enriching. One moves from one state or passage to the other. The world is the expression of the divine and this itself is proof for our salvation or liberation. This divine truth is expressed in scriptures and in fact, the scriptures are the outcome of a concrete experience of the people. Therefore, the scriptural sayings have the force of action. Vijñānabhikṣu states that "The very meaning of *śāstra* is action. Therefore, statements which do not culminate in action are futile and meaningless."[119]

There is an unbreakable inter-penetrating relationship (*avicchеda sambandha*) or unlimited conjunction (*avicchеda saṁyoga*) between creator and creation, between *puruṣa* and *prakṛti*. There is an indissoluble relation and conjunction between God and creation. This relation and conjunction, is expressed through human beings. Human being is a constituent that has become limited to fulfill the teleological purpose of God.[120] This integral vision of Vijñānabhikṣu is expressed in terms of *avicchеda saṁyoga*. The fact that pot is in touch with the earth does not denote that pot and earth have become one. At the same time without the contact of the earth, pot cannot exist on the earth.

Change takes place on the thing which has the ability to change; if the thing has no capacity to change, then it won't. A well ripe mango seed has the potentiality to change into a mango tree, but not a burnt seed even if it is matured. Add to this, the ripe seed needs a substratum and environment to actualize its potentiality. If the condusive atmosphere is not available, then the seed will either remain mummified or will get converted into some other energy form. The nature of *puruṣa* is unchanging and *prakṛti* is changing. A certain aspect of *prakṛti* will change, that is its very nature. Change takes place only by a particular contact. Every fusion or contact does not effect birth. This is the reason that certain contact gives rise to certain intellects to discharge the teleological function.[121]

There are two kinds of changes: change in the conscious state and change in the unconscious state, that is, *vikāras* in the mind and *vikāras* in the object (matter). *Buddhivikāras* are *caitanyamaya* or conscious, and material *vikāras* (*vastuvikāras*) are unconscious. The latter surmounts as the *saṁyoga* or conjunction ceases to exist as the wave in the sea.

This relationship could be termed as beginningless-endless relation between the possessor and possessed or experiencer and experienced. There is no change or mutation here. Because of the *avaccheda saṁyoga*, the unchangeable things will not change. Just as there cannot be the change in the space upon the contact of the pot with the earth in different places; similarly, the space does not change by a mere change of locus. Lotus leaf does not change upon its contact with water. But, water is essential for the lotus to exist. Likewise, a substratum is essential for a being to exist.

5.11 Practical Implications of *Avibhāga-Bhedābheda*

5.11.1 An Inclusive Reading of a Scripture

Vijñānabhikṣu's reading of the *Brahmasūtras* is based on *Sāṅkhya* School. He spots *Avibhāga-Bhedābheda* thread throughout the text. While reading and interpreting it, he makes use of both *śruti* and *smṛti* texts to show that they do not contradict each other. In the process, he highlights at the outset several seemingly contradictory passages in various scriptures. In fact, they are all in agreement with the general flow of the scripture. This allows us to read any scripture from the *Bhedābheda* perspective.

Vijñānabhikṣu quotes the *Bhagavad Gītā* to explain all that exists in the world as nothing but a part of divine manifestation. There is no end to the manifestation of

Brahman. All the glorious splendors are nothing but a spark of the divine splendor. Therefore, one needs to know all that exists as nothing but a fraction of that divine being, pervaded and supported by it.[122]

To read scripture from an inclusive perspective the following yardsticks are beneficial and effective.

a. *Establishing the authenticity of the scripture*: First and foremost, one must determine the text as valid and authoritative. For Vijñānabhikṣu, the Vedas are *apauruṣyea* and infallible. *Śruti* texts take precedence over the *smṛti* texts. However, both revealed texts as well as tradition, aid us in establishing the authenticity of the scriptures as pointed by Vijñānabhikṣu.

b. *Extracting the abheda śruti*: The first section of the *Brahmasūtras* deals with *abheda śruti* that gives the *brahmabodha*. Every scripture will have basic texts to confer the identity of Supreme Brahman with the other created beings.

c. *Extracting the bheda śruti*: The second section of the *Brahmasūtras* embarks upon texts which appear contrary to *bheda śruti*. They need to be reconciled with the first section.

d. *Extracting inclusive texts*: The third kind of text found in the scripture is the texts that speak in both inclusive and exclusive terms. They assist us to accommodate the differing views of other.

e. *Re-reading from an inclusive perspective*: Based on the previous three kinds of texts, the scriptures should be re-read and commented upon.

5.11.2 *Avibhāga-Bhedābheda Sambandha* as the Philosophy of Integral Relation

The relationship is a subject of experience. It is like the *vyāpti* (invariable concomitance) in a syllogism inherent (as *samavāya* in the *Nyāya*) between subject and object. Relations do not exhaust a thing, but a thing gains its significance because of the relation. In the same way, a personal relationship gives identity to a person, though the relationship does not exhaust the person.

At the outset, Brahman, *ātman* and *jagat* may seem abstractions and they do if taken as mere concepts. But, they are more than any ideal concepts. One cannot negate the fact that in relation they are real, and because they are real in the relationship, they are experienceable and knowable. Without relation, these are unknowable and not experienceable. However, in themselves, they are complete but incommunicable and unknowable.

Every School of Philosophy is unique. This uniqueness is the hallmark of *darśana*. True to the word *darśana*, 'vision of the reality,' Bādarāyaṇa codified it from the *Vedas* and *Upaniṣads*. The codification is so terse (that's why it is called *sūtra*) that they needed interpretations. Different scholars began to interpret 'according to their seeing,' some with monist way, some with dualistic way and some with integral way. Vijñānabhikṣu sees it from an integral way. But, the unswallowable chunk of Vijñānabhikṣu's vision is, 'why the *avibhāga sambandha* way?'

There are two ways in which a reality can be approached:

from the subject to object and from object to subject. Vijñānabhikṣu is aware that if he begins from the object, he will land up objectifying the subject and land up in materialism and physicalism. On the contrary, if he begins from the subject, he will land up in *Kevala Advaita* (pure monism) or idealism. The strategic point of departure, therefore, which can accommodate both systems without trouble, is the *Bhedābheda* way. For this purpose, there was a need to affirm a kind of relationship that would explain both the extremes. The main task in front of him, therefore, was to harmonize or to bring the unitary aspect of Brahman with the plurality of *puruṣas* and *jīva-jagat*. The *Sāṅkhya* way was an ideal platform to explain this very fact if the divine is made the principal-agent behind its evolution. Vijñānabhikṣu succeeds in achieving his purpose.

Absolute Brahman, as a unitary general concept is abstract and ineffectual in itself. Therefore, this general Unity (*ekam*) has to become Many (*bahuṇām*). The abstract has to become actual. On the other hand, plurality is an aggregate of multiple units of abstracts. When they are considered as multiple concepts, they are once again abstract and in effectual. So, the whole reality has to be considered an organic unity of convergences and divergences. This gives integrity, the *avibhāga*. In other words, *Avibhāga-Bhedābheda* of Vijñānabhikṣu posits *unity-in-diversity.*

This *Avibhāga sambandha*, the integral approach of the relationship of Vijñānabhikṣu invites us to probe further. It is a foundation of mutual communication, a relationship of involvement, a deeper interaction and an inter-penetration. Thus, it enables a new paradigm for understanding reality.

A being cannot communicate unless it establishes a relationship. The deeper the relationship, the more effective is the communication. The communication between the Supreme *Puruṣa* or the Brahman with the other *puruṣas* and *prakṛti* can be explained in terms of *aviccheda* or *avibhāga sambandha*. In the Christian Trinitarian understanding, it is like a perichoretic (circumincession) relationship. The more openness to the Universal Relationship a person establishes the more open one becomes towards the other. In the *Vedāntic* terms, *brahmāvid brahmaiva bhavati*, by knowing Brahman, one becomes Brahman.

There is reciprocalness in the *aviccheda sambandha*, i.e., there is an inter-penetration with each other. This reciprocalness impels one to act. In the Veda-Upaniṣadic terms, this impelling force is called '*codana-lakṣaṇa*.'[123] This is a relationship of mutual involvement. The purpose of this is to keep the *dharma*. Kaṇāda in his *Vaiśeṣika darśana* understands *dharma* as "well-being and perfect happiness."[124] Therefore, this reciprocal relationship when understood properly fosters a deeper unity. The divine attributes and the activity in the creation and the culmination of the latter in the former are understood to be the reciprocal relationship. The mutual penetration neither makes the secular a complete divine entity nor is the divine reduced to secular. Here, both integrities are healthily maintained. Sacred and secular can interact with each other without reducing the other.

By its very nature, Brahman intends to grow. Therefore, establishes a relationship with *puruṣa* and *prakṛti*. By the very fact of the proximity of *puruṣa*, the creation in *prakṛti* takes place. The created creation is now directed towards its freedom. This is achieved when it culminates itself in Brahman. The beginning of its return can only take place in the establishment of a relationship. Therefore, *puruṣa* must begin to realize that it is only an *aṁśa* of the *aṁśī*. *Anubhava*, the experience-after-the-*prakṛti* which Vijñānabhikṣu speaks about[125] in VAB 1.1.19 is very essential for the *puruṣa* to attain its original state.

When understood the dynamics involved here, the *Upaniṣadic* ideal of '*vasudaiva kuṭumbakam*' is not a farther reality. When the self is liberated, it acts as *sākṣin* for other-selves. This also paves the way for religious harmony. Every religion is an independent entity and at the same time, every member has a common destiny. Understanding the one is to understand the other (in Heideggerian sense), though the paths are different.

5.11.3 *Avibhāga-Bhedābheda Sambandha* as the Foundation of Manifestation of Mutual Communication

Vijñānabhikṣu speaks of three kinds of *puruṣas* in his *magnum opus*. These are integrally connected with *prakṛti*. And the connection is so intimate that one can neither find *bheda* nor *abheda* and simultaneously, they form one integral whole, called the 'wholesomeness' (*avibhājya*).

One might get lost or confused about the purpose and

meaning of it. But when it is observed from an integral perspective, one will become aware of the motive clearly. The purpose is to exhort the people about cosmic interconnected and well-being. This can be easily understood from the hymn to *Puruṣasūkta* (RV 90.10.1-16).

The *Puruṣasūkta* is a mythical poem. This myth can be understood as a manifestation of the multiplicity of this world as an organic whole called the *Puruṣa*. In it, everything is organically interconnected. *Puruṣa* is seen here as a huge organism in which everything is, moves and has its being. This is the reason, the entire thing is perceived as a sacrifice, the cosmic *yajña*. Creation is *yajña*. *Yajña* is a basic category of the Vedic time. Final fulfillment is realized through the acknowledgement of this *yajña*. The acknowledgement comes from the very fact that one lives as a part of this *yajña*, that is, by contributing to the cosmic rhythm. The interconnected has to be preserved and whatever the performance of the person (*puruṣa-strī*) has to align with this inter-connectedness. Doing away with this is to let the cosmos in chaos. This would then be the path of 'dis-integration' which the tradition calls the *pra]aya*. Therefore, living in harmony, coming-in-union (communion) and inter-personal build-up creates, re-creates and recharges the cosmos and thus cosmic energy is sustained.

Avibhāga-Bhedābheda is a philosophy of integral wholeness. It is the nature of Hindu philosophy *per se*. Anything that promotes an experience of this wholesomeness is a part of the integral wholeness.

Reparation for the wrong done is nothing but at-one-ment (atonement), i.e., process to be part of this wholeness process. *Attone* or *atoon* from which the word 'atonement' can be derived, is 'being in harmony ('at one') with someone not in consonance with.' Therefore, as a requirement for redemption and to re-establish the bond, there is a need for reconciliation, forgiveness, remorse, reparation, etc. In this way, *mukti* is nothing but removing divisions, dichotomy and diversions. These negative elements only cause dissipation of energy, loss of the centre of identity, loss of concentration and meaning. 'Part-iality' can only lead to meaninglessness, disintegration and exclusiveness. Integration of the whole (*sarvam*) will mean comm-union of the whole creation. Various parts, groups and quarters give meaning if they are harmoniously united with the one whole.

The dualism of the early *Sāṅkhya* symbolizes that the *puruṣa* is the principle of unity through awareness and *prakṛti* as the multiplicity of experience. If *puruṣa* is the unifying element, then *prakṛti* is the element unified. The etymological meaning *pra-kṛ-ti* reveals that *prakṛti* is a principle of 'process.' The entire universe (the *sthūlaśarīra*) is a process in which everything is connected organically by the *puruṣatattva*, the principle of unity (*sūkṣmatattva*). The senses (*pañcendriya* and *manas*), the will, understanding (*buddhi*) and their *tanmātras* are part of this great union. Whatever happens to this 'process-ing' affects the totality of everything. The process-ing involves the elements of goodness or light represented by *sattva*, elements of passions, dynamism, negative energy represented by *rajas*, and the elements of dullness, heaviness represented by *tamas*. It is their harmonious blend of relationships that keep the rhythm of creation in equilibrium. To keep the harmonious blend of the relationship, one has to experience the *puruṣa*. A mere identifying oneself with *prakṛtitattvas* (which is called *moha*) expressed above will only lead to bondage.

This discussion guides us to find out the worldview of Vijñānabhikṣu. The worldview depicted in the *Sāṅkhya* system is a cosmic. Vijñānabhikṣu is aware of it. However, he does not reject it, rather inserts a purposeful divine intervention to make it theo-centric. The title of Borelli's work on VAB 1.1.2 '*Theistic Non-Dualism*' is a confirmation of this fact and therefore needless to explain here. The human being is only a part of the cosmos and therefore, the world-view is not anthropocentric, but cosmocentric. However, both *puruṣa* and *prakṛti* are the powers (*śakti*) of Brahman. It is by the will of God the *sṛṣṭi, sthiti* and *laya* takes place. And so, the world-view of Vijñānabhikṣu is theocentric.

Since the divine is the centre of everything, nameless and formless, social stratifications for one's selfishness and the supremacy of a particular race and culture is meaningless and absurd. Upholding the creation is to endorse the divine (*Puruṣa*) with an open mind and heart (which is called *śraddha-bhakti*). And listening to the scriptural utterings (*śruti*) no matter which religion one sanctions, it's very crucial living a life of mutual understanding and cooperation (*nidhidhyāsana*).

Summary

From what has been assessed so far, we can enlist certain general characteristics of *Avibhāga-Bhedābheda*. The world is real with a divine beginning. There is a substantial identity between *jīva* and Brahman, yet different. Brahman is *adhiṣṭhāna kāraṇa*, the foundational cause of everything. He is also *kāraṇa* Brahman (Brahman as the cause) and *kārya Brahman* (Brahman as effect). Brahman is an Ultimate Being as well as a person displaying both *nirguṇa* and *saguṇa* forms. There is a strong sense of divine inter-penetration in the world, making the world divine. The difference is an attribute of identity manifested in difference. Thus, they co-exist in each other in a unique relationship. The relationship between Brahman and other beings is that of *avibhāga* (non-differentiable).

---

[1] Dasgupta, *A History of Indian Philosophy*, 471-72.

[2] Srinivasachari, *The Philosophy of Bhedābheda*, vi.

[3] Nicholson, *Unifying Hinduism*, 65.

[4] Srinivasachari, *The Philosophy of Viśiṣṭādvaita*, 228-231.

[5] Rukmani, "Vijñānabhikṣu: The Sāṅkhya-Yoga-Vedāntācārya," 24.

[6] VAB 1.1.2, p.35. Text is quoted under the subtitle, *tattvamasi.*

[7] VAB 1.1.2, p.26. *avibhāgaḥ saṁyogaviśeṣaḥ, svarūpasambandho vā ādheyatvādivat. Avibhāga* is a special relation, a particular relation and attributive nature.

[8] Rukmani, "Vijñānabhikṣu: The Sāṅkhya-Yoga-Vedāntācārya," 28-29.

[9] One such example is his explanation on *tattvamasi* itself. This we have seen in the previous chapter.

[10] VAB 4.1.3, p.305-06.

[11] Ludwig J. Wittgenstein, *Tractatus Logico-Philosophicus*, translated by D.F. Peers and G.F. McGuninnes (London: Routledge and Kegan Paul, 1965), 105.

[12] Bina and William C. Wilcox Gupta, ""Tat Tvam Asi": An Important Identity Statement or a Mere Tautology," *Philosophy East and West* Vol. 34, no. 1 (January 1984): 85.

[13] Gupta, "Tat Tvam Asi," 85-86.

[14] Gupta, "Tat Tvam Asi," 88.

[15] This concept is borrowed from Jaina theory of *syādavāda* to describe the reality as indescribable.

[16] Anand, *Hindu Inspriation for Christian Reflection*, 74-75.

[17] Swami Vireswarananda, *Brahma Sūtras* (Calcutta: Advaita Ashrama, 1962), xiii.

[18] George Thaibaut, *The Vedānta-Sūtras with the Commentary of Śaṅkarācārya*, 1968 ed., The Sacred Books of the East, vol. 34, 38 (Delhi: Motilal Banarsidass, 1904), pt.1, p.c.

[19] Dasgupta, *A History of Indian Philosophy*, 2.

[20] Richard De-Smet, "Śaṅkara's Non-Dualism (Advaita-Vāda)," in *Religious Hinduism: A Presentation and Appraisal*, edited by Richard De Smet and Josef Neuner (Allahabad: St. Paul Publications, 1998; reprint, 1998), 81-82.

[21] Anima Sen Gupta, *Essays on Sāmkhya and Other Systems of Indian Philosophy* (Kanpur: M. Sen, 1964), 73.

[22] *"asya tu jīva ādhyātmatvabādhena pāramārthika ātmā viṣaya iti."* VAB 1.1.2, p.36.

[23] *"nānyo'to 'sti dṛṣṭe"* (BU 3.7.23). VAB 1.1.2, p.36.

[24] *yathā śarīrasya keśādiraṁśo, rāśeścaikadeśo'śaḥ, pituśca putra iti.* VAB 1.1.2, p.27.

[25] *yasmāt parameśvara eva mukhyo brahmaśabdārthaḥ, "paraṁ jaiminirmukhyatvād."* VAB 1.1.2, p.20. The primary meaning of the word *brahma* is Supreme Lord only, as Jaimini thinks "it is the Supreme, for that is the primary meaning." *mukhyatvāt parabrahmaṇyeva brahmaśabdasya mukhyatvāt, gauṇamukhyayośca mukhye saṁpratyaya iti arthaḥ.* VAB 4.3.12, p.328. Primarily, Supreme Lord (Brahman) is the only primary meaning of the word, secondary meaning is only by conviction.

[26] *"yattat kāraṇamavyaktam nityaṁ sadasadātmakam, tadvisṛṣṭaḥ sa puruṣo loke brahmeti gīyate"* (Manu 1.11). VAB 1.1.2, p.20 and 4.3.9, p.328. As translated by Borelli, 36.

[27] Rao, *The Śrīkara Bhāṣya*, 179.

[28] *"ābrahmabhuvanāllokāt punarāvartito'rjuna, māmupetya tu kaunteya punarjanma na vidhyate"* (BG 8.16). VAB 4.4.22, p.340. As translated by Prabhupāda, 377.

[29] Again, this has the allegiance to Vijñānabhikṣu's *tattvamasi* interpretation.

[30] *asmanmate tu ahaṁśabdārthatvena prayokartrsaṅghāta adhyakṣatvādīnā sāmānyarūpeṇa eva ākāṅkṣāyāṁ tat ityādi viśeṣarūpeṇa upadeśa iti laukikī śabdamaryādā na hīyata iti. yadapi tat tvameva tvameva tat iti paraspara vyatihāravākyaṁ tadanya vaidharmyalakṣaṇam bhedaṁ nivartayati jīvasyāsaṁsāritva pratipādanāya paramātma svarūpa pradarśanāya ca, anyathā vyatihāra vaiyarthāt*. VAB 1.1.2, p.31. "In the understanding of the statement the word "I" has the general sense of agent and coordinator of aggregates, while the word "that" communicates a specific sense. In this way popular usage is not contravened. In the case of reciprocal statement "you are that, that you are," difference characterized through possession of mutually exclusive attributes is abolished in order to teach the highest Self." For the translation see, Borelli, "The Philosophy of Vijñānabhikṣu," 64-65. Also see, Rao, *Śrīkarabhāṣyam*, 171.

[31] *jīvād atyanta bhinna eveśvaro brahmaśabdārtha iti siddham*. VAB 1.1.2, p.32.

[32] Nicholson, *Unifying Hinduism*, 65-67. So much so, in the medieval philosophical system *māyā* was synonymously understood to be *prakṛti*.

[33] Kiran Singh, *Sāṁkhya Darśana: Text with Commentaries*, vol. I (Delhi: New Bharatiya Book Corporation, 2015), vii.

[34] *so'yaṁ brahmamīmāṁsasiddhāntaḥ saṅkṣepeṇa punaḥ smāryate—"tattvamasi ahaṁ brahmāsmi" iti evaṁ vidhānyeva vedāntamahāvākyāni ca na jīvabrahmābhedaṁ bodhayanti*. VAB 1.1.2, p.35.

---

[35] *sāṅkhyayogādibhyaścāsya darśansyāyaṁ viśeṣaḥ, yat śrutyavāntara vākyārtho vyāvahārikātmā jīvasteṣāṁ viṣayaḥ. asya tu jīvādyātmatvabodhena pāramārthika ātmā viṣaya iti.* VAB 1.1.2, p.36.

[36] Nicholson, *Unifying Hinduism*, 70.

[37] Nicholson, *Unifying Hinduism*, 67-68.

[38] Nicholson, *Unifying Hinduism*, 68.

[39] Vijñānabhikṣu, *Sāṁkhyasāra*, vi.

[40] Sen-Gupta, *The Evolution of the Samkhya School of Thought*, 8.

[41] *sāmānyamacetanaṁ prasavadharmi.* See, Īśvarakṛṣṇa, *Sāṁkyakārika: Sagauḍapādabhāṣya 'Abhinavarājalakṣmī' Bhāṣya Bhāṣāṭīkātrayavirājitā*, translated by Bala Śāstrī Sītārāma Śāstrī, Guru Prasāda Śāstrī, Chaukambha Surabharati Granthamala (Varanasi: Chowkambha Surabharati Publications, 2012), 26.

[42] *yatha—prakṛtiriti uccyate vicārotpādakatvāt, avidhyājñānavirodhatvāt 'māyā' sṛṣṭikaraṇatvāt.* See, Vijñānabhikṣu, *Sāṅkhya Pravacanabhāṣya*. Also see, Īśvarakṛṣṇa, *Sāṁkyakārika: Sagauḍapādabhāṣya 'Abhinavarājalakṣmī' Bhāṣya Bhāṣāṭīkātrayavirājitā*, 25.

[43] *"guṇānāṁ sāmyāvasthā prakṛtiḥ."* See, Vijñānabhikṣu, *Sāṅkhya Pravacanabhāṣya*. Also see, Vijñānabhikṣu, *Sāṁkhyasāra*, 79-89.

[44] *yathā "arvāg bilaṣcamas ūrdhvabudhna"* (BU 2.2.3) *ityasminmantre camaso yāgaśarīratvena eva pratipādito na svātantryeṇa tathā pradhānamapi jagatkāraṇabrahmaśarīratvena eva atra pratipāditaṁ na svātantryeṇa.* VAB 1.4.8, p.132.

In fact, about the *Upaniṣadic* statement mentioned in the text, Śaṅkara comments on *Bṛahadāraṇyaka Upaniṣad* concerning the inverted bowl as the head and the seven seers (altogether eight) sitting around it as the organs. Explicitly they are: the mouth as the opening, ears as auditory organs, eyes as organs of sight and nostrils as organs of smell. Tongue communicating the Vedas is the eight. It is in this head, various forms of knowledge are filled, just as soma juice is filled in the bowl. *Brahadāraṇyaka Upaniṣad with the Commentary of Śaṅkarācārya*, 1950 ed. (Almora: Advaita Ashrama, 1934), 324-26. Thus, these organs represent *indriyas* and *tanmātras* of the *prakṛti*.

[45] Nicholson, *Unifying Hinduism*, 88. For the original quote see, Vijñānabhikṣu, *Sāṅkhya Pravacanabhāṣya*, 2.

[46] Bapat, *A Study of the Vedānta*, 205.

[47] Vijñānabhikṣu, *Sāṅkhya Pravacanabhāṣya*, xii. Also see, Ram, *Integral Non-Dualism*, 168.

[48] Vijñānabhikṣu, *Sāṅkhya Pravacanabhāṣya*, 1. Also see, Singh, *Sāṁkhya Darśana: Text with Commentaries*, viii.

[49] Nicholson, *Unifying Hinduism*, 85. For original text see, Vijñānabhikṣu, *Sāṁkhyasāra*, 2.2 and 2.3.

[50] Sen-Gupta, *The Evolution of the Samkhya School of Thought*, 128.

[51] *yatraḥ pradhānapuruṣau yataścaitaścarācaṁ, kāraṇaṁ sakalasyāsya sa no **viṣṇustuḥ** prasīdatu*. Singh, *Sāṁkhya Darśana: Text with Commentaries*, 178. Stress is added for the word *viṣṇu*.

[52] *atra nānandamityānandarūpatāpratiṣedhaḥ, na nirānandamiti ca aupādhika ānanda-dharmakatvānumitiḥ*. VAB 1.1.2, p.34. Here, "not bliss" is a denial of a blissful essence. "Not without bliss" is an inference that bliss is only a temporary quality. Vijñānabhikṣu is refereeing to the contradictory statements of the scripture: TU 2.4.1 and 2.8.1, "He who knows the bliss of Brahman does not fear at any time, this is the one bliss of Brahman" and KauU 3.8, KaU 2.12 "Not bliss, not without bliss, the one who knows leaves both joy and sorrow." VAB 1.1.2, p.33-34.

[53] Vijñānabhikṣu, *Sāṁkhyasāra*, 2.3.6.

[54] Singh, *Sāṁkhya Darśana*, 188.

[55] "*pūrvabhāvitve dvayorekatarasya hāne'nyatarayogaḥa*." Singh, *Sāṁkhya Darśana*, 186-87.

[56] Vijñānabhikṣu, *Sāṁkhyasāra*, 2.3.6.

[57] For more details see Sen-Gupta, *Essays on Sāṁkhya and Other Systems*, 21-36.

[58] Singh, *Sāṁkhya Darśana*, 42.

[59] *yathā hi kevalo raktaḥ sphaṭiko lakṣyate janaiḥ, rajjukādhyupadhānena tadvat paramapuruṣaḥ*. KP 2.2.28.1-2. Singh, *Sāṁkhya Darśana*, 49.

[60] "*sa yadatra kiñcat paśyatyananvāgatastena bhavati asaṅgo hyāyam puruṣaḥa... padmapatrasthajaleneva padmapatrasyāsaṅgatāyaḥa puruṣāsaṅgatāyāṁ dṛṣṭāntatāśravaṇācca*." Singh, *Sāṁkhya Darśana*, 38.

[61] *puruṣaḥ prakṛtiśṭhohi bhuṅkto prakṛtijāt guṇāt*. Singh, *Sāṁkhya Darśana*, 52.

[62] According to Vijñānabhikṣu, *avidyā* is to be understood in two ways: a form of knowledge with subsequent bondage and a form of *vāsanā* or the acquired tendency of the self which the *advaitins* are busy with. Singh, *Sāṁkhya Darśana: Text with Commentaries*, 61.

[63] *avibhāgo vacanāt*. Singh, *Sāṁkhya Darśana*, 61.

[64] *"sadeva somyedamagra asīt... kathamasataḥa sajjāyet."* Singh, *Sāṁkhya Darśana*, 81.

[65] *na vijñānamātraṁ bāhyapratehe*. Singh, *Sāṁkhya Darśana*, 87.

[66] *"ato na sannāsadidaṁ jagat sadasātmakam, asadviṣayakatvācca tasya dhīstāttviko brahmaḥ."* Vijñānabhikṣu, *Sāṁkhyasāra*, 2.2.11.

[67] In *Yogavārttika*, Brahman is termed as *Ātman*, Soul as *Īśvara* and individual souls as *jīva*. In other words, *Ātman* or Brahman is the controller like *ether*, the divine principle is *Īśvara* and individual life is *jīva*. Rukmani, *Yogavārttika of Vijñānabhikṣu*, vol.1, 132. Īśvarakṛśṇa agrees with this insight in his *Sāṅkhyakārka*, *"puruṣasya = ātmanaḥa siddhiḥ."* *Kārika* 17. Further, he explains, "people find peace of mind in worshipping *prakṛti, buddhi, ahaṁkāra, indriya, pañcamahābhūta,* etc. *jaḍa tattvas* think that it is the real '*ātman*,' but they do not know the conscious *puruṣa tattva* as the *ātman*." See, Īśvarakṛṣṇa, *Sāṁkyakārika: Sagauḍapādabhāṣya 'Abhinavarājalakṣmī' Bhāṣya Bhāṣāṭīkātrayavirājitā*, 68. Translation is mine.

[68] *kleśakarmavipākāśayairparāmṛṣṭaḥ puruṣaviśeṣa īśvaraḥ... yathā jayaḥ parājayo vā yoddhṛṣu vartamānāḥ svāmini vyapadiśyate. yo hyanena bhogena aparāmṛṣṭaḥ sa puruṣaviśeṣa īśvaraḥ* (*Yogavārttika*, 1.24). Rukmani, *Yogavārttika of Vijñānabhikṣu*, vol.1, 127.

[69] *Yogavārttika*, 1.24. see, Rukmani, *Yogavārttika of Vijñānabhikṣu*, vol.1, 127.

[70] *prakṛtiṁ ca puruṣaṁ caiva praviśyātmecchayā hariḥ* (KP 4.13; VP 1.2.29). Rukmani, *Yogavārttika of Vijñānabhikṣu*, vol.1, 137. Also see, VAB 1.1.2, p.18.

[71] Rukmani, *Yogavārttika of Vijñānabhikṣu*, vol.1, 138-39.

[72] Here, *Ātman* is synonymously used as *Brahman*.

[73] *vijñātavācyavācakatvasya yoginaḥ*. Rukmani, *Yogavārttika of Vijñānabhikṣu*, vol.1, 159.

[74] SPB 4, 3. Also see, Borelli, "The Theology of Vijñānabhikṣu," 16-17.

[75] Borelli 17.

[76] Dasgupta, *A History of Indian Philosophy*, vol. 2, 42. Original parenthesis.

[77] *ato binnābhinnārūpam brahma iti sthitam*. Srinivasachari, *The Philosophy of Bhedābheda*, 12.

[78] Srinivasachari, *The Philosophy of Bhedābheda*, xi.

[79] It connotes that one of the two entities related is dependent upon the other, in the sense that it cannot exist without the other. One cannot be known without the other. One qualifies the other. This is the qualified non-dualism or the *Viśiṣṭādvaita*—unity with difference proposed by Rāmānuja. In other words, it is the qualified or the embodied that is one, while the factors qualifying or embodying it are quite distinct, though inseparable, from it.

[80] Jadunath Sinha, *The Philosophy of Vijnanabhikshu*, 70.

[81] Srinivasachari, *The Philosophy of Bhedābheda*, 250-316.

[82] Borelli, "The Theology of Vijñānabhikṣu," 140-74.

[83] The world-view of Plotinus is a kind of *Pariṇāmavāda* of *Bhedābheda*. According to him, the One overflows in a stream of activity in one direction, and on the contra direction, the material reality ascent towards the same One. Therefore, creation is not copies of the ideal world as Plato understood, rather a real transforming into real and merging back into it.

[84] He proposes *acosmism* and *naturalism*. *Acosmism* is the reality of the infinity and the unreality of the finite.

[85] Srinivasachari, *The Philosophy of Bhedābheda*, 255-58.

[86] Srinivasachari, *The Philosophy of Bhedābheda*, 267.

[87] Srinivasachari, *The Philosophy of Bhedābheda*, 267.

[88] For Derrida, anything can be a text. A text is that which 'is.'

[89] For more details and the basic works of Derrida, see, Jacques Derrida, *Dissemination*, translated by Barbara Johnson, 2005 ed. (London, New York: Continuum, 1981). Jacques Derrida, *Of Grammatology*, translated by Gayatri Chakravorty Spivak, 1994 ed.

(Delhi: Motilal Banarsidass Publishers, 1976). Jacques Derrida, *Writing and Difference*, translated by Alan Bass (Chicago: The University of Chicago Press, 1978). Robert Bernasconi David Wood, ed. *Derrida and Différance* (Evanston: Northwestern University Press, 1988).

[90] Jim Powell, *Derrida for Beginners* (Chennai: Orient Longman Ltd., 2000), 26.

[91] Marginalized word is a text, given least importance or a counter part of a binary opposite. For example, when we say 'light and shadow,' the central word here is light. But what gives prominence to light is its counter-part, the dark. The counter-part, the lesser given importance is the marginalized word.

[92] David Wood, *Derrida and Différance*, 48.

[93] *Logocentrism* represents a Platonic ideal world. The word is coined in 1920s by Ludwig Klages, a German Philosopher to denote a tradition which considers words as fundamental expression of external reality. It says that the logos is epistemologically superior, representing an original and irreducible object.

[94] *"Esse ex se est in ratione orginantis; esse secundum se in ratione exemplantis, et esse propter se in ratione finientis vel terminantis; id est in ratione principia, medii et finis seu termini."* *Hexaemeron* 1.12. (V.331). As translated and quoted by John W. Borelli, "Matter and Exemplar: Difference-in-Identity in Vijñānabhiskṣu and Bonaventure," in *Neoplatonism and Indian Thought*, edited by R. Baine Harris (Virginia: International Society for Neoplatonic Studies, 1982), 150,158.

[95] Borelli, "Matter and Exemplar," 151.

[96] Borelli, "Matter and Exemplar," 152-53.

[97] Doniger, *The Hindus: An Alternative History*, 21.

[98] After the death of Vallabha in 1587, his eldest son, Gopinath became the guru of his new sect. He was succeeded by his brother Goswami Vittal. Ṭoḍāramalla was the follower of Vittal. For more details about his works and contributions, see, Kumud Ranjan Das, *Raja Todar Mal* (Calcutta: Saraswat Library, no date), 222.

[99] *"yena mlecchapayodhimagnanigamoddhārakriyā kāritā..." "rājaneṣu tamomayena kalian krūreṇa nimlocito yasminn abhyudito jagadvimalayan sāmrājyatigmadyutiḥ."* Rājā Ṭoḍāramalla,

Ṭoḍārānandam, edited by P.L. Vaidya (Bikaner: Anup Sanskrit Library, 1948), xxx, xxii.

[100] Wujastyk, "Change and Creativity in Early Modern Indian Medical Thought," 110.

[101] *Collins English Dictionary*, 2018 ed. s.v. "Religion."

[102] Deontology is defined as an ethical theory that the morality of an action be based on whether the action itself is right or wrong under a series of rules, rather than based on the consequences of the action.

[103] *"dhṛtiḥ, kṣamā damo asteyaṁ śaucam indriyanigrahaḥ. dhīr vidyā satyam akrodho daśakaṁ dharmalakṣaṇam." Manu Smṛti* 6.92. *"daśalakṣaṇāni dharmasya ye viprāḥ samadhīyate, adhītya ca anuvartante te yānti paramāṁ gatim." Manu Smṛti* 6.93. Those Brāhmaṇas who thoroughly study the tenfold laws, and after studying obey them to enter the highest state.

[104] *"parahit saris dharm nahi bhāī, par pīḍā sam nahi adhmāī,"* (*Śri Rāmacaritamānas, Uttarakāṇḍa* 40.1). For the classical text used here, see, Tulsidas, *Śri Rāmacaritamānas: With Hindi Text and English Translation*, translated by Mādhava Śaraṇa, 1968 ed. (Gorakhpur: Gita Press), 1014.

[105] *vakṣyati cācāryaḥ sarvāsu vedāntavidhyāsu codanāṁ yogena ātmadarśanam.* VAB 1.1.1, p.1.

[106] Abu'l Fazl Allami, *The A'in-I Akbari*, translated by H. Blochmann, vol. 1 (Calcutta: Asiatic Society of Bengal, 1873), xxxii.

[107] Søren Kierkegaard, Howard V. Hong, Edna H. Hong, *Philosophical Fragments: Johannes Climacus* (Princeton: Princeton University Press, 1985), 38-47.

[108] Panikkar, *The Vedic Experience-Mantramañjarī.* For Panikkar any knowledge is sacred, every action is sacred, even eating is sacred. Secular implies "a temporal dimension of human and social life, with the character of human experience in a given age, including experience of the sacred and divine." Fred Dallmayr, "Rethinking Secularism (with Raimon Panikkar)," *The Review of Politics* 61, no. 4 (Autumn, 1999): 720.

[109] *Caturṛṇa* according to *Śatapatha Brāhmaṇa* are: 1. When he performs sacrifices, it is the debt to the Gods' concerned. It is on their behalf, therefore, that he doing this action when he sacrifices or makes an oblation. 2. And when he recites the Vedas, it is the debt to

the sages' concerned. It is on their behalf, therefore, that he is doing this action for it is said of the one who recites the Vedas that he is the guardian of the treasure store of the sages. 3. And when he desires offspring, it is the debt to the ancestors' concerned. It is on their behalf, therefore, that he is doing this action, so that their offspring may continue without interruption. 4. And when he entertains guests, it is the debt to the human' concerned. It is on their behalf, therefore, that he is doing this action if he entertains guests and gives them food and drink. The person who does all these things has performed a true work; has obtained all, conquered all. *Śatapatha Brāhmaṇa* 1.7; 2.1-5.

[110] *"bṛhaddhi jālaṁ bṛhataḥ śakrasya vājinivataḥ... ayaṁ loko jālamāsit śakrasya mahato mahān*." This world so mighty was the net of Sakra, of the Mighty One: With this, the net of Indra, I envelop all those men with gloom (Atharvaveda 8.8). Hymns of the Atharva Veda, by Ralph T.H. Griffith, [1895], at sacred-texts.com. Also see, Rajiv Malhotra, *Indra's Net: Defending Hinduism's Philosophical Unity*, 2016 ed. (Noida: Harper Collins Publishers, 2014), 4.

[111] Raju Felix Crasta, "Welcoming Newness," in *Francis Effect*, edited by Kuruvilla Pandikattu and Vadappuram M. Jose (Pune: Papal Seminary, 2018), 181.

[112] Pope Francis, *Laudato Si'* (Vatican: Liberia Editrice Vaticana, 2015), no.233.

[113] *"yogārambhe mūrtiharimamūrtamatha cintayet, sthūle vinirjitaṁ cittam tataḥ sūkṣme śanairnyet*" (GP 1.229.25). Vijñānabhikṣu, *Yogasārasaṅgraha of Vijñānabhikṣu*, 22,26,30.

[114] *"kāryarūpatāyā asthiratvena kāraṇarūpatāyā eva satyatvāt. vācārambhaṇaṁ vikāro nāmadheyaṁ mṛttiketyeva satyam*" (CU 6.1.4). Vijñānabhikṣu, *Yogasārasaṅgraha of Vijñānabhikṣu*, 23,27,32.

[115] When it concerns Jesus, there can be no neutrality! Yet, Jesus cautions his disciples when someone complained against an opponent performing an act of healing in His name, "For whoever is not against us is for us" (Mk 9:40; Mt 12.30). If someone discovers divine in one and does not topple down other's culture and tradition, but works for the welfare of all, also reveals God's power. In this sense, Murugan can also be a form of revelation of God. But the orthodox tendency is to limit the revelation "this way only." In the Christian tradition, the dictum *"extra ecclesia nulla salus,"* has in fact radicalized the original flavor of the Bible, stating that Jesus, the Truth should be the savior

for all, and therefore, all other religions lack *Truth*. Thanks to the *Nostra Aetates* which rectifies, "The Catholic Church rejects nothing that is true and holy in these [Hinduism, Buddhism, Islam] religions. She regards with sincere reverence those ways of conduct and of life, those precepts and teachings which, though differing in many aspects from the ones she holds and sets forth, nonetheless often reflect a ray of that Truth which enlightens all men. Indeed, she proclaims, and ever must proclaim Christ "the way, the truth, and the life" (John 14:6), in whom men may find the fullness of religious life, in whom God has reconciled all things to Himself." *Nostra Aetate*, no.2. http://www.vatican.va/archive/hist_councils/ii_vatican_council/documents/vat-ii_decl_19651028_nost-ra-aetate_en.html.

[116] Cambridge Dictionary, s.v. "Ingenuity." Dictionary online, available on https://dictionary.cambridge.org/dictionary/english/ingenuity, accessed on 19 March 2019.

[117] Wendy Doniger, *On Hinduism* (New Delhi: Aleph Book Company, 2013), 172.

[118] Srinivasachari, *The Philosophy of Bhedābheda*, 15.

[119] *"āmnyāyasya kriyārthatvādānarthakyamatadarthānāṁ...kinvanyaśeṣameva tad 'bhūtārthānāṁ kriyārthena samāmnyāya."* VAB 1.4.4, p.131.

[120] Ram, *Integral Non-Dualism*, 134.

[121] Ram, *Integral Non-Dualism*, 135.

[122] *"nānto'sti mama divyānāṁ vibhūtīnāṁ parantapa... athavā bahunaitena kiṁ jñātena tavārjuna viṣṭabhyāham idaṁ kṛitsnamekāṁśena sthito jagat"* (BG 10.40, 42). "O mighty conqueror of enemies, there is no end to My divine manifestations.... But what need is there, Arjuna, for all this detailed knowledge? With a single fragment of Myself I pervade and support this entire universe." See, the introduction to the second *pāda* of the first chapter, VAB 1.2, p.93.

[123] *Codanā lakṣaṇa* is a Vedic command that impels one to act. *Codanā* means, "sending, directing, throwing, urging or driving onward, promoting, inciting, encouraging, inspiration, a precept, sacred commandment, scriptural injunction." See, Apte, under the word "*codanā*"

[124] Jaimini in the *Pūrva-Mīmāṁsā darśana* defines *dharma* as, *codanalakṣaṇārthro dharmāḥ*. Kaṇāda in *Vaiśeṣika* system explains it as, 'well-being and perfect happiness.' The closest Hebrew word for dharma is 'shalom' meaning peace, harmony, wholeness, completeness, prosperity, welfare and tranquility.

[125] *atha tadanubhavāntaram eva sa vidvān saṁsārabhayād uttīrṅo bhavati.* VAB 1.1.19, p.84.

GENERAL CONCLUSION

There is only one blueprint of Reality, though it appears to be plural. This truth is the quintessence of the *Vedas* which the *Upaniṣads* and the *Brahmasūtras* reiterate. It is the teaching of the *Vedānta* no matter what tradition one endorses and propagates. The scripture, be it *śruti* or *smṛti,* does not categorically assert that what it upholds is only *Bheda* or *Abheda* nor *Bhedābheda*. Rather, the study reveals to us that the Reality is One. But this *ekaṁsat* (one truth) appears *aneka* (many) due to the characteristic feature of its amalgamation in the phenomenal world, making it true and real in as much as the former is. Therefore, what appears to be is neither an illusion nor a *vivarta* of the Real. This is the monotheism Vijñānabhikṣu investigates in all his writings, in particular the *Vijñānāmṛtabhāṣyam*. He does not propagate any religion here, rather the monotheistic belief that he practices.

Most scholars consider Śaṅkara's treatment of the *Vedānta* as sacrosanct, and a good number of people follow Madhva's dualist path, but a fair hearing is not given to the *Bhedābheda* tradition in the history, though several attempts were made to bring out the ethos of the *Vedic* and the *Vedāntic* teachings. The commentators and the followers of the former two schools begin with eisegesis on the *Upaniṣads* and deliberately endeavour to manoeuvre their teachings using linguistic and other tools. Vijñānabhikṣu is not an exception to this. However, neither the *Upaniṣads* nor the *Vedas* has one set of dogmas, rather they point to an indubitable *sat*. There is no 'only one way' to arrive at this *sat*. Various manifestations and deductions of this *sat* can be found in every scriptural passage. Vijñānabhikṣu's endorsement of *jñānakarmasamuccaya* as one of the paths to liberation testifies to this fact. There are other ways and means too, like *bhakti* and *karma* to reach the ultimate. Thus, it is the *Bhedābheda* tradition that defends better the spirit of *smṛti* and *sṛuti*.

The Advaitic thought pattern disregarded the materialistic well-being propounded by the Vedic religion and settled for the *Upaniṣadic* spiritual aspect. It is here that Vijñānabhikṣu, without negating the spiritual nature of the world, opposed the notion of the unreality and *māyāvāda*. On the contrary, he also resisted a strict dualism, and thus, resolved for a theistic outlook, having divine as essence dissolved both in physical and ontological spheres. The rationale used by him sufficiently explains the cosmotheandric inter-relatedness or the *jugalbandi* of sacred-secular within the reality. This can even satisfy and stitch in a common thread the agonistic and atheistic thoughts; people dissected by multi-religious ideologies, cultures and traditions. So the sacred-secular can uphold the integrity of whole humanity without disregarding any differences.

The Supreme Brahman is One without the second. He is *nirguṇa*. It is His will and desire that He should be many.

Therefore, He becomes *saguṇa*. Since the origin and foundation is in Him, He is called *adhiṣṭhāna*. As a cause, He is called *kāraṇa* Brahman. His becoming many is expressed in His active form, the *kārya* Brahman. This *saguṇa* form, in the words of scriptures, is *Īśvara, Hiraṇyagarbha, Viṣṇu, Śiva* or *Puruṣa*. This is also the deity people worship as 'the God' and *mumukṣus* find their union with.

The *nirguṇa* Brahman expresses Himself as *mūlacaitanya* and *mūlapadārtha* in the creation. In our ordinary understanding, they are *puruṣa* and *pradhāna* (*prakṛti*). These latter are not independent realities, but dependent realities. The *mūlacaitanya* can also be known as *puruṣa, ātman* and *jīva* under various *upādhis*. Since both *puruṣa* and *pradhāna* are in essence the power and the mode of Brahman, their coming closer is natural like magnet and iron. It is here, the creation begins. Therefore, essentially *brahmatattva* or *brahmātmatā* emanates from every created being and each one becomes the relative of the other. Upon the release of *jīvā* from its identity with *prakṛtitattvas, karmas* incurred till the present birth gets united with *kārya* Brahman, and thus retains *Bhedābheda* relation. Brahman's relation, exhibited in all these levels is indistinguishable (*Avibhāga*) like sea and wave, fire and its spark, father and son, water mingled in water, sugar or salt in water, river in sea, etc.

Concretely speaking, the *Avibhāga-Bhedābheda* relation is deeply rooted in *ātman*, Brahman and *jagat*. Just like the word *paṅkaja* is understood – by popular meaning (lotus) and by etymology (that which is mud born) – and in both senses refer to the same thing, so too Brahman and *ātman* or *jīva*. In the same way, when referred to *Puruṣa*, the other meanings of it – Brahman, *ātman* – are also understood; one is specific and the other is in general sense respectively. If there were to be only one meaning, the quality of one should be the quality of the other. In this sense, they cannot be one. They share the same locus, in the sense of their origin in the foundational and supporting cause.

Two things can be noted here: there is something unchanging, permanent, and something changing and impermanent. The *Brahmātmatā* expressed is that which never changes and can be inferred throughout in the ongoing creation. I translate this as the spiritual essence, the divinity or simply 'the essence' hidden which can never be negated. This is the indubitable starting point like Cartesian 'cogito' where one must hold on to while looking for an integral vision. The changing transient aspects are equally important to maintain diversity. At the manifested state everything looks diverse and thus *vibhāga* is understood, and at the unmanifested state, everything is *ekam, avibhāga*. Even *prakṛti* has concealed and unconcealed aspects: primordial concealed *tattva* and revealed material *tattva*. However, it is the *Brahmātmatā* that makes both *bheda* and *abheda* aspects as kinsfolks of each other, like in the relationship of father and son. Every son is a continuation of the father or has an essence of him. And, at the same time, both are two distinct individuals. So too, the material world and transcendental worlds are the *locus operandi* of the Ultimate Reality.

This furnishes us an added spiritual dimension to the world of sentient and non-sentient beings. Each one is distinct and the center of the manifestation of God. The Ultimate Being, matter and pre-matter are dissolved into spirituality. This leads us the way to consider not only human beings as sacred but also the world we live as spiritual to treat it with dignity.

The *Avibhāga-Bhedābheda* of Vijñānabhikṣu brings together divergent cultures and traditions. Everyone has the right to worship the divine. According to Vijñānabhikṣu, the divine is in the worship and not in the rituals of the worship. Rituals are secondary. Thus by reversing the performance of worship keeps both *jñāna* and *karma* on an equal pedestal. However, he doesn't abandon ritual altogether but keeps the spirit of it. According to him, if the actions performed are a hindrance to achieving Brahman, even if they are well-known religious rituals like *Agnihotra* should be abandoned, even by monks (VAB 1.1.1, p.4-6).

Further, the ingenuity of Vijñānabhikṣu lies in the fact of converting Īśvarakṛṣṇa's *svatantrapradhānakāraṇavāda* of Sāṅkhya into *Īśvarādhīnapradhānakāraṇavāda*, in other words, a leap takes place from *prakṛtipariṇāmavāda* to *brahmaśaktiprakṛtipariṇāmavāda*. This crafts atheistic *Sāṅkhya* into theistic *Sāṅkhya*. Here, the reversal of independence of *prakṛti* makes the system dependent on a principle that becomes a uniting factor between conscious and unconscious elements. For an agnostic or an atheist this uniting factor could be the deontological principle deeply embedded within, and for the theist it is the divine or spiritual power. Thus, the *Avibhāga-Bhedābheda* becomes a uniting factor of theistic and atheistic trends, or the diverse trends within.

Vijñānabhikṣu in three stages endeavours to prove the *Avibhāga-Bhedābheda* as the semantic axis of the *Brahmasūtras* (and thus the entire scriptures): *abheda, bheda* and *bhedābheda*. In the first stage, he considers *ruḍhi* or secondary power of meaning like *Advaita* and principle of *ekavākyata* (*śāstramārga*). To prove the *bhedaparatva* of scriptures, he takes hold of *padaccheda vṛtti* (grammatical technique) and *prakaraṇa saṅgati* (contextual relevance). And to establish simultaneous *bheda* and *abheda,* he employs *samavāya* (inherent relationship) as in *samānādhikaraṇyam.* This is even established by his interpretation of *tattvamasi.* Finally, he concludes that both dependent and independent realities are incapable of functioning separately due to the intrinsic nature of the relationship exhibited in *avibhāga sambandha*. Each stage is substantiated with scriptural assertions from *śruti, smṛti* and ordinary usage. This directs us to regard the nature of scriptures neither as *bheda* nor as *abheda*, but as *Bhedābheda*. Therefore, neither the scriptures in themselves are contradictory, nor their inter-textuality at the core is different. If it were different, the basic truth content of one scripture should have been different from the other.

A thought does not originate from the vacuum. It has a foundation of the past and the present. Vijñānabhikṣu, as a staunch Hindu believer rooted in the *Vedic* and the *Vedāntic* traditions, understood that Hinduism is under the threat of its existence. This threat is from both within and without. The Islamic invasion, the spread of Christianity, pluralistic religions of Akbar, emerging *Bhaktism,* increasing sectarianism, suppressed literature, Islamic rigorous monotheistic appeal and destruction of idolatrous practices, etc. compelled him to be a revivalist. The background analysis and his rootedness made him clear that the desire for another religion is not necessary. Hinduism, at the core, is the monotheistic religion. Idolatry understood by other people is not in fact polytheism. Hinduism is an accommodative religion. Every tradition and culture can have a peaceful cohabitation under its shelter. Therefore, he needed a strong foundation for his appeal and at the same time, he was required to answer *the modern's* critique sufficiently.

The present situation of the country is not far from the reality faced by Vijñānabhikṣu. True, that today Moghuls do not rule, but the majoritarian Hinduism prevails. The 'one nation, one language and one culture' meme of the majority religion are not without an agenda. The increasing population of minorities, demand for a separate religious status by Dalits, Liṅgāyats and tribals pose a serious threat to Hinduism as an '*akhaṇḍa dharma*.' An analysis of the census over the years in India can elucidate this fact clear. Added to this, the growing agnostic and atheistic trends due to globalization trigger a greater threat to Hinduism. It is from this point of view, one should read growing intolerance, religious fanaticism and persecution of minority religions. But, the mounting hatred towards others will only further damage the Hindu religion and disturb the fabric of harmonious relationships in society at large. If the accommodative feature which is the hallmark of its culture is preserved, then it would act as a salvaging factor for its revival. This book addresses to a certain extent that claim which negates the accommodation and plurality.

This book is groundbreaking one. Its topmost motif is unearthing the philosophy of Vijñānabhikṣu and thus it ventures into a pioneering task. So far, though the philosophy of Vijñānabhikṣu is exposed, his key concept is not investigated in detail. Besides, this work offers critique, application and appropriation of Vijñānabhikṣu. The use of primary source is another novelty of this significant work. Apart from this, there is lots of scope for further research. Some of them are enumerated below.

1. *Jñānakarmasamuccaya,* originally a *Mīmāṁsā* concept and later undertaken by the *bhedābhedavādins,* is a great concept to be probed from the *Avibhāga-Bhedābheda* point of view. This is another central issue in the philosophy of all the *bhedābhedavādins.* Vijñānabhikṣu gives a great deal of importance to this topic.

2. *Avibhāga-Bhedābheda* as a central theme of scripture/s is another theme for in-depth research. It can be dealt with, taking one scripture at a time or a group of scriptures of a tradition or any other religious texts or inter-intra research.

3. *Satkāryavāda*, as causality is central to *Vedāntic* philosophy. Vijñānabhikṣu draws on an amalgamation of various causalities of *Sāṅkhya* and *Vedānta*. It can be called *brahmaśaktiprakṛtipariṇāmavāda*. There is greater scope for this concept to be studied as a philosophical issue in Vijñānabhikṣu's writings.

4. So far no translation of *Vijñānāmṛtabhāṣyam* in any language is done, except a fraction of it, as said in the first chapter of this research. Therefore, there is a greater need to make the philosophy made available to the linguistic fraternity. The present work will surely aid in translating and editing the work. There is scope even to translate a section of the book and do the research.

5. Keeping the context and genre of *Vijñānāmṛtabhāṣyam* and that of the author, one can explore and make a real contribution in the field of inter-religious dialogue, which is a need of the hour today.

6. A comparative assessment can be made between *Avibhāga-Bhedābheda* and the Christian concept of the Trinity. For instance, the mutual interpenetration and inter-relation in Christian theology is known as '*perichoresis*'.[1] This would deepen the theological bond between these two diverse creeds. In fact, Borelli in his theological work has already hinted at this.

7. Another noteworthy feature of Vijñānabhikṣu is the mystical dimension. This would throw enough light on the spirituality and divine relationship.

Thus, Vijñānabhikṣu's philosophy can become an inspiration to envisage the entire cosmos and all that dwelling in it as *vasudaivaka kuṭumbakam.*

---

[1] In the Christian theology it is called perichoretic relationship. *Perichoresis*, the Greek term, literally means 'rotation' is a term used to explain the interpersonal relationship between the Persons—Father, Son and Holy Spirit—in the Trinity. It is sometimes understood as 'co-inherence.' H.S. Bettenson, *The Early Christian Fathers: A Selection from the Writings of the Fathers from St. Clement of Rome to St. Athanasuis* (Oxford University Press, 1956), 286. The Latin equivalent word for perichoresis is *circumincession*.

GLOSSARY

Abhāva	Non-existence, absence, negation.
Abheda	Non-difference, non-duality, identity.
Ācārya	Scriptural theologian, the great teacher, preceptor.
Acetana	Non-conscious, inanimate, matter.
Acintya	Inconceivable, unthinkable, incomprehensible.
Acit	Insentient, inert, non-conscious; matter.
Adhikaraṇa	A set of aphorisms dealing with a particular topic.
Adhiṣṭhāna	Basis, foundation, substratum, root.
Ādhunika	Modern.
Advaita	Not-two, Non-duality, name of a school of *Vedānta*. It also means the theory or system which is based on non-duality.
Āgama	'That which has come down,' revealed scripture.
Ahīkuṇḍala	The coiled snake.
Aikya	Oneness.
Ajñāna	Ignorance, nescience.

Ākāśa	Ether, space, sky.
Akhaṇḍa	Non-divisible, whole, undivided.
Akṣara	Imperishable, indestructible.
Amṛta	Elixir, immortality.
Aṁśa	Part, component.
Anādi	No-end, Eternity
Ānanda	Bliss, joy, delight.
Ananta	No-end, infinite, endless.
Aṅga	'Limb,' individual part, accessory, member.
Anitya	Non-permanent, transient.
Antaryāmin	Indwelling, inner ruler.
Anubhava	'That which comes after the world,' experience, knowledge.
Anumāna	Inference, one of the valid sources of knowledge.
Anyonyābhāva	Mutual absence.
Anyonya-sambandha	Mutual relationship.
Apauruṣeya	Impersonal, authorless. *Apauruṣeyatva* is a doctrine on Vedic scriptures which states that no human being is responsible for the creation of the Vedas.
Āraṇyaka	Literally it means 'forest born.' These are the part of Vedas that deal mostly

	with philosophical speculations on the ritual sacrifices.
Arhant	A liberated state.
Ariṣaḍvarga	Six-fold enemies such as *kāma*, *krodha*, *lobha*, *moha*, *mada* and *matsara*.
Āruruksa	The beginners.
Asat	Non-truth, non-being, non-existence.
Āśrama	The stages of life; there are four stages or *āśramas*. They are *brahmacarya* (student-hood), *gṛhasta* (house-holder), *vānaprastha* (forest-dweller or hermit) and *sannyāsa* (renunciant).
Āstika	Believer in existence.
Ātman	Self, 'soul.'
AUM / Oṁ	The Sacred syllable, the eternal.
Avaccheda	Discrimination, limitation, separation, distinguishing.
Avibhāga	Non-divisible, indistinct, non-separate.
Avicccheda	Uninterrupted, continuity.
Avidyā	Ignorance, nescience.
Bandha	Bondage, control.
Bhagavadgītā, Gītā	The Song of the Lord, one of the

	important scriptures of Hinduism, a portion of the *Mahābhārata*.
Bhakti	Devotion, Love.
Bhāṣya	Commentary.
Bhāva	State of being, existence, relation.
Bheda	Difference.
Bhedābheda	Difference and non-difference.
Bimba	Original, prototype.
Brahmā	Creator God (personal), one of the three gods of the Hindu trinity.
Brahmajijñāsā	Quest for Brahman. *Brahmajijñāsu* is the one who has taken up the quest for Brahman.
Brahmajñānā	Knowledge of Brahman.
Brahman	The Supreme Being, the Highest impersonal Self.
Brāhmaṇa	The portion of the Veda; one of the four classes of the caste system.
Brahmasūtras	Threads of the Absolute, aphorisms or terse sayings on Brahman written by Bādarāyaṇa.
Brāhmin	A member of the priestly class; one of the four castes.
Buddhivṛtti	Modes of the mind.
Caitanya	Pure consciousness, intelligence,

	spirit, awareness.
Catuḥsūtrī	The first four aphorisms of *Brahmasūtras*.
Cetanā	Consciousness, the animating principle of living beings.
Cit	Consciousness, intelligence, spirit, the individual self.
Dama	Self-control, control of the senses.
Darśana	Philosophical systems. They are six orthodox systems and three Heterodox systems.
Devata	A celestial, demigod.
Dharma	Literally "that which holds on" is generally understood to be a moral precept. It is also known to be a religion.
Dharmajijñāsā	The quest for *dharma*. For *Dharmajijñāsā* the goal is *dharma* and the method of sacrifice and other rituals. But, for *Brahmajijñāsā* the goal is self-realisation through the acquisition of knowledge.
Din-I-Ilahi	The Divine Faith, religion founded by Akbar.
Duḥkha	Suffering, pain, sorrow, grief,

	unhappiness.
Dvaita	Duality, dualism.
Ghaṭa	Pot.
Guṇa	Quality, attribute. There are three basic products of *prakṛti: sattva* (purity, brightness), *rajas* (active, passionate) and *tamas* (dark energy, inertia, ignorance).
Hiraṇyagarbha	Golden embryo, creative potency, principle and Lord of all creation, identified with *Brahmā*.
Icchā	Desire, divine will.
Indriya	Sense organ.
Īśvara	God, Lord, personal god.
Itihāsa	Literally, 'so it was' (*iti ha āsa*). History, story, the 'historical tradition,' the epic (the two great epics the *Mahābhārata* and the *Rāmāyaṇa*)
Jaḍa	Inert Matter, unconscious.
Jagat	Material universe, the world, cosmos.
Jijñāsā	Desire.
Jīva	Individual soul, embodied self.
Jīvanmukti	Liberation of an individual in the embodied state.

Jñāna	Knowledge; or the metaphysical or spiritual knowledge.
Jñānakāṇḍa	The parts of the Veda dealing with the knowledge.
Kāraṇa	'Instrument,' cause.
Karma	Work, duty, action, the result of an action. The law of *karma* means that every individual reaps the reward of his own efforts and actions, both good and bad. It implies also that the state, which we are, is the outcome of our past actions. *Karma* is of three kinds: what one is now doing; what one is now receiving, and what one has in store for the future.
Karmakāṇḍa	The section of Vedas dealing with actions, sacrifices and rituals.
Karmakartṛvirodha	Doer-knower difference.
Karma-phala	Result or fruit of action.
Karmatyāga	Abandoning actions.
Kārya	Effect, product.
Kṣatriya	Member of the warrior or ruling caste.
Kṣetrajña	Knower of the field (*kṣetra* = field; *jña* = to know).
Lakṣaṇā	Secondary or implied meaning of a

	word, meaning associated to the primary meaning.
Lakula	Mace.
Liṅga	Mark, characteristic, indication.
Lokasaṅgraha	Collection of the world(s), universal welfare.
Mahābhārata	The great epic that contains the *Gītā* depicting the fight between Pāṇḍavas and Kauravas.
Mahāvākya	Great saying of the *Upaniṣads.*
Manana	Reflection or reasoning on the scriptures.
Manas	Mind, the faculty of thinking.
Mantra	An instrument of thought, a sacred word or phrase of spiritual significance and power; form of sound.
Māyā	The mysterious power, wisdom or skill of the Gods, hence the power of deceit, illusion. In *Vedānta* it is used as a synonym for ignorance.
Mīmāṁsā	One of the six orthodox schools of philosophy which deals with the science of hermeneutics. The textual work of Jaimini is known as *Pūrva-*

	mīmāṁsā-sūtra.
Mokṣa	Liberation, absolute freedom, the final goal of human life wherein the individual soul enjoys complete bliss.
Mṛttika	Mud, earth.
Mukti	Liberation, release, freedom from Rebirth.
Nāstika	Believer in non-existence, atheist.
Nāstika darśana	Heterodox Systems of Indian Philosophy: Cārvāka, Jainism and Buddhism.
Nidhidhyāsana	Meditation, contemplation on the scriptures.
Nimitta-kāraṇa	Efficient cause.
Nirguṇa	Without attributes, without any form and qualities.
Niṣkriya	That which lacks action.
Nitya	Eternal, permanent.
Nyāya	Logical reasoning; a maxim, an axiom. One of the six orthodox schools of philosophy that is concerned with logic and epistemology.
Padaccheda	Dividing a word according to the grammatical rule.
Padārtha	Category, objects of experience.

Pañcarātra	*Vaiṣṇava Āgama*; authoritative scriptural source-books.
Pañcasūtrī	The first five aphorisms of *Brahmasūtras.*
Pāṇinisūtra	The aphorisms of Pāṇini.
Paṅkaja	That which is born in mud, lotus.
Paramamukhyavṛtti	Super-primary meaning, ultra or higher primary meaning.
Pāramārthika	Transcendental, absolutely real.
Paramātmā	Supreme Self, Brahman.
Parameśvara	Supreme Soul.
Paratantra	Dependent.
Pradhāna	Literally, "the most important," the chief of the material nature, creative principle of nature, *prakṛti.*
Prajāpati	Lord of creatures; creator.
Prajñāna	Consciousness.
Prakṛti	Primordial nature, Matter, the material cause of the world.
Praḷaya	Periodic cosmic dissolution.
Pramāṇa	Means of valid knowledge.
Prāṇa	Vital air, life-breath, vitality.
Prasthānatrayī	The triple foundation or canon–the *Upaniṣads*, the *Bhagavadgītā* and the *Brahmasūtras.*

Pratibimba	Reflection.
Pratyakṣa	That which is in front of the eye, perception, one of the valid sources of knowledge.
Pratyāṅga	Various manifestations.
Pṛthak	Separate, different.
Purāṇa	Sacred writings on Hindu mythology and folklore of varying dates and origin.
Puruṣa	'Person,' spirit, energy, cosmic person.
Pūrvamīmāṁsā	Known generally as *Mīmāṁsā*; it is the philosophical and religious system that belongs to the Vedic tradition. It emphasises the ritual aspect of the Vedas and gives priority for *saṁhita* and *brāhmaṇa* portion of the Vedas.
Pūrvapakṣa	The earlier view or the opponent's view.
Rāmāyaṇa	The epic-poem composed by sage Vālmīki.
Ṛgveda	One of the four Vedas.
Ṛta	Cosmic and moral order of the universe; harmony.
Rūḍhi	A conventional meaning.
Śabda	Verbal testimony; sound; word verbal

knowledge, one of the valid sources of knowledge.

Sādhanā Spiritual practice or discipline.

Sādhanacatuṣṭaya The four-fold virtues necessary for the quest for Brahman: *viveka*, *vairāgya*, *śamadamādisādhana-sampatti*, and *mumukṣutva*.

Sādṛśya Similarity.

Saguṇa With attributes, with qualities.

Sahodara The one who shared the same womb, the brother. The feminine gender is *sahodarī*.

Śaivism The religious system in which Śiva is considered the Supreme deity.

Sajātīya Of the same class.

Sākṣin Essential attribute of the self, purest internal sense organ, the witness consciousness.

Śama Sense control, tranquility.

Ṣadsampatti See *Śamadamādisādhanasampatti.*

Śamadamādisādhanasampatti Qualities such as *śama*, *dama*, etc. referred to as the wealth of six disciplines. The six spiritual virtues referred to as *śama*, *dama*, *uparati*, *titikṣa*, *samādhāna*, and

	śraddhā. It is also called *ṣadsampatti*.
Sambandha	Relationship.
Saṁhitā	Literally "Put together," is the collection of Vedic *mantras*, poems, prayers and rituals. Often they are called *karmakāṇḍa*.
Sampradāya	Tradition.
Sāṅkhya	Figure, number; one of the six systems or doctrines of Hindu philosophy attributed to sage Kapila.
Sant	Holy person.
Śarīra	'That which perishes,' the Body.
Śāstra	Scripture and tradition.
Sat	Being, existence, truth, reality.
Satkāryavāda	Theory that states that effect is not a new thing
Satya	Truth.
Siddhānta	The final view, the established conclusion.
Śiromaṇi	Crest jewel.
Śloka	Verse.
Smṛti	That which is remembered, the authored texts of later origin unlike the Vedas.
Śravaṇa	Listening to the scriptures.

Śruti	That which is revealed and heard, authorless and eternal Vedic texts, source of valid knowledge.
Sthitaprajña	Person of steady wisdom
Śūdra	A member of the fourth class in the Vedic system of *varṇa* classification of society.
Sūtra	Aphorism, condensed and cryptic statement.
Svabhāva	Essential nature, inherent property.
Svābhāvika	Natural.
Svarūpa	Natural form, essence.
Svatantra	Independent.
Syādvāda	It is a Jain theory of 'may be-ness,' which indicates the complex nature of reality.
Tattva	Category, reality, principle.
Triveṇi	The place where three rivers join, Prayag.
Tvam	Personal pronoun, second-person singular (you).
Upādānakāraṇa	Material cause.
Upādhi	Limiting adjunct or condition.
Upaniṣad	Sitting-near-with, the last portion of the Vedas; the mystical writings,

	revealing the knowledge and realisation of Brahman.
Uttaramīmāṁsā	A philosophical system of the Vedic tradition. It is generally known as the *Vedānta*. It takes the knowledge portion of the Vedas, mainly the Upaniṣads s primary. It considers knowledge of the Vedic truth, and not the rituals, leads one to liberation.
Vāda	Theory, debate.
Vaiśeṣika	One of the six Orthodox Schools of Indian philosophy.
Vaiṣṇavism	The religious system in which Viṣṇu is considered the Supreme deity.
Varṇa	Etymologically it is colour. In tradition, it is an order dividing society into four groups arranged in a hierarchy: the *brāhmana* (priestly class), *kṣatriya* (*rājanya* i.e. ruling/warrior class), *vaiśya* (cultivator and trader) and *śūdra* (servile/labour class).
Varṇāśrama	Literally, 'the order of colours.' *Varṇāśramadharma* indicates the duty of the four castes towards a society

	based on the division of labour.
Veda	Knowledge, revealed scripture, the four ancient Hindu Scriptures.
Vedāntin	Scriptural theologian of *Vedānta*.
Vijātīya	Of the different classes.
Viśiṣṭa	Qualification.
Viśiṣṭādvaita	Qualified non-dualism propounded by Rāmānuja.
Viṣṇu	The all-pervading, the Supreme Lord, One of the *trimūrti* or three principal deities of Hinduism, the protector.
Viveka	Discrimination between the eternal (*nitya*) and non-eternal (*anitya*).
Vṛtti	Relation between word and its meaning.
Vyāpaka	Pervade.
Yogarūḍhi	Derivative-conventional meaning.

Relations

Ādhāra-ādheya bhāva	Supporter and supported relation.
Aṁśa-aṁśin bhāva	Part and whole relation.
Aṁśa-avayava bhāva	Part and limb relation.
Aṅga-aṅgī bhāva	Part and whole relation.
Bimba-pratibimba bhāva	Relation between the original

	and its reflection.
Kārya-kāraṇa bhāva	Cause and effect relation.
Niyantā-niyamya bhāva	Ruler and ruled relation.
Prakāra-prakārin bhāva	Relation between the modes and that which has modes.
Rakṣaka-rakṣya bhāva	Redeemer and redeemed relation.
Śarīra-śarīri bhāva	Body and soul relation.
Śeṣa-śeṣin bhāva	Dependent and depended upon relation.
Viśeṣaṇa-viśeṣya bhāva	Substance and attribute relation.

APPENDICES

1. Evolution in the *Sāṅkhya*[1]

Prakṛti and its Evolutes

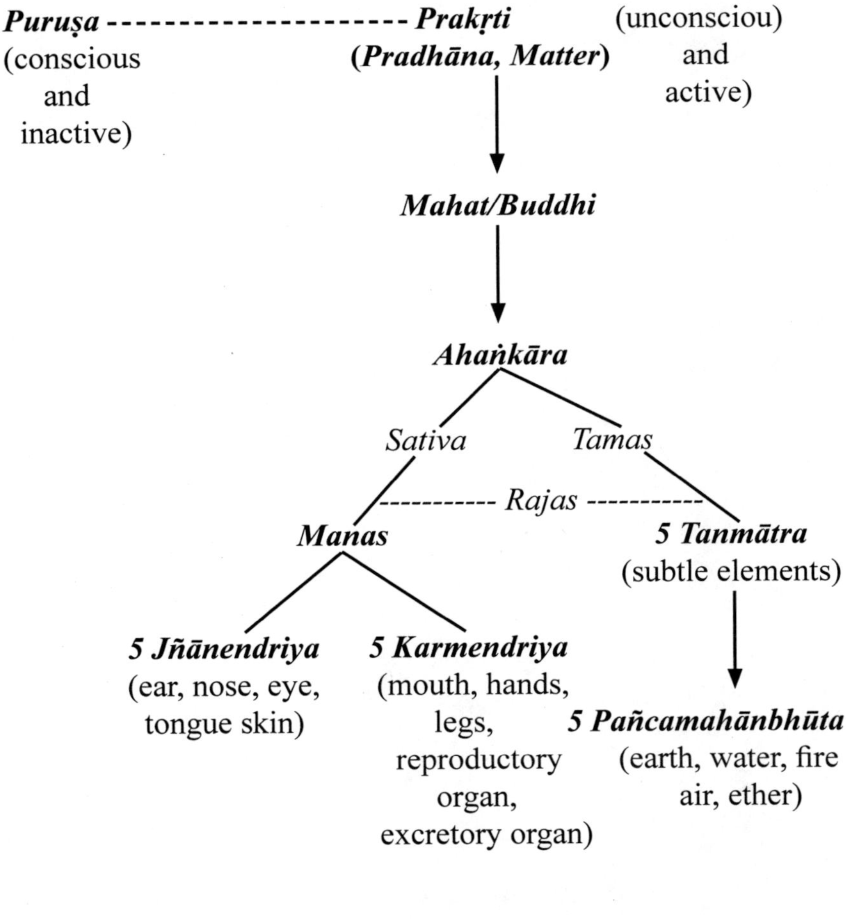

---

1 The purpose of this chart is to give an evolution in *Sāṅkhya*. Vijñānabhikṣu has presupposed that his readers know the philosophy of *Sāṅkhya*, and therefore, he does not enumerate it in his commentary on the *Brahmasūtras*. It is later he understood that without a detailed account of *Sāṅkhya* his theological position cannot be justified. Therefore, he writes commentaries on *Sāṅkhyakārika*.

BIBLIOGRAPHY

Primary Sources on Vijñānabhikṣu

Brahmasūtra-Vijñānāmṛtabhāṣyam. Prācyavidya Series, Edited by Kedāranātha Tripāṭhī. Varanasi: Banaras Hindu University, 1979.

Sāṁkhyasāra. Translated by Shiv Kumar. Delhi: Eastern Book Linkers, 1988.

Sāṅkhyapravacanabhāṣya. Edited by Richard Garbe. 2 Vols. Harward Oriental Series, Cambridge: Harward University Press, 1895.

Vijñānāmṛtabhāṣyam. The Chowkhmaba Sanskrit Series, Edited by Mukunda Shastri. Banaras: Chowkhamba Publishers, 1901.

Yogasārasaṅgraha of Vijñānabhikṣu. Translated by Ganganath Jha. Bombay: Bombay Theosophical Publication, 1894.

Yogasārasaṅgraha of Vijñānabhikṣu: Edited and Revised Edition with Sanskrit Text and English Translation. Translated by Ganganath Jha. Revised edition. Delhi: Parimal Publications, 1995.

Yogasārasaṅgraha of Vijñānabhikṣu: Sanskrit Text with Hindi and English Translation. Translated by Ram Shankar Bhattacharya and Goswami Prahlad Giri. Varanasi, Delhi: Bharatiya Vidya Prakashan, 1989.

Yogasārasaṅgraha: Hindi Vyākhyā Sahita. Translated by Sudhāṁśu Kumāra Saḍhaṅgī. Delhi: Bharatiya Vidya Prakashan, 2010.

Yogasārasaṅgraha: Mūla Hindi Anuvāda Evaṁ Vistṛta Vyākhyā Sahita. Translated by Pavana Kumari. Delhi: Eastern Book Ltd., 1981.

Yogavārtthika of Vijñānabhikṣu. Translated by T.S. Rukmani. 4 Vols. New Delhi: Munshiram Manoharlal Publishers, 1981.

Secondary Sources of Vijñānabhikṣu

Borelli, John W. "Matter and Exemplar: Difference-in-Identity in Vijñānabhiskṣu and Bonaventure." In *Neoplatonism and Indian Thought*, edited by R. Baine Harris, 137-160. Virginia: International Society for Neoplatonic Studies, 1982.

Borelli, John W. "The Theology of Vijñānabhikṣu: A Translation of His Commentary on Brahma Sūtras 1.1.2 and an Exposition of His Difference-in-Identity Theology." PhD Dissertation, New York: Fordham University, 1976.

Borelli, John W. "Vijñānabhikṣu and the Re-Assertion of Difference-in-Identity Vedānta." *Philosophy East and West* 28, no.4 (October 1978): 425-437. Available on https://www.jstor.org/stable/1398647, accessed on 27 July 2018.

Chattopadhyay, Narayana Kumar. *Indian Philosophy – Its Exposition in the Light of Vijñānabhikṣu's Bhāṣya and Yogavārttika*. Sanskrit Pustak Bhandar: Calcutta, 1979.

Gode, P. K. "The Chronology of Vijñānabhikṣu and His Disciple Bhāvāgaṇeśa, the Leader of the Citpāvan Brahmins of Benaras." *Adyar Library Bulletin* 7 (February, 1944): 20-30.

Hall, Fitz-Edward. *An Introduction to Sāṅkhya-Pravacana-Bhāṣya: A Commentary on the Aphorisms of the Hindu Atheistic Philosophy*. 1979 ed. Delhi: Bharatiya Book Corporation, 1855.

Hall, Fitz-Edward. *Sāṅkhyasāra: A Treatise of Sāṅkhya Philosophy*. Calcutta: Asiatic Society of Bengal, 1862.

Kapoor, Subodh. "The Philosophy of Vijñāna Bhikṣu." In *Encyclopaedia of Indian Heritage*. Delhi: Cosmo Publications, 2002: 2175-86.

Nicholson, Andrew J. "Reconciling Dualism and Non-Dualism: Three Arguments in Vijñānabhiskṣu's Bhedābheda Vedānta." *Journal of Indian Philosophy* 35, (2007): 371-403.

Nicholson, Andrew J. "Vijñānabhikṣu's Yoga." *Journal of Vaishnava Studies* 14, no. 1 (2005): 43-53

Nicholson, Andrew J. *Unifying Hinduism: Philosophy and Identity in Indian Intellectual History*. Ranikhet: Permanent Black, 2010.

Nicholson, Andrew J. "Bhedābheda Vedānta." In *Internet Encyclopedia of Philosophy: A Peer-Reviewed Academic Resource.* Available on http://www. iep.utm.edu/bhed-ved/#SH2b, accessed on 15 September 2016.

Ram, Kanshi. "Vijñānabhikṣu's Theory of Double Reflection." *Annals of the Bhandarkar Oriental Research Institute* 69, no. 1/4 (1988): 77-92.

Ram, Kanshi. *Integral Non-Dualism: A Critical Exposition of Vijñānabhikṣu's System of Philosophy*. New Delhi: Motilal Banarsidass Publications, 1995.

Rao, C. Hayavadana (ed.). *The Śṛīkara Bhāshya: Being the Vīrasaiva Commentary on the Vedānta Sūtras by Śrīpati*. Vol.1. New Delhi: Akshaya Prakashan, 1936.

Rukmani, T.S. "Vijñānabhikṣu: A Maverick Philosopher." *Journal of Indian Council of Philosophical Research* 24, no. 4 (October-December 2007): 131-143.

Rukmani, T.S. "Vijñānabhikṣu: The Sāṅkhya-Yoga-Vedāntācārya." *Journal of Indian Council of Philosophical Research* 27, no. 3 (July-September 2010): 21-38.

Rukmani, T.S. "Vijñānabhikṣu's Double Reflection Theory of Knowledge in the Yoga System." *Journal of Indian Philosophy* 16, no. 4 (December 1988): 367-375.

Rukmani, T.S. "Vijñānabhikṣu on Bhava-Pratyaya and Upāya-Pratyaya Yogis in Yogasutras." *Journal of Indian Philosophy* 5, no.4 (August 1978): 311-317. Available on https://www.jstor.org/stable/23440748, accessed on 27 July 2018.

Rukmani, T.S. "Vikalpa as Defined by Vijñānabhikṣu in the Yogavarttika." *Journal of Indian Philophy* 8, no. 4 (December 1980): 385-392. Available on https://www.jstor.org/stable/23440372, accessed on 27 July 2018.

Sinha, Jadunath. *The Philosophy of Vijnanabhikshu*. Calcutta: Sinha Publishing House, 1976.

Sinha, Nandalal (trans.). *The Sāmkhya Philosophy: Containing Sāmkhya-Pravacanasūtram, with the Vṛitti of Aniruddha, and the Bhāṣya of Vijñānabhikṣu and Extracts from the Vṛittisāra of Mahādeva Vedāntin; Tatvasamāsa;*

Sāmkhyakārikā; Pañchaśikhāsūram. 1979 ed. Delhi: Munshiram Manoharlal Publishers, 1862.

Śrīvāstava, Sureścandra. *Ācārya Vijñānabhikṣu Aur Bhāratīya Darśan Me Unkā Sthān* [*a Study of Vijñānabhikṣu and His Place in Indian Philosophy*]. Allahabad: Lokabharati Prakashan, 1969.

Other Secondary Sources

A. Dictionaries and Encyclopedias

Agrawal, M. M. and Karl H. Potter (eds.). *Encyclopedia of Indian Philosophies.* Vol.14. Delhi: Motilal Banarsidass Publishers, 2013.

Apte, Vaman Shivaram. *The Student's Sanskrit-English Dictionary.* New Delhi: Sri Sadguru Publications, 1890.

Bronkhorst, Johannes. "Yoga and Seśvara Sāṁkhya." *Journal of Indian Philosophy* 9, no. 3 (September 1981): 309-320. Available on https://www.jstor.org/stable/ 23440736, accessed on 27 July 2018.

Burtchaell, J. T. *New Catholic Encyclopedia.* Detroit, Michigan: The Catholic University of America, 2002.

Collins English Dictionary. Dictionary Online. Available in https://www.collins dictionary. com/dictionary/english, 1819.

Contributors. *New World Encyclopedia.* Encylopedia Online. Available in http://www. new worldencyclopedia.org/, last modified on 13 March 2016.

Dasgupta, Surendranath. "Vijñānabhikṣu." In *Encyclopedia of Indian Philosophies: Bhedābheda and Dvaitādvaita Systems.*

Vol.15, 2013 ed. Edited by M.M. Agrawal, Karl H. Potter (Delhi: Motilal Banarsidass Publishers, 1981): 417-460.

Dictionary of Spiritual Terms. Dictionary Online. Available in www.dictionaryof spiritualterms.com, 2003.

Encyclopedia of Religion. Encyclopedia Online. Available in https://www. encyclopedia.com, 2016.

Harper, Douglas. *Online Etymology Dictionary.* Dictionary Online. Available on https://www.etymonline.com/.

Harshananda, Swami, *Concise Encyclopedia of Hinduism.* Bangalore: Ramakrishna Math, 2008.

Jhalakīkar, Bhīmācārya. *Nyāyakoṣaḥ or Dictionary of Technical Terms of Indian Philosophy.* 2015 ed. Varanasi: Chaukhamba Surbharati Prakashan, 1928.

'Jñāna,' Baccūlāl Avasthī. *Bhāratīya-Darśan-Bṛhatkośa.* Delhi: Sharada Publishing House, 2012.

Kapoor, Subodh. *Encyclopedia of Indian Heritage: Vedānta Philosophy.* Vol.19-23. New Delhi: Cosmo Publications, 2003.

Kumar, Shashiprabha, Santhosh Kumar Shukla, Ram Nath Jha (eds.) *Dārśanik Sampradāy-Koś: Dictionary of Concepts in Indian Philosophy.* New Delhi: D.K. Printworld and Jawaharlal Nehru University, 2014.

Monier-Williams, M. *A Sanskrit English Dictionary.* New Delhi: Bharatiya Granth Niketan, 1899.

Potter, Karl H. and M.M. Agrawal. *Encyclopedia of Indian Philosophies, vol 15: Bhedābheda and Dvaitādvaita.* Delhi: Motilal Banarsidass Publishers, 1981.

Sūryakānta. *Sanskrit-Hindi-English Dictionary.* New Delhi:

Orient Longman Private Limited, 1975.

Vatsyayan, Kapila (ed.). *Kalātattvakośa: A Lexicon of Fundamental Concepts of the Indian Arts.* Delhi: Motilal Banarsidass Publishers, 1988.

Whitney, William Dwight. *The Roots, Verb-Forms and Primary Derivatives of the Sanskrit Language*. New Delhi: Motilal Banarsidass Publishers, 2006.

B. Books and Articles

(Avadhūta), Sadāśivendra Saraswati. *A Commentary on Bādarāyaṇa Brahmasūtra Named Brahmatat'tvaprakāśikā*. Translated by S. Kothandaraman. 2 vols. New Delhi: B.R. Publishing House, 2009.

Acharya, Ramakrishna. *Brahmasūtron Ke Vaiṣṇav-Bhāṣyon Kā Tulanātmak Adhyayan*. Agra: Vinod Pustak Mandir, 1960.

Aggarwal, Mamta. "15 Famous Saints of the Medieval India." Article Online. Available on http://www.historydiscussion.net/, accessed on 6 September 2018.

Agrawal, Madan Mohan (ed.). *Brahmasūtranimbārkabhāṣyam: Vedāntakaustubha-Vedāntakaustubhaprabhā-bhāvadīpikāvyākhyātrayopetam.* 4 Volumes. The Vrajājvana Prācyabhārati Granthamāla, no.94. Delhi: Chaukhamba Sanskrit Pratishthan, 2000.

Agrawal, Madan Mohan. *The Philosophy of Nimbārka*. Varanasi: Chowkhambha Surabharati Publication, 1982.

Allami, Abu'l Fazl. *The A'in-I Akbari*. Translated by H. Blochmann. Vol.1. Calcutta: Asiatic Society of Bengal, 1873.

Anand, Subhash. *Hindu Inspriation for Christian Reflection: Towards a Hindu-Christian Theology*. Anand: Gujarat Sahitya Prakash, 2004.

Ānandatīrtha, Śrī. *Viṣṇutattvavinirṇaya of Śrī Ānandatīrtha*. Translated by K.T. Pandurangi. Bangalore: Dvaita Vedanta Studies and Research Foundation, 2011.

Andrijanic, Ivan. "Bhartṛprapañca and the Eight States of Brahman." *Revista Científica Guillermo de Ockham* 14, no. 1 (2016): 57-66.

Andrijanić, Ivan. "Quotations and (Lost) Commentaries in Advaita Vedānta: Some Philological Notes on Bhartṛprapañca's 'Fragments'." *Journal of Indian Philosophy* 43, no. 2 (2015): 257-276. Available on http://link.springer.com/ journal/volumesAndIssues/10781, accessed on 25 January 2017.

Annambhaṭṭa. *Tarkasaṅgraha*. Translated by Gopinath Bhattacharya. Calcutta: Progressive Publishers, 1983.

Anonymous. "Aum or Om," *The Hindu Universe*. Available on http://www.hindunet. org/aum/, accessed on 7 December 2016.

Anonymous. "Six Mahāvākyas," *The Hindu Universe*. Article Onlne. Available on http://hindunet.org/scriptures/ mahavakyas/index.htm, accessed on 30 November 2016.

Anonymous. *Chāndogya Upaniṣad: With the Original Text in Sanskrit and Roman Translation, Translation with an Extensive Commentary*. Translated by Swami Muni Narayana Prasad Rediscovering Indian Literary Classics, no.15. New

Delhi: D. K. Printworld (P) Ltd., 2006.

Anonymous. *The Bṛhadāraṇyaka Upaniṣad: Containing the Original Text with Word-by Word Meanings, Running Translations, Notes and Introduction*. Madras: Sri Ramakrishna Math, 1968.

Bachrach, Emilia. "In the Seat of Authority: Debating Temple Spaces and Community Identity in a Vaiṣṇava Sampradāy of Contemporary Gujarat." *Journal of Hindu Studies* 10, no. 1 (2017): 18-46.

Ballantyne, R. James (trans.). The Sāṅkhya Aphorisms of Kapila. 3rd ed. London: Trubner and Co, 1885.

Bapat, Shailaja. *A Study of the Vedānta in the Light of Brahmasūtras*. Delhi: New Bharatiya Book Corporation, 2004.

Bettenson, H.S. *The Early Christian Fathers: A Selection from the Writings of the Fathers from St. Clement of Rome to St. Athanasuis*. Oxford: Oxford University Press, 1956.

Bhandarkar, R.G. *Vaisnavism, Saivaism and Minor Religious System*. Varanasi: Indological Book House, 1913. Available on https://archive.org/details/VaishnavismShaivismAndOtherMinorReligiousSystemsR.G.Bhandarkar.org//, accessed on 2 February 2019.

Bhardwaj, Surender Mohan. *Hindu Places of Pilgrimage in India: A Study in Cultural Geography*. Berkeley: University of California Press, 1973.

Bhāskarācārya. *Brahmasūtrabhāṣyam*. Chowkamba Sanskrit Series Nos.70, 185 & 209. Edited by Vindhyesvari Prasada Dvivedin. Banaras: Chowkambha Sanskrit Book

Depot., 1915.

Bhāskarācārya. *Siddhāntaśiromaṇiḥ*. The Kāshī Sanskrit Series, no.149. Edited by Muralidhar Thakur. Banaras: Jaya Krishna Das Haridas Gupta, 1950.

Bhatt, S.R. *The Philosophy of the Pancharatra: Advaitic Approach*. Madras: Ganesh and Company, 1968.

Bhattacharyya, Krishnachandra. *Studies in Philosophy*. Vol.I. Calcutta: Progressive Publishers, 1956.

Bholebābā, Yativara (ed.). *Brahmasūtram: Saṭīkabhagavatpāda Śaṅkarapraṇīta Śārīrakamīmāṁsābhāṣya, Bhagavatpāda Rāmānanda Praṇīta Ratnaprabhā Samalaṅkṛtam*. 3 Volumes. Varanasi: Chowkhamba Vidhyabhavan, 2006.

Borde, Victor. *Puruṣasūkta: An An A-Religious Inquiry into a Sacred Text* (Indiana: LifeRich Publishing, 2021)

Bose, Roma (trans.). *Vedānta-Pārijāta-Saurabha of Nimbārka and Vedānta-Kaustubha of Srinivāsa: Commentaries on the Brahmasūtras*. Calcutta: Royal Asiatic Scoeity, 1943.

Brahadāraṇyaka Upaniṣad with the Commentary of Śaṅkarācārya. Almora: Advaita Ashrama, 1934.

Chandra, Satish. *History of Medieval India*. 2018 ed. Hyderabad: Orient Blackswan Private Limited, 2007.

Chandramouli, C. "Census of India 2011–A Story of Innovations," *Press Information Bureau*, Government of India, 23 August 2011. Available on http://pib.nic.in /newsite /feacontent. aspx?relid=74556.

Chattopadhyaya, Shyama Kumar. *The Philosophy of*

Sankar's Advaita Vedanta. New Delhi: Sarup and Sons, 2000.

Chinmayananda, Swami. *Aitareya Upaniṣad: Truth Before and After Creation*. Mumbai: Central Chinmaya Mission Trust, 2015.

Chinmayananda, Swami. *Discourses on Kenopaniṣad*. Mumbai: Central Chinmaya Mission Trust, 2013.

Chinmayananda, Swami. *Īśavāsya Upaniṣad: God in and as Everything*. Mumbai: Central Chinmaya Mission Trust, 2015.

Chinmayananda, Swami. *Kaivalya Upaniṣad*. Mumbai: Central Chinmaya Mission Trust, 2015.

Chinmayananda, Swami. *Kaṭhopaniṣad: A Dialogue with Death*. Mumbai: Central Chinmaya Mission Trust, 2014.

Chinmayananda, Swami. *Māṇḍūkya Upaniṣad with Gauḍapāda's Kārikā*. Mumbai: Central Chinmaya Mission Trust, 2015.

Chinmayananda, Swami. *Muṇḍakopaniṣad: Tale of Two Birds: Jīva and Īśvara*. 2016 ed. Mumbai: Central Chinmaya Mission Trust, 1953.

Chinmayananda, Swami. *Praśnopaniṣad*. Mumbai: Central Chinmaya Mission Trust, 2013.

Chinmayananda, Swami. *Taittirīya Upaniṣad*. Mumbai: Central Chinmaya Mission Trust, 2016.

Chaudhuri, Roma. *Ten Schools of the Vedānta.* Kolkata: Rabindra Bharati University, 2012.

Crasta, Raju Felix. "Lokasaṅgraha, the Welfare of the Worlds: A Hermeneutical and Exegetical Exploration." MPh Dissertation, Pune; Jnanadeepa Vidyapeeth, 2013.

Crasta, Raju Felix. "Welcoming Newness." In *Francis Effect*, edited by Kuruvilla Pandikattu and Vadappuram M. Jose, 181-184. Pune: Papal Seminary, 2018.

D'Souza, Ivan. "*Paramamukhyavṛtti* (Super-Primary Meaning) in *Dvaita Vedānta* of Madhva: A Hermeneutical Probe into Its Scriptural Application and Significance." PhD Dissertation, Pune: Jnana-Deepa Vidyapeeth, 2017.

Dallmayr, Fred. "Rethinking Secularism (with Raimon Panikkar)." *The Review of Politics* 61, no. 4 (Autumn, 1999): 715-735.

Das, Kumud Ranjan. *Raja Todar Mal*. Calcutta: Saraswat Library, no date. Available on https://archive.org/details/in.ernet.dli.2015.149505, accessed on 12 September 2018

Dasgupta, Surendranath. *A History of Indian Philosophy*. 5 vols. Delhi: Motilal Banarsidass, 1973.

Dattatreya, Rishi. *Avadhūta Gīta*. Translated by Kannoo Mal. Madras: S.R. Murty and Company, 1920. Available on https://archive.org/details/Avadhuta_Gita _with_English_Translation, accessed on 15 December 2017.

Dattatreya, Rishi. *Dattatreya, Song of the Avadhut: An English Translation of the Avadhut Gita with Sanskrit Transliteration.* Translated by Swami Abhayananda. Book Online. Available on abhayananda@bellsouth.net, 2009, accessed on 15 December 2017.

Derrida, Jacques. *Dissemination*. Translated by Barbara Johnson. 2005 ed. London, New York: Continuum, 1981.

Derrida, Jacques. *Of Grammatology*. Translated by Gayatri Chakravorty Spivak. 1994 ed. Delhi: Motilal Banarsidass Publishers, 1976.

Derrida, Jacques. *Writing and Difference*. Translated by Alan Bass. Chicago: The University of Chicago Press, 1978.

De-Smet, Richard. "Śaṅkara's Non-Dualism (Advaita-Vāda)." In *Religious Hinduism: A Presentation and Appraisal*, edited by Richard De Smet and Josef Neuner, 80-96. Reprint. Allahabad: St. Paul Publications, 1998.

Devananda, Swami Vishnu. *Meditations and Mantras*. 2003 ed. Delhi: Motilal Banarsidass Publishers, 1978.

Doniger, Wendy. *On Hinduism*. New Delhi: Aleph Book Company, 2013.

Doniger, Wendy. *The Hindus: An Alternative History*. 2015 ed. New Delhi: Speaking Tiger Publishing Private Limited, 2009.

Ekka, Philip. *Tribal Movements: A Study in Social Change*. Jashpur: Tribal Research and Documentation Centre, 2003.

Eliade, Mircea. *Yoga: Immortality and Freedom*. Translated by Willard R. Trask. London: Routledge and Kegan Paul, 1958.

Francis, Pope. *Laudato Si'*. Vatican: Liberia Editrice Vaticana, 2015.

Gambhirananda, Goswami (trans.). *Brahmasūtrabhāṣyam of Śrī Śaṅkarācārya*. Calcutta: Advaita Ashrama, 1965.

George, Vensus A (ed.). *Self-Realization (Brahmānubhava): The Advaitic Perspective of Shankara*. Indian Philosophical

Studies Series, edited by George F. Mclean. Washington: The Council for Research in Values and Philosophy, 2001.

Ghate, Vinayak Sakharam. *The Vedānta; a Study of the Brahmasūtras with the Bhāsyas of Sáṁkara, Rāmānuja, Nimbărka, Madhva and Vallabha*. Poona: Bhandharkar Oriental Research Institute, 1960.

Gosvāmī, Śrīla Rūpa. *Śrī Bhakti-Rasāmṛta-Sindhu: The Eternal Ocean of Nectar of Devotion*. Vol.1. Edited by Gaurahari Dāsānudās Bābājī. Book Online. http://esoteric teaching.org, no date. Available on https://archive.org/ details/SriBhakti-rasamrta-sindhu/, accessed on 24 September 2018.

Goswami, Lalit Krishna. *Śrī Nimbārka Vedānta*. Prayāga: Nimbārka Peeṭha, 1965.

Gupta, Anima Sen. "Ramanuja on 'Tat Tvam Asi'." *Philosophy East & West* 12, no.2 (1962): 128-134.

Gupta, Anima Sen. *Classical Samkhya: A Critical Study*. Patna: Anima Sen Gupta, 1969.

Gupta, Anima Sen. *Essays on Sāmkhya and Other Systems of Indian Philosophy*. Kanpur: M. Sen, 1964.

Gupta, Bina and William C. Wilcox. ""Tat Tvam Asi": An Important Identity Statement or a Mere Tautology." *Philosophy East and West* Vol. 34, no.1 (January 1984): 85-94.

Gupta, Tripta. *Vedānta Kaustubha: A Study*. Delhi: Sanjay Prakashan, 2000.

Hara, Minoru. "Nakulīśa-Pāśupata-Darśanam." *Indo-Iranian Journal* 2, no.1 (1958): 8-32.

Hiriyanna, M. "Bhartrprapañca: An Odd Vedāntin." In *Indian Antiquary* 53 (1924): 77-86.

Hiriyanna, M. "Fragments of Bhartrprapanca." In *Proceedings of the All-India Oriental Conference 3*, 1924: 439-450.

Hiriyanna, M. *Indian Philosophical Studies. 2* vols. Mysore: Kavyalaya Publishers, 1957.

Hiriyanna, M. *Indian Philosophical Studies.* 2 vols. Mysore: Kavyalaya Publishers, 1972.

Hume, Robert Ernest. *The Thirteen Principal Upanishads.* New York: Oxford University Press, 1921.

Īśvarakṛṣṇa. *Sāṁkyakārika: Sagauḍapādabhāṣya 'Abhinavarājalakṣmī' Bhāṣya Bhāṣā-ṭīkātrayavirājitā.* Translated by Bala Śāstrī Sītārāma Śāstrī, Guru Prasāda Śāstrī Chaukambha Surabharati Granthamala. Varanasi: Chowkambha Surabharati Publications, 2012.

Iyer, M.K. Venkatarama. "The Methodology of the Upaniṣads." In *Studies in Vedānta Philosophy,* edited by R. K. Panda, 69-83. Delhi: Bharatiya Kala Prakashan, 2002.

Jha, Chandra Kumar. *Śrīmadbhagavadgītā: Ek Trik-Śāstrīya Pariśīlan*. Kurukshetra: Nirmal Book Agency, 2014.

Joshi, Maheshwar P. "Śaṅkarācārya, Lakulīśa-Pāśupatas and Uttarākhaṇḍa." *Annals of the Bhandarkar Oriental Research Institute* 70, no.1/4 (1989): 266-272.

Kandula, Satya Sarada. "Tat Tvam Asi: Vakya Vritti of Sri Adi Sankaracharya." In *Old Thoughts,* 2010. Available on https://oldthoughts.wordpress.com/ philosophy/tat-tvam-asi-vakyavritti-of-sri-adi-sankaracharya/, accessed on 12 December 2016.

Karmarkar, R.D. (ed.). *Śrībhāṣya of Rāmānuja*. University of Poone Sanskrit and Prākrit Series, 2 vols. Poona: Puṇyapatanavidhyāpīṭha, 1962-64.

Karnik, Vaishali Sunil. *Concept of Mokṣa: In Advaita Vedānta with Special Reference to Jivanmuktiviveka of Sri Vidyārañyaswāmī*. Delhi: Bharatiya Kala Prakashan, 2012.

Keay, John. *India, a History*. New York: Grove Publications, 2000.

Khanna, Madhu (ed.). *Thirty Minor Upaniṣads*. New Delhi: Tantra Foundation, 1914.

Kierkegaard, Søren, Howard V. Hong and Edna H. Hong. *Philosophical Fragments: Johannes Climacus*. Princeton: Princeton University Press, 1985.

Kumar, Bijendra. *Bhedābheda Darśana*. Delhi: Bijendra Kumar, 2013.

Linden, C.W.J. Van Der. *The Concept of Deva: In the Vedic Age of the Indian Literature*. Utrecht: Drukkerij Vesta, 1954.

Lingat, Robert. *The Classical Law of India*. Translated by J. Duncan M. Derrett. Berkeley: University of California Press, 1973.

Luke, K. "The Term Brahman in Modern Research." *Indian Theological Studies* 30, no. 2 (June 1993): 145-170.

Macdonell, Arthur Anthony and Arthur Berriedale Keith, *Vedic Index of Names and Subjects.* 2014 ed. Varanasi: The Chowkhamba Vidyabhawan, 1912.

Macdonnell, Arthur A. *A Vedic Reader for Students*. 1976 ed. Madras: Oxford University Press, 1917.

Mādhavācārya. *Sarva-Darana-Saṁgraha.* Edited by K.L. Joshi. Delhi: Parimal Publications, 1997.

Mādhavācārya, *Sarvadarśanasaṅgraha* Translated by E.B. Cowel and A.E. Gough. London: Trubner and Company, 1882.

Majumdar, A.K. *Caitanya: His Life and Doctrine*. Bombay: Bharatiya Vidya Bhavan, 1969.

Majumdar, B.P. "Lakuliśa-Pāśupatas and Their Activities in Mediaeval India." *Proceedings of the Indian History Congress* 13, (1950): 115-120.

Majumdar, B.P. "Lakuliśa-Pāśupatas and Their Activities in Medieval India." *Proceedings of the Indian History Congress* 13, (1950): 115-120. Available on https://www.jstor.org/stable /44140899, accessed on 19 January 2019.

Majumdar, Shridhar. *The Vedanta Philosophy*. 2000 ed. Chowkamba Sanskrit Studies, no.108. Varanasi: Chowkhamba Sanskrit Series Office, 1926.

Malhotra, Rajiv. *Indra's Net: Defending Hinduism's Philosophical Unity*. 2016 ed. Noida: Harper Collins Publishers, 2014.

Mallik, Girindra Narayan. *The Philosophy of Vaisnava Religion*. Vol.1. Lahore: Motilal Banarsidass Publishers, 1927.

Matthews, Warren. *World Religions*. 2010 ed. Belmont: Wadsworth, 2007.

Mehta, P. D. *The Heart of Religion*. 1987 ed. Great Britain: Element Books Limited, 1976.

Minor, Robert N. *Bhagavad-Gītā: An Exegetical Commentary*. Columbia: South Asian Books, 1982.

Mishra, Umesh. *Nimbārka School of Vedānta*. Allahabad: Tirabhukti Publications, 1966.

Müller, Fredrich Max. *The Vedas*. Calcutta: Susil Gupta Limited, 1956.

Nakamura, Hajime. *A History of Early Vedānta Philosophy*. Translated by Sengakul Mayeda Trevor Leggett, Taitez Unno and others. 2 vols. Delhi: Motilal Banarsidass, 1983.

Nakamura, Hajime. *A History of Early Vedānta Philosophy*. Vol.2. Delhi: Motilal Banarsidass, 2004.

Nandakumar, Prema. "The Bhakti Movement in North India." In *Enclopedia of History of Science, Philosophy and Culture in Indian Civilization*. Vol.2, part 3. Edited by R. Balasubramanian, 869-904. New Delhi: Centre for Studies in Civilization, 2003.

Nath, Pathikonda Viswambara. *Tat Tvam Asi: The Universal Message in the Bhagavadgītā*. 2 vols. 2002 ed. Delhi: Motilal Banarsidass Publishers, 1998.

Nath, Vijay. "From 'Brahmanism' to 'Hinduism': Negotiating the Myth of the Great Tradition." In *Proceedings of the Indian History Congress*, 61, 26-56. New Delhi: Indian History Congress, 2001. Available on https://www.jstor.org/stable/44148078, accessed on 7 September 2018.

Nath, Vijay. "From 'Brahmanism' to 'Hinduism': Negotiating the Myth of the Great Tradition." *Social Scientist* 29, no. 3-4 (March-April 2001): 19-50. Available on https://www.jstor.org/stable/3518337, accessed on 7 September 2018.

Nikhilananda, Swami. *Vedāntasāra of Sadānanda with Introduction, Text, English Translation and Comments.* Almora, Himalayas: Advaita Ashrama, 1931.

Nimbārkācārya. *Brahmasūtra Nimbārkabhāṣyam: Vedāntakaustubha Vedāntakaustubhaprabhā Bhāvaadīpikā Vyākhyātrayopetam.* Translated by Madan Mohan Agrawal. 4 vols. The Vrajajīvana Prācyabhāratī Granthamāla, Edited by Madan Mohan Agrawal. Delhi: Chaukambha Sanskrit Pratishthan, 2000.

Nimbārkācārya. *Śrībrahmasūtra Śrīnimbārkabhāṣyam: Vedānta Pārijātasaurabh of Nimbārkācārya and Vedāntakaustubha of Śrīnivāsācārya.* Kashi Sanskrit Series, Edited by Duṇḍirāja Śāstri. Banaras: Chowkamba Sanskrit Series Office, 1989.

O'Flaherty, Wendy Doniger (trans.). *The Rig Veda: An Anthology: One Hundred and Eight Hymns, Selected, Translated and Annotated.* 2000 ed. New York, Middlesex: Penguin Books, 1983.

Pahlajrai, Prem. "Vedanta: A Comparative Analysis of Diverse Schools." In *Asian Studies Graduate Student Colloquium.* Washington: University of Washington, 2003: 9-13

Panikkar, Raimundo. *The Vedic Experience–Mantramañjarī: An Anthology of the Vedas for the Modern Man and Contemporary Celebration.* London: Darton, Longman and Todd, 1977.

Pereira, Jose. *Hindu Theology: A Reader*. New York: Image Books, 1976.

Powell, Jim. *Derrida for Beginners*. Chennai: Orient Longman Ltd., 2000.

Prabhavananda, S. *Vedic Religion and Philosophy*. Madras: Sri Ramakrishna Math, 1983.

Prabhupada, A.C. Bhaktivedanta Swami. *Bhagavadgītā As It Is*. California: Bhaktivedanta Book Trust, 1972.

Prabhupāda, Bhaktivedānta Swami. *Teachings of Lord Caitanya*. Bombay: Bhaktivedānta Book Trust, 1974.

Purnima, P. "15 Popular Saints of Bhakti Movement." Article Online. Avalilable on http://www.historydiscussion.net/, accessed on 6 September 2018.

Radhakrishnan, Sarvepalli. *Indian Philosophy*. 2 vols. New Delhi: Oxford University Press, 2006.

Radhakrishnan, Sarvepalli. *The Brahma Sūtra: The Philosophy of Spiritual Life*. London: George Allen and Unwin, 1960.

Radhakrishnan, Sarvepalli. *The Principal Upaniṣads*. London: George Allen and Unwin Ltd., 1953.

Raghavendracharya, R. (ed.). *Brahmasūtrabhāṣyam of Sri Madhvācārya*. Vol.1. Government Oriental Library Series, no.39. Mysore: Government Branch Press, 1911.

Raghavendracharya, R. (ed.). *Brahmasūtrabhāṣyam of Sri Madhvācārya*. Vol.2. Government Oriental Library Series, no.47. Mysore: Government Branch Press, 1915.

Ranade, R.D. *A Constructive Survey of Upanishadic Philosophy: Being an Introduction to the Thought of the Upanishads*. 1968 ed. Bombay: Bharatiya Vidya Bhavan, 1926.

Rao, C. Hayavadana (ed.). *The Śrīkara Bhāṣya: Being the Vīraśaiva Commentary on the Vedānta Sūtras by Śrīpati*. Vol.1. New Delhi: Akshaya Prakashan, 1936.

Rao, C.R. Krishna. "The Supreme Text: Tattvamasi–That Thou Art." *Dharmaprakash Journal* 11, no. 9-10 (1982): 26-50; 17-28.

Runia, David T. "Ancient Doxography." Article Online. Oxford University Press, no date. Available on http://www.oxfordbibliographies.com/view/document/obo-978019538 9661/obo-9780195389661-0227.xml#firstMatch, accessed on 6 September 2018.

Sahu, Bhairabi Prasad. "Brahmanical Ideology, Regional Identities and the Construction of Early India." *Social Scientist* 29, no.7-8 (July-August 2001): 3-18.

Samuel, Geoffrey. *The Origins of Yoga and Tantra: Indic Religions to the Thirteenth Century*. Cambridge: Cambridge University Press, 2008.

Śaṅkara, *Brahmajñānavalīmālā*. Book online, https://sanskritdocuments.org. Available on https://sanskritdocuments.org/doc_z_misc_shankara/brahmajna .pdf, accessed on 15 August 2019.

Śaṅkarācārya. *A Thousand Teachings, the Upadeśasāharsī of Śaṅkara: Translation with Introduction and Notes*. Translated by Sengaku Mayeda. Tokyo: University of Tokyo

Press, 1979.

Śaṅkarācārya. *Ādi Śaṅkarācārya's Vākya Vṛtti*. Translated by Swami Chinmayananda. Mumbai: Chinmaya Mission, 2010. Available on http://www.astrojyoti.com/vakyavritti.htm, accessed on 12 December 2016.

Śaṅkarācārya. *Bṛhadāraṇyakopaniṣad: Sānuvāda Śānkarabhāṣyasahita*. Translated by Shattkarbashaysa. Gorakhpur: Gita Press, 1950.

Śaṅkarācārya. *Vivekacūḍāmaṇī*. Translated by Pranipata Chaitanya, Revised and edited by Satinder Dhiman. Tamil Nadu: Tiruchengode: Chinmaya Mission, no date. Available on https://realization.org/down/sankara.vivekachudamani.chaitanya.pdf, accessed on 10 March 2017.

Sankaranarayanan, S. (ed.). *Brahmasūtracatuḥsūtrī Śāṅkarabhāṣyam: Śrī Śaṅkarācārya's Commentary on the Catusūtrī of Brahmasūtra with Sanskrit Text, Transliteration, Word for Word Meaning, English Translation and Annotation*. 2 vols. Ernakulam: Chinmaya International Foundation, 2015.

Sarao, K.T.S. *The Decline of Buddhism in India: A Fresh Perspective*. New Delhi: Munshiram Manoharlal Publishers, 2012.

Saraswatī, Svāmī Dayānanda. *Ṛgvedādi-Bhāṣya-Bhūmikā: Being an Introduction to the Commentary on the Four Vedas*. Translated by Parmanand. New Delhi: Meharchand Lachhmandas, 1981.

Sastri, R. Ananthakrishna (ed.). *Pasupata Sutras with Pancarthabhashya of Kaundinya*. Trivandrum: The Oriental

Manuscripts Library of the University of Travancore, 1940.

Sastry, Alladi Mahadeva. *The Bhagavad Gita with the Commentary of Sri Sankaracharya*. Madras: Samata Books, 1979.

Satyanand, Joseph. *Nimbārka: A Pre-Śaṅkara Vedāntin and His Philosophy*. New Delhi: Munshiram Manoharlal Publishers, 1997.

Sawai, Yoshitsugu. "Rāmānuja's Hermeneutics of the Upaniṣads in Comparison with Śaṅkara's Interpretation." *Journal of Indian Philosophy* 19 (1991): 89-98.

Sen-Gupta, Anima. *Essays on Sāṁkhya and Other Systems of Indian Philosophy: Part 1 and 2*. New Delhi: Munshiram Manoharlal Publishers, 1977.

Sen-Gupta, Anima. *The Evolution of the Samkhya School of Thought*. Patna: Anima Sen-Gupta, 1953.

Shah, Jethala G. *Shri Vallabhacharya: His Philosophy and Religion*. Anand: The Pushtimargiya Pustakalaya, 1969.

Sharma, B.N.K. "Tat Tvam Asi." *Dharmaprakash Journal* 11, no.11 (1982): 17-37.

Sharma, B.N.K. *Brahamasūtras and Their Principal Commentaries: Critical Exposition*. 3 Vols. Delhi: Munshiram Manoharlal Publishers, 1974.

Sharma, B.N.K. *Mahātātparya of Mahāvākyas and Other Advaita Śrutis*. Bangalore: Anandatirtha Pratisthana of Akhila Bharata Madhva Mahamandal, 1999.

Sharma, Ramamurti. *Bhāratīya Darśan Kī Cintandhārā* Chowkambha Prācyavidhyā Granthamālā. Delhi:

Chowkambha Orientalia, 1999.

Sharvananda, Swami. *Māṇḍūkyopaniṣad: Including Original Verses, Constructed Text (Anvaya) with a Literal Word by Word Translation, English Rendering of Each Stanza, Copious Notes, Introduction and a Summary of Gauḍapāda's Kārikā* Upaniṣad Series. Madras: Sri Ramakrishan Math, 1943.

Sheth, Noel. "The Non-difference and Differnce of Human Beings and the World from God." *Budhi: A Journal of Ideas and Culture* 13, no.1-3 (2009): 123-130.

Shyamamanohar, Goswami. *Śrīmadbrahmasūtrāṇubhāṣyam*. 4 vols. Pune: Vallabhapīṭha Śrīviṭhaleśaprabhucaraṇāśrama Trust, 1983-84.

Singh, Kiran. *Sāṁkhya Darśana: Text with Commentaries*. 2 vols. Delhi: New Bharatiya Book Corporation, 2015.

Sinha, Jadunath. *The Philosophy of Nimbarka*. Calcutta: Sinha Publishing House, 1973.

Sinha, Kounteya. "More Indians have stopped believing in God: Survey." In *Times of India*, E-Paper 27 May 2013. Available on https://timesofindia.indiatimes. com/uk/More-Indians-have-stopped-believing-in-God-Survey/articleshow/20 284261.cms, accessed on 26 December 2018.

Somov, Pavel G. *The Lotus Effect: Shedding Suffering and Rediscovering Your Essential Self.* Oakland: New Harbinger Publications, 2010.

Srinivasachari, P.N. *The Philosophy of Bhedābheda*.

Revised and Enlarged, 1950 ed. Madras: Adyar Library, 1934.

Srinivasachari, P.N. *The Philosophy of Viśiṣṭādvaita*. Madras: The Adyar Library and Research Centre, 1970.

Tejomayananda, Swami. *Amṛtabindu Upaniṣad: A Drop of Immortality.* Mumbai: Central Chinmaya Mission Trust, 2012.

Tejomayananda, Swami. *Śvetāśvatara Upaniṣad.* Mumbai: Central Chinmaya Mission Trust, 2013.

Thadani, N.V. *Mīmāṁsā Sūtra of Jaimini: Text with Translation in English and Notes*. Delhi: Bharatiya Kala Prakashan, 2007.

Thaibaut, George. *The Vedānta-Sūtras with the Commentary of Śaṅkarācārya*. Vols. 34 and 38. 1968 ed. The Sacred Books of the East. Delhi: Motilal Banarsidass, 1904.

Ṭoḍāramalla, Rājā. *Ṭoḍārānandam*, Translated and edited by P.L. Vaidya. Bikaner: Anup Sanskrit Library, 1948.

Tripathi, K.D. "Lakṣaṇā." In *Kalātattvakośa: A Lexicon of Fundamental Concepts of the Indian Arts*. Edited by Kapila Vatsyayan. Vol.1: 135-144. Delhi: Motilal Banarsidass Publishers, 1988.

Tulsidas. *Śri Rāmacaritamānas: With Hindi Text and English Translation*. Translated by Mādhava Śaraṇa. Gorakhpur: Gita Press, 1968.

Upadhyaya, K.T. Pandurangi and Krishnacharya (eds.). *Gītātātparyanirṇayaḥ*. Vol.1. Bangalore: Dvaita Vedanta Studies and Research Foundation, 2007.

Upadhyaya, Tribuvan Prasad (ed.). *Bhāskarī: An English Translation of the Īśvara Pratybhijñā Vimarśinī with an*

Outline of History of Śaiva Philosophy. Vol.3. Princess of Wales Saraswati Bhavana Texts Series, 84. Lucknow: Superintendent of Printing and Stationery, 1954.

Uppal, Sveta. *Vedapārijāta*. New Delhi: NCERTC, 2014.

Vadakkan, Jaison. *Exclusion of Śūdras from Brahmajijñāsā: Re-Reading Apaśūdrādhikaraṇam of Brahmasūtra Śāṅkara Bhāṣya.* Delhi: Motilal Banarasidass Publications, 2019.

Van Buitenen, Johannes Adrianus Bernardus. *Rāmānuja's Vedārthasaṁgraha*. Michigan: Deccan College Postgraduate and Research Institute, 1956.

Varadachari, V. *Antiquity of the Term Viśiṣṭādvaita* Madras: Ramanuja Research Centre, 1974.

Vardhan, Varan. "Buddhist Compassion Towards Other Religions." In *Melodies from the Flute: Dialogue among Religions and Cultures: Memorial Volume for Indian Christian Philosopher Rev. Noel Sheth S.J.* Edited by Kuruvilla Pandikattu and Thomas Karimundackal, 290-308. Pune: Jnana-Deepa Vidyapeeth and Christian World Imprints, 2018.

Vasu, Srisa Chandra. *A Catechism of Hindu Dharma*. Allahabad: Sudhindra Natha Vasu, 1919.

Vidyatantra, Samaya Sri, "Mahavakyas: The Great Contemplations." Article Online. Available on http://www.swamij.com/mahavakyas.htm, accessed on 7 December 2016.

Vikrant, Swami. *Classical Indian Philosophy*. Bangalore: Kristu Jyoti Publications, 2007.

Vimalananda, Swami. *Tat Tvam Asi: Notes on Chāndogya*

Upaniṣad, Chapter Six. 2013 reprint ed. Mumbai: Central Chinmaya Mission Trust, 2000.

Vireswarananda, Swami. *Brahma Sūtras*. Calcutta: Advaita Ashrama, 1962.

Wittgenstein, Ludwig J. *Tractatus Logico-Philosophicus*. Translated by D. F. Peers and G. F. McGuninnes. London: Routledge and Kegan Paul, 1965.

Witzel, S.W. and M. Jamison. *Vedic Hinduism*. Book Online. Harward: Harvard University, 1992. Available on http://www.people.fas.harvard.edu/~witzel/ vedica.pdf, accessed on 10 October, 2018.

Wood, David and Robert Bernasconi (eds.) *Derrida and Différance*. Evanston: Northwestern University Press, 1988.

Wujastyk, Dominik. "Change and Creativity in Early Modern Indian Medical Thought." *Journal of Indian Philosophy* 33, no. 1 (February 2005): 95-118.

Zaehner, R.C. *The Bhagavad-Gīta: With a Commentary Based on the Original Sources*. Oxford-London: Oxford Univesity Press, 1969.

INDEX OF QUOTATIONS

brahma satyaṁ jagat mithyam	*Brahmajñānav-alīmālā* 20
brahma vā idam agra āsīt	BU 1.4.10
brahma veda brahmaiva bhavati	MU 3.2.9
daśalakṣaṇāni dharmasya ye viprāḥ	*Manu Smṛti* 6.93
dhṛtiḥ, kṣamā damo asteyaṁ śaucam	*Manu Smṛti* 6.92
dvā suparṇā sayujā sakhāyā samānaṁ	MU 3.1.1
ekam eva advitīyaṁ Brahma	CU 6.2.1-2
ekaṁ sadviprā bahudhā vadanti	RV I.164.46
ekastathā sarva-bhūtāntarātmā	KaU 5.9
ekasyātmano anye devāḥ atyaṅgāni bhavanti	Nirukta 8.4
eko hi rudro na dvitīyāya tasthuḥ	SU 3.1-2
eṣa ma ātman antḥhṛdaya etad brahma	CU 3.14.4
eṣā ta ātmāntaryāmyamṛtaḥ	BU 3.7.3
eso'ntar-hṛdaya ākāṣaḥ tasmiñ chete	BU 2.1.17
etānyapi tu karmāṇi saṅgaṁ tyaktvā	BG 18.7
etasmājjāyate prāṇo manaḥ sarvendriyāṇi	MU 1.3; KU 15
indraṁ mitraṁ varuṇamagnimāhuratho	RV I.164.46
indro māyābhiḥ puruṣa īyate	RV 6.47.18
īśavāsyamidaṁ sarvaṁ	IU 1
jñājñau dvāv ajāv īśanīśāv ajā	SU 1.9
jyotirdīpyate viśvataḥ pṛṣṭeṣu sarvataḥ	CU 3.13.7
kāyena manasā buddhyā	BG 5.11
kratau phalārthavādamaṅgavatkāṣṇājiniḥ	MS 4.3.17
kratau phalārthavādamaṅgavatkārṣṇājiniḥ	*Mīmāṁsā Sūtra* 4.3.17
mahābhāgyaddevatāyā eka eva ātmā	Nirukta 7.4

sa ma ātmeti vidhyāt	KauU 3.9
sa tatra paryeti jakṣan krīdin ramamāṇa	CU 8.12.3
sa yathaitāṁ devatāṁ sarvāṇi bhūtānyavanti	BU 1.5.20
sadeva somyedamagra āsīt	CU 6.2.1
sanātanam enam āhur utadya	AV 10.8.23
sarvabhūtādhivāsaṁ yat bhūteṣu ca vasatyapi	AbU 22
sarvabhūtastham ātmānaṁ sarvabhūtani	Manu 2.12; 43.2; BG 6.29
sarvadharmān parityajya māmekaṁ	BG 18.66
sarvagatvādanantasya sa evāyamahaṁ sthitaḥ	VP 1.19.15
sarvaṁ khalvidam brahma	CU 3.14.1
sarvaṁ samāpnoṣi tato'si sarvaḥ	BG 11.40
sarvavyāpinam ātmānam kṣīre	SU 1.15-16
sarve asmin devo ekavṛto bhavanti	AV 13.4.14-21
satyaṁ jñānaṁ anantaṁ brahma	TU 2.1.1
so aśnute sarvān kāmān saha brahmaṇā	TU 2.1
so'ham	IU 16
so'ryamā sa varuṇaḥ sa rudraḥ sa mahādeva	AV 13.4.4
tadevāgnistadādityastad vāyustadu candramāḥ	YV 32.1
tadviṣṇorvedaṁ sadā paśanti sūrayaḥ	SU 1.2; BG 6.10
tasmād vā etasmād ātmani sarve prāṇaḥ	MaiU 6.32
tasya priyameva śiraḥ	TU 2.5.2
tattvamasi	CU 6.8.7
te dhānayogānugatā apaśyan	SU 1.3
tena etasyai devatāyei sāyujyaṁ	BU 1.5.22
tileṣu tailaṁ dadhanīva sarpir-āpaḥ	SU 1.15-16
triṣu dhāmasu yad bhāgya bhoktā	KU 18

INDEX OF WORDS

Relation with Brahman, *jīva* and *jagat*	*Pāramārthika* and *vyāvahārika*	*Abheda* in *svarūpa*, essential nature, but different in *viśeṣa guṇa*. *Abheda* takes precedence. Brahman is whole and *jīva* and *jagat* are parts. Brahman being *antaryāmin* is the internal regulator	Brahman and *jīva* are identical in *svaūpa*, as cause and effect, but different in *guṇa*. The *abheda* and *bheda* are on par with each other	Absolute difference between Brahman, *jīva* and *jagat*	Absolute identity. Brahman is *sat-cit-ānanda*, *jīva* is *sat-cit* and *jagat* only *sat*. Brahman is *vibhū* and *jīva* is *aṇu*	*Jīva-jagat* are *bhinnābhinna* from Brahman during its *kāryāvasthā*, *saṁsāra*, but non-different during dissolution and liberation	Brahman and *jīva-jagat* are neither absolutely different, nor absolutely identical, nor both different and non-different. The relation is that of cause and effect, one is impossible without the other. The cause transcends the effect though it is immanent in the effect.	Brahman and *jīva-jagat* are distinct during state of bondage but in *mokṣa* they are identical- *Bhedābheda*. *Jīva* has no unknown eternal nature	Brahman is basis for *prakṛti* and *puruṣa*	There is *abheda* of *svarūpa* and *guṇa* between Brahman as the cause and *jīva* as effect. Yet there is *bheda* between them too regarding *svarūpa* and *guṇas* such as limitations of place, time, degree of perfection etc. This apparent contradiction *is acintya*.
Relation with Brahman, Īśvara	*Īśvara* is *saguṇa* Brahman, the *māyā* relected form of Brahman	Brahman is *Īśvara*, none other than Viṣṇu	Brahman is *Īśvara*, none other than Kṛṣṇa	Brahman is *Īśvara*, none other than *Viṣṇu*	Brahman is *Īśvara*, none other than *Kṛṣṇa*	Brahman is *Īśvara*, but non-theistic	Brahman is *Śiva*	Brahman is *Śiva*	*Puruṣa* and *prakṛti* are *upādhi* of *Īśvara* through which Brahman brings about creation	Brahman is *Īśvara*, none other than *Kṛṣṇa*, also *Viṣṇu*
Liberation	Identity already exists, but forgotten due to ignorance	Liberation is realisation of the *svarūpa* or identity with Brahman. Only *videha mukti*	Liberation is realisation of the *svarūpa* or identity with Brahman. But even after death, *mukta jīva* separate from Brahman	Even after liberation, liberated soul is different from Brahman. Only *videha mukti*	Identity already exists. *Jīva* is bound in *saṁsāra* due to *avidya*. But, a *mukta jīva* still differs from Brahman remaining *aṇu* and lacking powers of *sṛṣṭi*, *sthiti* and *laya*. *Jīvanmukti* is supported.	*Mokṣa* is not pure knowledge, but fullness of *ānanda*. *Jīva* is not *nitya mukta*. *Jīvan mukti* is not possible. *Mokṣa* is possible only after death of the body.	Mokṣa is attainment of *śivatva*. But *jīva* becomes similar and not identical with Śiva. Mukta *jīva* is all pervasive, but lacks the power of *sṛṣṭi*, *sthiti* and *laya*. *Mukti* is *nitya*.	Mokṣa is attainment of Śiva. This is *tādātmya* with Śiva, but still subservient to Śiva, lacking power of *sṛṣṭi*, *sthiti* and *laya*. *mokṣa* is *anitya*. Only *videha mukti*.	Ultimate mokṣa is non-difference with Brahman. In mokṣa jīva loses all the knowledge and consciousness. Avibhāga is not the same as tādātmya.	Mokṣa is the attainment of Brahman°s attribute except the *mukta jīva*, remains *anu*, and lacks the power of *sṛṣṭi*, *sthiti* and *laya*. *Abheda* in terms of *bhoga* alone, *bheda* everywhere. *Mukta jīva* takes refuge in *Īśvara* forever. Only *videha mukti*.
Means of liberation	*Tattvajñāna* of *ātman* and Brahman	*Bhakti* is a matured form of *jñāna*.	Emotional *Bhakti* involving contemplation	*Jñāna* leads to *bhakti*, bhakti to *dhyana*. *Dhyāna* and *bhakti* are direct means of liberation. But grace is needed.	Through *jñāna*, the *akṣara* Brahman is realized. Bhakti alone reveals ānanda. *Puṣṭi* bhakti requires only *Īśvara's* grace	*Jñāna* along with *karma* is needed for *mokṣa*. *Bhakti* on *nirākāra*, *nirviśeṣa nirākāra* Brahman needed.	*Jñāna* and *karma* is the means. *Jñāna* leads to *upāsana* or *dhyāna* on the *svarūpa* of Śiva being non-different from one°s own nature. Divine grace then leads to *mokṣa*	*Karma is citta śuddhi*. *Jñāna* must lead to *upāsana* or *dhyāna* on the manifest and *unmanifest* form of Śiva. Seeker needs outer marks of Śiva on body. Ultimately it is grace.	*Jñānakarma-samuccaya* is the means. But *bhakti* as love of *Īśvara* is also the means of highest realisation. There is mystical relation between *Bhakta* and Lord.	*Karma* causes *citta śuddhi*. *Satsang* is a direct means. *Jñāna*, bhakti also means. Liberation is through grace of God in the final stage.
Special features	Only pure *advaita*, at the *pāramārtika*	What is *pāramārtika* to Rāmānuja is *vyāvahārika* to Śaṅkara	Natural difference and non-difference	Eternally damn souls exist. *Abheda vākyas* are figurative. Viṣṇu *sarvottama*	Attempts to address weakness of *māyā* of Śaṅkara	*Upādhi*	*Māyā* as *Umā* is a *paraśakti* of Śiva.	*Viśeṣa* as *bheda* and *advaita* as *abheda*. But they do not eo-exist	*Avibhāga* as different from identity is a creative answer to *Bhedābheda* problems	More of *dvaita*, but understood as *advaita*.
External observations	*Māyā*, unreality of world is hard to accept. *nirguṇatva* is not amenable to senses	Hard to accept difference and non-difference at the same time.	Illogical appearance of *bheda* and *abheda*. Does Brahman suffer imperfection?	Duality is philosophically contradictory. Eternal hell and grace do not fit with *karma* theory	*Ekatva* with Brahman, but separation in liberation? Still *dvaita* then.	Peculiar definition of *upādhi*. Illogical *saguṇa* and *nirguṇa* concepts	Hard to accept difference and non-difference simultaneously.	Brahman is eternal but becoming?	Sāṅkhya theism appears philosophically untenable. Dualism still persists?	Critically seeing, *acintya* is not satisfying.

[i] Prem Pahlajrai, "Vedanta: A Comparative Analysis of Diverse Schools," in *Asian Studies Graduate Student Colloquium* (Washington: University of Washington, 2003), no page number. This chart is an edited and updated version.

Comparative Chart of Daśabhāṣyas of the Brahmasūtras[i]

Feature	*Kevalādvaita Nirviśeṣādvaita*	*Viśiṣṭādvaita*	*Svābhāvika Bhedābheda*	*Dvaita Tattvavāda*	*Śuddhādvaita*	*Aupādhika Bhedābheda*	*Viśiṣṭa Śivādvaita*	*Viśea Bhedābheda*	*Avibhāga Bhedābheda*	*Acintya Bhedābheda*
Proponent	Śaṅkara	Rāmānuja	Nimbārka	Madhva	Vallabha	Bhāskara	Śrīkaṇṭha	Śrīpati	Vijñānabhikṣu	Baladeva
Date	CE 788-820	CE 1017-1137	CE 1250	CE 1238-1317	CE 1479-1544	CE 1000	CE 1270	CE 1400	CE 1600	CE 1725
BS Bhāṣya	*Śārīraka mīmāṁsā bhāṣya; śāṇkara bhāṣya*	*Śrībhāṣya, Vedānta-dīpa, Vedānta-sāra*	*Vedānta-pāri-jāta saurabha*	*Brahma-sūtra-bhāṣya; Anu-vyākhyāna Nyāya-vivaraṇa, Aṇubhāṣya*	*Aṇubhāṣyam*	*Brahma sūtra bhāṣya or Śārīraka-Mīmāṁsā-Bhāṣya*	*Brahma Sūtra Bhāṣya or Brahma Mīmāṁsā Bhāṣya*	*Śrīkara-bhāṣyam*	*Vijñānāmṛta-bhāṣyam*	*Govinda-bhāṣyam*
Sūtras	555	545	549	564	550	541	545	544	554	558
Adhi-karaṇa	191	156	162	223	162	186	185	173	162	206
English equivalent	Absolute monism	Qualified monism	Natural difference and non-difference	Difference or Dualism or Plurality	Pure Monism	Adventitious difference and non-difference	Qualified monism with *Śiva* being central	Special Monism	Undifferentiable difference and non-difference	Inexplicable difference and non-difference
Doctrine	Monism 'illusionism'	Monotheism	Monotheism	Monotheism	Monotheism	Non-theistic monism	Monotheism	Monotheism	Monotheism	Monotheism
Speciality of Brahman	*Nirviśeṣa*	*Saviśeṣa*	*Saviśeṣa*	*Nirviśeṣa*	*Nirviśeṣa*	*Nirviśeṣa* in causal form; *Saviśeṣa* in effect form.	*Saviśeṣa*	*Saviśeṣa*	*Nirviśeṣa Saviśeṣa*	*Nirviśeṣa*
Quality of Brahman	*Nirguṇa*	*Saguṇa*	*Saguṇa*	*Saguṇa*	*Saguṇa*	*Saguṇa*	*Saguṇa*	*Saguṇa*	*Nirguṇa*	*Saguṇa*
Unity *Ekatva*	Total unity Or *tādātmya*	*Eka, jīva* and *jagat* are attributes of Brahman	*Eka, jīva jagat* are attributes of Brahman	Eka, *jīva* & *jagat are pratibimbas. Jīvas* are *kāraṇarūpa nānātva* of Brahman. Even in liberated state they don°t completely merge.	One regarding cause and effect. differ from Brahman in *guṇa* and śakti	One in, but as *kārya rūpa*	One	One	One with *jīva* as parts which are not identical, yet non-separate with Brahman	One, but ever separate from *jīva* even in liberation
Theory of Causality	*Vivartavāda*	*Pariṇāma vāda*	*Pariṇāma vāda*	*Pariṇāma vāda.* All things depend on Brahman. Brahman is *nimitta kāraṇa.*	*Pariṇāma vāda* and *avikṛta pariṇāma-vāda.*	Śakti *vikṣepa Pariṇāma-vāda*, transformation through projection of Brahman's powers. Brahman is *nimitta kāraṇa* and *upādāna kārañа.* Cause and effect are *bhinnābhinna*	*Pariṇāma vāda. Brahman is nimitta kāraṇa and upādāna kārañа*	*Pariṇāma vāda.*	*Brahma-*śakti*-prakṛti- pariṇāma-vāda.* Brahman is *adhiṣṭāana kāraṇa.* Effect is *Avibhāga* from Brahman	*Pariṇāma vāda.* Brahman is both *nimitta and upādāna kāraṇa.*
World	*Mithyā* due to *māyā* and *avidyā*	*Satya*	*Satya*	*Satya*	*Satya Māyā* is Brahman's *acintya śakti*	*Satya*, because the *upādhi* is real, though *anitya*	*Satya*	*Satya*	*Satya*, but of different order than Brahman	*Satya*